IRELAND'S TERRORIST DILEMMA

INTERNATIONAL STUDIES ON TERRORISM

Yonah Alexander, *General Editor*

Y. Alexander and A.S. Nanes (eds) Legislative Responses to Terrorism. 1986. ISBN 90 247 3213 1

IRELAND'S TERRORIST DILEMMA

edited by

Yonah Alexander
Alan O'Day

1986 **MARTINUS NIJHOFF PUBLISHERS**
a member of the KLUWER ACADEMIC PUBLISHERS GROUP
DORDRECHT / BOSTON / LANCASTER

Distributors

for the United States and Canada: Kluwer Academic Publishers, 190 Old Derby Street, Hingham, MA 02043, USA
for the UK and Ireland: Kluwer Academic Publishers, MTP Press Limited, Falcon House, Queen Square, Lancaster LA1 1RN, UK
for all other countries: Kluwer Academic Publishers Group, Distribution Center, P.O. Box 322, 3300 AH Dordrecht, The Netherlands

Library of Congress Cataloging in Publication Data

Ireland's terrorist dilemma.

(International studies on terrorism ; v. 2)
Bibliography: p.
1. Terrorism--Northern Ireland--History--Addresses, essays, lectures. 2. Northern Ireland--Politics and government--Addresses, essays, lectures. I. Alexander, Yonah. II. O'Day, Alan. III. Series.
HV6433.G7I74 1986 303.6'25'09416 86-2431
ISBN 0-89838-912-7

ISBN 0-89838-912-7 (this volume)
ISBN 90-247-3212-3 (series)

Copyright

PRINTED IN THE NETHERLANDS

Ireland's Terrorist Dilemma

CONTENTS

INTRODUCTION

Despite the massive attention accorded the crisis in Northern Ireland since late 1968, surprisingly few book-length studies of terrorism in that troubled country have been published. Recognizing this gap in scholarship, we have decided to publish this volume* to explore the roots of Irish terrorism and describe its impact on British and Irish life. This collection of thirteen essays represents no political point of view and engages in no special pleading. It seeks to place a range of questions and problems in the appropriate historical and contemporary context. There is no attempt to suggest magic remedies for the terrorist crisis but to explain to a general and academic readership the pitfalls of subscribing to easy solutions. A range of problems are considered in the book but several receive substantial emphasis: the roots of conflict; the media and propaganda; commercial and governmental policies and actions. Although no solutions are espoused the editors and contributors hope that a fuller examination of the Northern Ireland problem will add to the fund of knowledge required for the framing of a long-term satisfactory settlement of the dispute.

The purpose of the first chapter, written by George Boyce, is to illuminate a significant and at times dangerous theme in Anglo-Irish relations – the notion of the suffering Catholic people and the martyr figure. It suggests that the idea of the suffering people, so vividly expressed in 19th century nationalist propaganda, took on a new meaning when the civil rights movement of the 1960s was met by Protestant suspicion and then physical opposition. The hunger strikes of 1981, therefore, struck a deep note in the Irish people. Deeds of violence were forgotten, and attention focussed on the spectacle of young men willing to give their lives for Ireland. The initially sluggish response of the nationalist community and the efforts of the Catholic Hierarchy to end the strike quickly, could not allay the impact which another display of nationalist sacrifice made on a people that saw itself as did the Catholics in the whole of Ireland in the 19th century. Thus, the hunger strike powerfully reinforced the terrorist position and its legitimacy in the Catholic community.

Sheridan Gilley looks at the problem within the specific tradition of a prayerful Irish Catholicism, concentrating on the all-powerful event of the Easter Rising of 1916. He suggests that in Northern Ireland the vision of sacrifice established by Pearse retains its influence. Gilley notes that insofar as the Irish State was the creation of a Catholic revolution, there is undoubtedly an Irish Catholic imagery which speaks at a deeper level than self-interest, an imagery of sacrifice and suffering as in the pictures which

* For an earlier work, see Yonah Alexander and Alan O'Day, *Terrorism in Ireland* (London: Croom Helm, 1983, and New York; St. Martins Press, 1983).

appeared on Belfast and Derry walls during the hunger strikes of 1981. At this level, Irish Catholicism retains its revolutionary character: needing, as in Ulster, only the time and "favourable" harsh circumstances to leap from the past back into life. Gilley provides a pertinent reminder of the importance of the myth, imagery, and spirituality which underlie the contemporary crisis.

In the following chapter Maureen Hartigan, Alan O'Day and Roland Quinault deal with Irish bombings in Britain. The comparison between the terrorist threat of the 1860s and the post-1972 period sheds interesting light on what conditions are essential for an effective campaign of violence. It is argued that whereas the incidents of the 1860s were relatively successful in capturing the attention of British leaders and inducing changes of policy, albeit of a different sort than was sought by the extremists, the modern campaign has had little influence. It is suggested that 'history' has taught the I.R.A. that British Governments bend in the face of violence, but only when it stems from recognized injustice thus conferring a form of legitimacy on terrorism. Whereas the Fenians possessed a degree of legitimacy the I.R.A. has lacked it. Indeed, much of the heroism which Fenians exemplified has seemed merely cowardice in the I.R.A. terrorist offensive. In short, the I.R.A. has failed to strike the right chord in its violence on mainland Britain.

The essay by Patrick Buckland compares the creation of states in Ireland and the Middle East. It argues that though one can detect differences in specific policies, the strategy in all instances was the creation of new states which would safeguard imperial interests indirectly and cheaply, regardless of the cost to the citizens of the new political entities. Minorities were either ignored completely or found their future depended on the goodwill of dominant groups that had a long history of hostility to them. In taking little account of the distinctive political culture of the north of Ireland, British politicians ensured that Northern Ireland would suffer from prolonged disharmony. Present-day difficulties stem from the origins of the new regime and can only be understood through an examination of metropolitan policy considerations.

In the next chapter, Jonathan Kelly and Ian McAllister make an explicit test of some economic theories and their relationship to political violence by applying multivariate analysis to survey data collected in Northern Ireland in 1973, during the worst period of violence. Although the data were originally designed to focus on social mobility, a substantial portion were used to elicit respondents' exposure to political violence, attitudes towards politics, and attitudes to the conflict generally.

Ken Heskin considers from a theoretical and concrete perspective the attitudes and motivations of terrorists through the medium of an unusual interview with an active terrorist, published in November 1983. The object is to combat some of the myths concerning the character of individual terrorists and to prevent discussion of the question from being seen as simply a succession of essentially inexplicable, dreadful deeds perpetrated by unseen evil forces. The interview, as explained by the author, reveals the complex forces which motivate a modern terrorist.

The role of popular newspaper cartoons in shaping views of the present-day crisis is analyzed by John Kirkaldy. It points out that English cartoons during the current difficulties are not simply reflections of the past. The focus has changed from the whole of Ireland to an increaisng concentration on the North. Indeed, Protestants in the North have received a consistently critical treatment in cartoons, also. Unlike in the past, anti-Catholicism has not played a major part in English cartoons, though one can detect occasional traces of it. Overall, English cartoons have fulfilled their traditional function – expressing anti-Irish prejudice that in any other form would be publicly unacceptable in England. The cartoon has thus played a part in thwarting an understanding in Britain of the forces behind Irish terrorism.

John Hill deals with the British cinema and Ireland. No issue has plagued British broadcasting more in recent years than its coverage of the conflicts in Northern Ireland. Amidst a tortured history of overt and covert censorship, the fragile doctrine of 'balance' has never seemed more precarious. And, yet, many of the emphases and lacunae evident in the British media's coverage of Northern Ireland are not new, and find their parallel in the treatment accorded the Irish by the post-war British cinema, even when such images seem safely removed from contemporary political crises. The chapter deals with how some of the key British feature films have dealt with political violence in Ireland. It demonstrates how recurrent attitudes towards Irish history have emerged in an ongoing tradition, both typical of British cimema itself and of British political culture in general.

Propaganda and the manufacture of history by Ulster extremists is covered by Richard Davis. Since the division of Ireland, a fundamental intellectual problem for Ulster extremist groups has been the issue of one nation or two. During the contemporary crisis Protestant extremists have actively sought new justifications for the creation of a Northern Irish State different in kind from both its southern neighbour and Britain. Extremists have increasingly abandoned democratic, problem solving, social engineering attitudes in favour of absolutist solutions. One unexpected consequence has been a move towards a greater Protestant secularism. The essay examines the evolution of Ulster extremist outlooks from both an historical and contemporary perspective. It seeks to establish that the present situation can only be assessed by giving due weight to both. For what has emerged, and what must be considered in any resolution, is the position of those members of the Protestant community who now subscribe to the new ideology.

In his contribution, Richard Davis examines the propaganda war waged between the Provisional I.R.A. and the British Army, with the loyalist paramilitaries clumsily attempting to establish themselves as an argumentative third force. It is suggested that the mechanics of violence have a pathology of their own, sometimes divorced form supportive actions in the real world. The author argues that the Provisionals were probably more effective with the pen than with the bomb. Perhaps the principle reason why the Provisionals have done so well is because of the weakness and errors of the opposition. The chapter traces the sources of each side's successes and failures in the vital propaganda war.

The next chapter examines what conditions are essential for militarizing a society. Specifically, it looks at the development of the Ulster Volunteer Force in 1913 and 1914 and argues that the preconditions which existed then are absent today. The reasons why there is no equivalent now of the old UVF are several, and inlcude the fact that there is no threat at present of the Unionist majority being forced into the Republic of Ireland and the Unionist cause on mainland Britain does not appear to enjoy the public suport of the UVF. Moreover, it is probable that any attempt to build up a paramilitary army along the lines of the old UVF would be immediately prevented. Westminter's commitment to the present constitutional position of Northern Ireland, guaranteed by the security forces, is probably perceived as being sufficient protection by most of the Unionist majority. Yet it is clear that resuscitation of a 1913–14 type of situation is feasible if British guarantee appears to be in doubt.

Henry Patterson discusses the interface between British governments and the Protestant backlash (1969–74). Political violence in Northern Ireland is linked to the polarization of politics. This chapter seeks to explain an element of that polarization through an examination of Protestant responses to British government policy. It is argued that one important index of the inadequacies of British government policy has been the failure adequately to perceive the nature of popular Protestant politics. It is suggested that direct rule, by destroying the substance of the Unionist state, was a radical measure. However, British policy-makers have been unprepared to accept all its implications. Instead of making it clear that what was at stake was a process of reconstruction of the Northern Ireland state along more democratic and equitable lines, the desire to return as quickly as possible to a situation where British involvement was minimized, led to an attempt to create a non-sectarian coalition. This meant, at the very least, appearing to take nationalist aspirations seriously. The result was predictably disastrous. For while it might have been possible to at least secure Protestant acquiescence to a more substantial programme of internal reform, reforms which appeared to be linked to a process of gradual British disengagement were quite a different matter.

The final chapter by Brian Reid surveys the role of the British Army in Northern Ireland. Its deployment as an aid to the civil power in 1969 raised a number of difficult problems. Although the Army had gained considerable experience in counter-insurgency since 1945, this had been acquired in former colonial territories. Consequently, the doctrine and experience that the Army had built up under extremely difficult circumstances in other parts of the world was of little use in Northern Ireland, an integral part of the United Kingdom. This essay explores the way the Army coped with the political tensions arising from the 'troubles' in Northern Ireland and assesses the degree of adaptability it has shown in coming to terms with its complex task of countering terrorism in the province. It suggests that the mounting of a counter-subversion campaign with the expectation of totally defeating the terrorists in military terms within the context of Northern Ireland politics has not been possible. It is clear that the task of the Army has been an unenviable one and the manner in which its operations have constantly been readjusted has tested its professionalism.

The editors express their appreciation to the authors for their important contributions and cooperation. Yonah Alexander wishes to thank the Institute for Studies in International Terrorism, State University of New York (Oneonta, New York) and the Center for Strategic and International Studies, Georgetown University, for their continuing support. These institutions bear no responsibility for the views presented in this volume.

'A GALLOUS STORY AND A DIRTY DEED': POLITICAL MARTYRDOM IN IRELAND SINCE 1867

D. GEORGE BOYCE

I'll say, a strange man is a marvel with his mighty talk; but what's a squabble in your back-yard, and the blow of a loy, have taught me that there's a great gap between a gallous story and a dirty deed ... Take him on from this, or the lot of us will be likely put on trial for his deed today.[1]

J. M. Synge, in his 'Playboy of the Western World', prompts a consideration of one of the most important themes for students of a highly topical subject: the place of violence in Irish politics, and particularly the distinction in Ireland between ordinary crime and what almost seems an indigenous kind of crime. This distinction puzzled a British M.P. when, after the recent I.R.A. bombing of Harrod's store in London, he asked whether it was 'really conceivable that if the perpetrators of such an outrage ... were convicted and executed, anyone could in any circumstances think of them as martyrs?'[2] And it may be put in Synge's terms as one between a 'gallous story' and a 'dirty deed'; between an act of violence which the community might regard as in some sense acceptable or, even, admirable, and one which they would repudiate as simply criminal.

This paper is not concerned with political violence in a general sense;[3] it deals rather with the theme of acceptable or approved violence in the context of Irish nationalist politics since the mid-nineteenth century, and especially the development of the concept of the political martyr: the 'laughing gesture of a young man' who, one of its most effective exponents Patrick Pearse put it, 'is going into battle or climbing to a gibbet ... an eternal gesture in Irish history'.[4]

The eternal Irish gesture; but the gesture was not perhaps as eternal as all that. And the character of Irish violence cannot be lumped into one category, without distinction of time or motive. Agrarian violence by Whiteboy organizations and their like between 1760 and 1830 was limited, decided and practical; it was aimed at particular individuals to redress specific grievances, or to ensure that no-one broke the ranks of silence and solidarity necessary for such organizations to exist and to achieve their aims: a reduction in rents,

[1] J. M. Synge, 'The Playboy of the Western World' (London, the New Mermaids ed., 1975), p. 81.

[2] Sir Ian Percival, QC, MP, *The Times*, 22 Dec. 1983.

[3] For a recent and full discussion of which see Charles Townshend, *Political Violence in Ireland: Government and Resistance Since 1848* (Oxford, 1983).

[4] Quoted in Fr. Francis Shaw, 'The Canon of Irish History: a challenge', *Studies*, vol. LXI (1972), p. 137.

the waiving of tithes.[5] Such violence was not calculated to produce political martyrs, nor indeed martyrs of any kind, however much peasants might admire and support the men who fought a clandestine war on their behalf.[6] Its purpose was not to set an example for future generations, but to ensure that the present generation (or the local part of it in which the violence was perpetrated) maintained or secured the limited objectives necessary for subsistence and existence. It did not seek to inspire or create an ideology or self-sacrifice for an abstract cause, but to defend society against change. Like the 'Scotch Cattle' in South Wales,[7] Whiteboy organizations defined their target, used such methods as were necessary to effect the desired result, and lived under a cloak of anonymity. No great names of Irish political resistance echo down the years from the agrarian violence that was endemic in Irish society from the 1760s until the beginning of the present century.

Agrarian violence was not the stuff of which political martyrs, political messiahs, were made. And rural society was of course the dominant influence on the political development of modern Ireland. Another major influence, the Roman Catholic church, was unlikely, on the face of it, to accept or foster such notions. It is misleading to pretend that the Roman Catholic church in Ireland spoke with one voice on the subject of politics, especially violent politics;[8] but it is generally ture that the hierarchy, fearing the influence on the young Catholic of secret oath bound societies, concerned lest young men would be led into hopeless rebellion and fruitless slaughter, set their face against violence as a means of political expression. There was perhaps an equivocation in that they also condemned English or State violence which provoked young men into such dangerous action (thus in a sense equalling state and rebels as no better than each other).[9] But while Catholic leaders disliked the heretic English interlopers, they were, after O'Connell, placed firmly in the centre of the rising Catholic democracy, increasingly able to achieve its freedom and position by mass political movement. Priests became the guardians of the national tradition; yet here was a problem. For while nationalism in 19th century Ireland was esentially organized at the ballot box, the bullet was never excluded from the popular imagination. O'Connell was the least unequivocal opponent of violence, but even he could select great

[5] P. F. O'Farrell, 'Millenialism, Messianism and Utopianism in Irish history', in *Anglo-Irish Studies*, ii (1976), pp. 49–50; Townshend, *op.cit.*, pp. 12–13, 21–24.

[6] M. R. Beames, 'Rural conflict in pre-famine Ireland: peasant assassinations in Tipperary, 1837–1847', *Past and Present*, No. 81 (1978), p. 90.

[7] D. J. V. Jones, 'The Scotch Cattle and their Black Domain', in *Welsh History Review*, Vol. 5 (June, 1970), pp. 220–49.

[8] Sheridan Gilley 'The Catholic Church and Revolution in 19th century Ireland', in Yonah Alexander and Alan O'Day (eds.) *Terrorism in Ireland* (London, 1983), pp. 121–45. D. McCartney, 'The Churches and Secret Societies', in T. Desmond Williams (ed.), *Secret Societies in Ireland* (Dublin, 1973), pp. 68–78.

[9] For a recent example see Townshend, *Political Violence*, p. 394.

military heroes from Ireland's Jacobite past (Sarsfield) as examples of the nobility and courage of the fighting Irishman.[10]

A democratic and constitutional political tradition that nevertheless allowed a place for deeds of violence (even if they were past rather than present deeds); a Church that opposed rebellion but could recognize the grievances that inspired it; and both faced with an unsuccessful but modern history of insurrecitonary activity that began in 1798 and was reaffirmed in the risings of 1848 and 1867. In these circumstances it was difficult to repudiate in an unqualified way the revolutionary gestures of the United Irishmen, Young Ireland and Fenian organizations, for fear of forfeiting popular support and affection; as the balladeers of the 1798 rebellion recalled

They died for love of country; it was an honourable crime.[11]

But why was there such a degree of popular approval for the crime that was no crime, 'to love their country well'? Was it some trait in the Irish character, as Synge suggested, was it 'more directly due to the primitive feeling of the people, who are never criminals yet always capable of crime'?[12] It may be that the nature of agrarian violence hardened the rural population to the idea that to attack one's enemy physically was no crime, but a reasonable and even in a sense lawful retaliation; but this would not explain the way in which the urban population took Irish political martyrs to their hearts, for after all the popular broadsheets and songs were sold on the streets of towns and cities, not on the Aran Islands – and Synge for his part was of course referring to the people of the Aran islands, who were hardly typical of the Irish population as a whole. An historical rather than sociological explanation is more satisfying to explain the love and indeed need for a gallous story and its distinction form a dirty deed; and that is the influence of the myth of Irish nationalism.

Irish nationalism was not, like German or Italian nationalism, a matter of uniting a 'nation' in a triumphalist political destiny (however disappointing that destiny might prove in the event).[13] It was not a set of ideas that could reflect on past glories (however imaginary) and anticipate more to come. It was not based on a notion of the inexorable march of a nation to power and predominance, in the way that English nationalism from the Elizabethan age to the nineteenth century wsa inspired. On the contrary it was taught as a story of oppression, defeat, humiliation and degradation – a fate that had gradually

[10] D. G. Boyce, *Nationalism in Ireland* (London, 1982), pp. 137–8.

[11] G. D. Zimmermann, *Irish Political Street Ballads and Rebel Songs, 1780–1900* (Geneva, 1966), p. 66.

[12] Vivian Mercer and David H. Greene, *One Thousand Years of Irish Prose* Vol. 1, *The Literary Revival* (New York, 1953), pp. 135–6.

[13] Ernest Gellner, *Nations and Nationalism* (Oxford, 1983), p. 100.

overtaken the Roman Catholic from the 16th century and had culminated in the 'great disaster' of 1689–90. It was the story of a people struggling for their very survival, their existence, at a time when, as one nationalist put it, God seemed to have turned His face away from His people. The story of Irish nationalism was one of defeat, both in ancient and modern times. Such a tradition could look to an O'Connell or a Parnell for present gains and advances; but O'Connell did not win repeal of the Union, nor did Parnell succeed with home rule. And while political Ireland marked time on the issue of self-government (though other, more immediate gains were of course won), comfort and nourishment could be taken from the idea of the Irish political martyr.

The ground was indeed fertile for such a development. A church that saw itself as a kind of collective martyr for faith and fatherland; constitutional movements that sought to infuse parliamentary and popular politics with an aura of excitement and defiance of the Saxon foe; a nationality that was cast, or cast itself, in the role of a scourged and oppressed children of God – scourged and oppressed by the heretic/English persecutors, forced to live with a history of catastrophe, with the Great Famine of 1847 as the most recent and vivid example. Added to this was a sense of inferiority bred by this history and reinforced by the attitude of contempt and dismissal encountered by Roman Catholics at the hands of Irish Protestants and of many Englishmen. This contempt was not, of course, universal; and Catholic Ireland always enjoyed English sympathisers,[14] and even Protestant supporters. But it was sufficient to rub salt into the wounds inflicted on the nation by its consciousness of military and political (and, from the 1890s) cultural overthrow. A nation obsessed with its own deficiencies, conscious of its servile past, could never win its freedom unless its confidence in the face of its enemy's sense of superiority could be restored. And while O'Connellism and Parnellism might help to restore it in political action, yet it still needed some heroic and emotional focus for its politics: it needed to be told that failure did not imply inferiority, that death did not mean annihiliation, that trials, executions, imprisonments, transportations, all the paraphernalia of the British legal and police system, all the power and might of the British empire, all the traditional arrogance of Protestantism, could not destroy the noble soul of a nation.

Irish nationalism was, in a sense, a form of secular religion: it was told as a story (as one of its finest historians, P. S. O'Hegarty put it) of Ireland 'in

[14] I have tried to explore the contradictory attitudes to the Irish Roman Catholic in late 19th century England in a forthcoming essay, 'Marginal Britons', in P. Dodd and R. Colls (eds.) *The Idea of Englishness, 1880–1920* (London, 1984). An excellent survey is Sheridan Gilley's 'English attitudes to the Irish in England, 1780–1900' in C. Holmes (ed.) *Immigrants and Minorities in British Society* (London, 1978), pp. 81–110.

the last phase of her captivity'.[15] It was propagated as a kind of faith, and, given the tendency of nationalist politicians to faction (which only the monolithic figures of O'Connell and Parnell prevented by establishing a leadership that was virtually a dictatorship) it was perhaps inevitable that nationalists should seek to create unity by emphasizing the idea of a common bond of religion and history: a Catholic people who kept both their religious and political faith in the face of superior odds. Nationalism was popular because it managed to wrest concessions, educational, economic, political, from the British; but it would be an error to suppose that it was merely a tribute to mammon. For these concessions were wrung from the British, not in the name of progress or modernity, however much they might promote such desirable ends, but in the name of hardly adequate recompense for past brutal misdeeds and misgovernment. Irish nationalism was fashioned as a kind of faith, a secular parallel of the religious devotion that gripped Catholic Ireland after 1850; and it provided a background against which the first significant martyr-makers, the Fenian Brotherhood, could operate.

The Fenian Brotherhood was a secret organization dedicated to the destruction by force of British rule in Ireland. As its most recent historian has pointed out, it was but one of a number of patriotic societies founded in the 1850s in the rising swell of European nationalism, the nationalism that was shortly to lead to the unification of Italy.[17] It spread more widely than its contemporaries, and was particularly strong in the United States of America among Irish immigrants. But its place in the making of modern Irish nationalism lies less in its success than in its failure. It was an organization riven by personal rivalries and leadership disputes; its attempt at a rising in Ireland in 1867 was dogged by a series of misadventures; and its ideal of a non-sectarian and liberal Irish nationalism was, in the event, more honoured in the breach than the observance.[18]

What they lacked in political expertise and military planning however, the Fenians more than made up for in their understanding of the psychology of Irish national sentiment. It would be misleading to assert that Fenianism awakened a slumbering genius of Irish nationalism, for nationalism after the Famine and death of O'Connell had not restablished itself as a major force in Irish politics. But the Fenians were able to build on the foundations laid by O'Connell decades earlier. O'Connellism was a moral force movement, relying on the power of the word, and still more to the crowd, to exert

[15] P. S. O'Hegarty, *A History of Ireland under the Union* (London, 1952).

[16] For which see the standard works by Emmet larkin, especially his article 'The Devotional Revolution in Ireland, 1850–1875', *American Historical Review*, lxxvii (1972), pp. 625–52.

[17] R. V. Comerford, 'Anglo-French tension and the origins of Fenianism', in F. S. L. Lyons and R. A. Hawkins (eds.) *Ireland under the Union: Varieties of Tension* (Oxford, 1980), pp. 149–71.

[18] For a discussion of these points see Boyce, *Nationalism* pp. 176–83.

pressure on the British government. But amongst these words were frequent appeals to events and figures in the Irish, Roman Catholic past: stressing the long period of suffering 'since Luther lit the candle', and the calendar of venerated martyrs.[19] But the latter were distinguished by a significant omission – the men of 1798, whose martyrdom was too close in time to be held up as proper leaders of the Irish people.[20]

The Fenians revived the idea of the suffering people and its beloved martyrs. But they did not fear to speak of '98 (nor for that matter '48). And while O'Connell had accustomed people to the images of noble death, and graveyard glories, the Fenians were able to offer a concrete example of the martyr that the idea of a suffering people, mourning over its dead prophets, generated. The Fenians sought to establish their legitimacy in the face of indifference, and, in the case of the Roman Catholic hierarchy, serious concern about the activities of a secret oath bound society on the young men of Ireland. And they did so by convincing people that they were not a mere accidental manifestation, but part of the great tradition of rebellion for the cause of Ireland that stretched back to 1798 and 1848. Their greatest propaganda success was the funeral of Terrence Bellew MacManus, a rebel of 1848 who died in New York, and who was given a kind of unofficial state funeral by the Fenians in 1861. MacManus was not one of the household names of Irish nationalist martyrology. But his funeral was carefully planned, combining sombre music and dress with paramilitary parade, including two Roman Catholic clergymen, and passing a vernated spot – or rather, a spot now venerated – in Thomas Street, Dublin, where nationalist Ireland's most charismatic hero, the young Robert Emmet, was publicly executed in 1803.[21]

The MacManus funeral attracted a turn-out of thousands in Cork and Dublin; and at the graveside T. C. Luby affirmed (as Patrick Pearse was to affirm at the grave of John O'Leary) that the example of the dead would give 'faith and stern resolve to do the work for which MacManus died'.[22] But the success of the propaganda funeral prompts some hitherto unanswered questions about the success of the political martyr and the subsequent place of the political funeral in the Irish nationalist tradition. It was an obsession satirised by the playwright Sean O'Casey when he made Mrs. Gogan, in 'The Plough and Stars' declare, after witnessing a parade of the Irish National Foresters

> ... The loveliest part of the dress, I think, is th' ostriches plume ... When yous are goin' along, an' I see them wavin' an' noddin' and waggin', I seem to be lookin' at each of yous hangin' at

[19] *Ibid.*, pp. 136–49.
[20] *Ibid.*, p. 147.
[21] Townshend, *Political Violence*, pp. 28–9.
[22] Boyce, *op.cit.*, p. 183.

th'end of a rope, your eyes bulgin' an' your legs twistin' and jerkin', gaspin' an' gaspin' for breath while yous are thryin' to die for Ireland.[23]

And when Bessie Burgess (Orange and Protestant and, in her own eyes at least, British) expresses her sorrow for the same Mrs. Gogan who has lost her consumptive daughter, the more astute Fluther Good disabuses her:

A terrible blow? Sure, she's in her element now, woman, mixin' earth to earth, an' ashes t'ashes an' dust to dust, an' revellin' in plumes an' hearses, last days an' judgements.[24]

O'Casey's rage at the Irish cult of death, with the funeral as a form of grim celebration – especially of the dead nationalist hero – leads the theme into sociological rather than historical grounds. And it is beyond the scope of this paper to explore its origin. It was, perhaps, part of the Roman Catholic consciousness inspired by the idea that the sufferings of the people – under English rule, in the famine – were God's judgement, for which a death was the only proper and appropriate expiation.[25] It was more likely simply another aspect of the Victorian character of Victorian Ireland, for the 19th century was an age when death was elevated into a sombre and extravagant ceremony, full of ritual and symbol, with plumes, hearses and black crepe, as Mrs. Gogan acknowledged.[26] The Victorian way of death, when placed in an Irish political context, became a resounding public and nationalist spectacle. It was a reminder to the people that their only proper response to the man who had 'given' his life for them was to reverse his memory and emulate his deeds. It helped create a kind of 'tyranny of the dead'.[27] And it transposed the blame for Ireland's ills from God to man – or, more precisely, Englishman. It was a means of shifting the burden of guilt away from the Catholic Irish to the Protestant English, reminding them grimly of what they had, (allegedly) done to the Irish nation, and were still doing. It thus served a double purpose of arousing the people and discomfiting the enemy.

The use of heroes who had died in their beds was one thing; the present given to the Fenians, and to Irish nationalism generally, by the creation of newly immolated martyrs was quite another. Or, rather, it was a continuation, but in a more immediate, dramatic, and decisive form, of the cult of death created by the Fenians in 1861. Nationalist popular songs were wont to weep

23 Sean O'Casey, 'The Plough and the Stars', in *Three Plays* (London, 1963 ed.), p. 167.

24 *Ibid.*, p. 208.

25 O'Farrell, 'Millenialism, Messianism', pp. 54–5.

26 Hilary and Mary Evans, *The Victorians: at home and at work* (Newton Abbot, 1973), pp. 73, 78. For other examples of the 'Victorianism' of 19th century Ireland see M. J. McCormick *Sheridan Le Fanu and Victorian Ireland* (Oxford, 1980), pp. 5–6; W. F. Mandle, 'The G.A.A. and Popular Culture, 1884–1924', in O. MacDonagh, P. Travers and W. F. Mendle (eds.) *Irish Culture and Nationalism, 1750–1950 (London, 1983), pp. 104–21.*

27 The phrase is J. C. Beckett's; see his *Making of Modern Ireland* (London, 1966 ed.), p. 441.

the grave of the young and attractive hero; Robert Emmet (so shrewdly recalled by the Fenians in their routing of the MacManus funeral procession) provided a characteristic figure:

He dies to-day', thought a fair, sweet girl –
She lacked the life to speak.
For sorrow had almost frozen her blood,
And white were her lips and cheek –
Despair had drunk up her last wild tear,
And her brow was damp and chill,
And they often felt at her heart with fear
For its ebb was all but still.[28]

This was sentimental and poignant, lovelorn and romantic. But Emmet was a figure whose death, while remembered, had about it an air of tragic but essentially poetical circumstance. To be blunt, Emmet was a long time dead, and Irish nationalism needed the powerful and energetic myth which only a crop of newly-sown martyrs could cultivate. A dead hero of the past was material for song and verse; a dead hero in the present would send a thrill through the country, vividly recall links with the past, and arouse nationalist and anti-British sentiment in the present – and the future.

Such martyrs were created in Manchester in 1867, in an incident whose fame long outlived that of the unsuccessful Fenian rebellion of that year. In October a Fenian rescue attempt resulted in the shooting of a policeman; and the Fenians involved, Allen, Larkin and O'Brien, were tried, condemned to death and executed in public on 23 November for the murder. The defiant mood and noble bearing of the prisoners at their trial, where they faced

'Crown witness, Judge and Jury ...
Avaricious of their blood'

was linked with earlier heroes similarly subject to 'judicial murder':

As Emmett and Fitzgerald stood
Whose memory still is green
Addressing courts imbued with blood
Again we have such scenes ...[29]

The court room scene was depicted by popular artists, and was illustrated in one of the most influential books in 19th century Irish nationalist literature, *Speeches from the Dock*, first published in 1867, and reprinted (and brought up to date) regularly – indeed, it was reprinted as late as 1945 with new

[28] James N. Healy (ed.) *The Mercier Book of Old Irish Street Ballads* (Cork, 1969), pp. 73–4.

[29] L. O. Broin, *Fenian Fever* (London, 1971), Ch. XII; Healy, *op.cit.*, pp. 138–40.

material covering the period up to 1921, and ran into its forty-eighth edition as early as 1894.[30]

In this book the 'efforts of the Irish race to burst the fetters that foreign force and native dissensions imposed upon them' were traced through the trial speeches made by patriots from Wolfe Tone to John Martin. The nobility and eloquence of what its authors, A. M. and T. D. Sullivan called 'Irish political prisoners' bore witness to the desire for freedom that brought forth in each generation men who were prepared to lift the pike and raise the green flag. Their dock statements 'reach us ... like voices from the tomb, like messages beyond the grave, brimful of lessons of dignity and patriotism'. Their memory must ever be hallowed; not least that of Allen, Larkin and O'Brien, 'Three gallant sons of Ireland ... whose blood has sanctified the cause of Irish freedom'. It was, the Sullivans reflected, only seventy years since Tone, and only two thirds of a century since Emmet, and yet 'already what a hord of imitators and disciples have they had', which not even Poland, Hungary nor Venetia could boast.[31] 'So perished, in the bloom of manhood, and the flower of their strength, three gallant sons of Ireland' befoer 'the wolfish eyes of the brutal mob'. A mob that had already shown its 'chivalry' when it seized and beat one of the Fenians, thus showing English nature 'in its real colours'.[32]

This was all very well; but even the most sympathetic reader will perhaps inquire about the morality of thus describing three men who had murdered a policeman, and whose comrades were, a month later, to cause an explosion in Clerkenwell in which twelve Londoners were killed and 120 injured.[33] Why did crowds turn out to view respectfully the empty hearses drawn through Dublin in December 1867 to commemorate the three Fenians? Why did T. D. Sullivan (a constitutional nationalist, and a man disliked and distrusted by the Fenians) write the hymn entitled 'God save Ireland' (The Manchester Martyrs' defiant shout from the dock) which became a national anthem? And why did 23 November become a day of annual pilgrimage to the shrine of the Manchester Martyrs, and one celebrated as much by parliamentarians as by conspirators?

A. M. Sullivan's own dock speech, when he was prosecuted under the party processions act for taking part in the funeral procession of the Martyrs (or, rather, their empty coffins),[34] offers some clues. When Sullivan was tried in

[30] T. D. and A. M. Sullivan, *Speeches from the Dock* (1867: all references here are to the 1894 ed.). The book was published in a new and revised edition in 1945, covering the period up to 1921.

[31] *Speeches from the Dock*, pp. 7–12.

[32] *Ibid.*, pp. 241, 250. The chapter devoted to Allen, Larkin and O'Brien is especially emotional and bitter.

[33] Sheridan Gilley, English attitudes to the Irish in England, 1780–1900, p. 96; L. O. Broin, *op.cit.*, pp. 210–211.

[34] L. O. Broin, p. 205.

February 1868 he conducted his own defence. Much of it was a recital of his version of the history of Anglo-Irish relations; and he denied the charge that the Irish 'glorify murder'. It was English law that the Irish did not respect, because it was not their law. Hence opponents of that law were no criminals but heroes. Sullivan added colour to his argument when he declared that the English police were to blame for the shooting of their comrade because they had run away from the Fenians, whereas 'if that had occurred in Dublin, eleven men of our metropolitan police would have taken those three revolvers or perished in the attempt' (applause). Some noble hearted Englishmen, he conceded, had pleaded for clemency for the three; 'but the roar of passion carried its way'. Hence the Irish response – the three 'appeared in new character ... they rose into the dignity and heroism of martyrs'.[35]

Part of Sullivan's argument – that English law was not the law to the Irish – explains why the murder of English officials could be regarded, even by constitutional nationalists, as defensible (at least). 'Yes, in our own days men have endured, with heroic silent fortitude, sufferings I dare not trust myself to mention', claimed John O'Connor Power in Manchester in 1874.[36] Charles Stewart Parnell, whose career was devoted to the capturing of violent nationalism for the parliamentary cause, declared in Westminster that no murder was done in Manchester.[37] But the other half of the argument was equally important. The whole tenor of *Speeches from the Dock* was one that stressed the 'fetters' imposed on the Irish, their suffering, the indignities heaped upon them.[38] A comparison between popular Catholic and Protestant attitudes to martyrs is instructive: the Orangeman, or Nationalist who gave his life for his cause was presented in very different roles. To the Catholic, the martyr was depicted as a tragic, wistful, saintly figure, surrounded with images of religious devotion, presented as a helpless victim of the cruel enemy – a hero to lament over, a prophet of freedom which such sacrifice might yet win:

When those poor men they was condemned
And asked what they'd to say
Allen he got up and spoke
In a bold and fearless way.
He said that he was innocent

[35] *Speeches from the Dock*, pp. 329–32; for a parliamentarian's discussion of the contrasting Irish and English attitudes to the martyrs see R. Barry O'Brien, *The Life of Charles Stewart Parnell* (London, 1910 ed.), pp. 43–6.

[36] *Flag of Ireland*, 17 Jan. 1874.

[37] F. S. L. Lyons, *Charles Stewart Parnell* (Fontana paperback, 1978), p. 54. As late as 1914 Tom Kettle, in his compilation of *Irish Orators and Oratory* included the speeches of the Martyrs, together with other clebrated 'speeches from the dock'.

[38] *Speeches from the Dock*, p. 7. See the perceptive comments of Louis Paul-Dubois, *Contemporary Ireland* (Dublin, 1908), pp. 172–81.

But made this bold reply
For poor oppressed Ireland
On the gallows he would die.[39]

As Sullivan's 'God save Ireland' put it

But on the cause must go,
Amidst joy, or weal, or woe,
Till we've made our isle a nation free and grand.[40]

Protestant popular martyrology was very different. The murdered Orangeman was no saintly hero, his eyes cast upwards, his thoughts fixed upon a (self-evidently) better world. His death at the hands of his Catholic enemies was an immediate and practical warning against the Protestant ever relaxing his vigil, for

... I'll end as I began
Be on your guard both day and night, and murdering Papists shun;
They never would consent for to meet us man to man,
But as they served Mcbriars they would serve each Orangeman.[41]

And when the British state and its agents opened fire on Protestants, tried or imprisoned them, Protestants were exhorted to take immediate and drastic action, not weep over their dead, hold funeral processions, lament or keen: in an Orange song, written on the occasion of the death of a man shot in Sandy Row, Belfast, for being 'too loyal', Protestants were roused to

Tear down that flimsy Government, in weakness unsurpassed,
That makes one law for Dublin, and another for Belfast ... [42]

Such popular songs reveal the different mentality of nationalism and Unionism. For Protestants and Unionists, superior, triumphalist, conscious that their survival in the 17th century and in the '98 rebellion was thanks to their own strong right arms, the dead hero stood as a warning that Protestants must never relax their guard, and must hit back harder than they were hit themselves – and do so at once, here and now, for, as Oliver Cromwell advised,

For 'happy homes', for 'altars free', we grasp the ready sword –
For freedom, truth, and for our God's unmutilated Word.
These, these, the war-cry of our march, our hope the Lord on high;

39 O. Broin, *op.cit.*, p. 208
40 Zimmermann, *op.cit.*, p. 267.
41 *Ibid.*, p. 318. McBriars was Master of an Orange Lodge, murdered because he would not agree to the 'vile Papish creed'.
42 *Ibid.*, p. 305.

Then put your trust in God, my boys, and keep your powder dry.[43]

For Roman Catholics, burdened and frustrated with a history – some real, some manufactured, – of a downtrodden, failed and tragic people, left, like the Serbs after Kossovo, to sing about their defeats,[44] the dead hero was an example to them to keep the faith, to remember the sacrifice, and to store up emotions that would, at some future date, enable them to take revenge on their foes.

This vengeance was reserved for the future generations – after the failures of '98, '48 and '67 no one could be sanguine about the chances of another armed revolt against British rule. Indeed, while emotions about the Manchester Martyrs were at their height in Ireland in 1868–1869, the constitutional nationalist movement was on the eve of a reconstruction that was to lead it near to success under the virtual dictatorship of Charles Stewart Parnell. But Parnell owed much of his success not only to his gift of leadership, not only to the enlistment of the tenant farmers in the nationalist cause by way of the new departure in 1879, but to his ability to create a nationalist movement that, in his own words, partook of an 'illegal' as well as a constitutional character.[45] And essential to that revolutionary character was the Irish Parliamentary Party's ability to convince people that it stood for the same cause as the heroic dead – especially the Manchester Martyrs. Thus political martyrdom, which gave such a powerful emotional surge to Fenianism in 1869, became a weapon in the hands of the home rulers. Partly this was because armed rebellion seemed unlikely to succeed, and thus the Martyrs' cause would have to be achieved another way; but equally important was Gladstone's disestablishment of the Church of Ireland in 1869, which demonstrated that the Protestant Ascendancy (and thereby the British connection) could be undermined by peaceful means. John O'Leary remarked sardonically that it was

> clear as the sun at noonday that the heart of the country always goes out to the man who lives and dies an unrepentant rebel. The rebel can reckon upon nothing in life; he is sure to be calumniated; he is likely to be robbed, and may even be murdered, but let him once go out of life, and he is sure of a fine funeral.[46]

But if the home rulers could deliver the goods and get results: land reform, educational reform, and (above all) in the end self government, then there would be no new crop of political martyrs. Political action would suffice.

[43] H. Halliday Sparling, *Irish Minstrelsy* (London, n.d. [1888]), p. 456 (Lt. Col. Blacker, 'Oliver's Advice', 1834).

[44] K. O. Morgan, 'Welsh nationalism: the historical background', in *Journal of Contemporary History*, vol. 6 (1971), p. 172.

[45] Boyce, *Nationalism*, pp. 332–3.

[46] *Ibid.*, p. 184.

The home rulers, up to 1914, seemed able to satisfy nationalist opinin. Thus William A. Redmond, in Manchester at a commemoration ceremony in 1912, declared that Irish party of today was endeavouring by constitutional means, 'to bring about precisely the same objects as the Fenians of 50 years ago'. And in 1909 at a commemoration ceremony in Manchester, John Dillon stated bluntly that 'to us Irish Catholics the greatest Catholic question in the world is the emancipation of the ancient Catholic race of Ireland'. John Redmond for his part told his listeners at Waterford in 1909 that, although the party was using different methods, it could not have won its great successes without the Fenians, and 'it was the Fenian movement which made possible the Land League movement and the National League movement of today'. He was only a boy of nine or ten in 1867 but he admired the men of '67 'with feelings of absolute veneration and affection'.[47]

Political power in Ireland lay with the ballot not the bullet; but no Irish nationalist leader could ignore the popular appeal of the hero and the martyr; and this ambiguity in nationalism towards violence and self sacrifice in the nationalist tradition was one found in the Roman Catholic church as well as the Irish parliamentary party. The Roman Catholic hierarchy in the 19th century set its face against revolutionary nationalism from which the blood of martyrs flowed. But many Roman Catholics felt, and expressed, their dislike of the British rule whose iniquities provoked young men into following the dangerous path to secret societies. To be anti-Fenian was not necessarily to be pro-British. And there were always Irish ecclesiastics, from 1798 to 1916 (and beyond) to whom the physical force tradition was understandable, and (to some) desirable.[48] Even Paul Cullen, deadly enemy of the revolutionary virus that was sweeping Europe in his time, would have allowed a mass for MacManus in 1861 had he been promised that there would be no political demonstration.[49] Moreover the fact that the martyred dead were Roman Catholic martyrs – martyrs, therefore, as much for faith as for fatherland – allowed the church to distinguish what was Caesar's from what was God's. While condemning the politics, ecclesiastics could approve of the religious fervour and sincerity of the Roman Catholic – whether he were Allen, larkin and O'Brien, or Pearse, MacDonagh and Plunkett – or even the Catholic/Marxist Connolly. Here again the martyr figure, which might have, and in some respects did, divide the nationalist people from the church, could reconcile them: for a man of violence, responsible for the death of a

[47] National Library of Ireland, volume of press cuttings on the Manchester Martyrs, 1891–1912 (ILB 0822 Vol. 43). The extracts quoted are from the *Freeman's Journal*, 25 Nov 1912; *The Freeman*, 9 and 27 Sept 1909; see also *United Ireland*'s leader of 25 June, 1898.

[48] S. Gilley 'The Catholic church and revolution in 19th century Ireland;, pp. 123–45; O'MacDonagh, 'Ambiguity in Nationalism: the case of Ireland', in *Historical Studies* (Melbourne), Vol. 19, No. 76 (1981), pp. 347–9.

[49] Gilley, *op.cit.*, p. 125.

policeman in Manchester in 1867, or of soldiers in Dublin in 1916, could, if he died a good Catholic, redeem his soul and sanctify the cause *for which he died* – even if his use of force for that cause *which he lived* met with official ecclesiastical censure. 'The scaffold', the reverend Eugene Sheehy declared in August 1885, had through the efforts of generation after generation of patriots become 'the altar of Irish nationality'.[50]

This complexity of attitudes on the part of parliamentarians and priests towards what the reverend Sheehy called with some hyperbole 'the holocaust' might appear hypocritical. But the Roman Catholic church in Ireland, seeking always to preserve an influence that it quite naturally conceived to be its right, and for the good of its people, had to live in Ireland and cope with the ambiguities and complexities of Irish nationalist politics. The view from Rome looked very different to the view from Dublin or Tuam, or for that matter West Belfast. Thus the amnesty movement for Fenians launched in November 1868 by Isaac Butt quickly gathered clerical support, and a distinction was drawn by one ecclesiastic between sympathy for amnesty and support for violence. There could be no doubt that such sentiments, coupled with a 'chapel-door' collection (which, admittedly, Cullen would not sanction) ensured that the 'faith of a felon' was the Roman Catholic faith.[51] And when church, parliamentary party and local nationalist organization combined to advance the cause of the 'Irish People' after 1879, the annual commemoration of the Manchester martyrs became a ritual in which the clergy could safely and sympathetically share.

The martyr figure was no longer, therefore, a means of creating or fostering violence in Irish nationalism; and the annual processions to shrines built in memory of the martyrs became something of a ritual – perhaps, even a mere ritual – as the constitutional movement settled firmly into power, despite the splits of the post Parnell decade. But it was this ritualizing or absorption of martyrdom that so alarmed the new generation of revolutionaries in the early twentieth century. At an impressive demonstration in Dublin in 1903 to mark the centenary of the death of Robert Emmet, perhaps, after Tone, the most popular of Irish martyred heroes, the Fenian John O'Leary in a short but pointed address warned his listeners that

> We are not here to talk. Emmet desired that his epitaph should not be written till his country was free, and I hold that the best way we can do honour to his memory is to strive with might and main to bring about the time when the epitaph can be written. I have nothing more to say, but I and all of you have very much to do.[52]

By 1914 some nationalists felt that the failure of Ireland to produce a new

50 *United Ireland*, 29 August, 1885.
51 Boyce, Nationalism, pp. 184–5.
52 *Ibid.*, p. 274.

generation of martyrs was the root of the cause of nationalist Ireland's degeneracy. Sean MacDermott, addressing members of the Irish Republican Brotherhood in Kerry in 1914, warned that

> Nationalism as known to Tone and Emmet is almost dead in the country and a spurious substitute, as taught by the Irish Parliamentary Party, exists. The generation now growing old is the most decadent generation nationally since the Norman invasion, and the Irish patriotic spirit will die forever unless a blood sacrifice is made in the next few years. The spark of nationality left is the result of the sacrifice of the Manchester martyrs nearly half a century ago, and it will be necessary for some of us to offer ourselves as martyrs if nothing better can be done to preserve the Irish national spirit and hand it down unsullied to future generations.[53]

And at the grave of the veteran Fenian O'Donovan Rossa in 1915 Patrick Pearse declared that 'Life springs from death; and from the graves of patriot men and women spring living nations'.[54] And when the logic of this sentiment was realised in the Easter Rising of 1916, Pearse's Headquarters General Order of 28 April declared that 'If they do not win this fight they will at least have deserved to win it. But win it they will, although they may win it in death'.[55]

The impact of the martyrdom of the thirteen Easter rebellion leaders has been too often told to need repeating here. It transformed the Rising form a 'dirty deed' – a stab in the back of those Irishmen fighting for Ireland's cause in the Flanders front – to a 'gallous story': an episode that enabled the rebels to identify with the past, with Tone, Emmet, the Manchester Martyrs, and to create the future, a future in which their cause of an Irish Republic would forever shape Irish politics. As the Protestant home ruler Stephen Gwynn put it 'nothing could have prevented the halo of martyrdom from attaching itself to those who died by the law for the sake of Irish freedom; the tradition was too deeply ingrained in Irish history'.[56] The phrase 'nothing could have prevented' is perhaps too deterministic; but certainly the spectacle of British law destroying Irish rebels was one which nationalist Ireland could hardly fail to respond to. It appealed to 'values of self-sacrifice for the group, religious communalism, purity, respect for women, fear of external evils and idealism which were taught by Irish Catholicism of the period'.[57] Moreover the pathetic circumstances of the executions, their long drawn out process, the execution of Connolly strapped to a chair because he was too badly wounded to stand, completed the picture. Or nearly completed it. For Irish nationalism

[53] *Ibid.*, p. 308; *cf.* Zimmemann, *op.cit.*, pp. 68–9.

[54] Patrick Pearse, *Political Writings and Speeches* (1918; Dublin, 1966 ed.), pp. 136–7; Richard Kearney, 'Myth and Terror', in M. P. Hederman and R. Kearney (eds.) *The Crane Bag Book of Irish Studies* (Dublin, 1982), pp. 273–87.

[55] Quoted in Townshend, *Political Violence*, pp. 298–99.

[56] Boyce, Nationalism, p. 285.

[57] T. Garvin, *The Evolution of Irish Nationalist Politics* (paperback ed., Dublin, 1983), p. 104.

only one more item was needed and that was supplied by the Roman Catholic faith of the rebels – men who died in their faith, and therefore (it could be held) because of their faith.

The Roman Catholic church would in all probability have condemned the sacrifice of the rebels had the hierarchy been in possession of foreknowledge about the rising. But the rising once over, and the rebels executed, and, more important, public opinion moved to sympathise with them, the church could hardly take a stand in the face of such circumstances.[58] Rebels, religion and popular martyrology were too strong a combined force; and popular shrines at street corners to 'St. Pearse' were signs of the times. Thomas Kent, an Irish Volunteer shot in Cork on 9 May after court martial gave his temperance badge to the Dean of Cork with a request that it be given to the Reverend Michael Ahern of Castlelyons from whom he had received it and to whom he 'now returned it untarnished'. The rosary beads that he used at his execution were later returned to his family.[59] The church, while it could not condone the violence of rebellion, felt an instructive as well as a judicious sympathy with the dead. The bishops blessed armed rebellion;[60] Catholic Fenianism was the victor of the rising; and the non-sectarian, at times, anti-clerical Fenianism of the 1860s was replaced by a militant Catholic and Gaelic nationalism, inspired by the mystical religious beliefs of Patrick Pearse.[61]

The martyred dead, however, could not by themselves free Ireland; they could only create the political conditions upon which a new, more radically nationalist movement could be built. And once again the complex relationship between the heroic dead and the rather more prosaic living developed, this time in the character of Sinn Féin, a party that was based on the embers of Easter and yet sought political power by means of the ballot: in this case the 1918 British act of parliament enlarging the franchise throughout the United Kingdom. 'Easter week had achieved its object' Eamon de Valera told the Clare electors in 1917. 'Another Easter week would be a superfluity'. The vote was like the 'crack of a rifle in proclaiming your desire for freedom'.[62] The victory of Sinn Féin in 1918 alarmed the physical force men, who perceived yet another case of the martyred dead being exploited for the practical living politicians. 'The position is intolerable', Michael Collins complained in 1919,

[58] D. McCartney 'The Churches and Secret Societies', in T. Desmond Williams (ed.), *Secret Societies in Ireland*, pp. 77–8.

[59] F. O'Donoghue, 'The Irish volunteers in Cork, 1913–1916', in *Journal of the Cork Historical and Archaeological Society*, vol. 71 (1966), pp. 41–8; see also Thomas MacDonagh's alleged speech at his trial (E.W. and A. Parks, *Thomas MacDonagh* [Athens, Georgia, 1967], p. 69.

[60] S. Gilley, 'The catholic church and revolution', p. 125.

[61] See for example Terence MacSwiney on the necessity for nationalism to be 'In conformity with the law of God', (M. Chavasse, *Terence MacSwiney* [Dublin, 1961]), pp. 23–4, 118–21, 132–3.

[62] Boyce, *Nationalism*, pp. 315–6.

'the policy now seems to be to squeeze out any one who is tainted with strong fighting ideas or I should say I suppose ideas of the utility of fighting'.[63]

The utility of fighting showed both the extent and limitations of its effectiveness in the troubles of 1919–21. IRA activity, terrorism and guerilla warfare made it impossible for the British government to stay in most of Ireland; and it was the practical, hard-headed gunmen, not the mystical self-sacrificing poets of the Easter rebels, that won as much of the day as the IRA did succeeded in winning. Political martyrdom helped create a climate of opinion in which the gunman could operate; it was not of itself sufficient to destroy the hold of Britain on Ireland. Yet its importance in the struggle for independence is undeniable. And a new status of political martyr was soon to be created. The death after clumsy forced feeding of a Volunteer commander, Thomas Ashe, in 1917, linked yet again moral superiority and violence, and indeed endowed self-violence with moral superiority:[64]

Let me carry your cross for Ireland, Lord.[65]

Similarly the fast to death of the Lord Mayor of Cork, Terence MacSwiney, in 1920 (as an act of personal atonement for his failure to turn out in 1916) provoked world wide sympathy for, and interest in, the Irish cause, and the usual funeral rites and political propaganda.[66]

But political martyrdom was essentially the weapon of a struggling, oppressed, suffering people (to take Irish nationalism on its own terms and accept its own self image). It was not the stuff of nationalism once possessed of liberty and country (or most of it). Or, more accurately, the new Irish state, whether under the government of Fine Gael, or Finna Fail, only needed the martyred dead as the dominant home rule party had needed them between 1870 and 1914 – as important but essentially ritualistic figures, to be respected and honoured, but to act as guides rather than drivers of the Irish nation. But they were in turn confronted with political and military rivals, those of the republican movement who could not accept the legitimacy of the Irish State, whether Fine Gael or Finna Fail led, and whose commitment to the idealised republic of 1916 remained unshaken. Thus there developed an at times grisly struggle for the memories (and sometimes for the bodies) of Ireland's martyred dead, with, on one recent occasion, the Irish government finding itself obliged to secure the interment of a dead IRA man by pouring concrete over his grave (unsuccessfully, as it turned out – he was subsequently disinterred and reinterred by his comrades and given full 'military' and

63 M. Forester, *Michael Collins: the lost leader* (London, 1971), p. 104.

64 Townshend, *Political Violence*, pp. 315–6.

65 Zimmerman, *op.cit.*, p. 71.

66 P. S. O'Hegarty, *History of Ireland*, p. 743; D. Mcardle, *The Irish Republic*, (London, 1968 ed.), pp. 359–60.

republican honours).[67] In 1940 de Valera was confronted with a similar dilemma, when Brian O'Higgins, a volunteer who had fought in the general post office in 1916, published a pamphlet in which he identified the IRA men who had planted a bomb in Coventry, killing and injuring innocent bystanders, with the Manchester Martyrs. De Valera compromised by protesting against the death penalty passed on the Coventry bombers which 'will be looked upon as an act fitting only too sadly into the historic background of our relations', while warning the nation against IRA activity at a time of crisis when 'small nations throughout Europe are devoting alll their efforts to strengthening national unity'.[68] In 1969 the then Fianna Fail government led by Jack Lynch formally requested the return of the remains of the Coventry bombers, thus fending off nationalist criticism that his government was 'soft' on the British, and identifying himself with dead martyrs, but not living IRA killers.

The martyr figure then could still strike a response, however limited, even in independent Ireland; and the IRA cross-border campaign launched in 1956 caused a tremor, with a wave of popular sympathy aroused after the death of two IRA men, Sean South and Fergal O'Hanlon, in a raid on Brookeborough R.V.C. barracks.[69] But the revulsion of Fianna Fail, and the second thoughts of the public, were revealed in the 1957 election when, so far as public order was an issue at all, Fianna Fail and Fine Gael vied with each other in competing for the image of the anti-terrorist party.[70] Elections in the south since 1968 have similarly been devoid of any real issue of the violence in the north of Ireland.[71] The 1957 funeral procession for South and Hanlon, like the return of the Coventry bombers, proved after all to be an expression of ritual nationalist obesiance, not a real active and living force that could disturb the political waters of southern Ireland.

But in the north the case was very different. Here the idea of the suffering people, so vividly expressed in 19th century nationalist propaganda, took on a new meaning, as the civil rights movement of the 1960s was met by Protestant suspicion and then physical opposition. This paper has argued that the martyr figure was most effective because most essential to a cause that based its emotional appeal on the idea of a suppressed and downtrodden people. In the atmosphere of success that attended the home rulers after 1880,

[67] *The Times*, 17–23 Feb. 1976.

[68] Boyce, *Nationalism*, p. 357; Earl of Longford and T. P. O'Neill, *Eamon de Valera* (London, 1970), pp. 368–9.

[69] J. A. Murphy, 'The new I.R.A., 1925–62', in T. Desmond Williams (ed.), *Secret Societies*, pp. 162–3.

[70] Boyce, *Nationalism*, pp. 359–60.

[71] Ronan Fanning, *Independent Ireland* (Dublin, 1983), p. 212.

[72] For an unsuccessful P.I.R.A. attempt to exhort passers by outside the General Post Office in Dublin to 'remember the thirteen' after 'Bloody Sunday', 30 Jan, 1972, see C. C. O.' Brien, *States of Ireland* (London, 1972), p. 282.

and the steps towards full sovereignty made by Irish nationalists in independent Ireland after 1922, it became a fossilized and moribund ritual, still an essential ingredient of Irish nationalism's sense of identity, but no longer a vital and dynamic force – until 1916, and then again, in the North, after 1980. For in 1980 some Provisional IRA men, led by the youthful Bobby Sands, embarked on a hunger strike that led to a preoccupation of the media and people of Northern Ireland with their slow and painful death.

The IRA hunger strike which began on 1 March 1981 and ended after the death of ten prisoners between May and August provided the inevitable scenes that had surrounded the political martyr since the Fenians; indeed, IRA propaganda consciously looked back to earlier examples, to Fenian prisoners like Jeremiah O'Donovan Rossa ('Chained hand and foot and forced to lap his food from the floor') and Terence MacSwiney.[73] Deeds of violence were forgotten, and attention focussed on the spectacle of a young man willing to give his life for Ireland, just as the victims of Fenian acts in England in 1867 became anonymous numbers against the names and personalities of Allen, Larkin and O'Brien. The initially sluggish response of the nationalist community,[74] the Roman Catholic hierarchy's efforts to end the strike quickly, could not allay the impact which another display of nationalist sacrifice made on a people that saw itself in the same light as did the Roman Catholics in the whole of Ireland in the 19th century: the idea of the suffering people, redeemed by sacrifice of the few, so potent in 1916, and in 1917 and 1920 with the deaths of Ashe and MacSwiney, produced a response to the strike in the north quite unlike the general indifference felt in the Republic of Ireland. In the south, despite occasional intervention by politicians, and many expressions of concern, the hunger strike could not produce the dynamic effect that it exercised in the North, where the self-image of the Roman Catholic community was one susceptible to the old emotional appeal of the tragic hero: Bobby Sands' statement that 'we admit no crime unless, that is, the love of one's people and country is a crime,[75] was but the modern version of the balladeer of 1798 who declared that love of country was 'an honourable crime'. Even the spectacle of grieving mothers engaged on last visits to dying sons (Allen kneeling before his mother to ask her blessing) was repeated.[76] and so was the purpose. A leading Republican publicist explained that Bobby Sands saw his case as 'a microcosm of the way the Brits are treating Ireland historically and presently':

[73] *The H Blocks: an indictment of Brisih prison policy in the North of Ireland* (Belfast, n.d. [1981]), p. 20; *1920: Terence McSwiney (sic) 1980??* (London, n.d. [1981]).

[74] Paul Bew, 'The problem of Ulster Terrorism: the historical roots', in O'Day and Alexander, *op.cit.*, p. 242.

[75] *The H Blocks*, p. 15.

[76] Ken Heskin, 'The psychology of terrorism in Northern Ireland', in O'Day and Alexander, *op.cit.*, pp. 97–8.

He definitely believes that people will die to win political status. But he knows that if he dies, through his death what whill happen is that there will be so much anger stored up in the Irish people that it will fuel the struggle for the next ten years.[77]

In the event 'St. Pearse' was joined by yet another crop of nationalist saints, and the political effect of the crisis was soon to be disclosed: the election of Sands as M.P. and the electoral advance of Provisional Sinn Féin, with the inevitable comparison of the fate of the old Home Rule party at the hands of resurgent republicans in 1918, and that of the SDLP and its political opponents in 1982.[78]

The political implications of the 'gallous story' have at times been far from negligible in Irish political history. And the Taoiseach of the Irish Republic, Garrett Fitzgerald, was aware of the pressure of 'MacDonagh's bony thumb'[79] on his shoulder when he remarked in July 1981 that

It has been clear from the handling of the problem by the British authorities that their assessment of the gravity of the situation created by the hunger strike has not corresponded with ours, and that they have not recognised the well-founded character of our concerns for the further consequences that would flow from its prolongation.

Fitzgerald went on to stress that the deepening crisis was not wholly the responsibility of the British; he condemned also the efforts of the IRA to 'obstruct a solution' which, he perceived, 'redoubled' as the Irish government sought to resolve the issue.[80] It is not the purpose of this paper to apportion praise or blame in the past or present, but to illuminate a significant and at times dangerous theme in Anglo-Irish relations. Nevertheless, the words of an Irish prime minister are not lightly to be set aside when the subject of political martyrdom and its consequences are under discussion. When in 1940 Eamon de Valera allowed hunger strikers to die he was able to do so because there was within his state no combustible political material which an act of martyrdom could ignite.[81] But the Northern Ireland crisis illustrated yet again the point made by *The Times* when it pondered in 1867 on the reasons why the Irish applauded the horror of the Clerkenwell explosion, and concluded that it was because of 'the outrageous egotism, the utter selfishness ... of an exaggerated national sentiment, self-obsessed, deaf to pity and humanity'.[82]

77 *Bobby Sands: Portrait of a Hunger Striker* (Belfast, 1981).

78 Bew, in O'Day and Alexander, *op.cit.*, p. 242.

79 C. C. O'Brien, *op.cit.*, p. 242 discusses the impact in the early days of the Ulster troubles of the 'bony thumb'.

80 *Keesings Contemporary Archives*, pp. 31193–4.

81 Longford and O'Neill, De Valera, pp. 356–7; but even here the authors point out that de Valera's initial decision to relent, in October 1939, may well have helped him to win the support of a public opinion which might not at that earlier time have accepted Draconian measures. See also T. P. Coogan, *The I.R.A.* (LOndon, 1980 ed.), pp. 184–93.

82 Quoted in S. Gilley, 'English attitudes to the Irish', p. 96.

For it is this national sentiment, and not innate traits of national character, that lies at the root of the Irish distinction between a gallous story and a dirty deed. It is a sentiment that has embedded itself deeply in the Roman Catholic nationalist tradition; it has not yet become the formal ritual in the north that the different political experience has rendered it in the south: and the subculture of violence which has often disturbed Irish politics and Anglo-Irish relations feeds upon it.

PEARSE'S SACRIFICE: CHRIST AND CUCHULAIN CRUCIFIED AND RISEN IN THE EASTER RISING, 1916

SHERIDAN GILLEY
University of Durham

The cause of all the poor in '93:
  The cause of all the world at Waterloo:
The shouts of what was terrible and free
  Behind the guns of *Vengeance* and her crew:
The Maid that rode so straightly and so true
  And broke the line to pieces in her pride –
They had to chuck it up; it wouldn't do;
  The Devil didn't like them, and they died ...

Envoi

Prince, may I venture (since it's only you)
  To speak discreetly of The Crucified?
He was extremely unsuccessful too:
  The Devil didn't like Him, and He died.

Hilaire Belloc
'Ballade of Unsuccessful Men'

The idea of sacrifice occurs in Christian cultures in realms remote from high theology, and the invocation of the soldier's sacrifice in war became highly topical in 1982, when even sensitive Anglican bishops defended the British onslaught in the Falklands with the text 'Greater love hath no man than this, that a man lay down his life for his friends'. The pacifist might reply that Scripture does not say that a man should kill for his friends; yet it has needed only this little war to remind us of the power of sacrifice even in modern language, in the morally ambiguous willingness to give up one's own life while taking the lives of others. It was this understanding of sacrifice in war, while invoking the model of the passion of Christ, which inspired and justified the first ultimately successful 'anti-colonial' revolution of the twentieth century, the Irish Rising of Easter 1916; and the speeches and poetry of the leaders of the Rising, of Joseph Mary Plunkett and Thomas MacDonagh, and more especially of Padraic Pearse, drew upon the sacrificial Christ of a prayerful Irish Catholicism.

The Easter reference in the Rising has always attracted attention. As James Stephens declared at the time, on Easter Sunday in Dublin they cried 'Christ has risen' in the churches; they cried 'Ireland has risen' on Easter Monday

(Augustine Martin 1966, p. 38). 'Elsewhere Easter is celebrated as the Feast of the Resurrection', remarks Terence the Vere White. 'In Dublin it is celebrated as the Feast of the Insurrection' (O'Brien 1973, p. 308). The resurrection of Ireland at Easter derives its power from a long tradition: the identification of Ireland and the Irish people with Jesus, as the suffering Christ of the nations martyred by the British, runs deep through nineteenth-century Irish Catholic culture. Yet in the wider European setting, the metaphor, the metaphor of suffering like Christ was so far from revolutionary violence as to incur the Marxist indictment of religion for offering an otherwordly justification for present suffering, and certainly the political conservatism of the court of Rome, in its century of warfare with revolutionary Italian nationalism, discouraged even Irish Catholics from developing the case for a just war into an argument for armed rebellion. There *were* Catholic revolutions in the nineteenth century, in Poland and Belgium, as well as a strong movement of Catholic civil disobedience in Prussia and the German Empire; and in Ireland there was a minority of revolutionary priests, from the 'croppy' clerics of Wexford in 1798 to the irrepressible neo-Fenian Father Patrick Lavelle. But the Church in general opposed the Irish rebellions of 1798, 1848 and 1867, supporting instead the non-violent nationalism of O'Connell and later Home Rule (Lyons 1971; Norman 1965). Archbishop Paul Cullen, later a cardinal, as ruler of the irish Church for more than a quarter of a century from 1850, earned the undying hatred of the revolutionary Fenians by refusing them the sacraments (Norman 1965), yet deep-seated anticlericalism failed to develop (McCartney 1967; Newsinger 1979), and the bridges with constitutionalist, not violent, nationalism were mended by Cullen's episcopal successors. Despite the survival of an underground insurrectionary tradition in the tiny Irish Republican Brotherhood, founded and funded from America, the victory of the constitutionalist school seemed complete by 1900, through an alliance between the priesthood and the parliamentary politicians (Larkin 1975, 1978, 1979; Miller 1973; Tierney 1976). To the outward eye, the non-violent character of Irish Catholicism seemed secure until the very eve of the Rising, which satisfied none of the Church's conditions for a just rebellion (Horgan 1948, p. 285; Shaw 1972, p. 118); so that Pearse and his fellow rebels were in revolt not only against the British, but against the explicit teaching and the dominant element in Irish Catholicism itself.

Yet the Rising was overwhelmingly the work of Catholics; only one of the 1916 leaders, Tom Clark, an old Fenian and sometime convict in England, remained true to the Fenian past by dying without the last rites, and the principal Protestant connected with the Rising, Roger Casement, was received into the Church before his execution. Some other nationalists like Maud Gonne had already taken a nationalist path to Rome (Levenson 1977, p. 94).

Catholicism had baptised revolution: and that by means of an understanding of Christ which carried revolution into the heart of Catholicism.

The revolutionary ideal was no more exclusively Catholic or even Christian in origin than Irish nationalism itself. Irish constitutionalism was partly a product of English Utilitarian influence, and revolution came to Ireland from republican France, firing the imagination of the rebels of Protestant background if not Protestant conviction, like Robert Emmet and Wolfe Tone. The Irish nationalist pantheon was always an ecumenical one, and Catholic nationalists were never narrow sectarians, but readily accepted Protestant leaders like Isaac Butt and Parnell. Yet from the 1820s, the great majority of Presbyterians and Church of Ireland Protestants became militantly Unionist and often No Popery Evangelical, and so Irish Nationalism became Catholic in its mass membership, as the expression of the wrongs of an impoverished and persecuted people. This trend was enhanced in the second half of the nineteenth century as the ardours of Italianate devotion (Larkin 1972) warmed nationalist feeling (O'farrell 1971), and as the language revivalists set to work to rescue the dying tongue and culture of the Gael. Here again, in the revival of Gaelic culture, the leaders were often Protestants opposed by the great mass of their co-religionists: most of the professional Gaelic scholars were Catholics, some were priests, but Douglas Hyde, the famous President of the Gaelic League, and Standish O'Grady, whose histories of heroic pagan Ireland so stirred the emotions of the young Padraic Pearse, were both sons of Church of Ireland Rectors. The greatest writers of the literary revival, Yeats and Synge, were also Protestants by birth, while another, non-Catholic, element came into the revolutionary tradition through James Connolly, (Owen Dudley Edwards 1971), a curious Catholic Marxist who might be said, like many of the early Socialists, to have believed in a devout Christianity all his own (Ransom 1980, pp. 29, 94).

Yet the fires of 1916 burnt out the foreign matter in Catholic nationalism. The idealism of literary nationalism was accepted, but not its ventures towards the wild romantic realism of J. M. Synge's depiction of the peasantry. As Pearse's lieutenant in the Dublin Post Office, Connolly, crippled by British bullets, made his confession and was anointed by a Capuchin friar to die a Christian hero, and his Socialism never came to mean anything to the great mass of Irishmen. O'Grady's semi-pagan heroism and a Jacobin republicanism purged of anti-Catholicism and anticlericalism became part of the spiritual endowment of the most Catholic state in Europe, a state which was the creation of a Catholic revolution.

Pearse's life and thought lie at the heart of that transition, the translation of ideals not specific to Catholicism into language seemingly Catholic. Like many another an Irish rebel, Tone, Emmet, Davis and Mitchel (Horgan 1948, p. 9), he was of mixed English-Irish parentage, his father being an

Englishman, a successful ecclesiastical sculptor of radical London and Birmingham Unitarian background, converted with his English wife to Catholicism in Dublin (Ruth Dudly Edwards 1977). His second wife, Padraic's mother, was an Irish Catholic, and from Padraic's Irish great aunt, the boy got his taste for Irish folk culture. His Gaelic was an acquired tongue which he never spoke with the fluency of a native, and his schooling, by the Christian Brothers, though much more nationalist than Most Irish education, was wholly geared to a gradgrind English examination system which he later described as a 'Murder Machine'.

Pearse qualified as a barrister, but his one notable appearance in court, if an oratorical triumph, was a legal failure. His early work was as a teacher and Secretary of the Gaelic League's Publications Committee, and in both his educational and linguistic endeavours he showed an efficiency and wisdom out of sorts with his literary reputation as a dreamy idealist. As editor of a famous Gaelic journal from 1903, he was responsible for encouraging many practical good works. After 1908, he founded two schools, St. Enda's for boys and St. Ita's for girls, in which a wide-ranging curriculum emancipated students from the examination treadmill (and from coercion and corporal punishment), while under an honours system drawing its inspiration from the 'fosterage' practised in the courts of Irish kings, the students enjoyed considerable freedom from authority as a 'Child Republic' with its own elected officers (Ryan 1919, p. 80). Pearse is a clear exception to the rule that no man is hero to his pupils, who seem almost without exception to have loved their school. Like the Gaelic League itself, St. Enda's did not seek to be monolingually Irish, but was based on a bilingualism taken from Catholic Belgium. It is true that the pupils sometimes 'ran wild' (Thornley 1971, p. 343) and that the schools were in chronic financial difficulties, and because Pearse's programmes for expansion and building outran his meagre income, St. Ita's had to close. Yet here again, as F. S. L. Lyons declares in his Introduction to Séamas Ó Buachalla's recent collection of Pearse's letters (1980), Pearse was a man 'meticulous and systematic' (Ó Buachalla 1980, p. xvii) in his business arrangements, and was except perhaps in his own eyes by no means a wordly failure, when he took the path to hopeless revolution).

But the first paradox of Pearses' nationalism was that spiritual sucess was the reward of worldly failure. 'The Gael is not like other men,' he wrote in a famous early address: 'the spade, and the loom, and the sword are not for him. But a destiny more glorious than that of Rome, more glorious than that of Britain awaits him: to become the saviour of idealism in modern intellectual and social life, the regenerator and rejuvenator of the literature of the world, the instructor of the nations, the preacher of the gospel of nature-worship, hero-worship, God-worship ...' (Pearse 1924, p. 221). The passage might have been written by a Deist nationalist enthusiast like Mazzini on behalf of Young Italy; it is notable, moreover, for the uncompromising, superhuman standards which it sets for Irish nationhood. Pearse's idealist refusal of the decadent realism of contemporary European literature is just as absolute, for the Gaelic race is the only one possessing 'a literature natural and uncontaminated ... as different from the unnatural literature of to-day as the pure radiance of the sun is different from the hideous glare of the electric light ...' (Pearse 1924, p. 225). Though he was later to change his mind on the value of the realism of Synge, the young Pearse was a passionate believer in the purity and perfection of Irishness, and that made him no moderate Home Ruler, but an exponent of separatism from the very first. Yet the lesson here – 'the spade, and the loom, and the sword are not for him', is one of conquest by the spirit not the sword, by the weapons appropriate to the school-teacher and Gaelic Leaguer. Indeed the lecture concludes with Newman's vision of an international Catholic University in Dublin, and Pearse's early political intransigence remained firmly rooted in the realm of absolute ideas.

Pearse was, however, offering as severely censored a reading of the Gaelic inheritance as of foreign literature, a Puritan Victorian understanding of heroic Ireland common to the Gaelic movement as a whole. The considerable traditional elements of bawdy and eroticism (Connolly 1982, pp. 192–194) were strained out in the translation in the interests of an Ireland pure and holy; not so the violence, which it was impossible to purge, and which is so grandiloquently idealized as Christian chivalry in the rhetorical volumes of O'Grady (1878 and 1880). The hall of King Concobar Mac Nessa of the Red Branch of Ulster is hung with 'the naked forms of great men clear against the dark dome, having the cords of their slaughter around their necks and their white limbs splashed with blood' (O'Grady no date, pp. 3–4); and Concobar's court is the setting for the coming of the young Chuchulain whom Pearse was to make 'an important if invisible member of the staff' of St. Enda's (Ryan 1919, p. 90). 'A.E.', the mystic George William Russell, describes Chuchulain in his tribute to O'Grady, as '*that incarnation of Gaelic chivalry, (of) the fire and gentleness, the beauty and heroic ardour*' displayed in a hundred gory battles against overwhelming odds (O'Grady no date, p. xiii). Cuchulain's ending is like Christ's, 'strapped to a post and shedding his life's blood in the defence of his people' (Owen Dudley Edwards and Fergus Pyle 1968, p. 45). Pearse declared that 'the story of Cuchulain (*sic*) symbolises the redemption of man by a sinless God' (Pearse 1924, p. 156). He wanted an Ireland 'teeming with Cuchulains ... a Cuchulain baptised' (Thompson 1967, pp. 76–77), and the mingling of Christian and pagan elements appears in his ideal for St. Enda's:

> the knightly tradition of the macradh of Eamhain Macha, dead at the Ford 'in the beauty of their boyhood,' the high tradition of Cuchulainn, 'better is short life with honour than long life with

dishonour,' 'I care not though I were to live but one day and one night, if only my fame and my deeds live after me;' the noble tradition of the Fianna, 'we, the Fianna, never told a lie, falsehood was never imputed to us,' 'strength in our hands, truth on our lips, and cleanness in our hearts;' the Christ-like tradition of Colm Cille (*sic*), 'if I die, it shall be from the excess of the love I bear the Gael.' (Pearse 1917b, p. 7).

This famous 'non-Christian' saying of Colum Cille, St. Columba, inscribed on the walls of St. Enda's, with Cuchulain's 'better short life with honour' comes from a late and suspect source (Shaw 1972, p. 134); but even in a different idiom, the same mingling of warlike sentiment and patriotism with Christianity could be also found in schools in England, in the years before the First World War (Marrin 1974, pp. 127–128). There is, however, an easy transition in Pearse's work from the blood of Cuchulain to the blood of Christ, and from here to the blood of the Irish political martyrs, and so to a more explicit enunciation of the underlying doctrine that the shedding of blood makes men holy.

The full statement of this position belongs to the last years of Pearse's short life: as late as 1912, he welcomed the Home Rule Bill as a first step to separation, while warning 'that if we are again betrayed there shall be red war throughout Ireland'. (Ruth Dudley Edwards 1977, p. 159). There was, therefore, a significant turning of a minority of nationalists in this year to the physical force school (Martin and Byrne 1973, p. 108), out of disillusionment whith the power of the moderates to win Home Rule; and it was also in 1912 that Pearse published his canonization of non-Catholic rebels in a ferocious litany intended in no sense of blasphemy, but in deadly reverence:

In the name of God,
By Christ His only Son,
By Mary His gentle Mother,
By Patrick the Apostle of the Irish,
By the loyalty of Colm Cille,
By the glory of our race,
By the blood of our ancestors,
By the murder of Red Hugh,
By the sad death of Hugh O'Neill,
By the tragic death of Owen Roe,
By the dying wish of Sarsfield,
BY the anguished sigh of Fitzgerald,
By the bloody wounds of Tone,
By the noble blood of Emmet,
By the Famine corpses,
By the tears of Irish exiles,
We swear the oaths our ancestors swore,
That we will free our race from bondage,
Or that we will fall fighting hand to hand. Amen.
(Ruth Dudley Edwards 1977, pp. 161–162).

So Pearse saw no incongruity in proclaiming at the grave of Wolfe Tone, who had loathed Catholicism (Shaw 1972, pp. 128–129): 'We have come to the holiest place in Ireland; holier to us even than the place where Patrick sleeps in Down. Patrick brought us life, but this man died for us ... He was the greatest of Irish Nationalists; I believe he was the greatest of Irish men ... it must be that the holiest sod of a nation's soil is the sod where the greatest of her dead lies buried'. (Pearse 1922, pp.53–54). So too, Pearse on Davis, a Protestant: 'The highest form of genius is the genius for sanctity, the genius for noble life and thought. That genius was Davis's'. (Pearse 1922, p. 328). Last, there is the ringing peroration to Pearse's elegy over the grave of the Fenian O'Donovan Rossa:

> This is a place of peace, sacred to the dead, where men should speak with all charity ... but I hold it a Christian thing, as O'Donovan Rossa held it, to hate evil, to hate untruth, to hate oppression, and, hating them, to strive to overthrow them. Our foes are strong and wise and wary; but ... they cannot undo the miracles of God who ripens in the hearts of young men the seeds sown by the young men of a former generation. And the seeds sown by the young men of '65 and '67 are coming to their miraculous ripening to-day ... Life springs from death; and from the graves of patriot men and women spring living nations. The Defenders of this Realm have worked well in secret and in the open. They think that they have pacified Ireland ... They think that they have foreseen everything, think that they have provided against everything; but the fools, the fools, the fools! – they have left us our Fenian dead, and while Ireland holds these graves, Ireland unfree shall never be at peace. (Pearse 1922, pp. 136–137).

The theme of resurrection is a law of nature, as well as God's. 'It is murder and death that make possible the terrible beautiful thing we call physical life. Life springs from death, life lives on death', and death can give birth to life (Pearse 1917b, p. 61).

Pearse found the roots of his identification of Ireland's cause with God's in some of the seventeenth-century poetry (but see Shaw 1972, pp. 141–142) mourning over Cromwell's Ireland, which Pearse had translated from the Irish, as in 'Prophecy':

> Victory shall be to the host of the Gael
> Over Calvin's clan – the trickster, the thief, the liar;
> Their nobles shall triumph over heretics,
> And shout at the routing of Clan Luther ...
>
> I pray God, if He deign to hear me,
> I pray Jesus who seeth all this,
> And the Holy Ghost again with one will,
> Mother Mary and Patrick White-Tooth,
>
> Kindly Colum and Holy Brigid,
> that they may weld the Gael together,
> And that thus they may compass this deed:
> The banishment of the Gall and the freeing of Ireland.
> (Pearse 1924, pp. 69, 71).

The Irishman's emotion is hatred of the Gall. 'Just as in early Irish manuscripts', writes Pearse, 'Irish love of nature or of nature's God so frequently bursts out in fugitive quatrains of great beauty, so in the seventeenth and eighteenth century manuscripts we find Irish hate of the English (a scarcely less holy passion) expressing itself suddenly and splendidly ...' (Pearse 1924, pp. 34–35). If love of Ireland was holy, then so was hating England.

Yet Pearse's ferocity was directed against abstraction not individuals. No man of violence himself, but a radical deeply opposed to capital punishment, he would 'weep over a dead kitten, and once stopped gardening for a whole day because he had killed a worm by accident' (Ryan 1919, p. 126). His plays and stories about women and children have a tenderness verging on the lachrymose: of the dying Old Matthias, who loved children, and was rewarded with a vision of Iosagan, 'Jesus-kin', the Christ child, to fetch him a priest, though Matthias had frequented neither clergy nor mass: of the Virgin and Child's visit to a barren woman, who later conceives; of the Christ-devotion of Mary Magdalen:

O woman, of the snowy side,
Many a lover hath lain with thee,
Yet left thee sad at the morning tide;
But thy lover Christ shall comfort thee ...

O woman that no lover's kiss
(Tho' many a kiss was given thee)
Could slake thy love, is it not for this
The hero Christ shall die for thee?
(Pearse 1917a, p. 80).

'God loves the women better than the men', remarks Pearse with the voice of the narrator. 'It's to them He sends the greatest sorrows, and it's on them He bestows the greatest joy'. (Pearse 1917a, p. 135). Pearse's psychology is a passionate intensity of extremes, and his ferocity is near neighbour to tenderness; great hate is born of great love, hate of the Gall, love of the Gael.

A hostile critic roundly declares that these direct emotions arise from Pearse's immaturity of vision, which places children before adults, and favours the rustic culture of the peasantry over urban sophistication, primitivism over civilization, and an ideal moral and literary simplicity over realist complexity (Thompson 1967, pp. 58–82). All the favoured qualities, however, are also those of Irish Catholic devotion, whether in the joyous tenderness of Iosagan and his mother, or in the reiterated theme of the *mater dolorosa*, the sorrowing mother, who becomes the mother of Christ, and is also Mother Ireland. The Keening Woman cries for twenty years for her dead son killed by the British; the story ends with prayer for the soul of the son, and the saying of the Rosary. Mother Ireland bears Chuchulain to her glory, and traitors to her shame. In the three Mother poems written just before his execution, Pearse addressed his own mother on the dolorosa theme:

My gift to you hath been the gift of sorrow,
My one return for your right gifts to me, ...
(Ó Buachalla 1980, p. 382)

'The Mother' offers Pearse and his gentle brother Willie, the ecclesiastical sculptor who died with him, to God:

I do not grudge them; Lord, I do not grudge
My two strong sons that I have seen go out
To break their strength and die, they and a few,
In bloody protest for a glorious thing,
They shall be spoken of among their people,
The generations shall remember them,
And call them blessed; ...
(Pearse, 1917a, p. 333.)

These last lines recall the Magnificat. Willie Pearse's statue of the 'Mater Dolorosa' still stands in a Dublin chapel, and 'A Mother Speaks' is an address to the sorrowing Virgin, and was taken by the Capuchin Father Aloysius to Mrs. Pearse on the day of Padraic's death:

Dear Mary, that didst see thy first-born Son
Go forth to die amid the scorn of men
For whom He died,
Receive my first-born into thy arms,
Who also hath gone out to die for men,
And keep him by thee till I come to him.
Dear Mary, I have shared thy sorrow,
And soon shall share thy joy.
(Ó Buachalla 1980, p. 383).

Pearse's identification of his mother with Mary is also an identification of himself with the Christ of the Passion, a preoccupation which originally arose out of his brilliant Passion Play in Irish, performed by his family, friends and pupils on the stage of the famous Abbey Theatre in 1911, with the blessing of Yeats, and with women keeners to provide an Irish setting: 'the Irish medium', recalled Pearse's pupil Desmond Ryan, 'had not veiled but intensified the meaning and pathos of the story. Some of us, too, thought, though to many it may seem an irreverence, that our national and individual struggle was in ways a faint reflection of the Great One just enacted. Is it not so? The Man is crucified as the Nation ...' (Pearse 1917b, p. 108). This theme is made explicit in Pearse's morality play 'The King', again, enacted by his schoolboys, in which a sinless child-king from a monastic school takes the place of his sinful monarch to die in battle for the freedom of the people. 'Do you think', asks his teacher Abbot, 'I would grudge the dearest of these little boys, to death calling with that terrible, beautiful voice?' (Pearse 1917a, p. 55). There is, then, an identity among the nation, Christ, the victim who dies for it and Pearse. 'The people who wept in Gethsemane, who trod the sorrowful way, who died naked on a cross, who went down into hell, will rise again glorious and immortal, will sit on the right hand of God, and will come in the end to give judgment, a judge just and terrible'. (Pearse 1922, p. 345). These themes all come together in the hero of his play *The Singer*, the revolutionary schoolteacher MacDara, who loses his faith, but refinds it in the Passion of the people: 'The people, Maoilsheachlainn, the dumb, suffering people: reviled and outcast, yet pure and splendid and faithful. In them I saw, or seemed to see again, the Face of God. Ah, it is a tear-stained face, blood-stained, defiled with ordure, but it is the Holy-Face!' (Pearse 1917, pp. 34–5). And as the people are as Veronica's Veil to Christ, so MacDara is again the son of Mary 'on the Dolorous Way', and is Christ in his triumphant conclusion: 'One man can free a people as one Man redeemed the world. I will take no pike, I will go into the battle with bare hands. I will stand up before the Gall as Christ hung naked before men on the tree!' (Pearse 1917a, pp. 24, 44). Or, as Pearse said in his last address to his pupils at St. Enda's: 'It had taken the blood of the Son of God to redeem the world. It would take the blood of the sons of Ireland to redeem Ireland'. (Pearse 1917b, p. 98).

The means, then, to this salvation is by the shedding of blood. Pearse wrote of the carnage of the first years of the war that 'Heroism has come back to the earth ... The old heart of the earth needed to be warmed with the red wine of the battlefields ...' (Pearse 1922, p. 216). Or, as he declared in anticipation of his own coming revolution, 'We make mistakes in the beginning and shoot the wrong people; but bloodshed is a cleansing and a sanctifying thing, and the nation which regards it as the final horror has lost its manhood'. (Pearse 1922, pp. 95–99). This doctrine is not, again, specifically Catholic in origin, though it occurs in the popular novels of the Catholic Canon Sheehan (Lyons 1979, p. 86). Rather, it derives from Cuchulain and from the favourite Nationalist image of Ireland as the rose which needed to be watered with blood, as immortalized by Pearse's exchange with Connolly in Yeats's famous poem:

There's nothing but our own red blood
Can make a right Rose Tree.
(Yeats 1950, p. 206)

The rose, however, has its relation to the Passion, as in Joseph Mary Plunkett's 'I see His blood upon the rose' (Plunkett 1916, p. 50); and even Connolly, no conventional Cahtolic, had been impelled to give the idea a religious cast: 'of us, as of mankind before Calvary', he wrote, 'it may truly be said "without the shedding of blood there is no redemption"? (Lyons 1979, p. 86).

In a less dramatic form, the same idea existed in Protestant Britain in the generalised notion that the First World War would purge sin and selfishness through the redemptive shedding of blood (Wilkinson 1978, p. 188; Thornley 1971, p. 342). Some Irish Catholics also gave the war a religious justification, like the Irish M.P. Tom Kettle, who died on the battlefield, one of the half a million soldiers of Irish ancestry to fight in the British and Dominion armies;

Know that we fools, now with the foolish dead,
Died not for flag, nor King, nor Emperor,
But for a dream, born in a herdsman's shed,
And for the secret Scripture of the poor.
(Martin 1967b, p. 63;
Owen Dudley Edwards and Fergus Pyle 1968, p. 100)

But here again, there are links with Pearse: Kettle dies for the dream of the poor, not for the king, while as in the theme of the sacrifice of the fool, the connexion between the planned Rising and the Passion is completed by the boast of their holy foolishness. The Rising was a theatrical gesture, an act of imagination, rather than a serious military affair (Martin 1967b, p. 127; Martin 1968, pp. 110–112). It was the work of a tiny conspiracy within the wider separatist movement: Sinn Féin had no part in it, though Sinn Féiners were to reap the reward, Casement's German mission had failed, and the leaders of the Irish Republican Brotherhood had also failed in their attempt to trick the mass of Professor Eoin MacNeill's Volunteers to join them. They took on the British Empire knowing that they must be beaten: yet for that Pearse was already prepared. 'I speak that am only a fool ...' he had written:

I have squandered the splendid years that
the Lord God gave to my youth
In attempting impossible things, deeming
them alone worth the toil.

The impossibility of the Rising is part of its attraction, for the consummate Christian hero is the fool:

Was it folly or grace? Not men shall
judge me, but God ...

Sacrifice of self is the chief message of the Gospel:

For this I have heard in my heart, that a
man shall scatter, not hoard,

Shall do the deed of to-day, nor take thought
of to-morrow's teen,
Shall not bargain or huxter with God; or
was it a jest of Christ's
And is this my sin before men, to have
taken Him at His word?
The lawyers have sat in council, the men
with the keen, long faces,
And said, 'This man is a fool', and others
have said, 'He blasphemeth;'
And the wise have pitied the fool that hath
striven to give a life
In the world of time and space among the
bulks of actual things,
To a dream that was dreamed in the heart,
and that only the heart could hold.
(Pearse 917a, pp. 334–335).

The lawyers in council, declaring 'He blasphemeth', are the Sanhedrin, and respectable Society, they are also the enemy, with political economy, of Christianity, as well as the British legal system which Pearse the barrister had forsaken (Pearse 1917b, p. 81; McCay 1966, p. 45). They all stand for the judgment of the world on Christ, which forgets that he triumphed through failure. Pearse's final act – recalling MacDara's nakedness, – is one of total sacrificial 'Renunciation':

Naked I saw thee
O beauty of beauty,
And I blinded my eyes
For fear I should fail ...

I turned my back
On the vision I had shaped,
And to this road before me
I turned my face.

I have turned my face
To this road before me,
To the deed that I see
And the death I shall die.
(Pearse 1917a, pp. 324–325).

Pearse foresaw and chose this destiny, even to the final dereliction of rejection by his people. The image arose from his dream about one of his pupils of St. Enda's about to die for a cause, confronted by a silent indifferent crowd. Pearse applies it to himself in the person of MacDar (*stet*): 'I seemed to see myself brought to die before a great crowd that stood cold and silent; and there were some that cursed me in their hearts for having brought death into their houses'. (Pearse 1917a, p. 25). Again, Pearse was to experience this himself, in reading the Proclamation of the Irish Republic to indifferent bystanders on the steps of the Post Office, and in enduring the more actively hostile jeers of Dubliners outraged by the destruction of their city. Yet the initial hostility of both Church and Nation to Pearse was to pass, as British bullets immortalized him as hero. '"Kings with plumes may adorn their hearse", ran a popular tribute ... "but angels meet the soul of Patrick Pearse".' (Ryan 1919, pp. 1–2). And so the religious imagination made true the sub-title of Ruth Dudley Edwards brilliant life of Pearse – 'The Triumph of Failure', turning fine rhetoric and indifferent poetry into a nation's creed.

It was Yeats, of course, who saw that these mildly comic fools, poets and school masters, had been transformed by the power of their sacrifice into something deadly serious:

Being certain that they and I
But lived where motley is worn:
All changed, changed utterly:
A terrible beauty is born.
(Yeats 1950, p. 203)

The final immortal oxymoron is almost a quotation from Pearse: the Abbot's 'terrible, beautiful voice' of death. Yeats concludes on the theme of love and death:

And what if excess of love
Bewildered them till they died?
I write it out in a verse –
MacDonagh and MacBride
And Connolly and Pearse
Now and in time to be,
Wherever green is worn,
Are changed, changed utterly:
A terrible beauty is born.
(Yeats, 1950, pp. 204–205)

Pearse was not the finest poet of the Rising: that was Thomas MacDonagh. The dying tubercular Joseph Mary Plunkett, with his bejewelled fingers and bejewelled verses and eve-of-execution marriage, is also a more complex and interesting writer than Pearse, as he places Ireland's resurrection and Christ's against a background of cosmic imagery drawn from the mystic St. John of the Cross (Ryan, 1963). Yet Pearse was arguably 'the most influential thinker, the most inspirational personality of the Rising'. (Augustine Martin 1966, p. 39). One of his many brilliant and grateful pupils writes of him and his companions, with no sense of irony, that 'we are now living the dream they died for' – that is, modern Ireland'. (Reddin 1943, p. 241).

There was of course more to the Catholicism of the Rising than Pearse. The confessionals crammed on Easter Saturday with men and boys, 'the striking fact that the rank and file of the Volunteers, almost to a man, prepared for the rising by going to confession and holy communion' (Martin 1967b, p. 20); the steady pace of the Rosary through the British bombardment; the O'Rahilly kneeling for a final blessing; even, in lighter vein, the impression of a modern writer 'that a few hundred British soldiers, dressed as priests, could have walked into the Post Office unhampered and put a sudden end to the entire rebellion', and the anxiety of combatants confronted with Friday chicken, until their chaplain, Father Flanagan, had taken his fork to the bird (Coffey 1971, pp. 126, 202). For these men, the religious legitimation of the Rising, even in the face of clergymen whom they had often defied, was of desperate importance, and Pearse provided that legitimation through the very symbols of the Faith. The consequences for Ireland were of course disastrous. Foolish talk costs lives, and as some Irish historians now recognize, the rebellion discredited the constitutionalist tradition and permanently alienated the Protestants of Northern Ireland from Irish nationhood. The pasisonate purity of the young firebombers of Belfast is Pearse's legacy, and an increasing number of Irish Catholics, like the splendid Jesuit Professor Francis Shaw, in his posthumously published challenge to the canon of Irish history (Shaw 1972), have dared to say that Pearse's ideals were hardly Christian.

It has been for some of the novelists and poets to reject Pearse most unambiguously: Sean O'Casey's prostitute sourly remarking of the Nationalists, 'they're all in a holy mood tonight' (Augustine Martin 1966, p. 40); Joyce creating a deliberately bourgeois anti-hero and sure that 'heroism is, and always was, a damned lie' (Watson 1979, p. 221); Yeats withdrawing into the tower of his old-age poetry from the Catholic nation he had helped to make:

Did that play of mine send out
Certain men the English shot?
(Yeats 1950, p. 393).

or in another oxymoron which occurs in Pearse:

A revolutionary soldier kneeling to be blessed;
An Abbot or Archbishop with an upraised hand
Blessing the Tricolour. 'This is not', I say,
The dead Ireland of my youth, but an Ireland
The poets have imagined, terrible and gay'.
(Yeats 1950, p. 365)

Yet it was an Ireland dreamed of by the young poet Yeats, who had lived in fascinated horror to disown his dream. 'Too long a sacrifice can make a stone of the heart', and for Yeats that stone was the heart of Catholic Ireland:

Out of Ireland have we come.
Great hatred, little room,
Maimed us at the start.
I carry from my mother's womb
A fanatic heart.
(Yeats 1950, p. 288)

In that sense, of turning the heart to the stone of a fanatic hate, it must be said of Pearse's sacrifice that it was magnificent, but hardly Christianity. Perhaps there is a lesson here for the liberation theologies of our time, which can be so free with the blood of the oppressor. Yet I had written this conclusion when I heard an army chaplain in Falklands cathedral telling his men that war had changed them utterly, with a deeper knowledge of God and of themselves. How far is it from that to the doctrine that blood purifies? The crucified Christ has many contradictory faces in the history of the Church, and the true Christ is difficult to find. It is too hard a saying that even this Irish Christ-modelled sacrifice of a Christian man and nation should be accounted wholly wrong.

There is also the uncomfortable consideration that Pearse's sacrifice, like Christ's, succeeded by its failure:

O wise men, riddle me this: What if the dream come true?
What if the dream come true? and if millions unborn shall dwell
In the house that I shaped in my heart? ...

Certainly in Northern Ireland, Pearse's vision retains its power. The existence of his set of Roman Catholic devotional images which offer a sanction to revolutionary activity does not, of course, in itself provide an explanation of the violence of the para-militaries in Ulster. This has a far more complex explanation in the social ghettoisation of the Protestant and Catholic communities, in the long years in which Catholics suffered discrimination and disability, even in the weakening authority of the priesthood in the 1970s to keep communal violence within bounds: the Bishop of Down and Connor met very different reactions from his flock when he opposed barricade-building in 1970 and 1974. Yet insofar as the Irish state was itself the creation of a Catholic revolution, there is undoubtedly an Irish Catholic imagery which speaks at a deeper level than self-interest, an imagery of sacrifice and suffering as in the pictures which appeared on Belfast and Derry walls during the H Block hunger strikes. Surely there have been few stranger applications of the Beatitudes than the ascription of the text 'Blessed are they who hunger for justice's sake' in a tenement mural, to the martyrdom of Bobby Sands. The heart of the matter is this: the English historian of the working class, Raphael Samual has spoken of the way in which Englishmen sympathetic to revolution cannot but be influenced by the anti-revolutionary bias of English culture. For an intellectual Marxist reared on *A Tale of Two Cities*, 'revolution' can still call up Dickens' ghastly vision of *tricoteuses* and tumbrils. It is on this level, of the image which enshrines the whole experience of a culture, that Irish Catholicism retains its revolutionary character: needing, as in Ulster, only the time and favourable harsh circumstance to leap.

REFERENCES

Coffey, Thomas M. (1971) Agony at Easter The 1916 Irish Uprising, London: Penguin.

Connolly, S. J. (1982) Priests and People in Pre-Famine Ireland 1780–1845, New York: Gill and Macmillan.

Dangerfield, George (1977) The Damnable Question A Study in Anglo-Irish Relations, London: Quartet Books.

Edwards, Owen Dudley and Pyle, Fergus (1968) 1916 The Easter Rising, London: MacGibbon & Kee.

Edwards, Owen Dudley (1971) The Mind of an Activist – James Connolly, Dublin: Gill and Macmillan.

Edwards, Ruth Dudley (1977) Patrick Pearse The Triumph of Failure, London: Voctor Gollancz.

Egan, Desmond (1966) Attitudes to Catholicism in the Modern Irish Novel, M.A. thesis, University College, Dublin.

Horgan, John J. (1948) Parnell to Pearse: Some Recollections and Reflections, Dublin: Browne and Nolan.

Larkin, Emmet (1972) The Devotional Revolution in Ireland, 1850–75, *The American Historical Review* 77, pp. 625–652.

Larkin, Emmet (1975) The Roman Catholic Church and the creation of the modern Irish State, 1878–1886, Philadelphia: American Philosophical Society.

Larkin, Emmet (1978) The Roman Catholic Church and the Plan of Campaign in Ireland, 1886–1888, Cork: University Press.

Larkin, Emmet (1979) The Roman Catholic Church in Ireland and the Fall of Parnell, 1888–1891, Liverpool: University Press.

Levenson, Samuel (1977) Maud Gonne, London: Cassell.

Lyons, F.S.L. (1971) Ireland since the Famine, London: Weidenfeld and Nicolson.

Lyons, F.S.L. 91979) Culture and Anarchy in Ireland 1890–1939, Oxford: Clarendon Press.

McCartney, Donal (1967) The Church and the Fenians, *University Review* iv, pp. 203–15.

McCay, Hedley (1966) Padraic Pearse a new biography, Cork: The Mercier Press.

Marrin, Albert (1974) The Last Crusade The Church of England in the First World War, Durham, North Carolina: Duke University Press.

Martin, Augustine (1966) To Make a Right Rose Tree, *Studies An Irish Quarterly Review* pp. 38–50.

Martin, F.X., O.S.A. (ed.)(1967a) Leaders and Men of the Easter Rising: Dublin 1916, London: Methuen.

Martin, F.X. (1967b) 1916 – Myth, Fact and Mystery, *Studia Hibernica* 7, pp. 7–126.

Martin, F.X. (1968) The 1916 Rising – A *Coup d'État* or a 'Bloody Protest'? *Studia Hibernica* 8, pp. 106–137.

Martin, F.X. and Byrne, F.J. (eds.)(1973) The Scholar Revolutionary: Eoin MacNeill, 1867–1945, and the Making of the New Ireland, Shannon: Irish University Press.

Miller, David W. (1973) Church, State and Nation in Ireland, 1898–1921, Dublin: Gill and Macmillan.

Newsinger, John (1979) Revolution and Catholicism in Ireland, 1848–1923, *European Studies Review* 9, pp. 457–480.

Norman, E.R. (1965) The Catholic Church and Ireland in the Age of Rebellion, 1859–1873, London: Longmans.

O'Brien, Conor Cruise (1973) States of Ireland, London: Hutchinson.

Ó Buachalla, Séamas (ed.)(1980) The Letters of P.H. Pearse, Gerrards Cross: Colin Smythe.

O'Farrell, Patrick (1971) Ireland's English Question: Anglo-Irish Relations, 1534–1970, London: Batsford.

O'Grady, Standish (no date) The Coming of Cuchulain, Dublin: The Talbot Press.

O'Grady, Standish Jemes (1878 and 1880) History of Ireland: The Heroic Period, 2 vols. London: Sampson Low. Republished (1979) New York: Lemma.

Pearse, P.H. (1916) The Separatist Idea, Dublin: Whelan & Son.

Pearse, P.H. (1917a) Collected Works of Padraic H. Pearse Plays Stories Poems, Dublin and London: Maunsel.

Pearse, P.H. (1917b) The Story of a Success Being a Record of St. Enda's College September 1908 to Easter 1916. Desmond Ryan (ed.) Dublin and London: Maunsel.

Pearse, P.H. (1922) Collected Works of Padraic H. Pearse Political Writings and Speeches, Dublin and London: Maunsel & Roberts.

Pearse, P.H. (1924) Collected Works of Padraic H. Pearse Songs of the Irish Rebels and Specimens from an Irish Anthology Some Aspects of Irish Literature Three Lectures on Gaelic Topics, Dublin, Cork, Belfast: The Phoenix Publishing Co.

Plunkett, Joseph Mary (1916) The Poems of Joseph Mary Plunkett, Dublin: The Talbot Press.

Ransom, Bernard (1980) Connolly's Marxism, London: Pluto Press.

Reddin, Kenneth (1943) A man called Pearse, *Studies An Irish Quarterly Review* pp. 241–251.

Ryan, Desmond (1919) The Man called Pearse, Dublin and London: Maunsel.

Ryan, Desmond (1934) Remembering Sion, London: Arthur Barker.

Ryan, Desmond (ed.)(1963) The 1916 Poets, Dublin: Allen Figgis.

Shaw, Rev. Professor Francis, S.J. (1972) The Canon of Irish History – A Challenge, *Studies An Irish Quarterly Review* LXI, pp. 113–153.

Thompson, William Irwin (1967) The Imagination of an Insurrection Dublin, Easter 1916 A Study of an Ideological Movement, New York: Oxford University Press.

Thornley, David (1971) Patrick Pearse and the Pearse Family, *studies An Irish Quarterly Review* LX, pp. 332–346.

Tierney, Mark (1976) Croke of Cashel: the Life of Archbishop Thomas William Croke, 1823–1902, Dublin: Gill and Macmillan.

Watson, G.J. (1979) Irish Identity and the Literary Revival Synge, Yeats, Joyce and O'Casey, London: Croom Helm.

Wilkinson, Alan (1978) The Church of England and the First World War, London: SPCK.

Yeats, W.B. (1950) The Collected Poems of Yeats, London: Macmillan.

IRISH TERRORISM IN BRITAIN: A COMPARISON BETWEEN THE ACTIVITIES OF THE FENIANS IN THE 1860S AND THOSE OF REPUBLICAN GROUPS SINCE 1972

MAUREEN HARTIGAN, ALAN O'DAY AND ROLAND QUINAULT

Although comparisons between apparently similar situations has numerous pitfalls, they can also be instructive. History never exactly repeats itself but two sets of events can be sufficiently similar to afford illuminating comparison. Over the past 120 years Britain has experienced a number of outbreaks of Irish Republican violence. But the two episodes which have attracted most attention have been the Fenian activities in the 1860s and the terrorism of contemporary Republican movements. In the 1860s the activities of the Fenians in Britain encouraged Britain's political leaders to re-examine Irish grievances and to provide legislative remedies for some of them. In contrast contemporary Republic activity in Britain has been more extended in time and more violent in nature yet it has won few, if any, concessions for the Irish Republican cause. Why did violence in one era seem to reap a significant reward and so little in the next? Are there ways in which the Fenian outrages can illuminate our understanding of the strengths and defects of today's Irish terrorism on mainland Britain? This article will compare the two eras and the degree to which subsequent Irish terrorism has conformed to the myths and methods of the Fenians.

I

In the nineteenth century a large and permanent Irish community was established in Britain. The Irish were attracted to Britain by the prosperity and the employment opportunities afforded by industrial and urban development. The failure of the Irish agrarian economy to support the rapidly growing population encouraged large scale emigration to Britain. After the famine many Irish flocked to Britain in the later 1840s and early 1850s. Britain was a particularly attractive destination for the poorer Irish who could not afford the fare across the Atlantic to the United States. Moreover, the political union between Britain and Ireland ensured there was no restriction on movement between the two countries. By 1861 there were over 661,000 Irish born in England and Wales, who constituted 3% of the British population. But the Irish community in Britain was at least twice as large as this if we include the children born in Britain of Irish parents. Irish settlement in Britain was heavily concentrated in the developing urban and industrial and urban areas. Most of the Irish lived in Lancashire, London or Glasgow, but there were also important Irish communities in the West Riding, on Tyneside and in South Wales. In 1841, 4% of London's population was Irish born and 175 of the population of Liverpool: the port with closest ties with Ireland. The majority of the Irish community in Britain occupied inferior positions in the economic and social hierarchy. Most were employed in unskilled jobs, many of the men being day labourers and many of the women domestic servants.

Irish Catholics formed the great majority of the Irish in Britain and their faith set them apart, socially as well as religiously, from the Protestant majority in Britain. Catholic endogamy together with Cathoilc welfare and social provision helped to preserve the distinct identity of the Irish in Britain and delayed assimilation into the mainstream of British society. But this situation was also encouraged by the political outlook of the Irish in Britain. In general, their politics, like their religion, was taken from their homeland. Although some Irish participated in English radical movements such as Chartism, they played virtually no official part in British public life at either a national or a local level. Most of their political interests revolved round specifically Irish movements such as Daniel O'Connell's Repeal Party which was active in the 1830s and in the 1840s. By the 1860s the Irish in Britain had begun to take an active interest in the revolutionary Irish republican movement of the Fenians.

Numerical estimates of the Fenian movement's active support in Britain ranged from the exaggerated claims of James Stephens, 'the Fenian chief', that 80,000 had enrolled to the innocent belief of the chief constable of Liverpool, that no actual organisation existed in his town.[1] Possibly the more realistic figure was that disclosed to the Home Office by the British consul in Philadelphia which estimated that some 18,000 Fenians existed on the mainland. According to the consul's informant there were some 7,000 in England, 8,000 in Scotland, and 3,000 in Wales actually sworn onto the Fenian muster rolls of subscribers.[2] Whatever the true numbers, they were sufficiently large to permit the establishment of branches or 'circles', as they were called, in most towns and cities where the Irish had settled. Yet, it seems probable that most of the circles must have been small and committed Fenians never constituted more than a tiny proportion of the Irish population. The clandestine nature of the organisation makes anything more precise than rough estimates impossible. The limited evidence available does not sustain the allegation of *The Times* that Fenians were drawn from the 'lowest and poorest of the Irish immigrants' for those charged with offences between 1866

[1] Head Constable of Liverpool to Mayor of Liverpool, 26 Sept. 1865, Public Recored Office, HO45 7799 Pt. I.

[2] Charles Kortwright to Home Office, Sept. 1865, *ibid.*

and 1868 were men with skilled trades.[3] Shoemakers and tailors seem to have been particularly involved in Fenianism.[4] Michael Davitt, who in the 1870s was to become the most celebrated of the Fenian prisoners in English prisons, was an educated clerk.[5] British Fenians appear to bear a resemblance to their brothers in Ireland and may be presumed to have joined for similar reasons. Some of the non-ideological motivations for membership in Ireland have been stressed by R. V. Commerford.[6] It seems likely that the isolated character of Irish life in Britain, particularly in an era before mass participation in politics or widespread involvement in team games, made Fenianism a form of socially attractive association to the young. The apparently substantial number of Fenian recruits, then, did not mean that those who subscribed could be termed hard-core activists.

Fenian activities in Britain were intimately linked to plans for a rising in Ireland.In 1866 the Fenian leaders hoped that many Irishmen in Britain would soon return to Ireland to assist with the armed struggle. Manyof those who returned to Ireland at Christmas 1865 (a tradition for Irishmen in all ages) stayed on afterwards for the purpose of aiding the uprising. Daniel Ryan, Dublin's ever-vigilant Chief of Police, found that 38 out of the 91 Fenians arrested in the swoop of February 1866 were 'strangers from England'.[7] The role assigned to the Fenians who stayed in Britain was strictly subsidiary. They were expected, when the Irish rising broke out, to create a universionary 'conflagration' on the mainland by systematically firing docks, gasworks and warehouses.

The homeland orientation of the Fenians in England was evident in February 1867 when they raided Chester Castle. They hoped to seize arms which could be used in the approaching Irish rising. But the suspicions of the authorities were aroused by the large number of Irishmen who travelled by train to Chester and the plan was foiled. Hitherto the government had paid little attention to Fenianism in Britain. Indeed the government was far more concerned with Fenian activities in the United States where they mounted several attacks on Canada and sought to embroil the republic in a war with Britain. Although the Chester episode alerted the English authorities to a domestic problem, the suppression of the Fenian uprising in Ireland, in March 1867, engendered a sense of complacency in England. Hence the dramatic events in England in the latter part of 1867, caught the government, the police, the press and the public by surprise.

Early on 11 September Captain Thomas Kelly, recently elected chief

[3] *Times*, 4 March 1868.
[4] See, Daniel Ryan to Home Office, Feb. 1865, P.R.O., HO45 7799 Pt. I.
[5] See, T.W. Moody, *Michael Davitt and the Irish Revolution* (Oxford, 1980).
[6] R.V. Comerford, *The Fenians in Context* (Dublin, 1984).
[7] See above n. 4.

executive of the 'Irish Republic' and Timothy Deasy, another Fenian leader, were arrested in Manchester.[8] A week later they were rescued by Fenian friends who attacked the police van which was transporting them to court. The rescuers shot open the lock of the van, but the bullet ricocheted and fatally wounded one of the policemen guarding the van, Sergeant Brett. However, both Kelly and Deasy escaped and neither man was subsequently recaptured. Thus from a Fenian point of view the Manchester rescue was a success which ranked with the earlier escape of Stephens from Richmond gaol in Dublin. Indeed the incident gave Fenianism a new lease of life at a time when it badly needed it. The Dublin *Freeman's Journal* observed that 'had this clever and daring manoeuvre been accomplished in an Irish town or even the Irish metropolis, it would create little surprise; but the rescue of an "Irish rebel" from the hands of the police in one of the great centres of England is a strange if not an alarming illustration of the extent of the orgnasiation and of the capacity of those who direct it'.[9]

But the death on duty of the unarmed Sergeant Brett did not produce any English sympathy for Fenianism. Moreover, many Irishmen in England displayed no sympathy for the Fenian action. While the trial of the Manchester 'murderers' was in progress, a thousand Irish workers employed in the Derbyshire iron and coal industries denounced Fenianism and expressed their desire to live on good terms with their English neighbours.[10] But the subsequent execution of three Fenians for the alleged murder of Brett was regarded by many Irish in Britain and even by many English people as an act of injustice. For the convicted Fenians had been brave men who had not set out to murder Brett but merely to rescue Kelly and Deasy. Moreover Richard O'Sullivan Burke, the organiser of the rescue, restrained two of his men from killing the informer who had identified Kelly and Deasy since it would only effect the 'ruin and failure of the purpose then in mind'.[11] Thus after the execution of the three Fenians, thousands of Irish men and women marched in funeral processions in Manchester and London to honour the 'martyrs'. Yet most were probably motivated more by anger at the miscarriage of justice than by Fenian commitment. For they were joined in their protests by substantial numbers of English radicals who had little understanding of and less sympathy with Fenianism. The belief that no premeditated murder had been committed at Manchester became in the 1880s an article of faith upheld by Parnell and the Irish parliamentary party in the House of Commons.

It was initially assumed that London, like the rest of Britain, was immune from the dangers of Fenianism. In January 1866 two Fenians were charged

8 See, P. Quinlivan and P. Rose, *The Fenians in England, 1865–1872* (1983).
9 *Freeman's Journal*, 19 Sept. 1967.
10 *Times*, 13 Nov. 1867.
11 John Devoy, *Recollections of An Irish Rebel* (Shannon, 1969), pp. 240–42.

with inciting Irish soldiers at Woolwich to join them, but the incident did not create alarm. Indeed, the defending barrister at their trial declared that it was 'a most absurd thing to suppose that Fenianism would succeed in London in the midst of a population devoted to the Queen, the constitution and the country'.[12] Yet, within two years, a single explosion at Clerkenwell was sufficient to create 'Fenian fever' in London. In December 1867 – while the protests against the executions at Manchester were in progress – a group of Fenians tried to rescue Richard Burke from the Clerkenwell House of Correction in London.[13] But the explosives they used to knock down the prison were badly placed and the blast backfired destroying many houses in the vicinity. Six civilians were killed and many others injured. The public outcry that the explosion provoked was understandable and extended even to those English groups broadly sympathetic to the Irish. The radical newspaper, *Beehive*, which had merely expressed 'regret' at the accidental shooting at Manchester, announced its 'deep abhorrence' of the Clerkenwell operation.[14] Those papers which were hostile to Irish nationalist aspirations regarded the Clerkenwell explosion as merely one incident in a much wider Fenian terror campaign in Britain. Thus *The Times* believed that the Fenians were determined to 'coerce us in this country ... by isolated acts of violence more or less murderous as the occasion prompts'.[15]

London was gripped by Fenian fever for over a month after the Clerkenwell explosion. The would-be rescuers of Burke were damned as 'maniacs' and 'unprincipled miscreants' who had come over to England to 'cry havoc, hell and destroy'.[16] Major buildings in the metropolis, such as the Tower of London, St. Paul's Cathedral, the Bank of England and the gasworks were believed to be the objects of probable bomb attacks.[17] It was even alleged that thousands of Irish labourers were constructing a tunnel under London in which they were placing explosives intended to destroy the city.[18] Even ordinary crime was now attributed to the evil designs of the Fenians, such as an attempt to set on fire a tailor's shop in Bishopgate.[19] The London correspondent of the *Freeman's Journal* noted 'We hear no more of trade outrages, of rattening, of picketing or vitriol – all are merged into Fenianism'. He observed that one of the few recent fatalities in London not attributed to the Fenians was the death of a walrus at the London Zoo.[20] Certainly the

12 *The Beehive*, 4 Jan. 1868.
13 See, Quinlivan and Rose, *The Fenians In England.*
14 *The Beehive*, 4 Jan. 1868.
15 *Times*, 14 Dec. 1867.
16 *Ibid.*, 18 Dec. 1867.
17 See, J.R. Vincent (ed.), *The Political Journals of Lord Stanley* (Sussex, 1979), p. 325.
18 *The Beehive*, 4 Jan. 1868.
19 *Times*, 16 Dec. 1867.
20 *Freeman's Journal*, 17 Dec. 1867.

panic in the metropolis soon acquired a humourous dimension. Thus at Woolwich Arsenal a sentry on duty mistook two horses for Irish intruders.[21]

The popular panic engendered by the Clerkenwell explosion obliged the government to take seriously the threat of further Fenian outrages in Britain. The Tory cabinet of Lord Derby considered the suspension of Habeas Corpus.[22] Lord Stanley recorded the attitude of Queen Victoria: 'she wants Habeas Corpus suspended, militia embodied, in short preparation to meet an armed insurrection notwithstanding which, she resists obstinately all suggestions that she should allow herself to be attended to when driving about, especially after dark'.[23] Although the government was anxious about the safety of the Queen it wished to avoid taking any action which might boost the prestige of the Fenians. When a minister suggested that the Queen's route from Balmoral should be altered to foil a possible kidnapping attempt, the prime minister disagreed. Lord Derby observed that 'nothing could give the Fenians a greater triumph than to be able to boast that, from fear of them, the Queen, in moving one part of her dominions to another, was obliged to do so secretly and as it were surreptitiously. The public impression caused by such a course, would, I am sure, be most unfortunate'.[24]

The outbreak of Fenian fever reflected a lack of public confidence in the police. The Metropolitan Police had been tipped off, in advance, about the Clerkenwell rescue attempt, but they had still failed to prevent it. In the light of this failure the Home Secretary took steps to increase the size and efficiency of the force. A thousand extra men were recruited and a special detective force was created. This was directed by Colonel Fielding who was brought over from Ireland where he had experience of counter-insurgency work. The special detective force developed into the Special Irish Branch which was set up in the 1880s in response to the Irish-American dynamite campaign in Britain.[25] To assist the police in coping with the Fenian threat, thousands of part-time special constables were enrolled at vestry and parish meetings after the Clerkenwell incident. Enrolment of special constables peaked at the end of January 1868 by which date over 166,000 men had volunteered.[26] The special constables had ill defined duties and powers of arrest, but their enrolment alarmed the English radicals who feared that an 'armed political *gendarmerie*' was in the making which might impose a continental-style 'reign of terror'.

In the wake of Manchester and Clerkenwell, anti-Irish prejudice

21 *The Beehive*, 4 Jan. 1868.
22 N.E. Johnson (ed.), *The Diary of Gathorne Hardy* (Oxford, 1981), p. 57.
23 Vincent (ed.), *The Political Journals of Lord Stanly*, p. 325.
24 G.E. Buckle (ed.), *The Letters of Queen Victoria* (2nd Ser., 1926), I, p. 468.
25 K.R.M. Short, *The Dynamite War* (Dublin, 1979), pp. 5–6.
26 *Times*, 13 Jan. 1868.

mushroomed in Britain. A week after the killing of Sergeant Brett, a Barnsley factory worker was found guilty of Fenian sympathies by a kangaroo court of his workmates and was briefly strung up.[27] But most Irish workers in Britain suffered loss of employment rather than personal attacks. After Clerkenwell, employers at the London docks showed a reluctance to take on Irish labour.[28] This was perhaps understandable in the light of reported Fenian designs on commercial premises. Yet few members of the Irish community in England had any direct involvement with the Fenians. Moreover, many Irish in Britain were appalled by the Clerkenwell explosion. Soon afterwards, for example, over five hundred Irish catholics met at Woolwich to express their abhorrence of Fenian terror. A similar meeting was later held in Swansea.[28] In February 1868 more than 22,000 Irish men and women resident in London sent an address to the Queen, which condemned the Clerkenwell outrage and pledged their loyalty to the throne.[30] Even Fenians had reservations about the Clerkenwell operation. Unlike Manchester, it did not free a Fenian leader. Moreover, the *Beehive* was probably correct in attributing the plot to a small group, rather than to the main Fenian leaders.[31] Certainly John Devoy later claimed this was the case.[32] In stark contrast to the Manchester 'martyrs' the perpetrators of the Clerkenwell explosion were never honoured in Fenian or nationalist circles. Yet the objectives of the Clerkenwell conspirators were precisely the same as those of the Manchester men: to rescue their leader from prison. Moreover, the success of the Manchester operation obviously encouraged some of the Fenians to try to repeat it in London. The Fenians who organised the Clerkenwell explosion did not have the 'murderous designs' attributed to them by *The Times* and other newspapers. As at Manchester, the death which resulted form the Clerkenwell escape plot was accidental, though clearly such an outcome might have been anticipated by the Fenians. But it is easy to see why Clerkenwell generated more anti-Fenian feeling than Manchester. Many civilians were killed at Clerkenwell as opposed to one policeman at Manchester. Moreover, an explosion is more terrifying and more random in its effets than a single shot. Yet the Fenians were not engaged in a campaign of indiscriminate murder and destruction. Moreover the Fenians were still intent on fomenting rebellion in Ireland rather than mayhem in England. When Michael Davitt, the Fenian secretary in Britain was arrested he was charged with buying arms for shipment to Ireland, not with planning terrorist

27 *Ibid.*, 25 Sept. 1867.
28 *Ibid.*, 8 Jan. 1868.
29 *Ibid.*, 24 Dec. 1867; also, 2 Jan. 1868.
30 *Times*, 12 Feb. 1867.
31 *The Beehive*, 4 Jan. 1868.
32 Devoy, *Recollections of An Irish Rebel*, pp. 248–50.

operations in Britain.[33]

The Irish orientation of Fenianism was not overlooked by Gladstone who sought to persuade English politicians to sponsor reforms in Ireland. Only six days after the Clerkenwell explosion Gladstone spoke at Stockport on the need to attack the roots of Fenianism as well as its manifestations. In particular he insisted that the time had come to deal with the old problems of church establishment and land tenure in Ireland. He tried to divorce these questions from the recent Fenian outrages, stating that crime should not be considered 'a legitimate ground for concession'.[34] But the timing of his speech suggested to both his colleagues and his critics that his reform proposals had been prompted by the recent Fenian outrages in England. Gladstone himself admitted that he had not taken up the question of the disestablishment of the Church of Ireland before since 'circumstances were not ripe, insofar as we did not know as much as we do now with respect to the intensity of Fenianism'.[35] In 1869 Gladstone privately admitted that the Fenians in both Ireland and England 'have had a very important influence on the question of the time for moving upon great questions of policy for Ireland'.[36]

The Fenians were probably surprised by Gladstone's response to the outrages. John Devoy later observed that Gladstone's remarks at Stockport 'proved a stronger argument in favour of physical force and even of terrorism on the part of Ireland to secure justice and freedom than any Irishman ever made'.[37] Certainly the Fenians had not expected that violence in England would reap political dividends. For all they had done in England was to try to rescue their leaders in order to continue the struggle in Ireland. Yet it soon became a truism in England as well as in Ireland that the Fenians had forced England to introduce Irish reforms. Even *The Times* admitted in 1881 that the Fenian outrages in England in the 1860s had 'indirectly brought important results in the end'.[38] Yet Gladstone's Irish reforms of 1869–70 were designed to divide the mass of the Irish people from the Fenians. British sponsored reform of Irish institutions was inimical to the separatist aims of the Fenians. The main beneficiary of Gladstone's reforms was the Roman Catholic Church in Ireland. This institution like its sister church in England, was hostile to Fenianism which it associated with the secular and anti-clerical secret societies of the continent. Moreover the Catholic Church had been largely instrumental in thwarting the Fenian rebellion in Ireland in 1867. Thus Fenian activities in England had only served to buttress the position of one of their principal

33 Moody, *Michael Davitt and the Irish Revolution.*
34 *Times*, 9 Oct. 1867.
35 See, Monypenny and Buckle, *The Life of Disraeli*, IV, p. 575.
36 See, Mark Ryan, *fenian Memories* (Dublin, 1945), p. 127.
37 Devoy, *Recollections of An Irish Rebel*, p. 250.
38 *Times*, 28 March 1881.

opponents in Ireland. Yet it is also true that if the Fenians had no intention of instigating constitutional reforms they were subsequently little loath to be credited with their achievement. The result may have been ironic but posterity rightly judged the Fenian version of political violence to have been effective.

II

A comparison between the Fenian activities in Britain in the 1860s and the IRA bombing campaign in Britain since 1972 is instructive. Both phenomena had a common origin: they were a by-product of recent unrest and violence in Ireland. Initially the IRA, like the Fenians before them, had no intention of starting a general terrorist campaign in Britain. The first IRA bomb attack in England – at Aldershot in february 1972 – was a direct reprisal for the recent killing of unarmed demonstrators by soldiers of the Parachute Regiment at Derry. The bombing was carried out by the Official IRA which made no further attacks in Britain and which, soon afterwards declared an unconditional cease-fire. But in the 1970s, as in the 1860s, some militant Irish Republicans realized that Britain offered them some temptingly 'soft' targets. Just as the minimum force used at Manchester in 1867 was followed by the indiscriminate Clerkenwell explosion, so the 'legitimate' reprisal at Aldershot was followed by the indiscriminate bombing campaign of the Provisional IRA. In both cases the recourse to increasingly ruthless tactics was probably a pragmatic response to the increasing security measures of the British police. In the 1970s, as in 1867, the British public reacted angrily to the death of innocent civilians and unarmed policemen at the hands of Irish Republicans.

It would be wrong, however, to over-stress the similarities between the Fenian and IRA campaigns in Britain. Although the modern IRA looks back for inspiration to the Fenians and share their desire for an all-Ireland Republic, it has had to resort to very different tactics in the struggle with the British government. For over a decade the IRA has been engaged in a deliberate terrorist campaign against the public and government in Britain for which the Fenians provide no precedent. The Fenian 'outrages' in 1867 were attempts to free their own leaders, they were not deliberate acts of murder or terrorism. These two incidents, in which seven people in total were accidentally killed, have little in common with the numerous bombings by the IRA in Britain which have caused the deaths of more than eighty people. These have been deliberately staged to inflict death, injury and terror: often on members of the general public who are quite unconnected with the government or the security services. Even the more selective attacks on soldiers and senior politicians – such as the attempt to kill the Conservative Cabinet at Brighton in 1984 – have no Fenian precedent from the 1860s. While it is true that in the 1880s a small group of Irish-American militants organized the so-called 'Dynamite War' in Britain, the attacks were aimed at government buildings and other important places with the purpose of committing symbolic destruction of property rather than to kill or maim.

The recent IRA campaign in Britain has been ruthless and protracted yet it has failed to provoke a positive response from successive British governments comparable to that which was elicited by the much more limited actions of the Fenians. There are many reasons why this has been the case. It must not be overlooked that the character of British rule in Northern Ireland today differs in some crucial respects from the way Britain governed the whole of Ireland a century ago. But, also, there can be no doubt that the IRA campaign in Britain has been ill-conceived and counter-productive. By bombing civilian targets such as shops, pubs and restaurants the IRA clearly intended to provoke popular pressure for a British withdrawal from Northern Ireland. However, in London and other large cities the level of IRA attacks has been too limited to frighten seriously or inconvenience the general public. Londoners and others who withstood the Blitz in the Second World War were unlikely to panic as a consequence of the infinitely lower level of IRA bombing. But the random attacks on civilian targets have been sufficiently numerous to generate a strong current of public opinion against the IRA while contributing nothing favourable to the achievement of Republican aims. For example, the Birmingham pub bombings of November 1974, provoked a spontaneous outburst of anger on the part of the car workers in the city. This scarcely advanced the traditional Irish nationalist strategy of soliciting the help of the British working class in their struggle against an allegedly elitist British government. Though it is true that the IRA have often concentrated their attacks on the more fashionable parts of the West End of London even this limitation has failed to achieve any significant class objective. For today London's fashionable shopping and recreation areas are used by all classes and all nationalities, all of whom are equally at risk of suffering from a bomb blast. Thus the explosion at Harrod's, London's most famous department store, in December 1983, caused casualties across the social scale and killed an American citizen. This hardly helped the IRA fund raising campaign in The United States and was a propaganda coup for the British government.

The majority of IRA attacks on Britain since 1972 have been directed at so-called 'legitimate targets' rather than at the general public. But even these bombings have been far too indiscriminate to effect significant practical, political or propaganda advantages. The slaughter of army bandsmen and horses while they entertained the public in the London parks in July 1982 cannot be described as a blow against the forces of oppression. Other attacks on military coaches, pubs and barracks all have resulted in civilian as well as military casualties. In any csae, soldiers and police personnel accept that their lives may be at risk in a way which the rest of the population does not. By attacking the police and army in Britain, the IRA have insured that their own activities on the mainland have been watched zealously by the security services. This may partly explain the relative lack of success which the Irish terrorists have had in their attacks on top politicians. Their one signal success was the killing of Airey Neave, the friend of Mrs Thatcher and the Conservative 'shadow' Secretary for Northern Ireland, in 1979. But Neave had not played an official role in the evolution of British policy on Northern Ireland and his death only made Mrs Thatcher all the more determined not to make concessions to Irish terrorists when she came into office soon afterwards. The failure of the IRA to blow up the prime minister and her other Cabinet colleagues at Brighton in October 1984 was due to chance more than incompetence. The IRA's use of a pre-timed bomb reveals the continued absence of selectivity in Irish terrorism and a reluctance of the perpetraters to be willing to sacrifice themselves for their cause. Certainly the murder of Mrs Thatcher would be a publicity coup for the IRA but it is unlikely to alter the policy of the British Government on Northern Ireland. Indeed 'Margaret the martyr' might become a potent Unionist symbol, whereas Margaret the elder statesman may yet be able to win important concessions for the nationalist minority in Northern Ireland.

It is clear that there is little political or military justification for the modern IRA campaign in Britain. This campaign is essentially counter-productive and diverts Republican energies away from the crucial arena of events – Ireland. But it may be argued that it is still justified on other grounds – it provides mass publicity for the IRA in Britain and shows that they are 'a force to be reckoned with'. However, Irish Republicans have always gained far better publicity and respect from the apparent mistakes of British policy in Ireland (or towards the Irish in Britain) than they have from their own direct actions in Britain. For example the introduction of internment in Northern Ireland in 1971 and the 'Bloody Sunday' massacre in Derry in 1972 were far better propaganda for the Republicans than the bombings in England. If present day Irish Republicans had pondered the lesson of Fenian activities in 1867 they would have learnt that far more support and prestige came from the 'Manchester martyrs' than from the 'Clerkenwell massacre'. It may, of course, be argued that the modern Irish militants are not interested in local or constitutional politics, but are essentially an anarchic group who wish to 'spoil' the situation not only for the British government but also for moderate nationalists in Ireland. But if this really is the case then they are hurting themselves as much as anybody. For the 50 plus Irish Republicans in British gaols (and the far larger numbers imprisoned in Northern Ireland and the Irish Republic) are paying a heavy price for Irish terrorism. Today there is no British based campaign for the release of the Irish Republican prisoners in any way comparable with the Amnesty movement which supported the release of the Fenian convicts in the 1870s. By forsaking the Fenian code of practice in Britain, modern Irish terrorists have forfeited any widespread sympathy from the British public. The Fenians obviously modelled themselves on the old Irish heroes, but the IRA activists in modern Britain are largely unknown and unsung: they are certainly not heroes in the Fenian mould.

BRITAIN'S RESPONSIBILITY FOR VIOLENCE IN IRELAND AND THE MIDDLE EAST: STATE CREATION AFTER THE FIRST WORLD WAR

DR PATRICK BUCKLAND
Reader in Modern History, University of Liverpool

It is often said that it is impossible for individuals to escape from their origins. The same can be said of states and regimes. Much of their history can be explained in terms of the circumstances of their birth and this is particularly true of those areas of the world for which Britain was responsible after the First World War, whether they were as near to Westminster as Ireland or as remote as the Middle East. Indeed, an historian of Ireland, critical of the thoughtless nature of partition in 1920–1, cannot on turning to the Middle East fail to be struck by the similarities in the British policy of state creation in Northern Ireland, Iraq and Palestine. These were places where Britain created new regimes after the First World War and the underlying theme of the process was the determination to safeguard British interests as indirectly and as cheaply as possible with scant regard for the internal workings of the new regimes. Internal problems, particularly divisions within society and conflict between communities, were never fully acknowledged, let alone resolved or managed. They were merely ignored or brushed aside with the result that all the three regimes so hastily erected after the First World War eventually collapsed in violence.

To develop the argument that British policy towards Northern Ireland after the First World War was of a piece with the policy of state creation pursued elsewhere and that policy contained the seeds of the violent destruction of the new creations, this paper will pose and partially answer three questions. How valid is the comparison of Northern Ireland with parts of the Middle East? How well considered were British attempts at state creation in Northern Ireland, Iraq and Palestine? How concerned was Britain to compensate for the deficiencies of the new regimes, particularly in respect of the potential for conflict and instability created by the existence of minorities and other disadvantaged groups. Such a consideration of British policy after the First World War not only contributes to an understanding of the course of violent conflict in Northern Ireland, Iraq and Palestine. It also puts into perspective current debates about the effectiveness of decision-making processes in the formulation and execution of British foreign policy. It was not information that government departments lack: rather they lacked a sufficiently broad perspective to enable them to respond to and interpret such information.

I

It might at first glance seem misleading to talk about Northern Ireland in the same breath as such areas as Iraq and Palestine with very different histories and with very different relationships with Britain. The links between Northern Ireland and Britain were much closer and of longer standing, for Britain's involvement with Ireland dated from the twelfth century. Ireland had been ruled directly from Westminster since 1800 under the act of union, and the Irish economy was intimately bound up with that of the rest of the United Kingdom. Moreover, when Britain abandoned the union after the First World War, it bestowed wide self-government on only part of Ireland, the twenty-six county Irish Free State. The remaining six counties of Northern Ireland were given a regional parliament and government with limited powers and remained an integral part of the United Kingdom. By contrast, Britain's direct involvement in Iraq and Palestine was of recent origin and was a matter of international concern and responsibility. Having occupied these two parts of the Ottoman Empire during the First World War, the British authorities gradually came to appreciate the desirability of securing continued oversight of areas of such strategic importance to the empire. Accordingly, the peace conference and the League of Nations handed them over to Britain, subject to the condition that it should bring these areas to full independence at some unspecified time. Under the mandate system, Britain was supposed to guide both territories towards independence and representative self-goverement, and within Palestine this trust was made the more complicated by the provision for a National Home for the Jews, a provision which many interpreted as turning Palestine into an independent Jewish state.

Nevertheless, the three areas had much in common. In none was there a political consensus on the nature of the state to be established. Rather, each area was riddled with sectarian, ethnic and regional divisions, and, to cap it all, in the 1920s and 1930s their economies were hardly healthy, with ailing agriculture and few industries in the case of Iraq and Palestine, and inefficient agriculture and ailing industries in the case of Northern Ireland. In fact, in all three areas Britain was faced with similar problems of establishing a regime which would be self-supporting and would survive manifold divisions. What is more, in each area Britain failed to find adequate solutions to these problems. However different the attempts to create new foci of political loyalty, they also had this in common – they failed to secure acceptance by all sections of their respective communities and all eventually came to a bloody end.

In Northern Ireland, Britain determined both the boundaries and the form of government in the 1920 Government of Ireland Act. The controversial six counties included a large Catholic minority, some one-third of the population within Northern Ireland, including some predominantly Catholic areas on the borders with the Irish Free State, such as Londonderry city, Newry and South Armagh. The form of government was modelled on Westminster and a subordinate regional government and parliament were given restricted financial powers but almost unlimited power over such vital matters of community interest and potential conflict as education, local government and law and order. In effect, the 1920 settlement gave the two-thirds Protestant and Unionist majority a virtual free hand, was never fully endorsed by the substantial Catholic minority, and ended in anarchy with the fall of Stormont in 1972.[1]

It was similar story in Iraq, though Nemesis came fourteen years sooner. Britain determined both the boundaries of Iraq and its form of government. British influence ensured that Iraq would consist not only of the Arab provinces of Baghdad and Basra but also of the northern province of Mosul, with its oil resources and its large and restless Kurdish population. Moreover, Britain determined that Iraq should be a constitutional monarchy, and, rejecting all internal candidates for the new throne, actually, in 1821, imported a monarch from the outside in the shape of the Hashemite King Faisal, one of the leaders of the so-called Arab revolt on behalf of the allies during the First World War. Finally, Britain speeded Iraq on the way to independence. In 1932 Iraq achieved independence and became a member of the League of Nations, albeit in close treaty relationship with Britain to protect British imperial and strategic interests.

Iraq's independence may have been only nominal but it did give the very small ruling elite of politicians and officers surrounding King Faisal a much freer hand in exercising control over internal affairs, and they soon used this hand most heavily to eliminate one minority problem, the Assyrian question, by the simple expedient of the systematic massacre of members of this Christian community in the village of Simmel in August 1933. Indeed, the internal history of Iraq was never a happy one, and the system of representative and responsible government failed to strike root. Politics were dominated by a small self-interested clique, were prone after 1936 to military intervention, and the whole edifice came to a grisly end in 1958 with the massacre of the royal family and leading officials. Thus the prime minister, caught while trying to escape disguised as a woman, was quickly done to death by an air force soldier and buried. But his body was disinterred by an angry crowd, dragged through the streets, strung up, torn to pieces and finally

[1] P. Bew. P. Gibbon, & H. Patterson. *The state in Northern Ireland 1921–72: political forces and social classes* (1979); P. Buckland, *A history of Northern Ireland* (1981): R. Harris, *Prejudice and tolerance in Ulster: a study of neighbours and 'strangers' in a border community* (1972): R. Rose, *Governing without consensus: an Irish perspective* (1971).

burned. As the leading historian of Iraq has asked and answered.

Inhumaneness? It is perhaps not appropriate to pass judgment, but it must be added, not to justify but to explain, that ... [the rulers of Iraq] ... were never tender with the lives of their people.[2]

Britain's sojourn in Palestine was more prolonged and more bitter. Britain remained in Palestine until 1948, when it unilaterally and ignominiously abandoned its mandate and left the country in chaos, having been unable to reconcile the conflicting claims of Arabs and Jews. The root of the trouble was that the Arabs, who at the beginning of the twentieth century comprised over ninety per cent of the population of Palestine, opposed the policy sponsored by Britain since 1917, when, in an effort to rallyj Jewish world opinion to the allied war effort, and in the hope of securing British interests in Palestine, the British government authorised the so-called Belfour Declaration, pledging support for the establishment in Palestine of a national home for the Jewish people.

Various efforts were made to erect political institutions which would encourage Jews and Arabs to develop a common loyalty to a new bi-national Palestinian state, but these efforts came to naught as violence increasingly became the hallmark of Palestinian politics. In face of rioting, rebellion and terrorism, both Arab and Jewish, Britain struggled to govern through separate Jewish and Moslem agencies, and succeeded only in re-inforcing existing divisions and preparing the way for the partition of Palestine, the foundation of Israel in 1948, and the first Arab-Israeli war of 1948–9. Indeed, the last few months of the mandate in 1948 make dismal and familiar reading. Hundreds of British nationals were killed and British soldieres and policemen, hardened by Jewish acts of terrorism and demoralised by the general disintegration, committed random acts of violence against Jewish civilians. As one former chief of police wrote while visiting Palestine during those last few months.

I found all the urban areas divided into small security zones. Syrian roving bands infested the contryside. As we returned by cars to Jerusalem one evening, the irregulars stopped us at a roadblock, thrusting their rifles in the windows. A police superintendent was turned out of his car and made to walk home. Control of the country was visibly lacking. I won't describe the situation further. It's too shaming.[3]

[2] H. Batatu. *The old social classes and the revolutionary movements of Iraq. A study of Iraq's old landed classes and commercial classes and its communists. Ba thists and Free Officers* (1978), p. 801–2. On the history of Iraq, see also P.W. Ireland, *Iraq, a study in political development* (1937); E. & E.F. Penrose, *Iraq: international relations and national development* (1978); P. Sluglett, *Britain and Iraq 1914–1932* (1976).

[3] N. Bethell. *The Palestinian triangle. The struggle between the British, the Jews and the Arabs 1935–48* (1979), p. 353. For Palestine and British policy in this period, see also M. Cohen, *Palestine: retreat from the mandate. The making of British policy 1936–45* (1978) and *Palestine*

II

The dismal fate shared by these three British efforts at state creation after the First World War thus raises a second question. How well-considered were these various efforts at state creation? Or to put it another way, how far-seeing and responsibly formulated were British plans and policies? Was British policy based upon a sound grasp and an accurate assessment of local conditions? Did the British policy-makers anticipate difficulties and take steps to avoid them?

The simple answer to this string of questions is 'No'. British policy was ill-conceived both in principle and in detail. Decisions to set up particular forms of government took too little account of local difficulties and, furthermore, the actual details and execution of those policies compounded all the difficulties. The decisions to create separate political entities in Northern Ireland and in Iraq and to assist Zionist aspirations in Palestine took too little account of the manifold obstacles to good government and civic contentment in those areas.

As far as Northern Ireland is concerned, there is no evidence that the British government even remotely contemplated the possible evil consequences of setting up a separate regional government and parliament. Ignoring sectarian and ethnic divisions and taking little account of the distinctive political culture of the nort of Ireland, British politicians simply assumed that parliamentary institutions would operate there as they did within the rest of the United Kingdom. In dismantling the union, the main preoccupation of the British government was not the internal development of Ireland but rather the nature of Britain's relations with the two parts of Ireland. In the case of the north the concern was financial – to ensure that Northern Ireland did not enjoy home rule at the expense of the rest of the United Kingdom.[4]

Such short-sightedness and lack of perception were paralleled in both Iraq and Palestine. For example, the Balfour Declaration was a masterpiece of miscalculation and wishful thinking. The timing and content of declaration were the products of particular circumstance, designed to maintain the war effort and to safeguard an essential British interest in the Middle East, but it was sheer folly not to have tried to assuage the fears and apprehensions of the Arab majority in Palestine. Instead the Balfour Declaration simply stated that 'Nothing shall be done which may prejudice the civil and religious rights of

---

and the Great Powers (1982): N. Lucas, *The modern history of Israel* (1974): L. Stein, *The Balfour declaration* (1961); B. Wasserstein, *The British in Palestine. The mandatory government and the Arab-Jewish conflict 1917–1929* (1978).

[4] R.J. Lawrence, *The government of Northern Ireland: public finance and public services 1921–1964* (1965): R.B. McDowell, *The Irish convention 1917–18* (1970).

existing non-Jewish communities in Palestine'.[5]

Such a declaration completely ignored the long history of antagonism between Jews and Arabs in Palestine. The Balfour Declaration is often condemned with hindsight, but there was plenty of evidence available at the time to warn the British politicians of the dangers of their policy, for, contrary to popular belief, the Arab-Jewish conflict did not 'leap fully armed out of the Balfour Declaration like Athene out of Zeus's head'.[6] Rather, the position of Jews in Ottoman Palestine had been particularly degraded, for, as one observer had put it in 1840, 'the Jew in Jerusalem is not estimated in value much above a dog',[7] and such Arab contempt turned to active hostility with the heightened pace of Jewish immigration after 1880 and with the claims of Zionism. So vehement was Arab hostility towards Zionists before 1914 that some Zionist leaders began to recognise Arab nationalism as a serious force to be reckoned with, but discussions aimed at a *modus vivendi* had come to nothing by the outbreak of the First World War.[8]

In the light of this history of antagonism, the Balfour Declaration appears almost incredible, but it becomes less so when the British attitude to the Palestinian Arabs is taken into account. Basically, Arab hostility was ignored because the British were by and large dismissive of the Palestinian Arabs. They were not the real, noble Arabs of the desert, but rather they were regarded as levantines of mixed race and questionable character. As Gilbert Clayton, the first head of the British military administration in Palestine wrote in 1918 to a friend, herself a champion of the Arabs:

> The so-called Arabs of Palestine are not to be compared with the real Arab of the Desert or even of other civilised districts in Syria and Mesopotamia. He is purely local and takes little or no interest in matters outside his immediate surroundings.[9]

Not only did the Balfour Declaration ignore palestinian Arab susceptibilities, but it was also launched in the most unpromising circumstances. Quite apart from Arab-Jewish hostility, Palestine was hardly the most propitious place for political experimentation. It has been aptly described as a 'disaster zone' in 1917.[10] During the previous four years its inhabitants had undergone a succession of natural and man-made calamities. The population had been depleted by perhaps one-quarter as a result of deaths in battles, forced conscription, deportations and acute famine, while the peasant economy had collapsed under the weight of locust plagues, army requisitioning, huge losses

[5] Stein, p. 22.
[6] Wasserstein, p. 2.
[7] *Ibid.*, p. 2.
[8] N. Mandel, *The Arabs and Zionism before World War I* (1976).
[9] Wasserstein, p. 12.
[10] *Ibid.*, p. 1.

of livestock and the disruption of markets. Palestine certainly presented administrative challenges, but the very last thing it needed was the political turmoil involved in the Balfour Declaration.

Just as culpable, perhaps even more so, was the decision to create a new state in Iraq and to speed it on its way to independence. Conditions in Iraq were scarcely suited to the establishment of a unified and centralised state, let alone an experiment in constitutional monarchy. Iraq was even more divided than Northern Ireland and Palestine. The Iraqis, as they came to be known, were not one people or one political community. In the first place, there were numerous ethnic and religious minorities. The Kurds were the most obvious minority, concentrated in the northern province of Mosul and speaking an Indo-European language, but there were many others, such as Turkomans, Persians, Assyrians, Armenians, Chaldemans, Jews, Yazidis, Sabeans and others. In the second place, the majority of the inhabitants of Iraq, the Arabs, might have shared some common characteristics, but they were otherwise divided into congeries of distinct, discordant and self-involved societies. For instance, a wide social and psychological chasm separated urban Arabs from tribal Arabs living in the countryside. The life of the former was, on the whole, governed by Islamic and Ottoman laws, but that of the tribal Arabs was regulated by Islamically tinged ancient tribal customs.

Moreover, the divisions of the Arab community were further increased by the fragmentation of both the urban and tribal societies. Geography not only separated the cities by time and space – the journey from Baghdad to Basra took a week and travelling itself was an adventure– but it also determined their economic orientation. The ties of Mosul were with Syria and Turkey: those of Baghdad and the Shi-ite holy cities were with Persia and the western and south-western deserts: while Basra looked to the sea and to India. The result was a strong tendency towards localism, and such localism was even more pronounced in the countryside, where the old tribal confederations had broken up in the course of the nineteenth century, and relations between tribes were dominated by raids and forays.

On top of all this came the divisions within Islam. Just as in Northern Ireland, religion was a source of division rather than of integration. Most Iraqis were Moslems, but some belonged to the Sunni rite and others to the Shi-ite rite. Socially they seldom mixed, as a rule they did not inter-marry, and in most cities they lived in separate quarters and led their own separate lives. What is more, Shi-ite political theory scarcely assisted the process of state formation, since the Iraqi Shi-ites, awaiting the return of the Twelfth Imam, tended to regard all earthly power as a usurpation of the authority of the Imam who would one day return to bring peace and justice to the world. At its simplest, Shi-ite political theory refused to accept the legitimacy of any earthly government.

Such was the condition of Iraq after the First World War. It was a fragmented and divided society. It might well be argued that such divisions could have constituted favourable conditions for the creation of a new state and the assertion of state authority on the principle of divide and rule. This was not, however, the case, because these divisions reflected the strength of local ties which served a definite purpose. There may have been many groups in Iraq, but each of these groups or communities was cohesive and represented for their members a source of strength and protection. As one Baghdad politician wrote in 1910.

To depend on the tribe is a thousand times safer than depending on the government, for whereas the latter defers or neglects repression, the tribe, no matter how feeble it may be, as soon as it learns that an injustice has been committed against one of its members readies itself to exact vengeance on his behalf.[11]

The implications of such divisions for the process of state creation were largely ignored by British policy makers. A unified Iraq with a representative constitution was in British interests, and contrary arguments were simply ignored on the few occasions they were fully articulated. This gap between reality and aspiration, this wishful thinking, is strikingly illustrated in the changing opinions of the remarkable Gertrude Bell, scholar and explorer of the Middle East turned influential colonial administrator during and after the First World War. Her travels in the Middle East and her knowledge of Mesopotamian society had early convinced her of the unsuitability of that area for constitutional government. Thus in 1919 she wrote judiciously,

Men who have kept the tradition of a personal independence, which was limited only by their own customs, entirely ignorant of a world which lay outside their swamps and pastures, and as entirely indifferent to its interests as to the opportunities it offers, will not fall into step with European ambitions, nor welcome European methods. Nor can they be hastened ... In our own history from the Moot Court through Magna Carta to the Imperial Parliament was the work of centuries, yet the first contained the grain of all that came after.[12]

Within a few months, however, her scholarly detachment and understanding soon evaporated as she became caught up in the rhetoric and urgency of international peace-making and as she became exposed to the charm of King Faisal. As a result she began to think that it would, after all, be possible to establish a model state in Iraq. Indeed, she ended up advising Faisal on his household and other arrangements, enthusiastically writing home on one occasion that

I was having tea with HM this afternoon, it was the loveliest Oriental scene. He was sitting in

[11] Batatu, p. 21.
[12] H.V.F. Winstone, *Gertrude Bell* (1978), p. 194.

the garden near a fountain in full Arab dress, the white and gold of the Meccan princes.[13]

The case of Iraq was thus of a piece with British policy elsewhere. Insufficient regard was paid to the peculiarities of the areas in which new political entities were established. And what is more, this initial error was compounded by the failure to erect adequate political and governmental institutions. The phrase 'constitutional gerrymandering aptly describes such institutions as were established in Northern Ireland, Iraq and Palestine.

This was most obvious in the case of finance, where from the start both Northern Ireland and Iraq were hamstrung by the financial conditions imposed by the British Treasury. In Northern Ireland, the terms of the 1920 government of Ireland act were unfair and so unrealistic that for much of the inter-war period Northern Ireland was on the verge of insolvency and was forced to undertake repeated begging expeditions to the British Treasury.[14] It was the same story in Iraq. The Treasury made almost impossible and not always justified demands on Iraq, and when Iraq was on the point of bankruptcy in 1926, the Treasury solution was not that Iraq should pay less to Britain, but that it should spend less on irrigation – a perverse recommendation, since the chief means of increasing Iraq's revenue at that time was through irrigation to increase agricultural productivity.[15]

Britain's financial demands hampered the new states. So, too, did the political mechanisms established. Such mechanisms were hardly sensitive to local conditions. In Palestine, rivalries were enflamed by the appearance that the governmental system discriminated in favour of the representative agencies of Zionism which were given semi-official or quasi-governmental status.[16] In Northern Ireland, no real thought was given as to how Westminster might exercise the sovereignty it maintained in the event of a clash of interests between Westminster and Belfast, while even less thought was given to the question of the distribution of powers and responsibilities within Northern Ireland, particularly in relation to the plethora of apathetic and partisan local authorities. The effect was both to hamper the development of the new regional government and to accentuate the myopic and sectarian tendencies inherent in Ulster politics and society.[17]

In Iraq the British even seemed bent on destroying the system of government they hoped would flourish. The failure of representative and responsible government was almost guaranteed with the importation of an

[13] *Ibid.*, p. 247.

[14] P. Buckland, *Factory of grievances: devolved government in Northern Ireland 1921–39* (1979), pp. 81–104.

[15] Sluglett, pp. 125–30.

[16] See, *e.g.*, the status accorded to the Zionist Commission in 1918. Wasserstein, pp. 24–5.

[17] Buckland, *Factory of grievances*, esp. pp. 36–50, 266–7.

outside ruling family. It was not just that the Hashemites had little standing or popularity in Iraq, but the British attempt to smooth Faisal's way into Iraq actually served to undermine the rule of law and to bring representative institutions into disrepute. The only serious Iraqi rival to Faisal, Sayid Talib, was arrested immediately after taking tea with the British High Commissioner and subsequently deported. To say the least, the manner of his arrest, as much as the arrest itself, was a matter of social and political insensibility, the only saving grace being the embarrassment of the arresting officer and fellow guest at the High Commission who told Talib: 'I regret that I have orders to arrest you.[18] Moreover, a so-called referendum was gerrymandered in an attempt to obscure the fact that Faisal was being foisted on Iraq.[19] After such an auspicious introduction to democratic methods it was, perhaps, not surprisingly that the rigging of elections became the norm as Faisal and his entourage sought to find a power base in the country by aligning themselves with certain tribal chiefs whom they converted into landowners with almost unrestricted rights over their tribesmen and former tribal lands. In such a manner, the ruling elite in Iraq became completely isolated from the rest of society.[20]

Indeed, the creation of the kingdom of Iraq has been desribed as 'wretched political architecture and constitutional jerry-building of the flimsiest and most dangerous kind' and it can be cogently argued that the seeds of the eventual collapse of Iraqi monarchy lay in its very beginnings.[21] The sad fact is that this was no glaring exception. Rather, British policy towards Iraq was similar to British policy elsewhere at that time. Important, even fateful decisions were made with scant regard either to local conditions or to likely local consequences. Not only in Iraq but also in Northern Ireland and Palestine, the ill-conceived and ill-considered settlements devised by Britain after the First World War contained, so to speak, their own self-destruct mechanisms. Such a conclusion cast doubts not only upon the competence of British officials and politicians, but also upon the efficacy and validity of the whole decision-making process in British politics – at least in the inter-war period.

[18] P. Graves, *The life of Sir Percy Cox* (1942), pp. 290–1.

[19] E. Kedourie, 'The kingdom of Iraq, a retrospect, *The Chatham House version and other Middle-Eastern studies* (1970), pp. 239–42; Sluglett, pp. 43–50, 67–8.

[20] Batatu, pp. 53–152.

[21] E. Kedourie, p. 239.

III

Such a pessimistic answer to the second question leads naturally to a third question – the extent to which Britain tried to remedy its initial errors. How far did Britain try to compensate for the deficiencies of the regimes it had established, particularly in relations to minorities or otherwise disadvantaged groups. How concerned was the British government to ensure that .equal treatment and fair representation were accorded to individuals and to each section of society. Whether they majority or minority communities?

The answer is that Britain became painfully aware of such problems, but hoped that all communities would accept the legitimacy of the new creations, and that the new administrations would help to create a new political community by ensuring the equal treatment for all members of their respective states. That was the theory but the practice was very different. In Northern Ireland and in Iraq, Britain was prepared to do very little to ensure such equal treatment. In both areas Britain confined its efforts to exhortations and refused to take any steps which might embroil it directly once again in the internal affairs of either area.

From the beginning the British government was anxious that the Catholic/nationalist minority in Northern Ireland should accept the legitimacy of the new creation and to that end Westminster did urge the government of Northern Ireland to adopt a friendlier and more accommodating attitude towards the minority, particularly in respect of law enforcement, local government and education. Nevertheless, in the last analysis, it refused to exercise its sovereignty to block such divisive measures as the abolition of proportional representation in local government elections or to counteract sectarian tendencies in education and law enforcement.

The reason that Westminster did not do so was that any firm stand would have meant the resignation of the unionist government and, in view of its in-built majority, its immediate return to office. Such an eventuality would have presented Westminster with two equally unpalatable alternatives: a humiliating climbdown: or the resumption of direct reponsibility for the government of the six counties – the very thing that the 1920 government of Ireland act had been designed to avoid. As far as Westminster was concerned, minority rights in Northern Ireland had to be subordinated to the broader interests of the United Kingdom and British empire.[22]

It was the same story in Iraq, where British attitudes towards groups not in power was determined first by the need to establish a unitary Iraqi state and then by the desire to withdraw as completely as was compatible with imperial interests. Shi-ite complaints about the sectarianism of Faisal's government

[22] Buckland, *Factory of grievances*, pp. 179–275.

provoked little action, partly because, according to one official British report, the theocratic ambitions, obscurantist detachment and Persian loyalties of the leading ulama gave them no motive for refraining from sacrificing the interests of Iraq to those which they conceive their own and rendered them incapable of gauging 'the needs oa state which is striving in the path of progress and enlightened self-government'.[23]

In respect of the Kurds, the British government laid itself open to charges of duplicity and deceit. In the 1920s, it was only too aware that special measures were needed to secure both the loyalty and fair treatment of the Kurdish minority, which was disaffected and none-too-kindly treated by the Iraqi government. Fair treatment for such minorities as the Kurds had been one of the conditions upon which the League of Nations had decided that Mosul should be part of Iraq rather than of Turkey, and, under pressure from Britain, the Iraq parliament had enacted some measures to ensure the use of the Kurdish language and the public employment of Kurds. The trouble was that, much to the concern of British officials in Iraq, these laws were not being implemented and on the very eve of independence the Royal Air Force was used to bring to heel the more militant of the Kurdish leaders.[24]

This was a serious matter, for the Permanent Mandates Commission was far from happy about the fate of the Iraqi minorities, and public discussion of the question could have prevented Iraq from achieving independence in 1932, so delaying the relese from the mandate, which Britain eagerly sought. This in stark contrast to its private expressions of concern, the public statements of the British government painted an optimistic picture of the prospects of the Kurds. Accordingly, the British government re-iterated a soothing extract from the 1925 report on the administration of Iraq.

> The system of employing Kurdish officials in Kurdish districts has long been accepted together with the use of the Kurdish language in the schools, and local correspondence is conducted in Kurdish if desired. In respecting Kurdish susceptibilities the Iraq government has rightly comprehended that a united state can be built up of diverse elements and has set an example among Near East countries.[25]

It was the same with the Assyrians, that Christian minority whose demand for a degree of local autonomy in Iraq had seemingly been endorsed by the League of Nations. Caught between a desire to do some sort of justice to the Assyrians, soothing the League of Nations and not offending the *amour propre* of the Iraqis, the British government contented itself with obscuring from public view the extent of Iraq's failure to meet Assyrian demands. Even after independence Britain was more concerned to cover up for the Iraq

[23] Kedourie, p. 250.
[24] Sluglett, esp. pp.35–8, 73–5, 86–7, 116–25, 199–206, 211–16.
[25] *Ibid.*, p. 193.

government than in deploring their sins of commission, so that in 1933, the British ambassador in Baghdad recommended that Britain should do its utmost to prevent a League of Nations commission of enquiry into the Assyrian massacre. As he put it, 'The orchestra at Geneva should be prevented and not merely discouraged from starting a tune the last bars of which are likely to be played solo by a British bugle.[26]

Britain's record in relation to the internal workings of its new creations in Northern Ireland and Iraq was hardly a creditable one, especially on the question of the treatment of minority groups. In Palestine, by contrast, where Britain remained in direct control until 1948, more sustained efforts were made to involve all communities in the affairs of state. In particular, a deliberate policy was adopted of trying to ensure that the composition of the civil service and the police truly reflected the ethnic and religious composition of the population at large. The motives behind this policy of communal equilibrium sprang partly from considerations of natural justice, but mainly from political necessity. Government patronage provided a way of keeping different factions in line, and, more importantly, with the failure to establish effective representative bodies, civil servants played a vital role in providing a link between the British administration and the different communities. This was particularly true of Arabs, for, in the absence of civil institutions of any kind representative of the Arabs between 1923 and 1948. Arab officials were pushed willy-nilly into the role of ersatz representatives of their community within the government of Palestine.[27]

Government by arithmetic, as one Royal Commission critically described it.[28] was not, however, an outstanding success. Admittedly, the composition of the public services more or less reflected the ethnic and religious composition of the population as a whole, but the almost political use of civil service and police appointments did not help to create a new political community in Palestine. Instead, it tended to undermine and discredit government and set up intolerable conflicts within the civil servants themselves.

In the case of Arab officials, their primary duty was not to the government which employed them. However conscientiously they may have tried to perform their official duties, the interests of family, community and party more often than not proved paramount over those of government. Thus it was said that schools were turned into seminaries of Arab nationalism, since, according to one official,

26 *Ibid.*, p. 298.
27 Wasserstein, p. 165.
28 *Ibid.*, p. 167.

An Arab teacher could not, even with a severe stretch of imagination, have been expected to foster loyalty to a governmentthat, in his opinion, was daily undermining the nationalist existence of his people.[29]

Similarly, Jewish officials experienced a conflict between public loyalty to the administration and private loyalty to the ideals of Zionism. The primacy of the latter over the former was most obviously manifest in the almost complete absence of official secrecy in Palestine. As if by magnetism copies of top secret and highly sensitive official documents found their way to the Zionists offices,[30] and the services Jewish officials were expected to perform for zionism went far beyond the infringement of governmental secrecy and included the pilfering of arms and the manipulation of justice. In fact, well-meaning British attempts to associate all communities with the government of Palestine had the very opposite effect from that which had been intended.

The contrast between the policy pursued by Britain in Palestine and that pursued in Northern Ireland and Iraq in respect of minorities and representation in government raises a number of questions, not least the question why did Britain pursue different policies in Northern Ireland and Iraq and show less practical solicitude for minority interests there. The reason was that it saw no need to take practical steps to safeguard minority interests in those areas, while there was a compelling argument against doing so. Quite simply, to have shown more practical concern might have jeopardised Britain's relationship with the established governments of Northern Ireland and Iraq. In Palestine, on the other hand, imperial interests demanded a different policy, not on humanitarian grounds but in pursuit of a plausible form of government which would enable Britain to abandon direct responsibility for Palestine.

Indeed, even the differences in policies confirm the view that after the first world war British policy towards Northern Ireland was of a piece with the policy of state creation pursued in other parts of the world under British control. It was a policy designed to safeguard imperial interests indirectly and cheaply, regardless of the cost to the citizens of the new creations. As one of the foremost commentators on Iraq put it in the 1930s,

It cannot be denied that individual officials and even the mother country itself are often genuinely concerned for the well-being of the peoples they have taken in charge ... In a conflict of interests ... it is very natural that those of the mother country should come first and that the good of the people must, in reality, be subordinated to the expected material and political returns.[31]

[29] *Ibid.*, p. 178.
[30] *Ibid.*, pp. 201, 202.
[31] *Ireland*, pp. 34–5.

ECONOMIC THEORIES OF POLITICAL VIOLENCE IN THE NORTHERN IRELAND CONFLICT*

JONATHAN KELLEY, IAN McALLISTER
Institute of Advanced Studies
The Australian National University
Canberra, A.C.T. 2600

I Introduction

There have been various attempts to synthesise the range of theories which have been put forward to explain the Northern Ireland conflict and to relate these to practical remedies and solutions to the problem (Darby, 1976: Ch 7; Douglas and Boal, 1982: Ch 1; Lijphart, 1975; Whyte, 1978, 1981, 1983). The diversity of the theories which have been put forward have necessarily limited attempts to test them concisely using empirical data (Douglas and Boal, 1982; McAllister and Rose, 1983; Moxon-Browne, 1982: Ch 10). For example, aside from the theories such as religion and class which have been most widely canvassed, explanations as diverse as Freudian social psychology and caste have been put forward. Clearly, it is impossible to attempt to test all these theories using survey data, and for the purposes of this analysis, only the major theories are examined.

There is a fundamental dichotomy in these theories between those which are economic in nature, and those which are non-economic. Each has particular implications for the future and for the possibility of solving the conflict. From the economic interpretation it logically follows that the conflict is essentially bargainable, and that a change in socioeconomic conditions will alter the intensity of the conflict. Better living conditions, more jobs and material affluence will, it is argued, make people less interested in an atavistic conflict centring on religion. By contrast, most non-economic theories imply that it is a non-bargainable, zero-sum conflict: the gains of one side will always be exactly proportional to the losses of the other. These theories are summarised in Rose's (1976: 139) words: 'the problem is that there is no solution'.

Economic theories of problem normally focus on class relations within

* We thank Professor John Jackson for allowing us access to his 1973 Social Mobility Survey, Mariah Evans and F.L. Jones for comments, and Penny Lockwood for research assistance. Data collection was supported by Grant HR1340/1 from the Social Science Research Council. Neither the original investigators nor the granting agency are responsible for the opinions expressed here. This paper draws heavily on two previous papers (McAllister and Kelley, 1984; Kelley and McAllister, 1984).

Northern Ireland, or on aspects of relative deprivation and discrimination between the two communities. For example, in a traditional Marxist analysis, Farrell (1976; see also O'Dowd, Rolston and Tomlinson, 1980), argues that the problem is essentially class-based, and that the physical conflict between the two religious communities is spurred on by discrimination against the Catholics. However, recent research has shown that the whole question of discrimination is much more complicated than had previously been thought, and that economic inequalities were either non-existent or could be largely explained by factors other than religious identification (Hewitt, 1981; Kelley and McAllister, 1984). Moreover, other empirical research has indicated that 'it is impossible to account for mobilisation in Ulster in class or other economic terms' (Thompson, 1983: 14;6). Other Marxists have attempted to explain the problem in terms of differential levels of economic development between the two parts of Ireland (Bew, Gibbon and Patterson, 1979).

Among the non-economic theories of the Ulster conflict, religion has been the one most frequently put forward. While the sense in which the problem is a conflict between groups with different religion *affiliations* cannot be doubted, it has shown that religion *commitment* and *belief* have little or nothing to do with the problem (McAllister, 1982). The importance of religious affiliation has led some writers to emphasise the territorial dimension to the problem, and the strong correlation between the national identities of the two religious communities (Moxon-Browne 1983; Rose 1971, 1976). Viewing the problem as a territorial one further serves to portray it as a conflict more akin to others in the western world, rather than a conflict which is simply *sui generis*. One final non-economic explanation which deserves mention is the plural society approach, originally suggested by Lijphart (1975) and more recently developed by Thompson (1983). This approach explains the eruption of the conflict by combining class and ethnic factors, but distinguishing clearly between them (Thompson, 1983: 146).

In this paper, we make an explicit test of some of these theories and their relationship to political violence by applying multivariate analysis to survey data collected in Northern Ireland in 1973, during the worst period of violence. Although the data were originally designed to focus on social mobility, a substantial portion were used to elicit respondents' exposure to political violence, attitudes towards politics, and attitudes to the conflict generally. More details can be found in McAllister (1982), and McAllister and Rose (1983). The data used to examine the economic differences between the two religious communities in Section III come from the 1968 Loyalty Survey (see Rose, 1971).

II Background: the level and incidence of violence

The violence which erupted in Ulster in 1969 quickly reached a level far surpassing even Ulster's bloody past and clearly exceeding that found in any other modern industrial society. In a population of only one and a half million, there have been some 2,400 sectarian killings and over 50,000 injuries since 1969. By comparison, the racial unrest which shook the United States between 1964 and 1970 caused only some 240 deaths and 9,000 injuries in a population in excess of two hundred million (Gurr, 1979:54). The level of violence in Ulster more nearly approaches that of a war, with 1.6 deaths per thousand persons. This is more than five times the American war deaths in Vietnam (0.3 per thousand) and about half those of World War II. The violence was at its height at the time of the survey analyzed here, 1973, when there were 250 deaths, 1,007 bomb explosions, and 5,018 shooting incidents, a level surpassed only by the previous year when there were 467 deaths.[1]

The intensity of the violence and its impact on ordinary citizens is also shown by the experiences of our survey respondents (Table 1). More than one person in 5 had experienced some form of property loss by 1973,

Table 1: Percentage of Men Exposed to Violence in Northern Ireland, 1973

Type of violence	All %	Catholic %	Protestant %
Property Loss			
1. House or shop bombed: self	7	6	8
2. House or shop bombed: family	10	10	9
3. Loss of property or goods: self	9	11	8
4. Loss of property or goods: family	11	14	9
5. Summary: percent experiencing any form of property loss[a]	22	25	21
Injury or Death			
6. Injured: self	3	4	2
7. Injured: family	6	7	6
8. Family member killed	2	3	2
9. Summary: percent experiencing any form of injury[a]	10	11	9
Rioting			
10. Rioted: self[a]	33	39	31
(Number of cases)	(2,370)	(849)	(1,521)

Source: Irish Social Mobility Survey, 1973, Northern Ireland Subset.
[a] These variables are used in subsequent analysis, scored 1 = yes and 0 = no.

[1] The literature on political violence is voluminous, but for useful introductions, see Eckstein (1964) and Gurr (1980). For a review of Northern Ireland work, see Carrol (1981).

while one in 10 had themselves been injured or had a family member injured or killed (lines 5 and 9). In addition, a third of the respondents had themselves rioted. Differences between Catholics and Protestants were slight, with Catholics only fractionally more likely to have been exposed to violence or to have rioted. The prevalence of violence is striking; this is violence on a scale which regularly affects the everyday lives of ordinary people.

While communal violence on this scale is common in an historical perspective, individual level survey data on them are exceedingly rare. Most of Europe's violent conflicts lie in the past, before the development of modern survey methods in the 1930s. Contemporary conflicts (for example, in Lebanon) have been in developing societies where surveys, rare and difficult in the best of times, are impractical in the midst of conflict. Fortunately, Northern Ireland is an exception and there are good data available for 1973 when Professor John Jackson conducted a large survey with support from the Social Science Research Council; he has kindly made these data availabe for the present analysis. These extensive data permit an unusually detailed analysis of the causes and consequences of violence for individual citizens, an analysis rare in the literature of violence and unparalleled in the study of conflict between Cathoilcs and Protestants.

Terrorist violence in Northern Ireland has not usually been directed specifically at leaders of the opposing parties or other expressly targeted individuals, but rather it has been aimed indiscriminately at members of the opposing religious community. The main form has been bomb and gun attacks on shops, bars, and other public places. As a consequence, the victims of terrorism are an almost random cross-section of the population, as can been seen from Table 2, which gives the results of a regression analysis predicting exposure to terrorist violence on the basis of various social and ascribed characteristics. It shows that only 6 percent of the variance in property loss, and a very modest 2 percent of the variance in injury, can be explained by these 14 variables. The loss of property is a little more likely among capitalists (mostely bar owners and other small businessmen who have more property at risk); they are 12 percent more likely to suffer loss (column 2). Professionals similarly have more property at risk and are 15 percent more likely than unskilled workers to suffer losses. Presumably for similar reasons, each year of education increases the chance of loss by a modest one per cent. Injury and death strike people in all social positions almost equally, regardless of education, occupational status, or ownership of the means of production; only the unemployed are slightly distinct, being 3 percent more likely to be injured.

In all, what is striking is how violence and property loss strike almost indiscriminately at people in all socio-economic positions. This can be compactly summarized by the sheaf coefficient of .03, which summarizes the

Table 2: Variations in Exposure to Violence[a]

Independent variables (scored from 0 to 1, unless otherwise noted)	Loss of property: Sheaf (1)	Loss of property: Metric regression (2)	Injury or death: Sheaf (1)	Injury or death: Metric regression (2)
Social and Economic Position	(.03)		(.03)	
Education (years)		1**		0˙
Occupational status		15**		4
Manager		2		0
Capitalist		12**		1
Experienced unemployment		−1		3*
Religion	(.04)		(.03)	
Catholic		8**		2
Church attendance		10**		1
Religious self-image		4		0
Belief in supernatural		2		0
Region[b]	(.13)		(.11)	
Belfast or Londonderry		17**		7**
Smaller towns		7**		5**
West or River Bann		5**		0
Age	(.07)		(.05)	
Under 25		5*		5*
25 to 49		4*		2
(Constant)		(−14)		(1)
(Percent of variance explained)		(6%)		(2%)

a Multiple regression analysis predicting the percent experiencing political violence, giving metric regression coefficients and standardised sheaf coefficients. The dependent variables are scored as the *percent* experiencing one or more types of political violence; see Table 1 lines 5 and 9.

b Omitted categories are rural and East of the River Bann.

*,** Significantly different from zero at (*) $p < .05$ or (**) $p < .01$.

effect of all five social position variables in a single standardized regression (or path) coefficient. The sheaf coefficient of .03, for example, shows that all aspects of social position together explain no more than would a single variable with a standardized regression coefficient of .03, which is a very small influence indeed. Catholics are a little more likely than Protestants to loose property, as are church attenders. But there is no religious difference in injury and the overall effect of all religious variables is small (sheafs of only .04 and .03).

The one way in which violence is clearly not random is in its geography: there are appreciable regional differences for both property violence and injury, reflected in sheaf coefficients of .13 and .11 respectively (Poole, 1983). More concretely, residents of Belfast and Londonderry are 17 percent more likely to experience injury or death, other things being equal. Violence is also 7 percent more likely in small towns than in rural areas, and more likely west of the River Bann than east of it. The urban nature of the violence has been frequently noted (Hewitt, 1977; Schellenberg, 1977). But apart from that, terrorist violence has been essentially indiscriminate. Religious differences are minor, as are differences between young and old. The concentration of violence in Belfast and other densely settled areas may reflect the greater ease of mobilizing political resources in settings where there is a large pool of potential supporters, communications are easy, and urban anonymity provides some protection against retaliation or arrest by security forces. There is substantial aggregate level evidence for such resource mobilization considerations in other contexts (e.g. Gamson, 1975; Obershall, 1973; Tilly, 1975) and the Ulster results offer further confirmation based on individual level data withextensive controls for possibly confounding characteristics.

These results also bear out other findings which have characterised the damage to property violence as largely indiscriminate in nature, caused in large part by the intense car bombing campaign carried out by the Provisional IRA and to a lesser extent by the Protestant paramilitaries. Similarly, most civilian deaths came as a result of random violence, particularly in 1972 and 1973 when these data were collected. During that period hundreds of people were murdered by sectarian gangs the only distinguishing characteristic of the victims being their religion – the *wrong* religion (Dillon and Lehane, 1973; McKeown, 1972).

III Socio-economic theories

The Extent of Economic Discrimination against Catholics[2]

The eruption of sectarian violence in Northern Ireland in 1969 is normally traced to the emergence of the civil rights movement in 1967 and to the street demonstrations and protests that followed in 1968. With its largely Catholic membership and demands for an end to discrimination based on religion, the civil rights movement was seen by Protestants as merely masking yet another republican attack on the Northern Ireland state, and as a result, precipitated a strong sectarian backlash. Catholics, on the other hand, viewed the movement as an attempt to redress their long-standing grievances within the

[2] This section draws heavily on Kelley and mcAllister (1984), which also describes the data, methods and measurement in more detail.

existing constitutional framework and a legitimate method of forcing the Unionist government to grant them equal treatment with Protestants. Moreover, in the early stages of the civil rights demonstrations, the movement had unparalleled success in gaining concessions from the government.[3]

Catholics argued that discrimination operated at three levels. Firstly, at the political level there were restricted franchises and, up to 1968, plural voting and residential and property qualifications restricted the size of the local government electorate. There was also extensive evidence of the manipulation of electoral boundaries to give Protestants political control in areas where Catholics constituted a numerical majority. Secondly, at the social level Catholics alleged discrimination in the allocation of council housing, and argued that Protestant families were frequently given houses in preference to needier Catholics. Finally, discrimination was alleged to have taken place at the economic level, through refusing Catholics the same job opportunities as Protestants. Although accurate information is sparse, it has been shown that there is a marked paucity of Catholics in the higher levels of the Northern Ireland Civil Service, and in certain traditionally Protestant industries, such as shipbuilding and engineering.[4]

It was the corpus of these allegations that motivated the civil rights movement in 1967 and 1968. Most of the anomalies were swiftly rectified after the British intervention in 1969, at the political level by bringing the electoral law into line with the rest of the United Kingdom, and at the social level by centralizing housing and determining allocation on a points system. However, while the anomalies at the political and social levels were easily changed, it has proved more difficult to assess both the extent of job discrimination and identify possible legal remedies. This was implicitly recognized by the British government in 1976, when they formed the Fair Employment Agency, a statutory body charged with examining the occupational structure of the Province and making recommendations for a more equitable allocation of jobs.

Even now, a decade and a half since the allegations were made, there remains scholarly disagreement on how extensive economic discrimination was in the late 1960s in Northern Ireland. For example, Common (1971) found that Catholic subregions in Ulster were significantly worse off than

[3] Rose (1971:124) states that the concessions gained by the civil rights movements were, in sum, 'greater than Catholics had won in 47 years of parliamentary opposition'. For accounts of the civil rights movement see, *inter alia*, Feeney (1974), Kane (1971), Power (1972) and Rose (1976).

[4] For general collations of the evidence by the civil rights movement itself, see Campaign for Social Justice (1969), Farrell (1976:86–91) and Fermanagh Civil Rights Association (1969). Earlier evidence is to be found in Gallagher (1957). For more objective discussions, see Barritt and Carter (1972), Bew *et al* (1979), Buckland (1979), Cameron (1969), Mertens (1969) and Whyte (1983).

Protestant areas in terms of viable farm business, industrial development and average incomes. Similarly, Elliott and Hickie (1971:42) have argued that discrimination produced an occupational structure displaying 'marked differences between the two communities'. By contrast, there is an extensive literature to suggest that the occupational differences between the two religious communities were small. Hewitt (1981:368) argues that 'the claim that Catholics are severely disadvantaged in consequence of Protestant discrimination is not born out by a comparison of the occupational structures of the two communities'. In an analysis of his 1968 survey data, Richard Rose (1971:280) concluded that there was 'a limited tendency for Protestants to have a higher occupational class than Catholics; the median Protestant, like the median Catholic, is a manual worker'.

Two comprehensive analyses have been conducted. The first, by Aunger (1975), uses the 1971 census to argue that there is a three-way stratification between Protestants and Catholic occupations. Firstly, there is a marked tendency for Protestants to dominate upper occupational groups, Catholics the lower groups. Secondly, he shows that while Protestants tend to be concentrated in higher status industries, such as shipbuilding, Catholics are concentrated in lower status industries such as building. Finally, even within the same occupations and working contexts, Protestants are more numerous in superior positions. Overall, Aunger (1975:5) concludes that 'while there is a very distinctive tendency for Catholics to fall into a lower occupational class than Protestants, it would be misleading to overemphasize this tendency'. Secondly, Covello and Ashby (1980:93) use Rose's (1968) data to conclude that while Catholics were not disadvantaged in terms of occupation or education, there were substantial differences in income which were 'far too great to be attributed to differences in social origins or prior status characteristics'.

In large measure this lack of consensus indicates a dearth of methodological sophistication. For example, while an aggregate profile of the occupational structures of the Protestant and Catholic communities shows some Catholic disadvantage, this canont be taken as evidence of discrimination *per se*, since occupational attainment depends on a variety of factors such as family

5 See also Birrell (1972) and De Paor (1970) for similar arguments.

6 For similar evidence, see Birrell and Murie (1980:144–6) and Fair Employment Agency (1978).

7 The data for the British estimates are the 1964 electorates cross-section of the Political change in British Survey.

8 See Rose and McAllister (1982:155). In 1961, for example, weekly wages in Northern Ireland were only 78 percent of the average of the whole United Kingdom, by 1971 this figure had risen to 89 percent.

background and education on which Catholics and Protestants differ, all of which must be taken into account before any firm conclusions can be drawn. In this paper we examine religious differences in status attainment in Ulster and control for these potentially confounding factors by multiple regression procedures. The data come from Rose's 1968 Loyalty Survey, collected on the very eve of the Troubles, while comparable results are also presented for Britain. We argue that there *were* substantial differences in attainment between Protestants and Catholics which could not be explained by family background, education or regional differences, but that the pattern is much more complex than has previously been thought.

The status a person attains in the occupational structure depends on many things. Most obviously, it depends on their ability and education, but indirectly family background is also of prime importance. It is the family that launches the individual into the occupational structure, provides an education, and inculcates the child with a range of socioeconomic expectations. Since there is little disagreement that Catholics have a lower status than Protestants in Northern Ireland (the disagreement being exactly how much lower), we would expect Catholics to do less well than Protestants, even in the absence of discrimination, as they come from lower status families. However, once we take this into account by controlling for family background (and other disparities such as educational level), any differences remaining can plausibly (albeit not certainly) be attributed to discrimination.

The actual differences between Protestants and Catholics in years of education, occupational status, and income are shown in Panel A of Table 3.

Table 3: Socioeconomic Differences Between Protestants and Catholics

	Education (men and women)	Occupational status (men and women)	Family (men and women)	Income[a] (men and women)
A. Baseline: Actual Differences				
1. Protestant mean	10.2	37	21.6	22.9
2. Catholic mean	9.7	30*	17.8*	18.0*
B. Adjusted for differences in family background and education				
3. Adjusted Catholic mean	—	36	19.0*	18.7*
C. Adjusted for difference in family background, education, and occupation				
4. Adjusted Catholic mean	—	—	19.1*	19.0*

* Difference between Catholic and Protestant means statistically significant at $p<.05$ by a one-tailed T test.

[a] In pounds sterling, at 1968 prices.

Source: 1968 Loyalty Survey.

Protestants average 10.2 years of education (line 1), compared to 9.7 years for Catholics (line 2); thus Catholics have only 94 percent as much education as Protestants. In terms of occupational status, the gap is larger. Protestants average 37 on the 0 to 100 occupational status scale (a typical job at this level would be a foreman) compared to only 30 for Catholics (for example, a sales clerk). This means that on average Catholics status is only 81 per cent of Protestants. Family income (in punds per week at 1968 prices) also shows large disparities. The mean family income for Catholics is almost 3 pounds a week less than the mean for Protestants.

There are, then, evident disparities between Protestants and Catholics, particularly in occupational status and income. But to what extent are these variations attributable to differences in family background?

Occupational status and income also depend crucially on the amount of education a person has. Panel B of Table 2 estimates Catholic status and income, controlling for both family background and education. We have already noted that Catholics receive about 6 months less education than Protestants, and this helps to explain some of the Catholic disadvantage in status. Line 3 shows that a Catholic with the same education and family background as the average Protestant could expect to attain a status of 36 or around 98 percent of the Protestant mean. There is, therefore, little evidence of occupational discrimination. However, educational variations make only a minor contribution to explaining religious differences in income: the mean Catholic income becomes 19 pounds per week, still only 88 per cent of the Protestant figure.

Our final estimates predict income, taking into acocunt family background, education and occupational status (Panel C). The results show that there is a marginal increase in Catholic mean income, but a substantial gap still remains. These figures imply that even after a wide range of factors which directly determine income are taken into account, there remains considerable variation between the two religious communities: in 1968 a Catholic family equal in family background, occupation and education to a Protestant family, could have expected to receive two pounds and 10 shillings less per week. This represents only 88 per cent of the average of Protestant family income – a real and significant disadvantage.

So far we have examined the effects of these factors at the level of the whole community – that is, assuming that these results hold for the various subgroups within each religious community. This is not necessarily the case, and in Figures 1 and 2 we present detailed graphs based on regression estimates to show how attainment varies for separate groups. To put the findings in a broader perspective, comparable figures for Britain in 1964 are also shown.

While Catholics are generally at a disadvantage compared to Protestants,

Figure 1

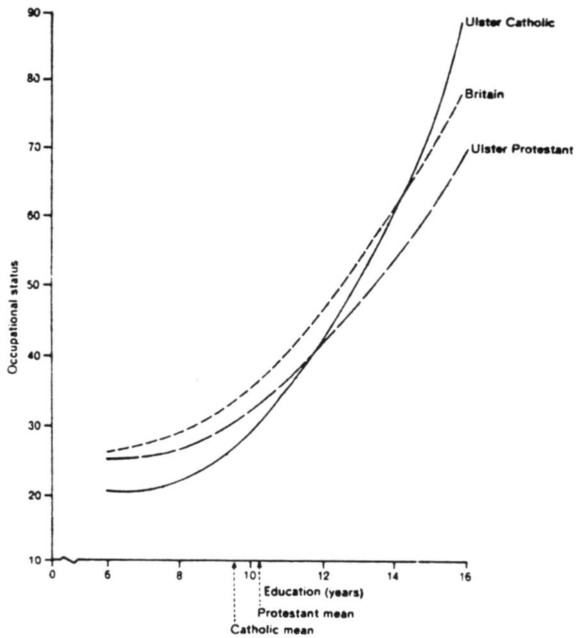

The effect of education on occupational status. Estimated from a regression equation controlling for family background and region. Men only.

Figure 2

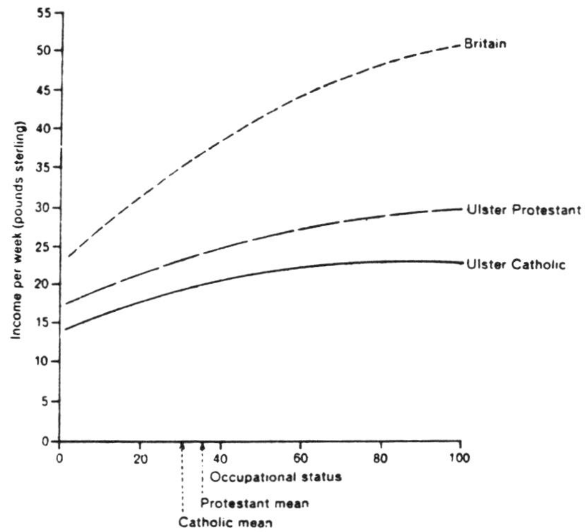

The effect of occupational status on income. Estimated from a regression equation controlling for family background, education and region. Men only.

Figure 1 suggests that highly educated Catholics actually surpass Protestants in occupational status. For those with 10 years of education the difference between the two religions is small – some 3 or 4 points of occupational status – and disappears altogether after 12 years of education. However, above that level, Catholics actually do better than Protestants. Catholics with 14 years of education could expect to return about 8 points more than an exactly similar Protestant, and for those with university education (16 years), the gap increases to almost 20 points. Conversely, Catholics with very low levels of education do slightly worse than Protestants. Once again, the British results aid interpretation. Education offers greater status in the more developed British economy than in the more impoverished Ulster economy, as would be expected. However, at the higher levels of education (around 14 to 16 years), the British do worse than Ulster Catholics. This suggests that it is well educated Ulster Catholics who are atypical, gaining a greater than usual advantage from their education. There are two possible explanations for this. Firstly, it may be that the sharp religious cleavage in Ulster provides a protected job market for Catholic professionals who serve their own community as doctors, lawyers, and the like. Similar 'enclave' economies are well known in other contexts (Wilson and Portes, 1980). Secondly, it may well be that once Catholics have gained further or higher education, they become more motivated than their Protestant counterparts to convert this into a job carrying prestige and status.

Figure 2 examines the financial returns that accrue to education and occupational status. It shows that there is a Protestant advantage at almost all levels. In converting occupational status into income, Protestants again have a consistent advantage among the middle and upper middle class groups of around 4 to 7 pounds per week. This suports Rose's (1971:289) conclusion from the same data that educated Protestants with qualifications were 'likely to enjoy higher wages than educated Catholics'. The results also show the depressed nature of general Ulster wage levels compared to the mainland. Indeed, in all cases the differences between the wages of the Ulster groups and the British sample are appreciably larger than the difference between the two Ulster groups themselves, a tendency which is particularly notable among the better educated and higher status groups.

Two main conclusions therefore emerge form this part of the analysis. Firstly, Catholics tend to have lower status jobs than Protestants but once we take differences in family background and education into account, the disadvantage disappears. There is no evidence of occupational discrimination. Secondly, in terms of the financial returns of work, Catholics receive a lower wage than Protestants, and this persists even after family background, education and occupation are held constant. There are a variety of explanations which could account for this pattern, none of which, unfortunately, can be tested by the data to hand. Firstly, as Aunger shows (1975:13), Protestants tend to predominate in well paid, capital intensive industries, such as engineeering and shipbuilding, while Catholics aer concentrated in more marginal and competitive industries, such as building and contracting, with generally lower wage rates. Consequently, it is possible for a Protestant to receive a high wage for performing the same tasks as a Catholic working in another industry. Secondly, since most of these capital intensive industries are more extensively unionized than their counterparts, it could be argued that Protestant bargaining power, and hence wage levels, are greater than similar non-unionized Catholic workers.[9] Finally, these differences in incomes could be interpreted as the direct result of religious discrimination against Catholics, with Catholics simply being paid less than Protestants in the same jobs.

There is, therefore, not much of an economic basis for the Ulster conflict – insofar as actual differences between the two communities can be substantially explained by family background and inherited privilege. There remains, however, the possibility that it is less the objective economic differences that cause the conflict than individual subjective perceptions of those differences. It is to this possibility that we now turn.

Economic position as a cause of violence.

It is often argued that economic deprivation is a major cause of rioting, with Catholics feeling economically deprived compared to Protestants, becoming frustrated, and venting their frustration through aggression; much of the British government's policy for Northern Ireland has focussed on alleviating the economic deprivation of the Catholic minority. But in fact socio-economic considerations have little to do with rioting either for the population as a whole, or among Catholics and Protestants considered separately (Table 4, second panel). The combined effect of all socio-economic variables, reflected in the sheaf coefficient, is a negligible .04. Only one of the five socio-economic variables has a statistically significant effect. Unemployment has no significant effect, in spite of the prominent role it plays in official thinking.[10]

On this evidence, it seems unlikely that economic changes will reduce conflict in Northern Ireland. It is, however, possible that economic improvements for the Catholic community would affect the climate of

[9] The Northern Ireland trade union movement has, at times, accepted the sectarian nature of the society, and at other times, taken extensive steps to try and counter it. Althoug no figures are available, union membership is probably greater within the Protestant community than within the Catholic. See Rose (1971:504).

[10] For a more detailed analysis of the effects of various social structural changes on the conflict, see McAllister and Rose (1983) and Moxon-Browne (1983).

opinion among Catholics as a whole, and hence reduce conflict, even though they have no effect on the Catholics actually affected by the changes.[11] Our data cannot rule out such a possibility, although neither can they support it.

The fact that economic deprivation has no demonstrable effect on rioting in Ulster is further evidence against the plausible and once supported deprivation-frustration-aggression theory. The weight of evidence in the United States is clearly against it as well (see especially McPhail, 1971). Nor is the opposite 'expectational' hypothesis supported (Berkowitz, 1968). It implies that people with *higher* socio-economic status should be more likely to riot. But in fact they are no more likely to riot either in Ulster (with the possible exception of the highly educated) or in the United States. Violence seems not to have economic roots.

IV Non-economic theories of violence

Religion

Religion *per se* does not have much to do with rioting. Catholics, in particular, are not significantly more likely than Protestants to riot. The recent troubles may have been presaged by Catholic civil rights activity in 1968 and 1969 which led to violence, but in 1973 the violence had escalated and spread to both communities more or less equally. Nor do religious beliefs have any significant effect; the devout are neither more nor less likely to riot than their less devout compatriots. In this, as in other ways, the conflict is not one of religious belief (McAllister, 1982; McAllister and Rose, 1983).

Geography

Our data confirm the urban nature of rioting. The geographical localism of riots is a major factor, as shown by its substantial sheaf coefficient. Belfast and Londonderry are by far the most likely locations for riots: other things being equal, Belfast and Londonderry residents are 30 to 35 per cent more likely to riot than residents of the relatively peaceful areas lying to the east of the River Bann. Residents of smaller towns are also comparatively peaceful – they are only 11 to 15 percent more likely to riot than are people living in rural areas east of the Bann. This great concentration of riots in Belfast is, we suspect in part a consequence of the sheer number of both Catholics and Protestants in the city. For potential rioters, it would seem that power,

[11] Such a possibility is at least consistent with evidence in other contexts that voters' reaction to political parties reflects not only whether the voter expects to gain personally if the party comes to power, but also whether the voter expects the community as a whole to benefit.

Table 4: The Causes of Rioting[a]

Independent variables (scored from 0 to 1 unless otherwise noted)	All: Sheaf (1)	All: Metric regression (2)	Catholic: Sheaf (3)	Catholic: Metric regression (4)	Protestant: Sheaf (5)	Protestant: Metric regression (6)
Economic Position	(.04)		(.08)		(.06)	
Education (years)		1*		1		1
Occupational status		3		−6		1
Manager		2		1		2
Capitalist		−6		−6		−8
Experienced unemployment		1		0		1
Religion	(.07)		(.07)		(.06)	
Catholic		5		n.a.		n.a.
Church attendance		−6	−12		−9	
Religious self-image		7		−5		9
Belief in super-natural		5		4		7
Region[b]	(.23)		(.26)		(.19)	
Belfast		30**		39**		24**
Smaller towns		11**		19**		6*
West of River Bann		1		0		4
Age[c]	(.18)		(.13)		(.18)	
Under 25		24**		21**		25**
25 to 49		13**		12**		12**
Exposure to Past Violence	(.18)		(.19)		(.19)	
Loss of property		16**		17**		16**
Injury or death		14**		10**		15**
Potitical Attitudes	(.05)		(.12)		(.06)	
Blame Protestants for conflict		7*		18**		−9*
(Constant)		(−1.7)		(11)		(−14)
(Percent of variance explained)		(17%)		(25%)		(14%)
(Number of cases)		2,370		849		1,521

*,** Coefficient significantly different from zero at (*) $p<.05$ or (**) $p<.01$.

a Metric partial regression coefficients and standardized sheaf coefficients predicting percent who have rioted.

b omitted categories are rural and east of River Bann.

c omitted category is 50 or older.

publicity, and safety lie in numbers. It is easier to find large numbers of the like-minded in a large population than in a small one; easier to organize in a densely populated city than in rural areas; and easier to escape retaliation and arrest. These results offer indirect, but not entirely unpersuasive, support for resource mobilization theories (e.g. Gamson, 1975; Obershall, 1973; Tilly, 1975)[12]

Age

Like war and crime, rioting is disproportionately an affair of the young. Young men are some 24 percent more likely to riot than those over fifty, while the middle aged are 13 percent more likely to do so. In this Ulster is again broadly similar to the United States (McPhail, 1971:1066).

Attitudes

Finally, political views about the origins of the conflict are important for Catholics but not as much for Protestants. Let us examine Catholics first, beginning with the comparison of two extreme groups: those who think Catholics are entirely to blame for the troubles and those who think no blame at all attaches to Catholics. The first group is some 18 percent less likely to riot than is the second group. So for Catholics, rioting seems to have strong *instrumental* overtones in that those who have well-defined views that attribute blame to Protestants are much more likely to riot. Their riots, like many black riots in the United States, are in part a means of seeking redress for grievances. But for Protestants, the interpretation placed on the conflict is much less important. Those who think Protestants themselves are entirely to blame are only 9 percent less likely to riot than are those who think Catholics are entirely to blame. Protestant rioting thus seems to be more *reactive*, in the sense that it stems not so much from a coherent view about their aims, or their adversaries' aims, or the nature of the conflict, as it does from other sources, notably reaction to Catholic violence (Nelson, 1975, 1984).

Violence as a cause of violence

The Ulster data suggest that exposure to violence is one of the major causes

[12] Furthermore, in Belfast large numbers of Protestants and Catholics live close together. This means there is an opposition to riot against ready to hand, and perhaps a greater chance that provocative but initially peaceful demonstrations will be physically opposed by the other community. Historically, the sheer physical proximity of the two communities seems to have been a catalyst in parking off riots (see Boyd, 1969; Stewart, 1977).

of further violence (see the sheaf coefficients in the first column of Table 4). In concrete terms, loss of property increases the chance that someone will riot by 16 percent (see line 2). Similarly, having been injured in the troubles increases the chance of rioting by 14 percent. These are substantial and statistically significant effects ($p < .01$). These effects do not come about because those exposed to violence have low status jobs, or because they are poorly educated, or are unemployed; such socio-economic characteristics are controlled in the analysis. Nor is it because they live in Belfast and other urban areas where both violence and rioting are common, or because they are young, or Catholic; these factors too are controlled. Rather it is that indiscriminately destroying property and inflicting injury, largely by bombing and sectarian shootings, provokes violent rioting in reply. Terrorists sow dragon's teeth and reap a harvest of violence in return.[13]

In spite of their manifest differences in other respects, Catholics and Protestants react very similarly to violence (columns 4 to 7). Violence is a major cause of rioting in both communities. These results offer strong support for Gurr's (1973) important hypothesis that violence against people who believe they are in the right increases their resistance. This is an important point because it implies that violence will tend to escalate. If the forces tending to produce violence and those tending to inhibit it remain unchanged, then the occurrence of violence at one time makes its occurrence later more probable. Once began, violence begets a cycle of further violence.

We suspect that the reason for this is what might be called the 'injury-frustration-aggression' thesis (in honour of its origins in deprivation-frustration-aggression arguments). It has long been known that the moblization of a large number of people for political action frequently engenders collective violence (Synder and Tilly, 1972; Tilley *et al.*, 1973). Once large groups are organised for action, there is considerable potential for demonstrations and protests to become violent, to become riots, often by the mere force of circumstances. We suspect that previous exposure to violence makes people frustrated and angry and hence more likely to demonstrate,

[13] It is somewhat puzzling that injury has less of an effect than property damage; intuitively it would seem that having an injury in the family would generate more hostility to the opposing community than mere property losses. The reason may be that many injuries are not in any direct sense caused by the opposition. Some 7 percent of the deaths were terrorists blown up by their own bombs and at least a further 26 percent, and perhaps as much as 34 percent, of those killed were engaged in terrorist activities when killed by the security forces (Peroff and Hewitt, 1980: 595). So in all roughly 40 percent of the deaths, and presumably some comparable proportion of the injuries, were a consequence of the terrorist activities of the injured rather than the terrorism of the opposition. The anger and hostility generated by those injuries would presumably not be directed, or at least not directed solely, at the opposition. If so, then the effect of injuries caused by the opposition would be greater than we have estimated, perhaps (if it arises solely from the remaining 60 percent of the injuries) as high as .23. It is also likely that some injuries are serious enough to preclude future rioting.

which in itself increases the risk of riot – that violence (rather than economic deprivation) leads to frustration and aggression. Furthermore, while the potential for violence is often close to the surface in many avowedly peaceful street demonstrations and protests, the prior exposure of the participants to violence reduces the normative and emotional constraints against violence and so violence makes it more likely that a peaceful demonstration will grow into a riot.

V Conclusion

It has often been suggested that violence is merely a symptom of economic deprivation; that deprivation leads to frustration and aggression. Much of the British government's policy is predicated on the hope that reducing unemployment and improving job opportunities will reduce violence, a policy which is applied not only in Northern Ireland but also in connection with racial violence in both Britain and the United States. Our results suggest that the prospects of success are dim. Using regression standardization procedures, we estimate that changes would have little effect on rioting. Consider, for example, the effect of reducing unemployment by three-quarters; increasing Catholic educational levels until they equal Protestant's; improving the jobs available to Catholics to the level of those available to Protestants; bringing the proportion of Catholics who own their own businesses up to the Protestant level; and increasing the proportion of Catholics in high-ranking managerial jobs to match Protestants' representation. Such dramatic changes would completely eliminate any socio-economic disadvantages Catholics face and, moreover, bring the level of unemployment down well below that of Britain. But the effect on violence would probably be negligible; only a one percent decrease in rioting. In this, as in many other ways, religious violence in Ulster seems strikingly similar to racial violence in United States where the evidence against the deprivation – frustration – aggression thesis is equally clear (McPhail, 1971; Spilerman, 1970).

Finally, the results emphasise the general failure of economic theories to explain the Ulster conflict. Class, measured by occupational status, or through a combination of SES factors, has no effect on how ordinary Protestants and Catholics attribute blame for the conflict. What does matter is religion – in the sense of affiliation, rather than commitment or belief. Unfortunately, it is not possible to reliably introduce national identity into the empirical analysis, because of the way the question was asked in the 1973 survey. However, other work on data collected in 1978 has shown that national identity is an even stronger predictor of political attitudes about the conflict than religious affiliation suggesting that the conflict is indeed one of national identity and territoriality, for which religious affiliation acts as a surrogate. The findings presented here further suggest that once violent political conflict commenced, a major cause of its continuation is yet more violence, in a continuing and seemingly unending conflict.

REFERENCES

Aunger, Edmund A. (1975). 'Religion and Occupational Class in Northern Ireland' *Economic and Social Review* 7:1–18.

Barritt, Denis P. and Charles F. Carter, (1972), *The Northern Ireland Problem* (Oxford: Oxford University Press).

Berkowitz, Leonard (1968), 'The Study of Urban Violence: Some Implications of Laboratory Studies of Frustration and Aggression' *American Behavioral Scientist* 2:14–17.

Bew, Paul, Peter Gibbon and Henry Patterson (1979), *The State in Northern Ireland, 1912–1972* (Manchester: Manchester University Press).

Birrell, Derek (1972), 'Relative Deprivation as a Factor in Conflict in Northern Ireland' *Sociological Review* 20: 317–343.

Birrell, Derek and Alan Murie, (1980), *Policy and Government in Northern Ireland* (Dublin: gill and Macmillian).

Boyd, Andrew (1969), *Holy War in Belfast* (Dublin: Anvil).

Buckland, Patrick (1979), *The Factory of Grievances* (Dublin: Gill and Macmillian).

Cameron, Lord (1979) (Chairman), *Disturbances in Northern Ireland* (Belfast: HMSO, Cmd 532).

Campaign for Social Justice in Northern Ireland (1969), *The Plain Truth* (Dungannon: Campaign for Social Justice in Northern Ireland).

Carroll, Terrance G. (1981), 'Disobedience and Violence in Northern Ireland', *Comparative Political Studies* 14:3–29.

Common, R. (1971). 'Some Concerns of Regional Geography: With

Illustrations from Northern Ireland' *Scottish Geographical Magazine 87:* 166–84.

Covello, Vincent T. and Jacqueline A. Ashby, (1980), *'Inequality in Divided Society: An Analysis of Data from Northern Ireland' Sociological Focus* 13:87:98.

Darby, John (1976), *Conflict in Northern Ireland* (Dublin: Gill and Macmillian).

De Paor, Liam (1970), *Divided Ulster* (Harmondsworth: Penguin).

Dillon, Martin and Denis Lehane (1973), *Political Murder in Northern Ireland* (Harmondsworth: Penguin).

Douglas, J. Neville H. and Frederick W. Boal (1982), 'The Northern Ireland Problem' in J. Neville H. Douglas and Frederick W. Boal (eds.), *Integration and Division: Geographical Perspectives on The Northern Ireland Problem* (London: Academic).

Eckstein, J. (ed.) (1964), *Internal War: Problems and Approaches*

Elliott, R.S.P. and John Hickie, (1971), *Ulster: A Case Study in Conflict Theory* (London: Longmans).

Fair Employment Agency (1978), *An Industrial and Occupational Profile of the Two Sections of the Population in Northern Ireland* (Belfast: Fair Employment Agency Research Report No. 1).

Farrell, Michael (1976), *Northern Ireland: The Orange State* (London: Pluto).

Feeney, Vincent, E. (1974). 'The Civil Rights Movement in Northern Ireland' *Eire-Ireland* 9:30–40.

Fermanagh Civil Rights Association (1969), *Fermanagh Facts* (Enniskillen: Fermanagh Civil Rights Association).

Gallagher, Frank (1957), *The Indivisible Island* (London: Gollancz).

Gamson, W.A. (1975), *The Strategy of Social Protest* (Homewood: Dorsey).

Mertens, Claude (1969). *'Report on Civil and Social Rights in Northern Ireland' Human Rights Journal* 2: 507–550.

Moxon-Browne, E.P. (1983), *Nation, Class and Creed in Northern Ireland* (Aldershot: Gower).

Nelson, Sarah (1975), 'Protestant "Ideology" Reconsidered: the Case of "Discrimination"' in Ivor Crewe (ed.), *British Political Sociology Yearbook* Vol. 2 (London: Croom Helm).

Nelson, Sarah (1984), *Ulster's Uncertain Defenders* (Belfast: Appletree).

Oberschall, A. 1973, *Social Conflict and Social Movements* (Englewood Cliffs: Prentice-Hall).

O'Dowd, Liam, Bill Rolston and Mike Tomlinson (1980), *Northern Ireland: Between Civil Rights and Civil War* (London: CSE).

Peroff, Kathleen and Chris Hewitt (1980), 'Rioting in Northern Ireland: The Effects of Different Policies' *Journal of Conflict Resolution* 24: 593–612.

Poole, Michael (1983), 'The Demography of Violence' in John Darby (ed.), *Northern Ireland: Background to the Conflict* (Syracuse: Syracuse University Press).

Power, Paul F. (1972), 'Civil Protest in Nortern Ireland' *Journal of Peace Research* 9: 223–36.

Rose, Richard (1971), *Governing Without Consensus* (London: Faber).

Rose, Richard (1976), 'On the Priorities of Citizenship in the Deep South and Northern Ireland' *Journal of Politics* 38: 247–91.

Schellenberg, James (1977), 'Area Variations in Violence in Northern Ireland' *Sociological Focus* 10: 69–78.

Snyder, David and Charles Tilly (1972), 'Hardship and Collective Violence in France, 1830 to 1960' *American Sociological Review* 37: 520–532.

Spilerman, Seymour (1970) 'The Causes of Racial Disturbances: A Comparison of Alternative Explanations' *American Sociological Review* 35: 627–649.

Stewart, A.T.Q. (1977), *The Narrow Ground* (London: Faber).

Thompson, John L.P. (1976), 'The Plural Society Approach to Class and Ethnic Political Mobilisation' *Ethnic and Racial Studies* 6: 127–153.

Tilly, Charles *et al.* (1975), *The Rebellious Century: 1830–1930* (Cambridge, Mass.: Harvard University Press).

Tilly, Charles (1975), 'Revolutions and Collective Violence' in F.I. Greenstein and N. Polsby (eds.), *Handbook of Political Science* Vol. 3. (Reading: Addison-Wesley).

Whyte, John (1978), 'Interpretations of the Northern Ireland Problem: An Appraisal' *Economic and Social Review* 9: 257–282.

Whyte, John (1981), 'Why is the Northern Ireland Problem so Intractable?' *Parliamentary Affairs* 34: 422–435.

Whyte, John (1983), *Is Research on the Northern Ireland Problem Worthwhile?* (Belfast: Queen's University Inaugural Lecture).

Whyte, John H. (1983). 'How Much Discrimination was there under the Unionist Regime, 1921–68?' in James O'Connell and Tom Gallagher (eds.), *Contemporary Irish Studies* (Manchester University Press).

Wilson, Kenneth L. and Alexandro Portes (1980), 'Immigrant Enclaves: An Analysis of the Labor Market Experiences of Cubans in Miami' *American Journal of Sociology* 86: 295–319.

THE TERRORISTS' TERRORIST: VINCENT BROWNE'S INTERVIEW WITH DOMINIC McGLINCHEY*

KEN HESKIN
Trinity College, Dublin

One of the frustrating aspects of an academic interest in terrorism in Ireland, or anywhere else for that matter, is that access to one's subject of study is usually very indirect. Because of the obvious practical difficulties of meeting and talking to active terrorists, one has to make do with data relating to the known consequences of terrorist activity (undisputed reports of shootings, bombings etc. on public record), a variety of second-hand accounts of terrorists' feelings, attitudes and personal characteristics by people who have met or associated with them, information on their backgrounds and families such as became available, quite unusually, in media coverage of the hunger strikes, and anything else that happens to come along. As Mallin (1978) has commented in the wider sphere of international terrorism, interviews with terrorists are virtually unobtainable.

A further difficulty arises in that, as Schlesinger (1984) has pointed out, the media, and broadcast media in particular have presented a very skewed and unintelligible picture of the conflict in Ireland. The information has been 'action-packed' but has lacked a story in the sense of a continuing analysis of the reasons behind the violence. Not only has there been no story but there have been no characters either because of the inability and/or disinclination of the media establishment to interview members of paramilitary organisations. In many ways, the media coverage of the conflict in Ireland resembles a cheap Hollywood horror movie, presenting a succession of essentially inexplicable, dreadful deeds perpetrated by unseen evil forces.

Both Elliott (1976) and Schlesinger (1978) have pointed to the gradual drift away from analysis as the policy of 'responsibility' in reporting Northern Ireland became generally accepted. In Britain, there is no specific legislation prohibiting interviews with members of proscribed organisations or members of their political wings, but the practice of not doing so, as a matter of course, has generally been adopted and interviews with Republicans are relatively rare. In the Republic of Ireland, Section 31 of the Broadcasting Act makes such interviews specifically illegal for the broadcast media. This state of affairs has led to the ironic situation that in those areas of the Republic which

* I am indebted to Vincent Browne and the Sunday Tribune for permission to use the interview material presented here.

currently receive British television (border areas and much of the eastern seaboard, including Dublin) the only occasions on which the public are ever likely to see a television interview with, say, Gerry Adams, M.P., leader of Provisional Sinn Fein, is on a British television channel.

However, newspapers are not subject to the same self-imposed or legally enforced restrictions as are the broadcast media and interviews with political representatives of paramilitary organisations do occasionally appear. Nonetheless, it has been very rare indeed in recent years that an interview with a currently active terrorist has been published. Hence, the publication by the Dublin newspaper the Sunday Tribune (27 November, 1983) of an interview with such an individual marks a singular opportunity of a currently active Irish terrorist. The main burden of this chapter will be to present details of that interview, with clarifying comments, to a wider readership.

The Sunday Tribune is a 'quality' Irish Sunday paper directed towards the educated middle classes. It has a very heavy bias in content towards political and economic news and analysis and is aggressively radical in its stance. The editor of the Sunday Tribune, Vincent Browne, has a considerable reputation for what might be termed 'jugular journalism' and has, for several years, been a thorn in the flesh of the establishment in the Republic of Ireland. Browne himself conducted the interview below. He states that, in the course of his work, he has met 'numerous killers from the IRA, INLA, UVF, UDA etc. during the last decade'. The interviewee on this occasion was Dominic McGlinchey, leader of the Irish National Liberation Army (INLA) which grew from the ashes of the Official IRA after its move away from violence towards political action. The political wing of the INLA is the Irish Republican Socialist Party (IRSP).

Background

The interview took place in the aftermath of a particularly horrible incident in Darkley, a small border village in Co. Armagh, in Northern Ireland. A gang of men forced their way into a Protestant gospel hall during a service and sprayed bullets into the congregation, killing three people and wounding seven others. In a subsequent statement, the gang, calling itself 'The Catholic Reaction Force', stated their purpose as 'token retaliation' for the recent murders of Catholics. Ballistics evidence indicated that one of the guns used in the Darkley attack had been used in previous INLA attacks and thus the media focussed its attention on 'mad dog McGlinchey' whose reputation for ruthless killing had made him the most wanted man by security forces North and South of the border. It was widely speculated in the media that McGlinchey was either directly or indirectly responsible for the grisly attack on helpless Protestant worshippers.

It appears that McGlinchey himself was anxious, in the light of media comments on the matter, and also perhaps in the light of the fact that the Provisional IRA had formally denounced the attack as blatant sectarian killing, to give an account of himself. I have reliable information to the effect that McGlinchey offered an interview to the BBC in Belfast at this time, but that the offer was declined. Vincent Browne, however, did avail of the opportunity presented and met McGlinchey in the Republic of Ireland during the week before Sunday, 27 November, 1983, when the interview was published.

The interview

The interview lasted for four hours, during which time McGlinchey and Browne were alone, except for times when somebody brought them refreshments. Much of the Sunday Tribune interview reports actual quotations but, as a consequence of the duration of the interview, sometimes the gist of a reply is given. Actual quotations, of course, appear inside quotation marks.

Some of Browne's comments on McGlinchey's demeanour are relevant to an assessment of his comments in the interview. Browne noted that he showed none of the 'mad dog' characteristics attributed to him by sections of the media, but that he spoke with a soft Derry accent, and was, for the most part, relaxed, composed and fairly articulate. Browne notes that McGlinchey did not strike him as psychopatic but that 'there is a coldness about him in relation to the consequences of his actions which is chilling'. One should be aware, however, that Browne uses the term 'psychopatic' as a layman and that one can set no store by such comments (see Heskin, 1984 for a discussion of this point).

Browne also comments that McGlinchey had never spoken to a journalist before and was 'quite devoid of the caution and guile that most interviewees evince in front of reporters'. He was apparently tired at the time of the interview and, in Browne's view, this caused him to be careless in his use of language. However, he perked up under pressure and became quite articulate, was 'unusually well able to carry the drift of an argument through several convolutions' and was anxious to broaden the discussion of political problems beyond the scope of his own involvement in the North's violence to topics such as neutrality, disarmament, liberation struggles around the world, Ronald Reagan and 'of course', Margaret Thatcher.

McGlinchey appeared uneasy about the concentration of the conversation on his own activity and repeatedly asserted that 'I am not a one-man army.

One man can do nothing on his own'. He also repeatedly asserted his abhorrence of sectarian assassinations and Browne noted that he was convincing in his denials of his involvement in the Darkley killings. However his initial denial of any INLA involvement was eventually contradicted by his admission that one INLA member was involved.

Q. How many people had he killed?
(After a few seconds pause)
A. 'I honestly don't know'.
Q. Was it 20, 30, 40, 50?
(Further pause)
A. 'Around the 30 mark, I would say'.
Q. Were they all members of the security forces?
A. 'I killed only one civilian and that was Dale, the informer, and he was killed for a very good reason. Never at any time have I killed or been responsible for killing any civilian. I am totally opposed to sectarian assassinations. It is not what this organisation is about and it is not what I am about'.
Q. But civilians were killed in some of the bombings he was responsible for?
A. 'I repeat that I have not been responsible for the killing of any civilians whatsoever'.
Q. How does he feel about his victims?
A. 'I often ask myself does this person really believe they are acting on behalf of the whole community as policemen or as members of the UDR or do they have any perception of the bigoted, repressive role they are playing. But generally as far as I am concerned I view them, be they members of the RUC, the UDR or the British army, as agents of a repressive and violent staet. I genuinely wish there were another way of dealing with repression in Northern Ireland, but I believe there is no other way. Therefore I do what has to be done and don't think about it thereafter'.
Q. Did he ever see the face of a victim before he killed him?
A. 'Usually, for I like to get in close, to minimise the risk for myself. It's usually just a matter of who gets in first and by getting in close you put your man down first. It has worked for me down the years. I wouldn't be as good as they are shooting it out over distances because I don't get the opportunity for weapons and target training like they do. So I believe in getting in close'.
Q. When had he last done that?
A. 'This was on the Cookstown job a while ago. I went up to the bunker outside the police station and just opened up on the policeman in the bunker'.

Q. Did he ever get nauseated by what he had done?
A. 'You don't really see nothing. You don't see people splattered all over the road or anything like that as you would after someone had been shot from a distance by a high calibre rifle. Usually you don't even see any blood. Your main concern is to make your get-away and you are not hanging around looking at the scene. It is, of course, unpleasant. I take no pleasure whatsoever in it as some people would like to suggest'. *McGlinchey was then asked if there was any killing he felt particularly bad about and a pause followed. He began talking about a Protestant boy he had grown up with who had joined the RUC and was subsequently killed by the IRA. McGlinchey said that he felt badly about that.*
Q. Would he have shot this lad if he had known he was a member of a patrol about to be ambushed?
A. 'I don't think I would. But I have shot members of the security forces I have known – a good number of them' (These were apparently people known from his youth and through his father's garage).
Q. Did he believe that all the appalling hardship he had inflicted on his victims, their wives and children was really worth it?
A. 'Times I have asked myself, I have asked if it is worth all the personal hardship I have inflicted on myself and on my own wife and children, but the alternative is to accept forever all the hardships and injustices'.
Q. But these are self-inflicted hardships, what about the hardships inflicted on the lives of others, for instance the children of his victims. They had done no harm to anyone, so why should he inflict suffering on them in the way he was doing?
A. (Browne notes that for the only time in the interview, McGlinchey became uneasy. He talked about his concern for children generally and for the kind of society he wanted to create for them, children being part of the future and so forth.)
Q. Isn't this just sentimentality and pretty meaningless if not entirely hypocritical, coming from him?
A. (in agitated tones) 'I'm not going to be blackmailed by the grief of children. The only way to end repression in the North is through violence against the security forces and the state itself. I am not going to be blackmailed by this talk of children from doing what has to be done'.
Q. Had he ever felt after an incident: 'Oh Christ no, I can't go on'?
A. 'I do often think about it all from the point of view of my own children. I would like to think there is a better future from what I am doing now. As I have said often to priests who condemn violence, if we can build a mass movement to end repression and if this movement got the support

of all those who say they oppose violence, then I would put down the gun in the morning. But don't forget, when the Northern people started a mass movement for reform Paisley and Bunting came out with clubs to beat them off the streets for demanding one man one vote'.

Q. Did he regret any of the killings he had done?

A. 'No, I don't. I would rather they didn't have to come about. There is no other way. But I don't hate people – that is not my motivating force'. *Newspaper reports during the week had claimed that, as a consequence of the Darkley killings, the Provisional IRA were looking for McGlinchey.*

Q. Are relations with the Provos tense?

A. On the contrary, relations with the Provos were very good. He had been in the Provos for a number of years and formed many friendships and no acrimony or competition with the Provos existed. Further, suggestions that the Provos were looking for him were ludicrous. The INLA and the Provos were involved in essentially the same struggle and since the new leadership in the Provos had asserted its dominance, there was a great deal of similarity between the two organisations.

Q. What sort of background did he come from?

A. He is aged 29 and comes from Bellaghy, Co. Derry. He was one of a family of eleven – seven boys and four girls. He was the third child. His father owned a garage in which he worked for a year from 1970 to 1971. His career as a mechanic was interrrupted by internment. He was interned on 14 August, 1971 along with five other youths from the area. Altogether, nine of the boys he was in school with were interned with him. Three of his brothers were in the Provos as well. Sean McGlinchey, who is a year younger, is serving a life sentence for bombing Coleraine (a largely Protestant town in Co. Derry). He has already served ten years. Another brother, Paul, has been in jail since 1976 for the attempted murder of South Derry Unionist politician Robert Overend. A third brother, Michael, served a sentence for membership of the IRA. He had no involvement in any paramilitary organisation and had been involved in no military activity up to the time of his internment. He attended some civil rights marches but that was the height of his involvement. He was brought to Ballykelly (a British security force base) on 14 August, 1971 and was given 'the treatment' there for over five days. Then he was taken to Magilligan Prison and later to Long Kesh (now the Maze Prison or 'H Blocks'). At this time he was seventeen years old. He was released from internment in May or June, 1972. 'My only involvement came through internment'. He immediately joined the Provisional IRA in South Derry and almost at once had to go on the run to avoid re-internment. He remained free for a year until he was arrested in a house where weapons were also found. He was charged in the Diplock Court with possession of weapons and served 18 months in Crumlin Road, Magilligan and Long Kesh prisons. During this year of freedom, he had been heavily involved militarily, attacking British Army personnel and planting a few bombs. He learned about explosives and weapons. 'I just picked it up as I went along'.

Q. Had he killed many people during that time?

A. 'Yes, there would have been soldiers – there wouldn't have been many at that time. (As an afterthought) And a few UDR men as well'.

After serving his 18 months, he returned to IRA involvement in South Derry.

'I was always on the run. They were hunting me right away. They know the mistake of letting me out'.

Between late 1975 and 1977, after a ceasefire during 1974, McGlinchey and a few close comrades caused havoc throughout Northern Ireland. ('We didn't confine ouselves to South Derry'.) He was one of three IRA men at the time who became the most notorious terrorists in the North. The others were Francis Hughes, who died on hunger strike in July, 1981 and Ian Milne, now in the Maze Prison.

'I was operations officer for the area in general. The South Derry was carrying the movement at that time. We were involved mainly in the killing of UDR men and policemen and we did a fair few bombings of police barracks and towns. We bombed Magherafelt and Toombebridge barracks to name just two'.

Q. What towns had he bombed?

A. 'I don't think a town wasn't blown up – they all got a touch. Killalea, Bellaghy, Portglenone, Magherfelt, Maghera, Castledawson, Ballymena and lots of others. There's more if I can think of it'.

He was involved in every single one of these operations himself.

Q. How many operations had he taken part in?

A. 'I couldn't count them, but I suppose I took part in over 200 operations'.

During this time, McGlinchey was also wanted in the Republic of Ireland. He had been involved in the hijacking of a police car and it was alleged that he had threatened a garda (policeman) with a gun. McGlinchey insisted that he had no gun at the time but did threaten the garda with a wheel brace. He served 4.5 years in prison in the Republic, until February, 1982 on the hijacking conviction.

Q. How did it come about that he left the Provisional IRA and joined the INLA?

A. It was during this period of imprisonment in the Republic (in Portlaoise Prison, where most of the political prisoners are housed) that he changed his political allegiance. He and his comrades in South Derry had been very critical of the Provisional IRA leadership during their activities in the 1975–1977 period for their failure to provide adequate supplies and weaponry. In gaol, he had also begun to read quite a bit – a few books by the Belgian Marxist economist, Ernest Mandel, those by James Connolly, and others. There was also a lot of political discussion in the gaol at the time and he claims that his politics developed significantly. There were also personal tensions in the prison and a number of rows broke out with people taking sides. This was a critical element in his decision to defect from the Provos and join the INLA.

Because of his status, he subsequently became a senior figure in the INLA and was instrumental in ending the factionalism within that organisation.

'I had moved up to Dundalk and started to organise the INLA in Armagh, Newry, Tyrone, South Derry and South West Antrim. Some Provo units came over to us but we also got many new recruits into the organisation'.

'We also started to build up the organisation in the 26 Counties. First of all this was to balance the movement in a manner that hadn't been the case before. Previously, the movement was centralised on Belfast and Dublin, now it was much more broadly based and the consequence of this was that many of the feuds that previously existed were defused'.

'The strength of the organisation, I think, can be established by the fact that the INLA exploded a 200 lb bomb in a pub in Strabane in the last few weeks. We were never able to do anything like this previously and it gives us the capacity to explode land mines to an extent that was not previously possible'.

'We have also been able to step up the military activity quite dramatically. Previously the INLA's activity was centred primarily on Belfast, now it's centred elsewhere. We launched attacks on police posts in Markethill and Cookstown in the last few weeks where three policemen were killed'.

Q. Did he have anything to do with the Darkley church killings?

A. He categorically denied that he personally had anything to do with it, but he did agree that he supplied the gun, a Ruger semi-automatic rifle, used in the killings. He commented, 'They were entirely innocent hillbilly folk, who had done no harm to anyone. There is no justification for the incident'.

He said that the gun was given to a member of the INLA to conduct an assassination on a known member of the UVF (Ulster Volunteer Force) in the Portadown area who had been responsible for a number of sectarian assassinations. Describing the INLA member to whom the gun was given he claimed, 'This INLA member was a brother of someone who had been killed some time previously and he must have been unbalanced or something to have gone and organised this killing. We are conducting an enquiry into the whole affair'.

Q. What action would be taken against this man, given that the organisation had executed reputed touts?

A. 'I can't really say but I would not be in favour of taking the kind of action against the lad because of the pressure he was under'.

Q. What kind of structure and support does the INLA have?

A. The INLA was broken down into cells and the old batallion structure had been done away with. There were well over 100 operators in the INLA at the moment with about 300 back-up people. The whole border area was strong for the INLA and it was much stronger in the South than it had ever been. 'In fact, there is nowhere in the South we couldn't carry out an operation, if we wanted to'.

Q. What is his attitude to the Republic of Ireland?

A. It must be done away with as the Northern state must be done away with. (As an afterthought) The Southern state will have to be brought down by a mass struggle rather than an armed struggle.

Q. Does the INLA carry out operations in the South?

A. 'Oh, it has'.

In the context of discussing operations in the North, Browne raised the topic of the INLA bomb placed in a public house in Ballykelly in December, 1982. The pub was patronised by British soldiers stationed nearby and 12 soldiers were among the 17 killed, with a further 65 people injured, some of them very seriously.

Q. How could such an operation possibly be justified in view of the inevitability of civilian casualties?

A. 'The owner of that pub was warned six times about entertaining members of the security forces there. He knew full well and the girls that attended the disco there knew full well that the warnings had been given and that the place was going to be bombed at some stage or another'.

Q. But the issue was that it was absolutely inevitable that planting the bomb in those circumstances meant that there would be civilian casualties and therefore does not a conflict exist with protestations of concern for civilians?

A. 'We didn't think we would kill civilians. The bomb was placed in a manner to avoid civilian casualties'.

Q. But how could you possibly place a bomb in a disco attended by a large number of civilians without expecting civilians to be killed?

A. 'We did give warnings again and again about this and the people that were there must have known what the consequences of it were likely to be'.

Q. Was he personally involved in the Ballykelly bombing?

A. He did not plant the bomb.

Q. Did he plan it or was he in any way involved in it?
A. Yes, he was.
Q. Doesn't that raise serious doubts about his previous protestation about avoiding civilian casualties or civilian assassinations and even about the Darkley affair?
A. 'My track record is good on avoiding civilians being killed'.
Q. What did he think was going to happen to him eventually?
A. 'I will probably get shot. There is a good possibility of my not seeing the end of the struggle. I could be lucky but just because I have been set up by the media as the most wanted man in Ireland,I suppose that increases the chances of my getting done in. But I don't really give it a lot of thought, I always try to avoid being shot'.
Q. What precautions does he take?
A. 'I stay out of the road. I avoid the enemy till it suits me to come into confrontation with them. I have been shot at hundreds of times in Cookstown; recently they shot 200 rounds at me. I would have a certain amount of fear. You need a certain amount of fear to keep you on edge. But you must be able to control your fear. I think I am better motivated than the enemy and that gives me an edge and therefore I think my chances of survival are high'.
Q. Is he a Catholic?
A. 'I am'.
Q. Is he a practising Catholic?
A. 'No, but I am a believing one'.
Q. What reaction did he have to the Pope's plea on bended knees to end violence?
A. 'I don't see the Pope as an authoritative moral figure. He is very misinformed, and about other struggles throughout the world. For instance he blessed the Guatemalan government and the Salvadorian government but he didn't bless the Nicaraguan government. He is a very conservative man. I certainly wouldn't take to heart his plea for peace'.
Q. What did he hope to be remembered for?
A. 'I will be remembered for nothing. I have no illusions about myself. There is no glory or anything to this. The only people who will remember me will be my family and particularly my children'.
McGlinchey's mother and other members of the family are members of the charismatic movement and are very religious. The family garage has gone out of business. None of the family were involved in Republican politics before the present trouble started.
Q. What is in store for us in 1984 from the INLA?
A. 'I believe that we are now better organised and better equipped to give the Brits a hard time in 1984. That's basically it. Only time is going to

tell. But it is not only the security forces that need to fear us in 1984. There are also those politicians who stir up sectarian strife – people such as Ian Paisley. They cannot escape much longer the consequences of their words and actions. I have high hopes for '84'.

At the time of the interview, McGlinchey was wanted on foot of a historic extradition order, which had gone through both the High Court and the Supreme Court in the Republic and which had broken new legal ground in Ireland by reflecting an interpretation of 'political offence' which precluded particularly heinous crimes. The effect of the order was such that, if apprehended, McGlinchey would be extradited to the North without further legal ado.

Q. What did he think of the extradition order?

A. 'They allege that I murdered a woman in Toombebridge, Co. Antrim in 1976. But the RUC know full well that I am innocent of this charge. The charge was merely a ruse to get by the extradition rules in the South and it has succeeded. There are lots of cases they could have sought my extradition on – murders of RUC and UDR men. They have identification, fingerprints, the lot. Instead they trumped up this charge of killing a civilian. I have never killed an innocent civilian in my life'.

Postscript

In the months subsequent to this interview, McGlinchey had a number of intercessions with the police in the Republic of Ireland. From all of these encounters he emerged with his freedom and, on two or three occasions, with the uniforms of the gardai concerned. Needless to say, these incidents were a source of great embarrassment to the police and to the government of the Republic.

However, he finally ran out of luck on the morning of Saturday, March 17, St. Patrick's Day, 1984. He was arrested along with three other men at a house in Newmarket-on-Fergus, Co. Clare after a brief but fierce gun battle in which a detective was wounded. After an attempt to legally forestall his extradition was brushed aside by a hastily convened Supreme Court, McGlinchey was handed over to the RUC on Sunday, March 18th, the first person claiming political motivation for his crime to be extradited from the Republic of the North.

REFERENCES

Elliott, P. (1976) Reporting in Northern Ireland: a Study of News in Britain, Ulster and the Irish Republic. University of Leicester: Centre for Mass Communication Research.

Heskin, K. (1984) The psychology of terrorism in Northern Ireland, in Y. Alexander & A. O'Day (Eds.) Terrorism in Ireland. Bedlenham, Kent: Croom Helm; New York: St. Martin's Press.

Mallin, J. (1978) Terrorism as a military weapon. in M.H. Livingston (Ed.) International Terrorism in the Contemporary World. London: Greenwood Press.

Schlesinger, P. (1978). Putting 'reality' together. London: Constable.

Schlesinger, P. (1984) Terrorism, the media and the liberal, democratic State: a critique of the orthodoxy. in Y. Alexander & A. O'Day (Eds.) Terrorism in Ireland. Bedlenham, Kent: Croom Helm; New York: St. Martin's Press.

ENGLISH CARTOONISTS; ULSTER REALITIES

JOHN KIRKALDY

In the drawing, the idiot Irishman amidst a scene of great destruction holds a pistol in each hand to his temple and the caption reads, 'I'm the last surviving Irishman – but not for long – my left hand won't allow my right hand to have the last word in the argument'. Is this a caricature from some dusty tome reflecting an anti-Irish outburst in the 19th century? – no, a typical Cummings cartoon drawn for the *Daily Express* in August, 1971,[1] and another reminder that the study of cartoons is one of the most neglected subjects of media reporting of the present troubles in Northern Ireland. Yet, these drawings provide some of the most blatant examples of anti-Irish feeling and give ample evidence of massive English prejudice.

Anti-Irish imagery in English cartoons has a long history.[2] John Derrick's *Image of Irelande* (1581) shows Irish Catholic priests blessing soldiers and encouraging murder, the killing of English Protestants in battle, and the stealing of cattle. One 17th-century broadsheet shows Irish 'Papists' sacrificing children taken from the wombs of their English Protestant mothers; the slaughter of Protestants by Catholics; the roasting of Protestant children on spits in front of their parents; priests anointing and giving absolution to those about to murder and rob; and the killing of Protestant children by dashing their brains out as if they 'were the pigges of the English sowes'. The English cartoonist Gillray drew grotesque Irish figures in his depiction of the 1798 rising. During the battle over Catholic emancipation in the 1820s, cartoons showed priests encouraging and exulting in the destruction of Protestant churches.

One typical drawing, showing the likely results of emancipation, depicted George IV kissing the pope's toes, grotesque cardinals and priests looking on, while, in the bakground, Protestant churches were being demolished and victims sacrificed on a 'Catholic gridiron', over all of which the devil was gloating. A cartoon dating back to te late 19th century shows a village priest tying a submissive female figure 'Erin' with a rope and warning of the wrath of God by pointing to heaven. The strands of the rope, labeled 'Home Rule' and 'Fenianism', illustrate a popular English misconception of the 19th century: although the Catholic church supported the nationalist movement, it

[1] *Daily Express*, August 11, 1971, 7. This is a slightly revised version of an article that first appeared in *Eire-Ireland* in Autumn, 1981. It is reproduced with permission.

[2] The following historical examples are taken from Howard Smith, *Ireland: Some Episodes From Her Past* (London: BBC Publications, 1974).

Cummings, The Daily Express, *August 11, 1971, p. 7. Reproduced by kind permission of the Daily Express, London, 1980. © London Express Service.*

opposed the physical force tradition. L. P. Curtis Jr. in his pioneering study of Victorian England's cartoons, *Apes and Angels*, has shown that the Irish were often drawn to resemble apes, Negroes, or Frankenstein monsters – protruding jaws, thick lips, bulging eyes and grizzled features.[3] *Punch* cartoonists, such as Sir John Tenniel and Harry Furniss, graphically reinforced the prejudices of the magazine's readership in this fashion.

It would be tempting to see these cartoons simply as an artistic version of

[3] L. Perry Curtis Jr., *Apes and Angels: The Irishman in Victorian Caricature* (Newton Abbot: David and Charles, 1971).

the Irish joke.[4] And it is true that they have, over the centuries, illustrated all of the crude racial stereotypes depicted in this traditional component of English humor.[5] Anti-Irish cartoons, however, do much more than this. Given artistic license and the relative immunity of cartoonists from prosecution for libel and slander, particularly during the last hundred years, such caricatures illustrate the very depths of English anti-Irish feeling. Take, for example, the Cummings cartoon mentioned above: no written comment nor even an Irish joke would seriously suggest that the Irish could inflict genocide on themselves. Yet, Cummings is only one of several English cartoonists who have so depicted the Irish during the present crisis. Cartoons of the Irish, therefore, allow all the irrationalities of English prejudice full and unchecked expression. They articulate feelings that the English, in more rational moments, know to be nonsense. If the *Daily Express* wrote an editorial on such lines, it would be a matter for the race relations board or the local asylum. As it wsa, the cartoon passed without protest in England. Its date – August, 1971 – importantly coincided with internment, which even the army itself and most British politicians now tacitly admit was a massive mistake, as internment did more in a few days to help the growth of the IRA than any other event in the crisis up to that moment. At the height of any Anglo-Irish crisis, English cartoonists have always revived all of the traditional images. *Punch*, for example, during the 1840s, 1860s, and 1880s was full of Irishmen in the guise of gorillas and orang-utans.

English cartoons depict the 'positive' and 'negative' stereotypes of the Irish even more extremely than Irish jokes. Before 1968, what little coverage there was of Irish affairs was of the traditional 'pigs in the parlour' kind. Since 1968, the Irish have been the target of an artistic venom characteristic of a 17th-century English broadsheet.[6] Indeed, cartoons have become the main

[4] Irish jokes are discussed by Andrew Brown, 'Anti-Irish Jokes', *The British Media in Ireland* (London: Campaign For Free Speech in Ireland, 1979), 16; John Kirkaldy, 'The Return of the Irish Jokes', *Quadrant* (May 1980), 10–15; and Sarah Nelson, 'Joke Irish', *Fortnight*, December 19, 1975, pp. 6–8, and January 9, 1976, pp. 13–14.

[5] For historical studies of English images of the Irish, see L. P. Curtis Jr., *Anglo – saxons and Celts* (Bridgeport: COnference on British Studies, 1968); Ned Lebow, 'British Historians and Irish History', EIRE-IRELAND, VIII 4 (Winter, 1973), 3–38, *White Britain and Black Ireland: The influence of Stereotypes on Colonian Policy* (Philadelphia: Institute for the Study of Human Issues, 1976); 'British Images of Poverty in Pre-Famine Ireland', in Daniel J. Casey and Robert E. Rhodes, eds., *Views of the Irish Peasantry 1800–1916* (Hamden: Archon Books, 1977); and Patrick O'Farrell, *England and Ireland since 1800* (London: Oxford University Press, 1975). Some similar points are also raised in Nicholas P. Canny, 'The Ideology of English Colonisation: from Ireland to America', *William and Mary Quarterly*, 3rd Series, 30 (Octobver, 1973), 575–98; Daniel D. Dorrity, 'Monkeys in a Menagery: The Imagery of Unionist Opposition to Home Rule, 1886–1893, EIRE-IRELAND, XII, 3 (Fall, 1977), 5–22; and W. R. Jones, 'England against the Celtic Fringe: A Study in Cultural Stereotypes', *Journal of World History*, 13 (1971), 151–71.

[6] For a brief study of English cartoonists and Northern Ireland, see Robert Taylor, 'Images of the Irish', *New Society*, November 28, 1974, pp. 556–57.

newspaper vehicle for this kind of comment, since it is no longer possible, as in previous centuries, to voice such prejudice in print. Irish cartoons in the English press not only combine general anti-Irish sentiments but also link these to a view of a particular incident or topic. Therefore, they act, like the Irish joke, as a method of reassuring the English that the Irish are wholly responsible for events in Northern Ireland since 1968, and so they exorcise any lingering doubts about British Government policy in the province. They also permit political comment of a kind that even the most biased Englishman would not find possible in other forms – even in the Irish joke. They grossly distort and simplify the problems of Ireland: Catholics and Protestants, North and South, the IRA and other paramilitary groups, and all the other political, social, and economic forces involved are lumped together in rude racism. These cartoons play an essential part in preventing English comprehension of the realities of Northern Ireland.

Three periods of cartoon and general reporting of Northern Ireland during the present situation can be discerned: general sympathy: October, 1968–August, 1969; growing alienation: August, 1969–December, 1973; and an increasing lack of interest, which has continued to the present. Like most historical generalizations, these categories oversimplify a more complex phenomenon, but a general pattern does emerge. Interestingly, whereas in previous Anglo-Irish disputes the Irish Question proved politically divisive, the present crisis has largely projected Ireland as a bipartisan issue at Westminster, reinforced by a widespread consensus among politicians and the media. Dominating English attitudes, with a few exceptions, has been a switch from 'positive' to 'negative' imagery. English cartoons have reflected, promoted, and intensified this shift.

English ignorance of Northern Ireland, prior to October, 1968, was almost absolute. In the decade before the civil rights movement touched off the major demonstrations, media stories about Ireland were intermittent and often mixed whimsy with a large dash of spurious local color. Details of more important events, such as elections were usually left to local 'stringers' or the occasional English journalist on a quick foray into the virtual unknown. Yet, as the *Cameron Report* and many other investigations have since demonstrated, Northern Ireland contained widespread discrimination against Catholics – in terms of housing, jobs, voting, and justice – systematically developed by the Protestant Unionist Party, which had ruled uninterrupted, since the creation of the province in 1921. Occasionally, newspapers such as the *Observer*, the *Sunday Times*, or the *Tribune*, tried to analyze more deeply, but most left their readers completely in the dark when it came to Irish affairs.

[7] *Punch*, October 16, 1968, p. 526.

Television and radio reporting of Northern Ireland was even more perfunctory.

The English reaction to the first few months of the crisis was symbolized by a *Punch* cartoon (October, 1968), by Norman Mansbridge, which shows a slab of stone, labeled 'Democracy', supported by three beautiful female pillars – England, Scotland and Wales – while a fourth figure, old and bent – Northern Ireland – cowered on her plinth.[7] Apart from the *Daily Telegraph* and, to a lesser extent, the *Daily Express*, and their Sunday versions, no newspaper felt that it could support the Protestants, and most were enthusiastic in their approval of the civil rights cause. Protestants were often depicted as dour, stubborn, and reactionary, as evidenced by an illustrated *Punch* 'Come to Ulster for that holiday with a difference' brochure by Mahood (January, 1969).[8] This was the first in a long and continuing series of anti-Irish cartoons by Mahood. One of the captions explains: 'If you like roses, fishing or beautiful scenery Ulster has the best. The same goes for religious maniacs, gerrymanderers and bigots'. Such cartoons had a double edge, for tourism in all of Ireland was soon affected by the disturbances in the North and by such notions about them.

Similar cartoons reflected a simplified and misleading view of Northern Ireland. It was certainly true that Protestants in the province had openly discriminated against Cathoilcs, but this had often been done with the connivance, open or tacit, of successive British governments. Northern Ireland remains part of Britain and is, therefore, ultimately a British responsibility. Section 75 of the 1920 Government of Ireland Act unequivocally gives ultimate jurisdiction over all matters in Northern Irish affairs to the British government of the day. If there are problems in the province, Britain is clearly accountable, however much she might try to evade the issue. This realization in 1968 led to efforts to present Northern Ireland as a remote country for which Britain had little or no responsibility. Northern Ireland had, however, been created by Britain; British arms and soldiers helped establish it in the bitter fighting of 1921–23; and blind British eyes had been turned to events there for half a century. Cartoonists played their part in the early months of the crisis by absolving the British from responsibility and placing the blame fully on Irish shoulders. Another feature in these cartoons continues to the present day: the ability of the English to find amusement in events in Ireland,however tragic. One of the pictures in the Mahood feature already quoted shows slogans being daubed on a wall over the caption: 'There are many cultural activities and one of the brighter sides of the unemployment problem is the unlimited time it gives the local inhabitants for artistic expression'. It is inconceivable to imagine an English

[8] *Punch*, January 15, 1969, pp. 88–89.

cartoonist extracting such delight in, say, London or Yorkshire. Yet, unemployment in Northern Ireland has consistently been higher than in the rest of Britain. In 1967, unemployment in Strabane was 25 percent and in Derry, 20 percent: there appears to be little cause for mirth.

By August, 1969, English impressions of Northern Ireland had changed dramatically: Catholics increasingly joined Protestants as figures of derision. In part, this represented a general, if unfounded, belief that most Catholic grievances had been met by reforms, but more important in this shift of opinion was the rising level of violence. The Burntollet ambush in January, 1969, and the sectarian rioting in Belfast and Derry during April and August, 1969, graphically illustrated a new dimension of the troubles. Finally, the introduction of the army in August, 1969, to take over security in the province, committed most English newspapers to support law-and-order demands. The B Specials and Royal Ulster Constabulary had received a generally hostile coverage from the British media until then. A full return to the traditional English stereotypes of the Irish first appeared in cartoons in the conservative press, but it quickly spread. Cummings, whose anti-Irishness deserves a study on its own, in the *Daily Express* (September, 1969) showed three seminaked Africans landing on the Northern Irish coast, complete with heathen artifacts, saying, 'We're pagan missionaries come to try to make peace among the bloodthirsty Christians'.[9] Mahood in *Punch* (October, 1969) drew a Catholic and Protestant fighting each other in a cage as part of 'The Human Zoo'.[10]

These increasingly hostile views of the Irish, personified in cartoons during this period, helped the English come to terms with a crisis of which they had little comprehension. English attention, at this time, almost exclusively focused on civil rights and on the details of the violence. Important though these undoubtedly were, they were only symptoms of a far more fundamental malaise in the province. The 'insane' image of the Irish promoted the idea that the violence in Northern Ireland was incomprehensible, that it could be explained only in terms of madness. Yet, the violence had a logical rationale, however terrible its results in human terms. Catholics had complained about discrimination since the province was created, but only with serious demonstrations and rioting was English attention for the first time captured and some reforms implemented. A fatal sympathy between the level of violence, the degree of media coverage, and political reaction appeared at the start of the crisis. 'Ireland' touched an awkward nerve in many Englishmen, as they had been assessed by conventional historical wisdom as the 'guilty party' in previous Anglo-Irish disputes. The presence of the army, now a

9 *Daily Express*, September 12, 1969, p. 10.
10 *Punch*, October 8, 1969, p. 569.

tangible British presence in the province, heightened the feeling of 'them' and 'us'. Hostile imagery of the Irish helped the English to ignore their contradictory position of maintaining that the crisis was an Irish affair, while, at the same time, the Labour government of Harold Wilson was intervening increasingly in Northern Ireland, bringing pressure to bear on the governments of Terence O'Neill and James Chichester-Clark. The hostile stereotypes had also something of a cathartic effect. As the English felt themselves being increasingly drawn into a situation they could not fully control, their rage and frustration grew. Finally, anti-Irish imagery conditioned the English for their increasing involvement in Northern Ireland: if the Irish were seen as 'mad', then the 'sane' English obviously needed to 'improve' matters.

After August, 1969, English cartoonists firmly reverted to all the old stereotypes of the Irish. No device seemed too low to be used to show them as perverse, irrational, stupid, mad, or generally unbalanced. Once again, the cartoons graphically illustrated all of the well-worn themes: love of violence, hatred of the principles of true Christianity, and an inability to comprehend the superior values of English norms of behavior. Such representations of the Irish employed two forms – dimunitive figures or horrific monsters – and both shared a common ugliness and the same semihuman features. Cummings, in the *Daily* and *Sunday Express* and Jak, of the *Evening Standard*, in particular, specialized in drawing cartoons of midget Irishmen snarling, fighting, generally behaving in a ridiculous fashion. Cartoonists showed even greater ingenuity when it came to depicting Irishmen on a larger scale, suitably exaggerating characteristics they wished to emphasize. Emmwood, in the *Daily Mail*, drew a King Kong-like figure, labeled 'Violence', clutching a club and smoking pistol, walking over an Ulster sketched in the form of a graveyard (June, 1970).[11] Rigby, in the *Sun*, showed 'Ulster' as a gorilla-like figure standing in a blood-stained boxing ring, clutching a rifle in one hand, while tossing sticks of gelignite into the air with the other (March, 1972).[12] Horner, in the *New Statesman*, illustrated Stormont, the former Northern Irish Parliament, as Frankenstein, complete with British politicians as perplexed laboratory attendants wondering what to do next (November, 1971).[13] Paramilitaries on both sides were not even illustrated as human on many occasions but as – a favorite device – snarling dogs panting for blood as, for example, in cartoons by Garland in the *Daily Telegraph* and Emmwood in the *Daily Mail*.[14] If they were drawn in human form, their ape-like nature was usually pronounced. English caricatures

[11] *Daily Mail*, June 30, 1970, p. 6.
[12] *Sun*, March 25, 1972, p. 5.
[13] *New Stateman*, November 12, 1971, p. 641.
[14] *Daily Telegraph*, July 15, 1971, p. 2, and *Daily Mail*, March 25, 1972, p. 6.

continued to show insensitivity towards the suffering involved during the disturbances. Mahood in *Punch* was to compile, for example, a light-hearted guide to the rioting, called 'Bigotry Cup 1970', a take-off modelled on World Cup football.[15] And, once Irish Republican Army (IRA) bombs began to explode in England, from 1972 on, the ape-like features of Irishmen in such caricatures became noticeably more pronounced.

English cartoons reflected a failure to understand a rapidly deteriorating situation. By the end of 1972, 467 people had been killed, including 146 soldiers. The central stratagem of British policy – the implementation of reform by a Northern Irish Unionist government – was demonstrated to be a failure, which was eventually conceded by the imposition of Direct Rule by the Conservative government of Edward Heath in March, 1972. Instead of reducing the tension in the province, the troops rapidly became part of the problem itself. Not even a massive army presence, which peaked at 21,000 men in July, 1972, was able to keep the peace. Despite mounting evidence that the soldiers had, on occasion, exceeded their powers and had used violence or brutal methods, the media generally continued to support the army's line that it was 'getting on top the gunmen', and an innocent looking Englishman began increasingly to be incorporated into many cartoons. English public opinion oscillated between two poles: supporting demands for a 'get-tough' policy, while at the same time wishing to see the army withdrawn from the province. A *Daily Mail* survey in September, 1971, showed that 59 percent of the people in Britain, excluding Northern Ireland, wanted the soldiers to leave.[16] Only occasionally did English cartoons reflect the true circumstances of the crisis, as in a Scarfe drawing in the *Sunday Times*, entitled 'How To Make The Irish Stew', which shows a cooking pot filled with two crosses and the artist's usual grotesque figures. Its caption reads:

> Take Ireland Mix Catholics and Protestants Add potato famine to reduce mixture Stir in English absentee landlords Bring to slow boil and simmer for four centuries – Later – Pour in British army Squeeze Catholics Add nail bombs and rubber bullets (lead if preferred) Cook on CS high speed gas and retire.[17]

By the time of the Sunningdale Agreement (December, 1973), the high point of British hopes in Northern Ireland, there was pronounced decline in media and cartoon interest in Northern Ireland. This had been a feature even earlier in popular and tabloid newspapers. Except when something startling took place, such as the Ulster Workers' Council (UWC) strike (May, 1974), or a particularly horrific death, coverage became increasingly perfunctory. Simon Winchester in his *In Holy Terror*, which describes the conditions of reporting

[15] *Punch*, July 8, 1970, pp. 59–61.
[16] *Daily Mail*, September 24, 1971, p. 1.
[17] *Sunday Times*, August 15, 1971, p. 8.

in Northern Ireland, noted that, as early as 1971, editors 'tended to want to know how long it would be before the total dead reached a certain, arbitrary figure, rather than the tragic circumstances of each death; funerals that rated a page in 1970 rated less than a couple of lines at the base of page three a year later'.[18] This not only reflects the common media phenomenon that repetition dulls any story, however tragic, but it also reflects the growing English feeling that the problem is impossible to solve. Anti-Irish feelings have not, however, diminished: cartoons, when they do appear, are still as hostile. McLachlan in *Punch*, for isntance, depicted a Roman arena with four lions contemplating some future victims involved in a general fight amongst themselves and saying: 'Oh dear, not the *Irish* Christians again' (January, 1977).[19] There seems to be a growing belief in Britain that, if the crisis in Northern Ireland is ignored, then it might go away.

The violence of the Irish has dominated both English cartoons and English reporting of the disturbances. The media have justifiably condemned the killing and wounding caused by the IRA, particularly the Provisionals, and by other paramilitary groups, but they have also oversimplified the causes of violence in the province. A feature of Irish media reporting, of whatever viewpoint, during the disturbances has been the provision of more explanation, unlike English reporting where emphasis has tended to rest solely on the gory details, as Philip Elliott's study of the content of British and Irish media during 1975–76 attests.[20] Thus, the IRA's involvement in the violence was exaggerated in the period 1968–69, when the IRA was weak, divided, and based mainly in the South. The walls of Belfast and Derry, always good barometers of Northern Irish opinion, often carried at this time the inscription 'IRA – I Ran Away'. The sectarian rioting, particularly in August, 1969, gave the impetus for the IRA's expansion and, later, its split between the Officials and the Provisionals in January, 1970. As Eamonn McCann, a leading Irish socialist and civil rights activist has pointed out in *The British Press and Northern Ireland*, Fleet Street has often ascribed almost every death or explosion, even without evidence, to the IRA.[21] The bombing of Castlereagh power station (April, 1969), for instance, was caused by Protestants, not the IRA, as was widely reported at the time. During 1972–73, the media greatly underestimated the involvement of such Protestant paramilitary groups as the Ulster Defense Association (UDA) and the Ulster Volunteer Force (UVF) in the sectarian assassinations that began at the time.

[18] Simon Winchester, *In Holy Terror* (London: Faber and Faber, 1974), p. 71.

[19] *Punch*, January 12, 1977, p. 55.

[20] Philip Elliott, *Reporting Northern Ireland: Ethnicity and the Media* (Paris: UNESCO, 1978).

[21] Eamonn McCann, *The British Press and Northern Ireland* (London: Northern Ireland Socialist Research Center, 1971).

"Oh dear, not the **Irish** Christians again!"

McLachlan, Punch, *January 12, 1977, p. 5. Reproduced by kind permission of Rothco Cartoons, Inc., New York, 1980.© 1977 Punch.*

"Sit down, Murphy, your Luger's showing!"

Jak, The Evening Standard, *May 8, 1970, p. 18. Reproduced by kind permission of the Evening Standard, London, 1980. © The British Library.*

In August, 1977, a member of the UVF was found guilty of bombing McGurk's Bar, in which fifteen people were killed. At the time, the media, despite strong evidence to the contrary, nearly unanimously sugested that it was the work of the IRA.

The contributions of English cartoons to this process has been largely twofold. Firstly, it has minimized any English responsibility for the Rights of using torture during internment, a charge found to be substantially true, Jensen in the *Sunday telegraph* drew a hooded IRA man holding a smoking gun with the caption 'Witness for the Prosecution' (September, 1976).[22] With certain excpetions – the *Guardian, Morning Star, Private Eye, Sunday Times* and *Tribune* – no newspaper is really prepared to concede that British troops have also, on occasion, contributed to the level of violence, as on Bloody Sunday (January, 1972). To criticize the government or the army means an almost certain charge of being an IRA sympathizer. Secondly, numerous cartoons have done their best to suggest that the Irish are naturally prone to violence and, even, seem to find some masochistic enjoyment in it. Cummings, in the *Daily Express*, drew dimunitive IRA and UDA figures firing at each other – a dove wounded in the crossfire – and depicted them both saying: 'Phew! That was a nasty moment – we nearly had a dangerous outbreak of peace that time!'[23]

English cartoonists depicted the army, in contrast, as patient, long-suffering, noble and virtuous – a direct contrast to the wild, impossible Irish. Yet, such imagery concealed that the soldiers had themselves soon become part of the complex ingredients of the problem itself. The English failed to realize that the circumstances of the army's introduction were unique: the Catholics, who traditionally viewed British soldiers as 'the enemy', saw them as a vindication of their cause and a pledge to end discrimination, while the Protestants, who traditionally have strong links with the forces, believed that the soldiers would be used in a 'get-tough' policy against what they saw as 'subversion'. These two views had no hope of being reconciled. The rising violence and reluctance of successive Unionist governments to introduce sufficient reforms meant that the so-called 'honeymoon' period was soon at an end. Relations between the troops and first the catholics and then the Protestants began to deteriorate rapidly. The troops, coming under increasing fire from mobs in the street, began to see their task more in terms of ending 'terrorism'. Despite a successful and efficient public relations campaign by the army, the circumstances in Northern Ireland began to contradict the official view.[24] Violence continued; a large military presence was necessary to keep

[22] *Sunday Telegraph*, September 5, 1976, p. 14.

[23] *Daily Express*, July 10, 1972, p. 6.

[24] Simon Hoggart, 'The Army PR men of Northern Ireland', *New Society*, October 11, 1973, pp. 204–05.

any semblance of law and order; and the troops began to trade force for force. The presence of the army itself, ironically, often became the cause for increased violence by street mobs. Only occasionally did cartoonists depict this situation, as in a Horner cartoon in the *New Statesman* after Bloody Sunday (January, 1972), which shows a soldier with a rifle at the ready, looking down a street festooned in black flags with the ironic caption parodying official pronouncements: "The Army is winning the war in Northern Ireland".[25] Some accusations against the soldiers were propaganda; many were not. Yet, most cartoonists continued to draw innocent soldiers and to repudiate any suggestion that the army was guilty of any misdemeanor, however small. Thus, Mac in the *Daily Sketch*, after the Lower Falls Curfew (July, 1970), drew an irate Irishman being dragged from his house by the soldiers, along with large amounts of arms, and the caption: 'There! What did oi tell yez! Lootin' again!'[26] Subsequently, however, the army did reluctantly admit that a number of incidents of looting had taken place. Most dangerous of all, the army presence in Northern Ireland has long become a substitute policy in itself, rather than a means to finding a policy.

It would be wrong, however, simply to see English cartoons during the present crisis as completed reflections of the past. The focus had changed from the whole of Ireland to an increasing concentration on the North. The South received an initially hostile press reaction, and many early cartoons were very critical, particularly when the IRA had a great deal of freedom in the country. During the Arms Trial (May, 1970), for instance, when two members of the Lynch Cabinet were accused of supplying arms to the IRA, Jak in the *Evening Standard* drew members of the Irish Parliament, sitting on crates of weapons and explosives clearly consigned to the IRA.[27] As the South began to take a tougher line against the IRA, so its image in English cartoons marginally improved, although this has been subject to setbacks, as in the aftermath of Bloody Sunday. The suspicion that the South and the IRA work hand in hand still remains in many cartoons. In August, 1979, Cummings in the *Daily Express* drew Jack Lynch, the Irish prime minister, sitting on a tortoise, marked 'Flying Squad', surrounded by dimunitive, ape-like members of the IRA, and commenting: '... and you can rest assured, my anti-terrorist flying squad will maintain its high-speed momentum to annihilate the IRA!'[28] Southern Irishmen have evoked feelings of suspicion and unease, but they have not been fully incorporated into English hostility towards the North. Protestants in Northern Ireland, who were often given support for their British sentiment in the past, have received a consistently critical press since

[25] *New Statesman*, February 4, 1972, p. 130.
[26] *Daily Sketch*, July 7, 1970, p. 11.
[27] *Evening Standard*, May 8, 1970, p. 18.
[28] *Daily Express*, August 29, 1979, p. 9.

Osbert Lancaster, The Daily Express, *November 23, 1971, p. 1. Reproduced by kind permission of the Daily Express, London, 1980. © London Express Service.*

1968. This perhaps reached its peak during the UWC strike, which was organized by Loyalists in May, 1974. Horner in the *Sun*, for instance, drew the skeleton of William II, dressed in court attire, being carried by the main figures of Ulster Unionism, watched by Protestant paramilitaries in masks and sun glasses, with the caption: 'The Loyalists'. A slogan on one wall in the cartoon – 'Queen Anne's Dad Is Dead Too'. – indicated English dislike of Protestant statements of loyalty.[29] Nor has anti-Catholicism played a major part in English cartoons, as in previous disputes, although Osbert Lancaster's character in the *Daily Express*, Father O'Bubblegum, shows that this tradition is not yet dead. O'Bubblegum, a swarthy and subversive figure, appeared in a number of cartoons, urging his flock to militant action. Such cartoons ignore repeated criticism by the Catholic hierarchy of any form of violence in the province. Thus, traditional suspicion of Catholic modes of worship and criticism of the priesthood were combined in a Lancaster cartoon which shows an English soldier saying knowingly to Fr. O'Bubblegum: 'If you say it's a rosary, Father, of course, it's a rosary – but it still looks very like a bicycle-chain to me'.[30] In general, English cartoons have fulfilled their traditional function – expressing anti-Irish prejudice that in any other form would be publicly unacceptable, even in England.[31] Perhaps English feelings were best summed up by a Jak cartoon in the *Standard* (October, 1982), which showed an innocent Englishman contemplating a billboard advertising 'The Ultimate in Psychopatic Horror – The Irish X X X X'.[32] On the poster for the film (produced by 'Emerald Isle Snuff Movies' and featuring 'the IRA, INLA, UDF, PFF, UDA, etc. etc.'), were a collection of figures that would have done credit to any horror movie.

[29] *Sun*, May 25, 1974, p. 6.

[30] *Daily Express*, November 23, 1971, p. 1.

[31] For Northern Irish cartoonists and the troubles, see Belinda Loftus, 'Laughter and Violence: The Northern Cartoonists', *Hibernia*, November 28, 1975, p. 27.

[32] *The Standard*, October 28, 1982, p. 18.

REPRESENTING VIOLENCE: THE BRITISH CINEMA AND IRELAND[1]

JOHN HILL

No issue has plagued British broadcasting more in recent years than its coverage of the conflicts in Northern Ireland. Amidst a tortured history of overt and covert censorship the fragile doctrine of 'balance' has never seemed more precarious.[2] And, yet, many of the emphases and absences evident in the British media's coverage of Northern Ireland are not new and find their parallel in the treatment accorded the Irish by the post-war British cinema, even when such images seem safely removed from contemporary political crises. In selecting some of the key British feature films to have dealt with political violence in Ireland I would hope to demonstrate how recurrent attitudes towards Irish history have emerged in an ongoing tradition, both typical of British cinema itself and of British political culture in general.

But, first, a note on methodology. A predominant temptation in the assessment of a film's treatment of Irelend – assisted here by a characteristic British preference for realist forms and resistance to more stylised modes – is the assumption that we can directly measure off the 'truth' of certain events and actions in a film against some external standard of reality or knowledge – in this case that of Irish politics and history. An example of this can be found in the reception accorded by the Guardian (29/11/79) to one of the most recent feature films to have emerged about Ireland: *THE OUTSIDER* (1979). On the arts page, as part of the conventional weekly review section, Derek Malcolm provided his presumably 'aesthetic' appreciation of the film while on the centre pages political reporter, Derek Brown, who had spent a large time reporting from Northern Ireland, was called upon to consider 'the political authenticity' of the film which presumably retained an independence from its 'aesthetics'. But, of course, what this division of labour projects is a false dichotomy. To take a fairly extreme example, a film about Ireland such as Douglas Sirk's *CAPTAIN LIGHTFOOT* (1954), a historical romance set

[1] This paper was originally commissioned as part of the Sense of Ireland programme at the ICA, London, March 1980. It has subsequently been delivered at the National Film Institute of Ireland Summer School, Clongowes Wood College, July 1980, the Cork Film Festival, October 1980 and the Department of Sociology, The New University of Ulster, January 1981. I am grateful to all those who participated in discussions at these events and wish to thank, in particular, Luke Gibbons and Jim Cook for their comments. An extended version of the paper is due to appear in a forthcoming collection of essays, *Cinema and Ireland*, co-edited by Kevin Rockett, Luke Gibbons and myself.

[2] For useful summaries of the details, see Liz Curtis, *Ireland: The Propaganda War*, Pluto, 1984 and *The British Media and Ireland*, Information on Ireland, London, 1979.

in nineteenth-century Ireland dealing with secret societies, is little illuminated by reflection upon its historical 'inauthenticity' – particularly when the deceits of Irish history are integrated with Sirk's characteristic concern with illusionism to form the very substance of the movie. This is not to say that the film is then outside the domain of politics, but rather than the political meanings it projects, must be understood on the basis of the artistic conventions it employs which may indeed be flagrantly anti-realist and historically anachronistic (as they are in '*CAPTAIN LIGHTFOOT* '), though the case remains the same even if they are not.

This is indeed the starting premiss of Thomas Elsaesser's work on the American cinema. Taking to task cultural critics of the left and right alike for their failure to 'understand Hollywood as an aesthetic phenomenon in its own right'[3], he argues that just such an understanding forms a necessary precondition to any ideological critique of that cinema, and to this end suggests the value of what he labels an 'affirmative-consequential' model of classical Hollywood cinema. Elsaesser's argument is that if we wish to understand the 'affirmative' ideology of Hollywood we must in turn come to grips with the aesthetic structure of 'consequence' in which it is embedded: that of narrativity sharpened and accentuated by generic dramaturgy. Narrative in itself is necessarily 'consequential' – not just linear (sequential) but causal (consequential) – which in turn is heightened by conventions of character (the central hero) and plot (the journey, the pursuit, the investigation) characteristic of the leading Hollywood genres. As Elsaesser puts it: 'there is a central energy at the heart of any good Hollywood film which seeks to live itself out as completely as possible ... the prevalent plot-mechanisms of the two major genres of the American cinema (the Western and the Gangster film) invariably conform to the same basic pattern. There is always a central dynamic drive – to get to the top, to get rich, to make it – always the same graph of maximum energetic investment'.[4] Irrespective of the specific inputs of content which might flesh out this pattern then Elsaesser suggests that what is revealed is 'a fundamentally affirmative attitude to the world it depicts, a kind of a priori optimism located in the very structure of the narrative about the usefulness of positive action. Contradictions are resolved and obstacles overcome by having them played out in dramatic-dynamic terms or by personal initiative: whatever the problem, one can *do* something about it'.[5]

And, of course, invariably bound up in this structure as part and parcel of

[3] Thomas Elsaesser, Why Hollywood, *Monogram*, April 1971, p.5.

[4] Thomas Elsaesser, Vincente Minnelli, *Brighton Film Review*, No. 15, December 1969, p.12.

[5] Thomas Elsaesser, The Pathos of Failure: American Films in the 70's, *Monogram*, October 1975, p.14.

its dynamic is violence. For by and large what one can do is a function of the means of force one has under command. As Andrew Tudor puts it after his consideration of three predominantly American genres – the western, the thriller and the horror movie – one element is completely shared: 'the use of violence as the ultimate necessary solution to crucial problems ... in terms of plot, in terms of emotion and in terms of morality, violence resolves all problems and tensions'.[6] Now I don't want here to debate the ethics of violence on the screen or the relationship this may or may not have to violence elsewhere but rather to indicate the dynamic function which violence performs in relation to American cinema and its contribution to the living through of the energies located by Elsaesser. For, in the American cinema, violence helps forward drives and ambitions, establishes character and identity, resolves problems and conflicts and ultimately affirms an ideology of advancement and development.

As a number of critics have indicated this can be instructively contrasted with the typical characteristics of the British cinema.[7] For while the British cinema has been no less in thrall to narrative than its American counterpart it has nonetheless not developed a native tradition of such essentially dynamic genres as the western or gangster. Far more characteristic have been the light comedy or domestic drama whose inner mechanics have not required the working out of energetic forces in quite the same way as their U.S. equivalents. As a consequence, if the American cinema has characteristically celebrated dynamism and forward movement, so as commonly has the British cinema opted for statism and acceptance of the status quo (take, for exmple, such apparently divergent movies as *BRIEF ENCOUNTER* (1945) and *SATURDAY NIGHT AND SUNDAY MORNING* (1960). The procedural logic of British cinema tends less to be forward than circular – the accumulation of experience on the part of characters tending to return them to base rather than to move them on. And this in turn can be linked to the British cinema's characteristic renunciation of violence. Reversing our earlier terms, violence in the British cinema habitually thwarts drives and ambitions, signals flawed character or lack of self-identity, compounds problems and conflicts and confirms an ideology of regression and fatalism (in turn a function of violence's lack of integration into the context and meaning of British film genres, or it being given a fundamentally different inflection as in the war movie).[8] And insofar as the British cinema's treatment of Irish

6 Andrew Tudor, *Image and Influence*, Allen and Unwin, 1974, pp.213–214.

7 See Charles Barr, *Ealing Studios*, Cameron and Tayleur, 1977, esp. pp.53–54.

8 Thus by a peculiar alchemy even British movies made during the war could find their morale-boosting tempered by an acute sense of passivity, such that Durgnat is able to remark, in the context of such late fifties films as *DUNKIRK* (and their special emphasis on 'a mood of near-defeat'), that:

politics conforms to these standards so we can see beginning to emerge some of its ideological parameters.

Fatalism, for example, is embedded in the whole structure and style of Carol Reed's *ODD MAN OUT* (1947). In a way reminiscent of Sophoclean tragedy the conventional dramaturgy of intrigue and suspense is marginalised with a displacement of focus away from what will happen to a display of how it happens. Intimations of doom are carefully marked from the beginning (e.g. the breaking of Johnny's shoe lace just as he announces 'it'll go fine') and then referred back to (e.g. Shell also breaks his lace) while interest in Johnny's fate correspondingly shifts from whether he will escape to just how and who will catch him. Accordingly, there is something of an absent centre at the heart of *ODD MAN OUT*. Unlike Elsaesser's ideal-typical portrayal of classical narrative cinema, there is no central protagonist whose drives and motivations structure the film's forward movement. On the contrary Johnny (James Mason) less acts than is acted upon (visually underlined by his increasing need for actual physical support), with the film's dramatic weight falling upon the series of characters whose responses and reactions constitute the terms upon which Johnny's fate is worked out.

Appropriately then the film's stylistic repertoire draws heavily upon the examples of German expressionism of the 1920's and French poetic realism of the 1930's whose formal strategies conventionally carry menaings of preordained fate and determinism. A preliminary aeriel shot of Belfast establishes an initial sense of openness quickly to be belied by the rest of the film. For once having set foot upon pavement the confines of the city remain the film's parameters. Action predominantly occurs within enclosed interiors, darkly lit, often cramped with people or objects, and shot low-angle to reveal the ceiling. As the film progresses studio exteriors replace actual locations and the combination of heavily shadowed lighting and constricting compositions minimise the changes between inside and outside. The subjective sequences only serve to make more explicit the meanings already sublimated into décor and composition (now buildings do literally bend over Johnny or turn into prisons) while dialogue makes verbally explicit the central thematic (thus, for example, Johnny becomes clearly identified with a bird in a cage in the conversation between Father Tom (W.G. Fay), Shell (F.J. McCormick) and Kathleen (Kathleen Ryan).

And most emphatic of all, perhaps, the imagery of the film works to create

---

'Wartime documentaries already stress Britain's capabilities of passive endurance; indeed, their apparent diffidence as to whether she could dish it out as well as take it worried some neutral nations From *LONDON CAN TAKE IT* through *SAN DEMETRIO LONDON* and *IN WHICH WE SERVE* to *WESTERN APPROACHES*, the British, with dire honesty, represent themselves as on the ropes. Although aggressive films weren't unknown the last shot of *THE WAY AHEAD* was characteristically subdued' (*A Mirror for England*, Faber, 1970, pp. 84–85).

a sense of almost natural ordination. Exterior changes of the elements (day to night, sunlight to rain and then snow) measure and map out Johnny's destination while the passage of time itself becomes a central motif. The film begins and ends at the same clock tower and its appearance as both sound and image punctuates the film's development throughout. The sound of its strokes reinforce and underline significant moments of action (e.g. the death of the two IRA men outside Teresa's) while visually there's no escaping it (in a geography of Belfast that makes no concessions to 'realism' it can be seen through windows from Kathleen's, Theresa's, Father Tom's and Lukey's as well as from most everywhere else). It's not then just a case of temporal concentration (eight hours) providing an acceleration of the drama but that time practically takes over as a dramatic agent in its own right. It may be Johnny's and Kathleen's death which closes off the action but it is an image of the clock striking twelve which actually ends the movie. As Frohock puts it with respect to 'the novel of erosion': 'Characters tend to be passive victims who change and evolve according to the will of time, and who act less than they undergo; the real agent, the active force is time itself'.[9] it becomes appropriate then that in such a universe the police become less the agents of laws created by people (and which thus it would be possible to challenge) than the agents of an abstract fate, whose language ('This time he has shot and killed a man ... he belongs to the law now') soon becomes little distinguishable from that of the church ('This is different ... he's killed a man and he must pay the penalty').

But what then is the tragic flaw which has wrought such inexorable nemesis? The answer seems clearly to lie in Johnny's association with violence. Very early in the film it is established that though Johnny had been serving a prison sentence for gun-running he no longer endorses his former means. Questioned by Dennis (Robert Beatty) on his commitment to the forthcoming robbery of the mill he responds (while ironically fitting his gun holster) that 'I believe in everything we're trying to do but this violence isn't getting us anywhere ... if only we could throw our guns away and make our cause in the parliaments instead of the backstreets'. The conversation is strategically important and is an addition to the novel which begins directly with the mill raid. It establishes an ethical and political frame for Johnny which differentiates him from his more gun-happy colleagues and thus provides the motor of Johnny's tragedy whereby it is he, who, despite his renunciation of violence, becomes the one to commit murder (sympathy for him largely resting upon this assumed moral innocence).[10]

[9] W.M. Frohock, *The Novel of Violence in America*, Southern Methodist University Press, Dallas, 1957, p.4.

[10] Although Johnny's downfall is inextricably linked with his use of violence, the film's condemnation of violence is by no means even-handed. For what the film implicitly endorses is

But if it is violence which has entrapped Johnny and denied him the possibility of freedom (Kathleen enquires portentously prior to the robbery – 'Johnny, will you ever be free?') so, in the film's terms, it would seem is the commitment to causes and its correspondent abandonment of a more prosaic human destiny. A crucial scene here is the one which takes place between Kathleen and Granny (Kitty Kirwan) following the Head Constable's departure from their home. Granny encourages Kathleen to heed the policeman's advice and tells the story of Hughie Fitzpatrick, also a gunman on the run, who had wished Granny to go with him. But she asks her granddaughter: 'Did I go out and look for him? I did not. I stayed and had my life', a life which was to include the bearing of eleven children. Granny falls asleep, however, and Kathleen removes the gun which the elderly woman had been hiding. And just as Johnny's fate had been sealed with the taking up of arms so now is hers. Hitherto associated with the house (home) she now too becomes a wanderer of the city's night streets. A repetition of camera set-ups (of the steps and alley) immediately associate her with Johnny and Dennis, while her march into and then out of the lively, noisy and well-lit dance hall decisively marks her rejection of the life that Granny had proffered. It's significant then that a film which sought to emphasize the affection of its characters and their desire for reunion (in a way which goes beyond that of the book) that they remain separated until the end. In the meantime, as Geduld points out Johnny's life is lived almost by proxy – the characters he meets becoming successively older as the night proceeds.[11] All that remains is death and this is exactly what the lovers find in their final embrace before a grilled fence, mocked by the sight and sound of their now departing ship.

At this point, however, it might be objected that to draw political conclusions from these observations would be to fall prey to the critical fallacies already outlined. For the narrative and stylistic strategies employed by the film tend to work against meanings reducible to socio-political values in favour of meanings preeminently universal and context-free. This is clearly the case as put by Ernest Lindgren:

> Occasionally an artist may define his purpose, Carol Reed did so at the beginning of *ODD MAN OUT* in the following introductory title: 'This story is told against a background of political unrest in a city of Northern Ireland. It is not concerned with the struggle between the law and

the violence employed by the police ('state violence') and which is responsible for the deaths of not only Johnny and Kathleen but also Pat (Cyril Cusack) and Nolan (Don O'Herlihy). This role of violence in bringing the narrative to a conclusion is downplayed by inter-linking the agents of law with an abstract fate or nemesis and the stylistic technique of editing away from violent acts to concentrate on the reactions to them and thus de-emphasizing the responsibility of those involved.

11 Quoted by James DeFelice, *Filmguide to Odd Man Out*, Indiana University Press, 1975, p.31.

an illegal organisation, but only with the conflict in the hearts of the people when they become unexpectedly involved'. Some critics ignored or over-looked this statement, and argued that Carol Reed, in omitting to dwell on the political issues which his heroes had at heart had evaded the very core of his subject ... One may feel that the director has realized his purpose well or ill, but that criticism is misguided which ignores a purpose no clearly defined, and tries instead to argue that the film should have concerned itself with something different'[12]

However, the example is hardly so clearcut. It's evident that the film strives to evacuate a number of concrete particulars – there is an imprecision ábout period and place, with neither Belfast nor the IRA explicitly named, compounded by an anti-naturalism of style and dialogue which by the end is openly allegorical. But, nonetheless period and place are not evacuated altogether and there is still sufficient sense of particulars for the conflicts in the hearts of people to have a specific as well as general content. The contention would be then not so much that the film omits political issues but that its handling of them effects a particular sort of displacement.

A common complaint against the realist mode in film and television is that through its necessary emphasis on the interaction of individuals it cannot adequately cope with broader socio-historical determinants (thus, in the case of Loach and Garnett's *DAYS OF HOPE* the form inevitably pushes then towards conspiracy theory in their delineation of the General Strike); by contrast it might be argued that the universalizing strategies of a film such as *ODD MAN OUT* likewise evacuates socio-historical determinants by pushing towards a level of abstraction where such categories become irrelevant, caught under a generalised blanket of 'humanity'. For ultimately all political problems in *ODD MAN OUT* become resolved at the level of humanism. This is surely the real import of the conventional designations of *ODD MAN OUT*'s concerns – it's being concerned with 'human charity' (Lindgren) or 'people retreating from involvement with a human problem' (De Felice). For 'human charity' and 'involvement with a human problem' are essentially meaningless in abstract – they only become moral and political problems at the level of specifics. *ODD MAN OUT* then does not so much evade politics as displace them onto a terrain where humanity becomes de-socialized and de-historicized and thus robs the causes and acts of its protagonists of a meaning outside of a fatal irrationalism.

And thus, while not directly 'about' Irish politics, it can nonetheless be seen how *ODD MAN OUT* – with its circulation of meanings around the terms of doom and entrapment, the curse of violence and blood sacrifice – begins to enforce not only a generalised humanism but an ideology of Ireland. Tom Nairn has commented on the paucity of explanations brought to bear in our understanding of the Northern Ireland situation and notes how in the face of

12 Ernest Lindgren, *The Art of the Film*. Allen and Unwin, 1963, p.169.

Ireland's apparent intractability to standards of reason the attitude can become all too readily one of historical despair: 'the myth of atavism' whereby only 'a specific historical curse, a luckless and predetermined fate, can account for the war'.[13] And it's this perceptual schema which *ODD MAN OUT* is in effect reproducing: Johnny's fate being precisely a luckless and predetermined one, motored in turn by those recurrent spectres of Irish history – violence and 'futile' causes.[14]

THE GENTLE GUNMAN, directed by Basil Dearden in 1952, can be seen as something of an inheritor of this ideological legacy. Stylistically it shares many of the former's aspirations. It's interiors are likewise dark and cramped with compositions frequently emphasizing divisions between characters or subordinating them to decor or surrounding objects, while exterior action predominantly occurs at night. The 'escape' to the openness of the Irish countryside is only to the gang's hide-out, a barren roadside petrol station, austere and desolate in a border limboland. Allegory is likewise not far from the surface with a prominent religious symbolism, with its intimations of martyrdom and sacrifice, culminating in young Johnny (James Kenney) again trapped into violence meeting his death in the glare of car headlights, arms outstretched to form a cross.

Once more the trap is that of 'the historical curse': the Irish struggle as a deathly ritual sustained through illusion and sacrifice. For the film Irish politics reduces to a game to be learnt and passed on to future generations (thus Matt (Dirk Bogarde) has to take the place of his brother Terence (John Mills) while Johnny replaces his father.) The film begins and ends with the arguments of an Irish doctor, Branigan (Joseph Tomelty) and an irascible Englishman, Truethorne (Gilbert Harding). They are introduced via a shot which begins in close-up on a chess board with the camera pulling back to reveal the two men in conversation. It soon becomes clear that the game is more than just a visual correlative of their dispute but a metaphor for the Irish themselves. A visually parallel shot shortly replaces the chessboard with a bomb in a suitcase, the camera this time pulling back to reveal two IRA men, Connolly and Maguire (Liam Redmond and Jack MacGowan). Branigan and Truethorne's game of chess is also a game played with bombs and the life of men. In a film which foregrounds its dialogue, this theme is made explicit by the script. Molly (Barbara Mullen) replaces Granny in *OLD MAN OUT*. On

13 Tom Nairn, *The Break-Up of Britain*, New Left Books, 1977, p.224.

14 This is not to suggest, however, that such characteristics are merely the disorted fruit of an alien British ideology, for clearly there are strong lines of continuity with Irish culture itself. The humanist dissolution of political problems into personal tragedies is clearly avident in the work of such writers of O'Casey and O'Connor while the notion of blood sacrifice has a continuing resonance within Irish political and cultural thinking. Richard Kearney, indeed, has suggested the necessary and systematic link between blood sacrifice, terror and fatalism at the 'mythical' level of nationalist thought in Myth and Terror, *The Crane Bag*, Vol.2, Nos.1/2.

the side of experience she is also on the side of 'life' and, as Granny was to Kathleen, is opposed to her daughter Maureen's (Elizabeth Sellars) apparently of the film loses her son. When she speaks it is with the weight of tragedy and with the film's evident support. In fact, she is allowed to make practically the same speech twice, first in relation to her husband and then her son:

'You killed his father, Shinto ... leave Johnny alone'.
'It was the English killed our father'. (Maureen) '
'No. It was Shinto. Joe was happy enough until he told him he was unhappy. And he was free until you told him he wasn't. And his fists were enough defence until you told him he needed a gun'.
'Matt didn't kill Johnny, Molly'. (Terence)
'No, it was the English. Like they killed our father'. (Maureen)
'No, it was you (to Maureen) and your Shinto. Johnny was only a lad. He'd still be playing hurley and football if you hadn't taught him the other game'.

Little wonder then that an exasperated Raymond Durgnat was to complain that the film's treatment of the Irish question was 'represented exclusively in terms of the Irish struggling against their own tendency to violence'.[15]

For the Irish alone have to accept responsibility, in the words of Terence, for 'making trouble'. Freedom and happiness are then if only the Irish could dispel their illusions and recognise it – a futility eloquently summed up for the film by an attack on an armed van in Belfast, at the cost of the lives of two men, in an attempt to rescue two prisoners who are in fact already 'free'.

But, as in the case of *ODD MAN OUT*, it's not so much that the film conveniently omits factors which might at least admit a small quotient of rationality to its characters' struggles (e.g. the legacy of English rule and partition) but that the film positively disputes their relevance by again dissolving political problems into a de-contextualised humanism. As Durgnat puts it, 'whenever ... complexity might threaten a generalisation, the team (Dearden and Ralph) unhesitatingly sacrifice the former to the latter'.[16]

For what pulls *THE GENTLE GUNMAN* back from the thoroughgoing romantic fatalism of *ODD MAN OUT* is Dearden's characteristic preoccupation with the generation of 'socially responsible' messages. If we draw on Elsaesser's remark 'that morality in the American cinema manifests itself in terms of aesthetic values and that ethical choices are elaborated not on basis of intellectual argument, but entirely by means of psychological pressures and needs'[17] we might argue in the example of Dearden that the opposite is the case, that the concern for elaboration of ethical choices tends towards narrative schematism and the foregrounding of intellectual

[15] Durgnat op.cit. p.108.
[16] Raymond Durgnat, Dearden and Ralph – Two on a Tandem, *Films and Filming*, July, 1966, p.27.
[17] Elsaesser (1971) op.cit. p.10.

argument. Thus, in *THE GENTLE GUNMAN* the narrative is organised to work against the final endorsement of the 'historical curse' by structurally locating Terence against the drive of the rest of the film 'saving' his brother and abandoning his former colleagues, and by making him, along with Molly, a spokesman for alternative values, a depressingly limp all-men-are-brothers humanism filtered through the little man collectivism of Ealing:

'I'm just as good an Irishman as ever I was ... but there's no future for a man, woman or child in the whole of the world till we've learned that an Irishman is the same thing as an Englishman, a Frenchman, a Russian, a German, an Italian or an American. When it comes down to it, man for man, there's little bit of difference. It's the way we're all separated out into different countries that causes the trouble ... I've lived over in England, I've lived with the people and worked with them. They've the same hopes as we have, the same fears. They pay too much rent and too many taxes, just like we do. They scrape and save for their kids in their old age just like we have to. It's not against people like that we should be working, it's with them. Can't you see it, man ... it's peace we want, and security and a decent life. And we'll not get them shouting 'ourselves alone' at the top of our voices.'

As Sartre observes, in a different context: 'His very declarations show the weakness of his position. ... He has no eyes for the concrete syntheses with which history presents him. He does not recognise the Jew, the Arab or the Negro, the bourgeois or the worker, but man alone, at all times in all places the same as himself.'[18] Social and historical particularity thus dissolves into a fetish of rhetorical universalism.

Much of this basic pattern is also to be found in *A TERRIBLE BEAUTY* (1960). Robert Mitchum inherits the mantle previously donned by John Mills and takes over the role of the IRA member, Dermot O'Neill, who turns his back on violence and thus enters 'the age of reason' as his confidante and adviser, Jimmy Hannafin (Cyril Cusack), insists on describing it. Once again this movement from violence and irrationalism to non-violence and reason [19] is associated with a break from nationalism in favour of the family and, in a novel input, with a contrast between aberrant sexuality and 'normality'.

One of the crucial differences here lies in the role allocated to Neeve (Anne Heywood), Dermot's sweetheart. Unlike Kathleen in *THE GENTLE GUNMAN*, whose sexuality had served as a reward for violent endeavour, Neeve's sexuality functions as a break on violence and as such stands in alignment with rather than in opposition to the older woman of experience

[18] Jean-Paul Sartre, *Portrait of the Anti-Semite*, Secker and Warburg, 1948, p.45.

[19] It would be a mistake to see this opposition between violence and reason as exclusive to the cinema. Roy Edgley (Reason and Violence, *Radical Philosophy*, Spring, 1973), for example, has located such an antithesis firmly within the more general assumptions of a liberal culture in which he suggests it seems to take on 'the force of an a priori opposition'. He goes on to outline the basic philosophical error in such an assumption: 'Though clubbing a victim to the ground is not reasoning with him, it does not follow that violence is contrary to reason ... violence is neither rational nor irrational ... is not un-reason but non-reason.' (p.21).

here represented by Dermot's mother, Kathleen (Eileen Crowe) after the fashion established by Granny in *ODD MAN OUT* and Molly in *THE GENTLE GUNMAN*. Kathleen interprets her son's involvement with the IRA in an offence against the 'natural law' of the family – 'You stay away from that gang. I don't want you dead or rotting in prison. It's not for that I raised you' – and this is paralleled by the 'unnaturalness' of the relationship between Dermot and Neeve which has dragged on for seven years without marriage (in contrast to the novel where they are only twenty and nineteen) and is increasingly becoming a parody of the family which Dermot's violent involvements are preventing them from having: 'You come to me a small boy with your tears for a hurt and I'm to wipe them away. Wash your face and comb your hair, so that you can go out and play soldiers again. You're not my child.'

This obstruction of violence to heterosexual union is underlined by the second change of emphasis effected by the film in relation to *THE GENTLE GUNMAN* – that of the treatment of the IRA leader Dan McGinnis (Don O'Herlihy). McGinnis falls into line with the characteristically cold and emotionless IRA men represented by Dennis in *ODD MAN OUT* and Shinto in THE GENTLE GUNMAN (both Robert Beatty), proud of his newly forged links with the Nazis and careless of his own men's lives; but what is novel about his portrayal is his association first with physical deformity (he is a cripple) and by extension sexual deformity. Violence in McGinnis becomes both a 'crippler' of his humanity and a surrogate for his sexual incapacity (and it is thus ironic that the film's representative of 'healthy' sexuality, Sean (Richard Harris), seen as cockily flirtatious at the movie's beginning, should likewise end up limping once involved in IRA adventuring). In this respect, McGinnis' perversity finds its clearest expression in relation to Bella, his love for whom can only manifest itself in voyeurism and violence. Reprimanded by Bella for trying to detain her and making 'marks' on her he responds that 'I love Ireland too. And watch the mark I leave on her'. It is appropriate then that McGinnis should end up killing Bella. Although unintended (he mistakes her for Dermot) it nonetheless symbolically fulfills McGinnis' fantasy of violation (the gun exchanged for the phallus) while bleakly underscoring the film's association of violence and family destructiveness

Necessarily, then, Dermot's retreat from violence is rewarded by reunion with Neeve. Ironically it is a reunion achieved by violence but what now justifies it for the film is that it is both in aid of and mobilising of the family. Having turned informer to protect the women and children at the barracks, Dermot is taken prisoner by his erstwhile colleagues. To free him the services are required of his brother Ned, hitherto identified as 'gentle as a lamb' and as a consequence of no use to the IRA. Unable to rouse himself in support of nation, Ned now finds a motivation in family: 'They hurt my brother and they'll feel the hatred of the O'Neills in me'. The resultant violence thus now becomes legitimate because of its just end – the family.

But if *A TERRIBLE BEAUTY* adds the notion of sexual pathology to its treatment of the IRA then it's brought to its summation in *SHAKE HANDS WITH THE DEVIL* (1959).[20] Like *A TERRIBLE BEAUTY*, *SHAKE HANDS WITH THE DEVIL* pivots around its central hero's involvement and disinvolvement with violence. Kerry O'Shea (Don Murray) is a young American student studying medicine in Dublin. Having fought in France during World War I he has'done all the killing I intend to' and now professes not to believe that 'violence ever solved anything'. What fuels his turn towards violence then (in a manner somewhat) similar to *HENNESSY*) is the death of his friend who had been trying to attend a wounded IRA man, shot while grenading an armoured car. Although his move to violence is thus endowed with initial rationalism, his subsequent repudiation of violence becomes associated with its opposite – when violence is seen as becoming an end in itself.

And again like *A TERRIBLE BEAUTY* it is also associated with the healing effects of romance. In this case the motivation is provided by Jennifer Curtis (Dana Wynter), the daughter of a British military governor. Kidnapped in retaliation for the imprisonment of IRA supporter, Lady Fitzhugh (Sybil Thorndike), the affection which begins to blossom between captive (Curtis) and captor (O'Shea) not only works to cut across the 'illusory' barriers of nation but provides the specific grounds for O'Shea's repudiation and then killing of his commandant, Sean Lenihan (James Cagney).

[20] Although the emphasis is on continuity, this new emphasis on pathological sexuality and violence in the male IRA characters clearly represents a certain discontinuity which would seem to have two main determinants. The 'external' impact of the IRA's renewed border campaign 1956–62 must have restored much of the organisation's hitherto dwindling threat and topicality while the 'interior' logic of the IRA film 'cycle' was likely to push the films towards a 'dept psychology' anyway. Alloway, for example, comments on the influence of psychoanalysis upon postwar Hollywood as follows:

'Conventions for depth were added to filter the stereotypes of earlier movies: characters could be either over-determined or pessimistically unexplained. In either case, the inference of complexity, of possessed and haunted intelligence, is inescapable. At the time the hero acquired memories, insomnia, and compulsions, villains acquired a naturalistically phased abnormality, a primal roughness.' (*Violent America: The Movies 1946–64*, Museum of Modern Art, 1971, p.25).

Thus, we find both the post-war Western (*Shane*, *3:10 To Yuma*, *Warlock*) and gangster movie (*Kiss Of Death*, *White Heat*) displaying an increasing preoccupation with psychological explanation and abnormality. *White Heat*, has James Cagney suffering from headaches and an Oedipus complex in a sort of loose prototype for his *Shake Hands With The Devil* IRA man. The labelling of 'deviants' as mentally ill is of course a commonly recognised phenomenon in the sociology of deviance, in part inspired by the work of Thomas Szasz, *The Manufacture of Madness*, Paladin, 1977.

It is in the characterization of Lenihan that those attitudes already implicit in the treatment of *A TERRIBLE BEAUTY*'s McGinnis are made most explicit. Again, sexuality is sublimated into vogeurism and violence with the IRA man's sadism finding expression in his treatment of Kitty (Glynis Johns), a good-natured prostitute to be found with an IRA unit in their Wicklow hide-out. Taunted for his vogeurism, Lenihan at first attempts to strangle her before finally killing her in a way both eloquent of IRA illusions (she is not the traitor he believes) and sexual aberration.

As such Lenihan's sexual pathology becomes the perfect metaphor for his similarly pathological politics, the two intertwining with his determination to shoot Jennifer Curtis (now wearing the dead Kitty's clothes) in retaliation for the death of Lady Fitzhugh. The fact that this occurs after the signing of the peace treaty giving Dominion status to a partitioned Ireland underlines for the film the perversity of his actions. 'You've forgotten what you're fighting for. It isn't Ireland or freedom ... it's just killing', claims O'Shea as he in turn is forced into killing him. But he then throws the gun away in a gesture to which the film has been cumulatively working – it being precisely such an image which was used over the film's opening titles. As Stuart Hall has observed, the linking of psychopathy with violence is not coincidental:

> 'Our unwillingness to acknowledge that there can be any rationality at all in collective social action which includes conflict and aggression, tempts us to label all social conflicts as 'violent' – implying that, because they are, by definition, 'irrational' they must also be illegitimate. They can therefore only be attributed to causes which aren't quite human – arising from primitive and pre-rational instincts and impulses. This is where such terms as 'animals' or 'psychopathic behaviour' arise'[21]

A sense of psychopathology also seems to carry over to Don Sharp's *THE VIOLENT ENEMY* (1969). It's basic pattern should by now be familiar. Like Johnny in *ODD MAN OUT* its central character, IRA man Sean Rogan ('the wild man ... the last of the heroes') has repudiated violence following a period in jail ('Look I've spent eight years thinking about this sort of violence, eight years in a cell thinking about where it got me ... Do what you like I'm finished with violence') but also like Johnny is forced into further acts of violence against his will. Once again the results of such acts are self-destructive and to be associated with illusion, fate and the rejection of marriage and family.

The irony of the film's appearance on the eve of a new outbreak of IRA violence is partly to be explained in terms of the novelty of the context in which the film's violence is located. Questions of the six counties are marginalised and re-routed towards the Republic, now viewed as a modern

[21] Stuart Hall, The Treatment of 'Football Hooliganism' in the Press, in Roger Ingham, et.al. '*Football Hooliganism*', Inter-Action Imprint, 1978, p.29.

industrialising state.[22] Indeed, for Colum O'More, the traditional IRA leader, affluence is now the new and crucial central enemy for which young Irishmen have sold 'freedom's birthright' in return for the 'regular wage, mortgages and refrigerators, cars on the instalment plan'. By way of 'an act of blood in defiance' he calls for the blowing up of an electronics factory as a 'gesture' and reminder that 'a free and United Ireland is still the one cause worth blood'. And as such he clearly conforms to the archetypical presentation of the blood-thirsty IRA man, prepared to see life wasted and for whom violence has become an end in itself.

However, the rhetoric of blood sacrifice is not shared by all the IRA. O'More (Ed Begley) is in fact isolated from his colleagues whose commitment to the new 'affluence' is rather less antagonistic. IRA man Danny indeed works in the very factory that O'More wishes to blow up and is prepared to betray him in order to defend the 'thousand men on good wages' working there.

Danny represents something of a doppelganger to Rogan (Tom Bell). He was with Rogan the night he was captured and their subsequent fates might easily have been interchanged. Danny is now 'looking prosperous' and has got to like it being 'quiet and peaceful'. As such he not only enjoys the conditions recommented to all Irishmen by John Mills but also apparently the life now aspired to by Rogan. For Rogan himself announces his desire for 'peace and quiet' and evidently approves of the new 'affluence'. Watching the townspeople leaving morning mass he comments approvingly: 'They look great'. Hannah (Susan Hampshire) retorts somewhat scoffingly, 'The affluent society', but he is not peturbed: 'Call it what you will. Neat Sunday clothes, a joint of meat waiting for them to go home to. It's good to see'. Indeed the movement of the camera at this point which has pulled down from the church steeple onto an anonymous but representatively 'prosperous-looking' couple before picking up the previously unseen Rogan and Hannah seems to suggest their potential interchangeability with such a couple, an idea given force by Archer's earlier advice to Hannah to 'look normal'.

And this prospect of romance and domesticity as a potential salvation for Rogan is further underlined by the drawing of a contrast with the Leary-s, the proprietors of the bar in which both Hannah and Rogan are staying. Bridget Leary is the archetypical older woman, repudiating the violence of her

[22] In this respect, the film reflects the modernisation and internationalisation of the Irish economy experienced in the sixties, under the premiership of Sean Lemass. A comparable programme of economic modernisation was also occurring in the North and, for a time, it did indeed seem to many as if the spirit of economic progress would bring North and South together, a view fuelled by the summit meetings of Taoiseach, Sean Lemass, and Northern Ireland prime minister, Terence O'Neill, in 1965. For further discussion see Terence Brown, *Ireland: A Social and Cultural History 1922–79*, Fontana, 1981 and Paul Bew and Henry Patterson, *Sean Lemass and the Making of Modern Ireland*, Gill and Macmillan, 1982.

surrounding menfolk. But even more importantly her association with men of violence is explicitly linked an 'unnatural' failure to have a family. Her husband, John Michael (Noel Purcell) was crippled during an IRA mission (and characteristically his post hoc version of how he received his injuries is appropriately romanticised) with the result that Bridget 'had the washing and feeding and cleaning of him for two years ... If he'd been a straight and peaceful man I'd have been nursing his babies instead' (cf. Neeve's complaints in *A TERRIBLE BEAUTY*). It's a revelation delivered in a scene between Bridget and Hannah and the scene's final two-shot of Bridget's forceful gaze upon the other woman sums up the alternatives of violence and non-violence offered by the film.

For it is not only Rogan's 'salvation' which is at stake but Hannah's herself. Like Maureen in *THE GENTLE GUNMAN*, Hannah is the daughter of an IRA man and in love with the 'cause' and her sexuality seems available in direct proportion to a man's violent commitment to that cause. Indeed, on receiving his first kiss Rogan has to ask whether it was for him or 'the legend'. But unlike Maureen, Hannah's commitment to violence and the cause changes during the course of the movie. She comes to recognise the 'unimportance' and 'meaninglessness' of the factory being blown up and the need to restrain rather than encourage Rogan's violence. However, like Maureen, she is alone at the end, not because of her own infatuation with violence but Rogan's inevitable entrapment within it.

Indeed, illusion and entrapment are the two dominant currents associated with Rogan's movement through the film. In fact, the very impetus for the narrative is compounded in deceit. Rogan is encouraged to break out of his British prison on the grounds that his remission has been revoked, a belief subsequently revealed as the malicious and untrue work of the two English criminals associated with O'More. The titles of the film then are overlaid on scenes of Rogan's 'escape'; the irony of the movie however is that any escape on Rogan's part is illusory, not only because he didn't need to, but because he has merely replaced one prison for another. And the second prison is the far more sinister one of violence. Many of the images of the film foreground this sense of enclosure by shooting through fences or intermediary surfaces (e.g. the shot of Hannah 'enclosed' in the telephone box while phoning to inform John Michael and O'More that Rogan has returned and 'the great days are back'). Most striking in this respect, however, is the representation of the electronics factory. This is introduced by an initially out of focus shot and loud, ominous music. The camera pulls focus to reveal barbed wire at the top of an electrified fence and as it zooms out reveals a car being let through a security barrier by a policeman. It then travels left along the fence, revealing tall perimeter lights, untilled soil and bare brick buildings, before picking up the car in which O'More, Rogan and the two Englishmen are arriving. At this point we have not been informed as to what we are looking at and, indeed, Rogan speaks for the audience when he asks 'what is it?' By its appearance it suggests nothing so much as a prison, and being told it's a factory does little to alleviate this sense, particularly as O'More's revelation is accompanied by an almost *MARIENBAD*-like travelling shot along the factory fence. This feeling is further reinforced by Rogan's attempt to enter the factory on the back of a swill cart. This is first shot through a double wire fence; the camera than zooms in to the point where the wires become a blur only to rapidly pull focus, reducing the horse and cart to a blur and bringing the first fence into stark definition. Another rapid piece of focus-pulling ensues – bringing the second fence in the rear into focus and revealing the arrival of the horse and cart behind it. At one level, a rather flashy piece of lensplay, but at another it is central to the film's meaning. Rogan has broken out of one prison only to break into another (at one point, Hannah refers to the factory as a 'controlled environment'). He is trapped as he was before (indeed, at one point, he is seen locked in his room by one of the Englishmen who had assisted in his 'escape'), his new-found freedom no more than an illusion.

But what precisely is the nature of his illusions and entrapment? At one level, it's his involvement in out of date causes and methods. Arriving at Leary's bar, where he is to stay and plan the raid, he is asked does he know the place. 'Like a prison cell' comes the reply. And the cell that the bar represents is its inability to adjust to the times. Time here has stood still (the clock on the wall noticeably never changes in stark contrast to the precision about timing required by the explosions) and the result is in Sullivan's words a 'museum' with its tricolour, military portraits and Countess Markiewicz posters adorning the bars drab brown walls.

But more centrally, it's Rogan's continuing involvement with violence.

'Change, there is no change'. This is not only O'More's verdict on IRA tactics but on Rogan himself. 'The violence is deep in him and it never ends'. As a character Rogan seems pulled apart by contradictory impulses. On the one hand, professing renunciation of violence and a desire for peace and quiet (though ironically he also found prison 'quiet') while on the other troubled by an innate violence which he can't quite control. On our very first encounter with him in the film he mounts an unwarranted assault upon the fellow prisoner who informs him of his revoked remission just as he is to brawl bloodily with one of the Englishmen in Leary's bar later. But it is the climactic violence at the end of the movie which in its very excess reveals the full force of his violent impulses. In pursuit of the two Englishmen, Austin (Jon Laurimore) and Fletcher (Michael Standing) he has already promised Hannah that there will be 'no more violence'. But upon their capture he inflicts a beating upon Fletcher far in excess of the needs of detention, culminating in a low-angle shot of Rogan ferociously thumping his nearsenseless adversary, which can only be stopped by the arrival of Hannah and the police.

The resultant effect, comparable perhaps to *STRAW DOGS*, is one of dislocation – of violence gone past the limit and a romantic relationship shattered.[23] Both Hannah and Rogan are marched from the scene by policemen, the camera moving in opposite directions as the two look across at each other. Brought together, Hannah tentatively but distraughtly puts her hand onto his face before the camera cuts to long shot, leaving the couple in the rear right of frame and zooming back onto the empty river. Rather than romantic reunion then the film seems to offer apartness and emptiness, in turn the effect of violence gone out of control and become its own end. 'We only pretend its something else. It's for its own sake most of the time' explains Rogan to Hannah at an earlier stage of the film. As if living through his own precepts Rogan's explosion of excessive and unnecessary violence underwrites the final illusion – that violence might ever be rational. But if violence truly 'runs deep in him' then Rogan is again more victim than willing agent – fated by the curse of his own violent instincts which defy control and deny his aspirations to a more settled domestic existence.

While continuing many of the former film's themes, Don Sharp's second Irish movie, *HENNESSY* (1975) was to face a considerably more awkward postproduction passage. For now its direct concern with Northern Ireland coincided with the advent of 'the troubles'. After a private viewing of the film by EMI chairman, John Read, and picture and theatre division head, Bernard Delfont, EMI decided it would not take up its first option on the film and show the film in their ABC cinemas on the grounds that it exploited the Northern Ireland 'troubles' in the interest of entertainment. 'Our decision is not a matter of commerce – it's a question of responsibility to the public and society in which we live' (quote from Daily Mail, 23/6/75). This lead was followed by Rank who refused to screen the film on their Odeon circuit, thus effectively preventing any mass exhibition of the film in the U.K. [24]

The grounds for their upset I think are readily apparent. The British Army, in a reference to Bloody Sunday, are shown as responsible, albeit accidentally, for the death of innocent bystanders in Belfast; the police are shown as brutal and ruthless and to be little distinguished in methods from the IRA (who on

[23] For an acute analysis of the treatment of violence in Straw Dogs see Charles Barr, Straw Dogs, A Clockwork Orange and the Critics, *Screen*, Vol.13, No.2, Summer 1972.

[24] As a footnote, it might be worth noting the Catch-22 situation besetting any film about Ireland. If made at a 'politically sensitive' time it risks banning or non-exhibition as with *Hennessy* and Brian Desmond Hurst's *Gurselves Alone*, which was banned in the North. Alternatively, make it as a less 'relevant' time and face perturbed questions as to why bother. Thus, Ray Durgnat felt *The Gentle Gunman* to be so 'untopical' that it must really be about the upsurge in the rate of juvenile delinquency (1966, p.30) while Milton Shulman proudly announced 'the trouble with the Irish question is that the English no longer care ... they might as well be listening to arguments about Schleswig-Holstein'. (Evening Standard, 23/10/52).

the evidence of the film are more efficient than them anyway); while sympathy is structured in favour of the modern day Guy Fawkes who only narrowly fails to blow up the Houses of Parliament as a vengeance for the death of his wife and child (the final playing of the National Anthem serving more as jokey irony than an upholding of traditional British values). In this respect, the film in part dramatises the threat to the British state through its continuing involvements in Northern Ireland. Whereas *The Violent Enemy* began in England and moved to Ireland, in *Hennessy* the direction is the reverse, beginning in Ireland and moving to England and as such transporting the 'despoliation' hitherto contained within Ireland to the heart of the British state. Thus, Hollis (Richard Johnson), the English police officer, is informed by his superior that 'the violence over there has corrupted you 'while it is significant that Hennessy should adopt the persona of an environmentalist (already seen complaining that 'this city stinks') in his attempt to blow up Parliament. Reinforcing this idea, a comment is made to Hollis later in the movie that 'there's not a smell of Irish any where'.

'It seems to me foolishly myopic', comments Anthony Arblaster, 'to see the extent to which always fragile liberal political traditions and freedoms have been corrupted and undermined by the Irish crisis in Britain as much as in Ireland itself'[25] and *Hennessy* can in part be seen to demonstrate this. Thus, for the film the military involvement in Northern Ireland becomes matched by the enormous security operation mounted to protect the State opening. That said, however, the difference of a film like *Hennessy*, when viewed in the context of other British films about Ireland, is on the whole more apparent than real. Like them its main force and dramatic weight is displaced from politics onto individuals with a corresponding suspicion, of 'abstract causes' and investment in the family.

Thus if *Odd Man Out*, *The Gentle Gunman* and *A Terrible Beauty*'s renunciation of violence can be associated with the attempt to 'humanize' their problems, in the same way the move towards violence in *Hennessy* can be associated with a similar displacement. The thesis is worked out with calculated obviousness. Hennessy on his way home from work as an explosives expert is stopped by his brother-in-law, Sean Tobin (Eric Porter). Inside the IRA hideout the two men discuss Hennessy's daughter's birthday and then Tobin asks Hennessy to supply gelignite for a job which is refused:

'I don't believe in it any more ...'
'I remember when they gave you medals for it'. (Tobin)
'Yes ... and now I put my family first'.

[25] Anthony Arblaster, Britain in Ireland, Ireland in Britain, in Ralph Miliband and John Saville (eds.), *The Socialist Register*, 1977, p.70.

'I put Ireland first'. (Tobin)
'Above everything? (Tobin nods) I wonder if you could?'

The scene ends with a mid-shot of Tobin looking down at Steiger watching him go, saying 'Wish her a happy birthday from me'. An abrupt cut follows to a children's clinic with the camera zooming in on swing doors as the daughter, previously unseen in the film, run forward to look out. The movement of boys running is reflected in the glass while banging and aggressive music is heard on the soundtrack. It's the beginning of a scene which culminates in a stunned soldier shooting randomly into a crowd and ending with Hennessy knelt over his dead wife and daughter in inarticulate anguish.

What legitimises Hennessy's desire for revenge and resultant violence then is not that it is in the name of Ireland (which is too abstract and devoid of emotion) but that it is a personal revenge for an atrocity against the family. As in so many of the films the decency and security of the family unit becomes the moral touchstone of the movie. And thus it is Kate (Lee Remick), in a role paralleling Molly's in *The Gentle Gunman*, who as a widow (and thus denied a family) stands for the weariness with Irish politics (but also like young Johnny is ultimately unable to escape it). Ironically, and again with echoes of *The Gentle Gunman*, her husband was blown up by his own bomb.

This individualization is enforced by the film's interlocking threads of plot, with its pursuer/pursued structure and suspence mechanics, forcing attention onto the loner. Hennessy, in a way which parallels *The Outsider*'s entrapment of Flaherty between the Provos and the Brits, is caught between the IRA and the police, just as Hollis is trapped between the IRA and his superiors (in a sort of *Dirty Harry* sub-plot). It thus becomes a case of 'man alone' and as such the political background only has meaning in relation to such projects. The significance of the deaths of Hennessy's wife and child is projected purely in terms of his psychology – no interest is shown in the events or causes leading up to the street battle. Likewise the IRA execution shown to us in a flashback, in a stylised and hallucinatory form, via first Hollis' memory and then Tobin's is abstracted of any meaning except the personal conflict between the two men and is given a 'dramatic balance' by the ending which finds Hennessy limping (as Hollis had been) and Hollis now holding the gun (as the IRA men had before). Thus, although, unlike so many of its predecessors, the adherence to violence is given some semblance of rationality, such violence is nonetheless circumscribed by a wider sense of irrationalism and unexplained happenings – once again, Ireland's 'historical curse'. And thus the essential meaninglessness of the series of shots with which the film opens, a succession of 'images of Belfast' unmotivated in any sense of establishing narrative, character or politics but just culturally familiar indices of the 'troubles', in the words of Tom Nairn, 'a freak side-show for la societé du spectacle'.[26]

This essential 'meaninglessness' is reinforced by one of the most recent British films about Ireland, *The Long Good Friday* (1979). Premissed upon a sort of *Performance*-type confrontation between two counterposing ethics (rational, quasi-capitalist East End gangsterism and no holds barred Irish terrorism), narrative focus is almost exclusively restricted to the increasingly perplexed responses of ganglord, Bob Hoskyns. As such the film affords no insight into the nature and background of the IRA and succesfully obscures their identity behind a veil of chic macho invincibility. Even allowing for allegories of the British state (the collapse of 'empire'), this absence of context merely reduces the IRA to the new bogeymen whose repeated assaults on Hoskyns remain as unexplained and inexplicable as the Indians'conventional attack on the stagecoach. Indeed, the conventions employed by the film directly parallel those of the Western. As Stam and Spence suggest: 'The paradigmatic encounters of whites and Indians ... typically involve images of encirclement. The attitude toward the Indian is premised on exteriority. The besieged wagon train or fort is the focus of our attention and sympathy, and from this centre our familiars sally out against unknown attackers characterised by inexplicable customs and irrational hostility'.[27] The authors could just as well be describing *THE LONG GOOD FRIDAY*

From here it is easy to see how other British films about Ireland conform to a basic pattern. *CAPTAIN BOYCOTT* (d. Frank Launder 1947), for example, is structured around a movement from violence to non-violence. Opponents of the Land League become converted to peaceful resistance following a speech by Parnell and become the first to implement the 'boycott'. An avuncular Alistair Sim, as the village priest, in what effectively becomes a direct address to the audience, benignly warns us 'to go home and leave violence be'. Durgnat, perhaps over-zealous in his pursuit of labour victory allegories, suggests the film to be 'unequivocally on the side of the rabble'.[28] On the contrary, the unity of purpose established at the beginning of the film is seen to degenerate into injust mob violnce as the villagers turn upon an innocent victim (the illusions of the Irish once more). In so doing the community is divided and we see the rise of the strong individual (Stewart Granger as Hugh Davin) who stands up to the mob, supported by the moral authority of the Church (Sim). Far from joining in with the rabble the film clearly forces our identification onto 'man alone' capable of taking a stand against the blood-thirsty mindlessness of his fellows (the 'curse' of the Irish).

It is a scene finding almost exact replication in *Ryan's Daughter* (d. David

[26] Tom Nairn, op.cit. p.223.

[27] Robert Stam and Louise Spence, Colonialism, Racism and Representation, *Screen*, Vol.24, No.2, March/April 1983, p.12.

[28] Durgnat (1970) op.cit. p.23.

Lean 1970). Again the unity of purpose, revealed in the rescue of arms from the storm, is dissipated into ugly mob violence as the villagers set upon Rosy (Sarah Miles), falsely accused of informing. Again justice is represented by the Church (Trevor Howard as the priest) and the individual prepared to stand up to the mob (Robert Mitchum as Charles Shaughnessy) who is subsequently forced out of the community. Of course, that the real informer goes unrecognized and indeed praised as a hero carries on the continuing thread of illusions embedded in Irish politics. In *I SEE A DARKK STRANGER* (d. F. Launder 1946), in a discovery similar to that made by Flaherty in *THE OUTSIDER*, the young Bridie Quilty (Deborah Kerr) finds her father not to be a hero of the 1916 Rising at all but a man who missed making Dublin because of the pubs on the way. The same character also overcomes her inherited hatred of the English, sufficient for her to spy for the Nazis, by falling in love with an English Officer. Again the humanist assumption that social institutions are reducible to their individual constituents and thus because a few Englishmen are personally nice in some way the injustices of England as a nation become eradicated.

RYAN'S DAUGHTER has a similar traversal of the Anglo-Irish divide via Romance, though whereas love triumphs in *I SEE A DARK STRANGER* it is the reverse in *RYAN'S DAUGHTER*. As such the effect is similar to that of *HENNESSY*: Anglo-Irish politics as a backdrop of fixed variables evacuated of substance except insofar as it sets the terms upon which the doomed passion must work itself out. Again, a decontextualising aesthetic strategy forges an ideology of fatalism, complemented by the characteristic British ending of renunciation with Rosy apparently accepting the prospect of a decent and secure existence in Dublin with Charles in exactly the moral lesson worked out by the same director's *BRIEF ENCOUNTER* some twenty-five years earlier.

What then emerges from such a general overview is the recurrence of certain predominant attitudes in the British cinema's treatment of Irish politics and history: a projection of problems (and solutions) as *solely* the problems of individuals or a diffuse humanity; an association of these problems with 'irrationalism' and 'false consciousness' and an almost blanket recoil from violence.[29] As such, the cinema's projection of Ireland inevitably drifts towards a fatalistic acceptance of events as just another human tragedy or perhaps even more insidiously as the holy anachronism outside of reason and hope. Of course the personalization and de-contextualisation of events and

[29] Such treatment has, of course, been extended to other colonial groups by the British cinema. The representation of Malaysian terrorism, for example, in such films as *THE PLANTER'S WIFE* (1952) and *THE SEVENTH DAWN* (1964) reveals a number of parallels. For a general discussion of 'the cinema of Empire' see, Jeffrey Richards, *Visions of Yesterday*, Routledge and Kegan Paul, 1973.

the denial of rationality to oppositional forces has a wide ideological currency within our political and media culture, but perhaps they reach a disturbing zenith in the treatment of Northern Ireland in continuing television and press coverage:

'In general, broadcasting presents us with a series of decontextualized reports of violence, and fails to analyse and re-analyse the historical roots of the Irish conflict. Such an approach is largely shared by the rest of the British media, and this cannot but contribute to the dominant public view of Northern Ireland's present troubles as largely incomprehensible and irrational'.[30]

If this is the case British commercial cinema must also share much of the blame.

[30] Philip Schlesinger, *Putting 'reality' together*, Constable, 1978, p.243.

THE MANUFACTURE OF PROPAGANDIST HISTORY BY NORTHERN IRELAND LOYALISTS AND REPUBLICANS

RICHARD DAVIS

Anatomy of 'two nations'

The Irish, according to popular account, are an intensely historically minded people. Present-day problems they explain by what seems to others an unnecessarily long and involved recital of events so distant as to shade into the gloom of prehistory. History indeed lies at the basis of the ultimate propagandist issue of contemporary Ireland: one nation or two? To many radicals, this issue is already an archaism in a world increasingly dominated by transnational capitalism. They prefer to substitute an analysis of 'divided class' [1] for an outdated propagandist device perennially adopted to split the workers. The ramifications of this position are considered elsewhere; here it will be useful to start with some popular notions and their exploitation in the second Irish revolution debate.

The idea of 'two nations' occupying the same territory has a long provenance throughout the world. Lewis Namier discerned numerous 'Ulsters' in Eastern Europe. In 1792, Edmund Burke, himself the offspring of a mixed marriage, complained that the Protestant 'garrison' of Ireland and the Catholic natives behaved, not as religious factions, but as 'two adverse nations'. Lord Durham's 1839 report on the French and English in Canada spoke of 'two nations warring in the bosom of a single state'.[2] D.O. Madden applied the phrase again to Ireland in 1843. Two years later Benjamin

Footnote Abbreviations

Protestant-Loyalist (Prot-Stat)		*Catholic Republican*	
C	= *Combat* (UVF)	AN	= *Andersonstown News*
LN	= *Loyalist News* (mixed loyalist)	AP	= *An Phoblacht* (Provisional Sins Fein)
OS	= *Orange Standard*	RN	= *Republican News* (Provisional Sinn Fein)
PT	= *Protestant Telegraph* (Paisley)	UI	= *United Irishman* (Official Sinn Fein)
U	= *Ulster* (UDA)		
UDAN	= *UDA News*		
UL	= *Ulster Loyalist* (UDA)		
UM	= *Ulster Militant* (UDA)		

[1] See Austen Morgan and Bob Purdie, *Ireland: Divided Nation Divided Class*, London (Ink Links), 1980.

[2] L. Namier, *Vanished Supremacies: Essays on European History, 1812–1918*, New York (Hayer), 1963, pp. 166–7. *The Report of the Earl of Durham, Her Majesty's High Commissioner and Governor-General of British North America*, London (Methuen), 1905, p. 8. Burke's *Works*, 111, London, 1872, p. 321 (to H. Langrishe, 1792).

Disraeli's *Sybil* portrayed the English rich and poor as two antagonistic nations. Neither Burke, Durham, Madden nor Disraeli regarded division as permanent or desirable. Burke sought the enfranchisement of Catholics; Durham hoped that English culture would soon swamp the French; Madden, a Protestant convert from Catholicism, considered that the two traditions had much in common; Disraeli aspired to a paternalist raising of the poor. The latter, moreover, was quoted against his protege,[3] Lord Randolph Churchill, who gave renewed momentum to the Irish 'two nation' division by his famous letter suggesting the 'Orange card' to defeat Gladstone's Home Rule Bill in 1886.

The 'Orange card' was of course not intended to partition Ireland, but to keep all Ireland an integral part of the United Kingdom, a pin to burst the nationalist balloon. Right up to the establishment of the partinioned Six County parliament in 1921, a settlement denounced by the Ulster Protestants' southern Irish leader, Edward Carson, the suggestion of separate nationhood was avoided; after all, the object was adhesion to the British Empire not the discovery of 'two nations' in Ireland. Carson, who had played Gaelic games at the University of Dublin, regarded himself as an Irishman. He was in reality a great deal less intransigent than the raised fist and pointed jaw of a famous harranguing photograph, later adopted by Ian Paisley, suggests.[4] Even by the 1960s, as M. W. Heslinga, whose acceptance of two basically religious nations is popular with loyalists, notes, Ulster Protestants rarely claimed national status.[5] Before the first Irish revolution, 1919–22, Arthur Griffith, founder of Sinn Fein in 1905, his Presbyterian friend, Robert Lynd, and their allies discussed the 'two nations' theory;[6] but the physical establishment of the Stormont regime in 1921 made 'two nations' a unionist dogma.

Protestant heritage or secular republicanism?

In his Ford Lectures, F. S. L. Lyons dissolved the two nations into four cultures – the dominant Anglo-American, the Anglo-Irish, the Irish-Catholic,

[3] Winston Churchill quoted Disraeli against the Two Nations in Ireland (1.1.13). See Cronin, *Irish Nationalism*, Dublin (Academy Press), 1980, p. 104. D.O. Madden, *Ireland and its Rulers, since 1829*, London (T.C. Newby), 1843, pp. 1–10, *Nation*, 4.11.43.

[4] A.T.Q. *The Ulster Crisis*, London, 1967, pp. 166–7, 179. Paisley superimposed himself on the photograph in the 1981 Carson trail. See Sam Wilson, *The Carson Trail*, Belfast (Crown) (1981), p. 64.

[5] M.W. Heslinga, *The Irish Border as a Cultural Divide*, Netherlands (Van Gorcum), 1971, p. 62. See also PT, 15.12.72. (Review of Tony Gray).

[6] Richard Davis, 'Ulster Protestants and the Sinn Fein Press, 1914–22', *Eire-Ireland*, St Paul, winter 1980, pp. 60–85.

and the Ulster Protestant – thus helping to develop wider perspectives.[7] Our concern lies less with historical reality than with the historical imagination of second revolution propagandists. The duel between extremes can be likened to that in the Roman arena between the hoplite and the reticularis, as two different levels of argument confronted each other. On the republican side what was presented was ostensibly a *secular* nationalism; against it was ranged, not so much a rival nationalism as the ideal of a *religious* heritage. How can such a generalisation be sustained? It is true that relations between republicanism and Catholicism were intimate, if antagonistic. Nevertheless it is undeniable that the republican tradition would be virtually non-existent if its Protestant progenitors were removed. When Padraic Pearse in his pamphlets before the 1916 Rising produced his 'apostolic tradition' of Tone, Davis, Mitchel, Lalor, and Parnell, he was not torturing his memory to discover, apart from Lalor, 'token Prods' to give his philosophy a non-sectarian veneer. The patriots cited did epitomise in their lives and works Ireland's claim to nationhood. Wolfe Tone, a deist contemptuous of the institutional papacy, Thomas Davis, an opponent of the Catholic church's desire for educational separation, John Mitchel, a Unitarian critical of the Catholic priesthood's role in 1848, and Parnell, whose final battle against priests and people baying for the defeat of an adulterer evoked memories of Cuchulain, the hero of the Irish sagas, were not crypto-Catholics. Ironically they represented in their actions the very demand that Ulster Protestants make on the present-day Irish Republic: reduction of Vatican influence, separation of church and state, legalised divorce, integrated education.

On the other side, can it be seriously maintained that, despite the Ulster Protestants' love for the symbolism of the union jack and the monarchy, heroic participation in Britain's ars, and glorification of their British character, their real cause is religious? Professor David Miller has written a stimulating essay on the conditional nature of the Ulster Protestants' British loyalism, juxtaposing against it the covenanting, or banding, tradition of Presbyterian democracy.[8] Dr Paisley, head of both the Free Presbyterian Church and the Democratic Unionist Party (DUP) put the issue succinctly when he declared that he would be loyal to the Queen, so long as she remained a Protestant.[9] Readers of his *Protestant Telegraph* soon discovered that there is disquietude over religious dealings by the monarch and more open

7 F.S.L. Lyons, *Culture and Anarchy in Ireland, 1890–1939*, (Oxford University Press), 1978.

8 D.W. Millar, *Queen's Rebels: Ulster Loyalism in Historical Perspective*, Dublin (Gill & Macmillan), 1978.

9 PT, 2.10.78. Paisley promised unswerving support for the union while the Queen remained a Protestant. Martin Smyth, Orange Grand Master, also asserted that loyalty depended on the Queen's Protestantism, see *The Christian Irishman*, Belfast (Presbyterian), 7–8.82, p. 12.

annoyance with the religious, or non-religious activities of her husband.[10] When he himself admitted in 1971 that religion was his chief objection to a united Ireland, Paisley endorsed the argument of Church of Ireland Canon J. O. Hannay earlier in the century. Indeed, when he talks of the conversion of all Ireland to Protestant fundamentalism,[11] Paisley implicitly sheds his unionism and becomes a religious nationalist who, in the Ireland of his dreams, would seek to preserve its ethos uncontaminated by English permissiveness. Though Paisley, despite his impressive popular vote, cannot speak for all Ulster loyalists in this regard, the idea of a 'Protestant heritage', however ill-defined, is probably common to most. William McGrath's Tara, 'a bizarre homosexual army', and his now disbanded Orange Lodge 1303 believed in an all-Ireland Protestant heritage, requiring the banning of the Roman Catholic church. This is but an extreme version of an attitude shared by a number of Northern Ireland Protestants.

At first sight the Northern Irish separate Catholic school system, confronting the state schools used by Protestants, belies the notion that the Irish republican heritage is basically secular. Political ideals filter through schools religious in orientation. Two points should, however, be made. First, the 'state' school system in Northern Ireland is as strongly Protestant as its counterpart is Catholic. Both must compete against F. S. L. Lyons' dominant Anglo-American culture.[12] Second, the important factor is not the religious formation provided by Catholic schools in Northern Ireland, but the type of political heritage transmitted. In the United States, for example, attendance at parochial schools hardly determines an individual's love of baseball, decision to join the navy, or membership of the Republican party. In Northern Ireland, sport, national identification, and party preference depend upon group loyalties associated with religious divisions. It can happen that these group loyalties, though partly transmitted through schools based on religious ideals, may nevertheless be in considerable conflict with those ideals.

In this chapter we shall look first at the secular republican tradition and its perception by loyalists. Discussion then covers those aspects of the 'Protestant heritage' which have evoked debate. These range from St. Patrick, through the Reformation to the Battle of the Boyne, and finally merge in opposition to the secular nationalist or republican tradition. But that is not the end of the story. Even before the suspension of Stormont in 1972 and the attempt

[10] PT, 17.2.68: (criticism of 'Queen's visit to pope'). 27.7.68: (attack on Duke of Edinburgh for Sunday sport, declaration of man's independence of God, support for EEC and involvement with Prince Bernhardt's international financiers). 10.4.71: (criticism of Duke's Australian suggestion that Partition was the cause of the Irish problem).

[11] PT, 2.3.68. For McGrath, see Liz Curtis, *Ireland: The Propaganda War: The Media and the 'Battle for Hearts and Minds'*, London (Pluto), 1984, p. 238.

[12] Lyons, *The Burden of Our History*, W.B. Rankin Memorial Lecture, Belfast, Queen's University, 1979, p. 16.

at power-sharing in 1973–4, there was increasing awareness by loyalist paramilitary extremists that Protestant and British interests were not identical. They had, therefore, to secure an identity of their own as 'Ulstermen'. But where were they to draw water to nurture this sapling? The ultimate answer was to divert their share of the nationalist stream of history. Eventually this diversion was to end in the channels of straight Gaelic appropriation, and the Cruthin pre-Gaelic tributary.

The united Irish and modern loyalists

But first consider the orthodox republican tradition, defined originally by Theobald Wolfe Tone and the United Irishmen in the 1790s. Basically, the United Irishmen was a Protestant movement, influenced by the French Revolution and heavily dependent on the radical Presbyterians of Antrim and Down. It aimed at democratising the Protestant ascendancy Irish parliament and working for the complete emancipation of Catholics, still hampered by vestiges of the early 18th century penal laws. However, the 1798 rebellion, despite risings in Antrim and Down, was more effective amongst the Catholic peasantry of Wicklow and Wexford, who, before their ultimate defeat, killed a number of Protestants at Wexford Bridge and Scullabogue. This, after the Act of Union in 1800, was to be a propagandist staple for the new 'unionists' as it had been for their predecessors. Tone, whose task was to obtain French aid, which arrived too little and too late, played small part himself. He was captured and anticipated the executioner by slitting his own throat. This 'Roman' death was to create some of the same controvery as hunger-strikes later. Was it suicide? Were gaolers fearing a reprieve responsible? Was Tone as non-Catholic exempt from condemnation for taking his own life? Paisley's *Protestant Telegraph* did not think so, denouncing Tone's 'cowardly' and 'ill-timed' death.[13]

During the current Ulster troubles republicans naturally emphasised the Northern Protestant United Irishmen. Tone, a southern Irish Protestant was always number one in the pantheon. His *Autobiography* is accepted even by the disillusioned novelist, Sean O'Faolain,[14] as defining the essence of republicanism. Arthur Griffith is probably the only eminent Irish

[13] PT, 2.9.61. For anti-Tone Catholic view, see Leo McCabe, *Wolfe Tone and the United Irishmen: For or Against Christ?* London (Heath Cranton) 1931, pp. 188 & 250. By contrast RN 3.71, was content to refer simply to Tone's death in gaol. PT, 2.9.67, for evocation of massacre of Protestants at Scullabogue. See also LN, 27.10.74, and 15.3.75, for Scullabogue and Wexford Bridge.

[14] Sean O'Faolain, ed., *Autobiography of Theobald of Wolfe Tone*, London (Nelson) 1937 p. XIX: 'His personality the man himself, is a definition of Irish Republicanism. It is the only sensible definition that exists'.

revolutionary to be mildly sceptical of a hero whom revisionist historians have shown to be much less wavering in his total opposition to Britain than admirers have insisted.[15] The doyen of northern republicanism was undoubtedly Henry Joy McCracken (1767–1798), a Presbyterian cotton manufacturer managing a mill in the Falls Road who commanded the United Irishmen in Antrim, and was hanged after defeat. Others were William Drennan (1754–1820), who withdrew from the movement after his sedition trial in 1794 but later played an important part in the development of Belfast, William Orr, a Presbyterian elder and Antrim farmer hanged in 1797 (b. 1766) for administering an illegal oath, the Rev. Dr William S. Dickson (1744–1824) Presbyterian minister of Portaferry, adjutant-general of the Down United Irishmen but arrested on the eve of the revolt, the Rev. James Porter (1753–1798) of Grey Abbey, hanged though an advocate of non-violence, Henry Munro (1768–1798) a linen merchant, hanged for commanding the United Irishmen at the Battle of Ballynahinch, and the luckier Samuel Neilson (1761–1803), linen merchant and editor of the *Northern Star*, who escaped death by plea bargaining. With such an array of Presbyterian republicans to recall, the Provisional Sinn Fein's *Republican News*, soon after its inception in 1970, ran a series of articles on Protestant patriots. The message was simple. Ours is clearly a non-sectarian cause, numbering even Presbyterian ministers amongst its heroic and revered martyrs. Let this generation of Ulster Protestants emulate them. Nationalists, moreover, needed the Protestant contribution of 'honesty, frankness and hard work' represented by Orr, Porter, and the heroic Betsy Gray, cruelly killed after inspiring the rebels at the battle of Ballynahinch. The presentation was naive. No real attempt was made to penetrate the outward actions of these people. No effective reply was made to Bob Cooper of Alliance who condemned Provisional violence as false to the ideals of Tone, McCracken and Hope.[16] Nevertheless, citation of Protestant republicans was good propaganda. To Paisley, who was outspoken in his insistence that most modern ecumenical Protestant churches were leading their flocks to perdition, the citation of such names was unimpressive; they were simply turncoats and Lundies. 'There has been a long line of Protestant traitors from Phelim O'Neill, through Wolf (sic) Tone, Robert Emmet, Charles Stewart Parnell and the Gilmore brothers, to Sir Roger Casement'. These were, however, usually idealistic and humanistic socialists

[15] See Jimmy Drumm's Bodenstown denunciations of politicians and 'pseudo-intellectuals' who 'take Tone out of his context to say he would not agree with our methods'. RN, 18.6.77. Frank MacDermott's *Theobald Wolfe Tone*, London (Macmillan) 1939, was an early neo-unionist work.

[16] AP, 9.71, A, 10.75.

or Unitarians and only nominally Protestant.[17] But the Protestant paramilitary journals sometimes took a different line in their post-1974 reaction against Britain and the 'fur coat' unionists. They asserted that the Protestant United Irishmen, though mistaken in their tactics, had some justice on their side against Britain.

Henry Joy McCracken's aphorism, 'the rich always betray the poor' was quoted frequently not only by republicans but also by John McKeague's *Loyalist News* associated with several paramilitary groups.[18] The latter used it in his anti-Paisley vendetta. Paisley, said McKeague soon after the suspension of Stormont, 'can now be counted among the Quisling throng'. The Provisional *Republican News* was delighted at this hint of working-class unity, suggesting that as McCracken was a Presbyterian and 'a very religious man', he was 'one person both Nationalists and Unionist workers can be very proud of'. But the *Protestant Telegraph* found 'his name stinking in the nostrils of every true Presbyterian as being a traitor and a renegade'.[19] The Ulster Volunteer Force (UVF) *Combat*, however, read its history differently. An East Antrim UVF officer was reared in a staunch Orange area of Sixmilewater where the United Irishmen had once been strong. To him McCracken, Dickson, Porter, Orr, Neilson, James Hope (1764–1816) and the Rev. Sinclair Kelburn (1754–1802), who preached with musket beside him, were not disloyal to the crown but to 'the English parasites and their Anglo-Irish henchmen', the forerunners of Heath, Wilson and Faulkner.

Loyalists in 1974 were likened to the United Irishmen in 1798, opposing treachery, corruption and the brutal treatment and internment of Ulster patriots. Modern loyalists would not make the mistake of alliance with Catholics, but 'stand alone and fight our own battles'.[20] Another article claimed that Protestant loyalists had more in common with the United Irishmen than modern republicans in that, apart from Wolfe Tone, few of the United men were separatists. Like William Craig's Vanguard party they saw separatism as a last resort. The writer claimed that United Irish leaders Arthur O'Connor and Samuel Neilson in fact welcomed the Union. Drennan, Archibald Hamilton Rowan, T. A. Emmet and Thomas MacNeven were against separation. Their object was 'the promotion of democracy, liberty and property'. McKeague's *Loyalist News*, sympathetic to the UVF, criticised modern republicans as false to the ideals of Tone and McCracken. It also used the Protestant leadership of early republicanism to demonstrate the

[17] PT, 27.2.71. In Paisley's *United Ireland: Never!*, Belfast (Puritan), (1972), p. (11) he suggests that 'some deluded Unitarian Presbyterians were caught in the trap'.

[18] LN, Belfast, 15.4.72. quoted in RN, 23.4.72.

[19] PT, 4.11.72.

[20] C, 1.4.74.

superiority of Protestantism over Catholicism.[21]

Though still antagonistic to republicanism, this was new thinking indeed by the UVF and marks a sharp break from the Paisley position. The Ulster Defence Association (UDA), the largest Protestant paramilitary force, was not then much interested in the United Irishmen but used Irish culture later for its own purposes. However, Sammy Smyth, a UDA founder member, rejoiced that Presbyterian United Irishmen had done the main fighting against the English. This indirect debate thus demonstrates the ease with which history can be manipulated. Both PIRA and the UVF were partly right in their analysis. The Provisionals correctly asserted the basic liberalism of the United Irish Presbyterians in the 1790s, but there was also truth in the suggestion of the *Combat* columnists that some were less than wholehearted in their approach to the Catholic majority. The mind of the latter, said Dr Wililam Drennan, was 'churlish soil'[22] requiring Protestant training. The Provisionals, however, argued reasonably that, although McCracken was proud to be an Ulsterman, he fought in the name of Ireland.[23]

There remained Wolfe Tone for whom none of the loyalists, except McKeague, felt much admiration. Tone provided the lynch-pin of the republican system. In dealing with Tone, the loyalists claimed, first, that he and his friend Thomas Russell (executed in 1803) were exceptions to the rule in their separatism. *Combat* argued that the policy of the constitutionalist Henry Grattan was far superior to Tone's as Grattan and the Irish Volunteers had fought bloodlessly for Irish independence, while Tone's sanguinary war was the death-knell of Ireland's freedom. Tone was 'nothing more than a disgruntled and unpatriotic revolutionary'.[24] Criticism of bloodshed was ironical, given the UVF record of Catholic assassination. The UDA was also contemptuous. Tone, declared *Ulster*,[25] 'has been held up as a famous person without too many people knowing his motives and objectives'. It accused him of having little feeling for the common people. Conversely, the Provisionals and Officials (OIRA) used Tone's appeal from the men of property to 'that highly respectable class, the men of no property' to prove Tone a socialist. Here the loyalists were closer to those analysts who argue that Tone was simply disillusioned with the gentry whom he regarded as the natural leaders of society.[26] The loyalists of both UDA and UVF were partly correct in their general argument that the United Irishmen had no real interest in Irish culture and accepted the Union. There are some exceptions such as Thomas Russell

[21] C, 2.76. and 8.4.74., LN, 26.10.74, and 29.9.73.

[22] Quoted in C.C. O'Brien, *States of Ireland*, London 1972, p. 39. For Sammy Smyth, UM, 7 1972.

[23] RN, 30.4.75.

[24] CC (1, 11) 74. McKeague's LN, 24.1.76. complained of Tone's instability.

[25] U, 1.79.

[26] Morgan and Purdie, *Ireland*, pp. 76–77.

and the Gaelic revivalist efforts in Belfast and Dublin in the early years of the United Irish movement.[27]

Though they agreed with Paisley's *Protestant Telegraph* in totally repudiating Tone, the two paramilitary bodies did so for opposite reasons. Paisley's technique for dealing with Irish nationalism in all its manifestations was the blanket assertion that it was simply an instrument of the ubiquitous Vatican conspiracy. Accordingly, he produced, out of context, a quotation in which Tone, depicted as leader of the United Irishmen in their butcheries, had 'described himself as a 'red-hot Catholic''.[28] In fact, Tone was 'red-hot' only in his opposition to religious monopoly. His *Autobiography* shows that Tone shared some of Paisley's own views on Catholicism when he sneered at priests, bishops, the 'trumpery' of the Mass, and the exiled Pope Pius VI. The Free Presbyterian would surely have agreed with the United Irishman in regretting the loss of 'an opportunity to destroy for ever the papal tyranny'.[29] Paisley's lack of finesse here missed a very good debating point which would have embarrassed republicans, usually most reluctant to mention Tone's attitude to Catholicism. The point, however, was taken by the more flexible UDA journal, *Ulster*, that if Tone did not like the English, he did not care for the Roman Catholic church either.[30] In 1971 loyalists attempted to blow up Tone's statue in St Stephen's Green, Dublin. The *Protestant Telegraph* had advertised the unveiling.[31]

This debate on Tone and the United Irishmen demonstrates an energetic effort to claim the same men for opposing 'heritages'. The very fact that such argument could take place indicates that the gulf between the 'two nations' is bridgeable. A relatively civilised debate over the motives or real intentions of the insurgents is far removed from the Paisleyite attempts, through derogatory cartoons and verbal caricature, to portray Irish Catholics as a sub-human species. To this viewpoint, Presbyterian rebel clergy of the 1790s and ecumenical Protestant parsons of the 1970s posed the same threat to the mythology of total division. Dr Ian Adamson, intellectual mentor of the UDA, celebrated the United Irishmen as the true members of the ancient Cruthnic people, whom he presented as the ancestors of Ulster Protestants.[32]

The republican apostolic succession moved from the United Irishmen to the Young Irelanders, whose leadership contained many Protestants such as Davis, Mitchel, and Smith O'Brien. Unlike the Presbyterian rebels, or

[27] I am indebted to Ms Nancy Curtin for this point.

[28] PT, 15.5.71. For 1791 context of 'red-hot', see MacDermot, *Tone*, p. 67.

[29] See O'Faolain, ed., *Autobiography of Theobald Wolfe Tone*, pp. 52, 56, 60, 216, 255, 258. McCabe, *Wolfe Tone and the United Irishmen: For or Against Christ?* was written to defend the bishops against Tone.

[30] U, 1.79.

[31] PT, 15.5.71.

[32] I. Adamson, *Cruthin: The Ancient Kindred*, Newtonards (Nosmada), 1974, pp. 85–7.

'blackmouths' whose lips were stained with berries eaten in hiding during the United Irish period,[33] these later Protestants had little appeal to any section of loyalist opinion in the 1970s. Though John Mitchel's father was a Presbyterian minister, the elder Mitchel belonged to Henry Montgomery's liberal wing which in 1829 deserted the Presbyterian synod dominated by Dr Paisley's hero, the anti-Catholic Henry Cooke. Apart from noting that Pearse had derived his ideas on violence from Mitchel, *Ulster*, the UDA monthly whose knowledge of violence was a great deal more practical than that of Pearse or Mitchel, had nothing further to add.[34]

From Davis to easter week: secular apostles or clerical marxists?

The most eminent of the Young Irelanders, Thomas Davis, who according to Republicans of the 1970s deepened and spiritualised the patriotism of the United Irishmen, did not appeal to loyalists either. Their apparent insistence on one of his chief objectives, integrated education made no difference. To Paisley he was simply 'the rebel', a tag applied to the *Protestant Telegraph*'s citation of RTE's regular Thomas Davis Lectures.[35] *Ulster* again came closer than the Paisley journal to the real issue by demonstrating that Pearse was impressed by Davis's ideas on reviving Irish culture, which the UDA journal categorised as 'romantic in the extreme'.[36] Davis, though not himself fluent in Gaelic, nor sufficiently conversant with the ancient Irish sagas to use their imagery in his patriotic poetry, does mark the beginning of a self-conscious binding of Irish republicanism to a cultural revival. In this sense he spiritualised and deepened Tone's message,[37] and produced the basic ingredients for what was to become the culture of Northern Irish Catholicism.

But what of Davis the educator who believed that without integrated education, there could in fact be no Irish nation? It is ironical that the Northern Ireland divided school system has a Catholic sector providing a cultural mix largely based on the ideas of such a Protestant. An even greater irony was to appear when, as will be described later, loyalists themselves attempted to emulate Davis's methods by asserting their right to Gaelic, and even pre-Gaelic culture.

Republicanism after the Young Irelanders was a coherent creed. The Fenians of the 1860s, who contained fewer Protestants of note,[38] saw

33 'Blackmouth' is sometimes used in a conservative sense.

34 U, 1.79.

35 PT, 1.5.71.

36 U, 1.79.

37 RN, Easter 72 (2.28).

38 T.C. Luby, prominent on the *Irish People* was a Protestant. According to Marx, 'Luby, etc of the Irish People were educated men who treated religion as a bagatelle'. Marx to Engels

themselves as the successors of the Young Irelanders; Pearse and the men of 1916 were in their turn linked through the IRB with Fenianism. The decline in the number of nationalist Protestants made it easier for subsequent loyalists to accept the Paisleyite rejection of Irish republicanism as a weapon of the Vatican. Thus the *Protestant Telegraph*, which partly owed its inception in 1966 to the celebration of the 50th anniversary of the Easter Week Rising by the Northern Irish nationalist community, used the age-old devices. Pope Benedict XV[39] was alleged to have blessed the Rising. Sammy Smyth's *Ulster Militant* agreed on the blessing and added that the Rising's socialist leader, James Connolly, was a priest.[40] The Irish tricolour was not, as republicans maintained, the visual symbol of Thomas Davis's ideal that 'Orange and Green will carry the Day', linked by the white band of friendship, but rather the pope's colours. Loyalist propaganda, like the conservative Ancient Order of Hibernians, paints the orange band yellow. Protestant loyalists, moreover, had their answer to the executed martyrs of Easter Week in the terrible casualties inflicted on the undaunted Ulster Division at the Battle of the Somme. Continued celebration of the Somme on Orange banners and by loyalist paramilitaries does not necessarily imply undeviating devotion to England; Gallipoli, remembered in the Antipodes with the same zest as the Somme in Ulster, is considered to mark the attainment of nationhood by Australia and New Zealand rather than increased subordination to the mother country. Republicans see the Somme as an argument for 'Brits out' as they believe it demonstrates that loyalists can fight only under British direction.[41]

On the republican side, 1916 provided the watershed. The pamphlets of Pearse and the 1916 Proclamation encapsulated the political philosophy of the United Irishmen, the Young Irelanders, and the Fenians, while the executions sealed them in blood, The only direct influence of an Ulster Presbyterian at this time can be found in the anonymous essay, 'If the Germans conquered England', published anonymously in the insurgents' single issue *Irish War News*. This article by the early Sinn Feiner, Robert Lynd, was equally popular with British officers as it demonstrated the soul-destroying character of an alien though efficient government. Revived by the Provisionals as applicable to Ulster in the 1970s, Lynd's essay superbly demonstrates the mirror-image

---

10.12.69., K. Marx and F. Engels, *Ireland and the Irish Question*, London (Lawrence and Wishart), 1978, p. 399.

39 PT, 31.5.69.

40 PT, 15.8.70. The yellow was the pope's colour or the emblem of murder. The contention does have some truth for the AOH who appear to prefer yellow to orange. UM, 3 and 4 (1972).

41 Gerry Adams believed that loyalists wre consistently out fought by the IRA, AP, 10.2.79. SP, 12.76, claimed that loyalist bluff against Britain had never been called and that their current actions depended on British support.

of nationalism and counter-nationalist patriotism.[42] The Provisionals depended on the 1916 Rising for their 'mandate'. Their very name attracted support by association with Pearse's 'provisional' government of Easter Week.[43] When informed in the 1970s and 1980s that they had no mandate from the people to take life, Provisionals pointed to the fact that Pearse had no mandate either, but was nevertheless endorsed by posterity, in his case only two years later at the 1918 general election. On the other side, organisations like the UVF of today and the UDA, whose efforts at the polls have been ineffectual, are concerned to claim continuity with the old UVF of 1914, mainly absorbed into the Ulster Division of the Somme. This continuity is scornfully rejected by *Visor*, a British Army magazine produced by the 'psyops' headquarters at Lisburn.[44] After the 1916 Rising the republican tradition was identified with the IRA which fought the guerilla war against Britain, 1919–21. Paisly claimed that Michael Collins, organiser of ruthless urban operations, was a Catholic priest working under the direction of the Vatican. Similar beliefs in the 1920s inspired loyalist attacks on Catholics known as the 'pogrom'[45] and the Altnaveigh massacre of Protestants.[46]

Northern republicans could not but reject the Treaty by Collins and Griffith in December 1921, which, as it turned out, accepted partition and the consequent unfinished business. The vicissitudes of the post-civil war IRA have been chronicled by J. Bower Bell and T. P. Coogan, the former to the annoyance of the *Protestant Telegraph*, the latter to the irritation of *An Phoblacht*.[47] The Provisionals continued the quest for apostolic succession from the first and second pre-treaty Dails by securing the adhesion of Thomas Maguire. As the last survivor of the 2nd Dail, elected in 1920, Maguire was appointed to the PIRA army council in 1970.[48] Thus a Bourbon sense of legitimacy compensated for the votes won in Catholic areas by the SDLP.

This brief survey of some aspects of the Irish republican tradition likely to provoke loyalist interest or hostility shows, first, that the tradition was, despite the clumsy diversionary tactics of the *Protestant Telegraph*, basically

[42] AP, 1.2.77, and Richard Davis, 'Robert Lynd: A Man for all Seasons', *Pace*, Belfast, Vol. 41, No. 2, Summer/Autumn, 1982, pp. 20–22.

[43] S. MacStiofain, *Memoirs of a Revolutionary*, Great Britain (Gordon Cremonesi), 1975, pp. 138 and 142.

[44] PT, 28.12.68. – links it with Bible Protestantism. 12.7.76. C, 7.74. UL 31.1.74. The British forces journal, *Visor*, 27.6.74 rejects this identification: 'There is no connection between the original UVF and the bunch of gangsters and psychopaths who nowadays use the same name'. Curtis, *Ireland: The Propaganda War*, p. 232.

[45] Between July 1920 and July 1922 453 people had been killed in Belfast (37 Crown forces, 257 Catholics, 157 Protestants and two doubtfuls). See Michael Farrell, *Northern Ireland: The Orange State*, London (Pluto), 1980, p. 62.

[46] At Altnaveigh near Newry, 18.6.22. six Protestants were killed by Catholics. See PT, 19.10.68., OUDAN (2,9) 73.

[47] PT, 2.1.81., AP, 16.11.77.

[48] RN, 11–12.70.

secular, or at least non-denominational. Separation of church and state was included in the Provisional's Eire Nua programme.[49] The Proclamation of 1916 did invoke God, but hardly in any sectarian sense, and promised to cherish 'all the children of the nation equally'. Second, the insistence that divisions were the work of the British government provided substance for the Provisional 'Brits out first' philosophy, more clear-cut than the Tone and Davis belief in Irish unity as a prerequisite for independence. Third, by setting their nationalist philosophy in the form of a historical imperative, republicans could continue the struggle in the teeth of majority opinion in their own community and at the same time assert a moral superiority over that community, conditioned as it was to accept force as the fulcrum of nationalist development.

Historians confront Provisionals

In this context the bitter hostility of the Provisionals to the revisionist historians of the 1970s is understandable. 'History books are to be rewritten 1984-style'.[50] The chief enemy was Dr Conor Cruise O'Brien, 'the Nepot of Howth' whose excellent study of Parnell's party was written before a highly controversial career in the United Nations, Ghana, and Dail Eireann. O'Brian was a member of the Cosgrave government of 1973–77, vital years of the Ulster troubles. As minister controlling communications O'Brien put historical revisionism into practice by reinforcing earlier legislation banning advocates of violence from Radio Telefis Eireann.

Developing from a relatively orthodox Irish patriotic position, O'Brien became increasingly convinced that the Ulster unionists, too often ignored in the polemic of those like Tone who saw only British divide and rule at work, were actually the determining factor in the Irish equation. By the time that O'Brien had lost his dail seat and resigned the compensatory Senate position after becoming editor of the London *Observer*, his popularity with loyalists had risen in proportion to its decline among nationalists. Republican journals were full of cartoons, wisecracks and straight invective against the errant doctor who quipped that, after being beaten up by an Orange crowd in 1970, he had been offered another thrashing by Belfast nationalists: 'an oecumenism of vindictiveness'.[51]

The revisionist case was the work of many historians who, since World War II, had been steadily nibbling away at some of the foundations of the

49 RN, 30.10.71.

50 RN, 1.6.74.

51 C.C. O'Brien, *Neighbours: The Ewart-Biggs Memorial Lectures 1978–1979*, London (Faber), 1980, p. 25.

republican tradition. In 1939 Frank McDermott reinterpretated Wolfe Tone as a reluctant revolutionary; forty-three years later Tom Dunne depicted Tone as a Whig pragmatist, representative of the colonising Irish rather than the colonised; in 1945 Professor Denis Gwynn found Thomas Davis an aggressive Protestant at fault in his disputes with the long-suffering O'Connell; Alf MacLochlainn subsequently argued that Davis was a racist. In the 1950s and 1960s Drs O'Brien and F. S. L. Lyons destroyed the republican view of Parnell as a separatist at heart. Suggestions were made that John Mitchel was a Fascist. Gradually, the new scientific historians, who dropped capitalisation to indicate their objectivity, approached the republican holy of holies, the Easter Week Rising. Fr F. X. Martin demonstrated that republicans opposed to the Rising had an excellent case and that Pearse and his colleagues had used morally dubious tactics to dispose of their objections. In a *Studies* article in 1972 Fr Frank Shaw attacked the whole canon of Irish history, arguing that the ideas of men like Tone and Pearse were quite unacceptable. Modern writers insisted that the black diaries of Sir Roger Casement, executed for his efforts to obtain German help for the Rising, were genuine and he was in fact a promiscuous homosexual. Worse still for republicans, Pearse himself was found to have homosexual inclinations.[52] Even the 'Official' republicans objected to his 'canonisation'.[53]

Some of this was of course mere range-finding for more serious criticism. Historians now asked whether the 1916 Rising was necessary, whether sufficient attention had been given to the problem of Ulster, and whether the Irish people had ever really sanctioned violence or even republicanism itself. Complaining that only Professor David Greene and the Christian Brothers were on their side,[54] republicans could not allow such suggestions, totally destructive of their historical case, to go unanswered in the 1970s; *Republican News* and *An Phoblacht* were assiduous in their savage reviews of books and television documentaries critical of the argument that only by forcing out the British could Ireland ever hope to be pacified or united. Occasionally, loyalist periodicals made use of modern research to answer the Provisionals,[55] but the

[52] D. Gwynn, *O'Connell, Davis and the Colleges Bill*, (Cork University Press), 1948, A. MacLochlainn, 'Thomas Davis and Irish Radicalism', *Irish Times*, 20.11.73. C.C. O'Brien, *Parnell and his Party, 1880–90*, London (Oxford University Press), 1957, Lyons, F.S.L., *The Fall of Parnell, 1890–91*, London (Routledge & Kegan Paul), 1960. F.X. Martin, 'The 1916 Rising – coup d'etat or a bloody protest?', *Studia Hibernia*, No. 8, 1968. Fr Francis Shaw, 'The Canon of Irish History – a Challenge', *Studies*, Summer 1972. Brian Inglis, *Roger Casement*, London (Hodder & Stoughton), 1973 (criticized by RN 9.6.73.). R. Dudley Edwards, *Patrick Pearse: The Triumph of Failure*, London (Faber), 1977, p. 127 (for Pearse's homosexuality). Tom Dunne, *Theobald Wolfe Tone: The Colonial Outsider: An Analysis of his Political Philosophy*, Cork (Tower Books), 1984 (1982), 53.

[53] UI, 11–12.79.

[54] RN, 1.6.74.

[55] Especially the works of Ian Adamson.

Protestant Telegraph Vatican conspiracy theory had no point of contact with the results of serious scholarship. As republican theory moved further from the original 'green' nationalism of the past towards greater emphasis on socialism or multinational dominance, dependence on history diminished. At present it is still important to find republican forerunners like James Connolly, himself reinterpreted, capable of bridging the gap between early nationalism and the new. Moreover, the Provisionals are aware that what gives their movement its long-lived tenacity, while other socialistic urban guerilla movements come and go, is its firm base in the historical education and tradition of its community.

The Protestant heritage: back to St Patrick

What of the loyalist as opposed to the republican tradition? In tracing its development we have found the Free Presbyterians dogging its footsteps, as they did physically to the People's Democracy (PD) marchers on their way to Derry in 1969. Is there a 'Protestant' version of Irish history to offset the republican? Like republicans, Protestants are concerned to ground their philosophy firmly in the past. Christianity, in all its forms, is after all an historical religion, basing its theology on events in this world. The 'Protestant' tradition would appear to derive from the Reformation of the 16th century, but Dr Paisley claims that there were Free Presbyterians before that.[56] He means that there existed 'born-again' Christians before Martin Luther.

The issue is best illustrated by the Irish Protestant attitude to St Patrick. Not only Free Presbyterians, but even members of the Church of Ireland have insisted that Patrick (a saint by usage not formal canonisation) was indeed a Protestant. He never, they maintain, received an official commission from the papacy for Irish evangelisation, though they admit that he studied in Catholic institutions on the Continent. In 1968, prior to the Civil Rights marches, the *Protestant Telegraph* published a characteristic article on St Patrick, denying that the Roman Catholic church had any claim to him.[57] There was, it maintained, no evidence in Patrick's *Confession* or elsewhere that he practised aural confession, advocated clerical celibacy, believed in purgatory, or glorified the Mass. It was true that in the 5th century some of these practices and beliefs had not been defined with their subsequent precision. However, the argument went further, citing chroniclers like Baronius who declared all Irish bishops of the time schismatics separated from Rome. The

[56] I.R.K. Paisley, *Paisley: the Man and His Message*, Belfast (Martyrs Memorial), 1976, p 159. The dying thief crucified with Jesus was claimed as a Free Presbyterian.

[57] PT, 2.3.68.

article also insisted that Ireland was genuinely Christian from the days of St Patrick to the 12th century when Henry II conquered Ireland, not only for himself, but for the Roman church. 'And popery was forced upon an unwilling people at the point of a bayonet'. This necessitated a long struggle, but 'Patrick's vision of Ireland, both North and South, is now a reality. May we in the Protestant North seek to complete the vision by evangelising the rest of the island before Popery envelopes us too'. The 'vision' seems to imply a mustard seed of pure Protestantism growing to unfold the whole island, as in the Tara/LOL (Loyal Orange Lodge) 1303 theory previously mentioned.

The emergence of the Provisional IRA was still two years away. Yet the *Protestant Telegraph*'s article described a clear ideal for a united Ireland, albeit in Free Presbyterian terms. Paisley's 1971 admission that only religious difficulties stood in the way of unity should be seen in this perspective. Its implications were every bit as revolutionary as those of the subsequent republicans, whose militancy was to some extent a by-product of the Paisleyites' attempt in 1968–69 to realise by forceful means their own vision of the future. But this was not all. By invoking the conquest of a contented 'Protestant' Ireland – presumably St Malachy and the Celtic reformers were Free Presbyterians in Paisley's book – Paisley mirrored the '700-years-tyranny' of traditional nationalists: Anglo-Norman invaders confronted solid, religious Celts. Even this did not end the convergence. If Paisley denounced the imperialism of the papacy which used Henry II to destroy traditional Irish liberties, the Provisionals did likewise in their journals. In replies to Catholic bishops and clergy who had decried their violence, Provisional journals referred repeatedly to the Irish hierarchy's long history of collaboration with Britain in the denial of Irish popular liberties. They had no hesitation in dating it back to the Bull *Landabiliter*, granted by the Englishman, Nicholas Breakespeare, who as Pope Adrian IV had conveniently handed over, for needless ecclesiastical reform, Ireland to the English king.[58] Nowhere else did the mirror-image reflect so brightly.

The ecumenist challenge: Bishop Hanson

Later in 1968 a Nottingham University professor of Irish extraction published a scholarly and judicious *Saint Patrick: His Origins and Career*.[59] It accepted Patrick's 'truly evangelical understanding of the Christian faith', admonishing those wishing to use him for their own purposes. Patrick was neither a modern Roman Catholic bishop nor a Protestant evangelist, merely

58 AP, 9.5. and 18.7.75.
59 Oxford UP, 1968. p. 203.

a 5th century bishop: 'He does not have occasion to mention the eucharist and the papacy', but would probably have accepted the idea of the real presence in the sacrament and acknowledged the pope.

No analysis could have been further removed from the emotional fundamentalism of the Free Presbyterians and their Northern Irish fellow travellers. By a quirk of fortune, or perhaps intention, two years later the author, Professor R. P.C. Hanson, was appointed by the Church of Ireland bench of bishops to the diocese of Clogher and became an outspoken opponent of Paisleyism. He denounced the Orange Order as unchristian, lamented the bullying tradition of Ulster Protestantism, and insisted that the duty of parish clergy was not to 'make the people happy at any cost but to lead them to the truth'. Free Presbyterians demonstrated against Hanson, who, accused of lacking political finesse, returned to academic life in 1972. His episcopal successor was a conservative.[60] As a bishop attacking the 'Protestant tradition' Hanson mirrored Catholic Bishop Edward Daly's rejection of the 'Republican tradition' of 1916. Hanson's experience illustrates the paradox, well known to sociologists, of using religion as the basis for tribal identity, while rejecting its inconvenient doctrines.

In his earlier writings Professor Hanson had already struck the heart of Biblical fundamentalism when demonstrating that 'the Bible does not preach itself. If you place a Bible in the market-place it does not expound itself; it does not behave like a gramophone'. Moreover, the Bible could not be separated from the tradition of the church. 'Tradition is, in short, the deposit left by the Church in interpreting the Bible'.[61]

Biblican criticism raises the essential question of 'Protestant tradition' grounded in the Reformation. Bishop Hanson, representing the ecumenical movement of the 1960s, exhibits a form of Christianity closer to Roman Catholicism than Free Presbyterianism in its recognition of church tradition rather than the Bible enthroned in its apparent meaning. The problem is not solved by declaring Hanson the pope's right hand man for the subversion of British Protestantism. Hanson's writings are critical of a number of Roman Catholic positions.[62] Moreover, the exact nature of the 'Protestant tradition'

[60] Hanson, though a Dubliner, was then professor of theology at Nottingham University. A strong opponent of clergy in politics, he talks of the 'Babylonish captivity to political ideologies'. See 'It is a Religious Issue', *Encounter*, Vol. XV, No. 4., October, 1980, p. 19. For lack of finesse, E. Gallagher and S. Worrall, *Christians in Ulster, 1968–1980*, (Oxford University Press), 1980, G and W, pp. 57 and 75. Opposition to clergy in politics, Richard Hanson, 'Politics and the Pulpit', *Community Forum*, Belfast, Vol. 3., No. 3., 1973, pp. 14–18. Duty of clergy, Hanson's review of D.H. Akenson, *The Irish Education Experiment, Irish Theological Quarterly*, Vol. 39, No. 2., April 1972, pp. 201–2.

[61] *The Bible as a Norm of Faith*, Durham University, 1963, pp. 10 and 12.

[62] PT, 4.11.72. See A.T. and R.P.C. Hanson, *Reasonable Belief*, (Oxford University Press), 1981, passim.

must be defined. Is there indeed a basic common denominator 'Protestantism' which Paisley can claim, rightly or wrongly, to represent, or is this concept in itself based on confusion? The ***Protestant Telegraph*** not only attacked its editor's ecumenical opponent, the Methodist Lord Donald Soper, for claiming that Dr Paisley was not a traditional Protestant at all[63] but denounced the former Archbishop of Canterbury, Geoffrey Fisher, for his desire to drop the word 'Protestant' completely.[64] These statements, inconsistent with each other, nevetheless indicated a trend towards the dissolution of Protestant certainties outside Ulster.

Fundamentalism or consensus Protestantism?

What then was the Paisleyite conception of the 'Protestant heritage' and how was it located in the 16th century and subsequent history? A very clear distinction appears between the ultimate doctrine of Bible Protestantism and their contrived Protestant consensus. As Paisley himself insisted, 'those who claim to be Protestants but freely confess that they are not born again Christians ... are in grave error'. Moreover, 'you can be orthodox upon every doctrine, and be lost forever'. Though John 3: 3–7 might be subject to different interpretations, the Free Presbyterian gloss could not. This is what the sociologist of religious sects, Bryan Wilson, has described as a 'heart experience', which 'must occur at a given time' and is 'essential to salvation'.[65] Such a doctrine has a very long tradition behind it, but in no sense provides a consensus for the churches which have conventionally accepted the label 'Protestant', with, as in the case of high church Anglicans, some opposition. The implications of the born-again doctrine must be faced. There are no gradations. As pointed out by R. A. Torrey in the extract cited above, orthodox belief is no help. Weekly attendance at the Martyrs Memorial would prove no more effective than Sunday golf in Ormeau Park or eight o'clock Mass at St Mathews Church, Newtownards Road, were the vital experience of spiritual rebirth lacking. Thus to talk of a 'common Protestantism' should make no sense to a Free Presbyterian. Nor was there any logical reason for denouncing Rome rather than any other church that believed, say, in intellectual conversion, the maintenance of a religious inheritance, a purified personal life, or the ultimate salvation of all sinners. For Paisley to stride about with his Biblical bludgeon seeking ecumenists and

[63] PT, 14.12.68.
[64] PT, 11.5.74.
[65] R.A. Torrey in PT, 12.5.73. Bryan Wilson, *Religious Sects: A Sociological Study*, London (Weidenfeld and Nicholson), 1970, p. 38. I.K.R. Paisley, *No Pope Here*, Belfast (Martyr Memorial Publications), 1982, p. 79.

Romanists to devour was only logical if regarded as a crusade for his own church; it was irrelevant as a defence of a 'Protestant consensus'.

Yet Paisley's political activities required the ultimate advocacy of such a Protestantism, despite the fact that he would merely be saving the pseudo-Protestant damned from the Catholic damned. John Calvin had faced this particular problem in 16th century Geneva, arguing that the elect had the right to force the reprobate to preserve outward decencies. Dr Paisley, however, was less willing to make this explicit. An elaborate Protestant consensus positon was put forward in the *Protestant Telegraph*, though the spectacular diversionary attacks on the harlotries of Rome and the inequities of ecumenists (surely a logical and natural union of the reprobate?) distracted attention from it. Greatest emphasis was placed on the notion of civil and religious liberty, Paisley asserting the Catholics, far from having anything to fear from political Protestantism, should support it.[66] The Protestant heritage was summed up in one illuminating article.[67] On four levels Protestant freedom asserted itself against Roman Catholic thraldom. First, the soul of a Protestant was free to meet its maker without intermediary. Second, the home of the Protestant was inviolate against the intervention of a priestly class. Third, the Protestant was untrammelled at the ballot box by ecclesiastical supervisors. In addition, church and state were completely separated.

This list was indeed an effective assertion of what a Protestant probably believed his or her tradition to imply. It was supported by allegations of Roman Catholic denial of these propositions in the Irish Republic or further afield. The 'sin box' confessional, repeatedly pilloried in article and cartoon as a means to political terrorism and clerical debauchery,[68] underlined the first Protestant assertion. Birth control (Humanae Vitae) and restrictive mixed marriage regulations (Ne Temere) were prime indications of the second. The Irish censorship board immediately evoked number three. Finally, the Mother and Child Health scheme of Dr Noel Browne, which failed in 1951 because of hierarchical opposition, was on the tip of every Northern Protestant tongue, to indicate the fourth category.

So far so good. In all these matters the Northern Irish Protestant heart could be said to beat in tune with that of Dr Paisley, whose *Protestant Telegraph* was certainly foremost in asserting the dangers to be feared from the Vatican. But was it really so simple? Did the four propositions mark a

66 PT, 9.2.74. (guarantee liberty). See also Sarah Nelson, *Ulster's Uncertain Defenders: Protestant Political, Paramilitary and Community Groups and the Northern Ireland Conflict*, Belfast (Appletree), 1984, p. 71 on Calvinist opposition to freedom.

67 PT, 3.6.74.

68 See PT. 3.12.66. on the confessionals which are 'in reality sin-boxes leading to greater villainies between confessors and penitents'.

clear distinction between the ethos of the Falls Road and that of the Shankill? Were they inherent in Bible Protestantism as the true descendant of the real Reformers of the 16th century? The first and second questions can easily be dealt with. The confessional, according to strict Roman Catholic doctrine, does not demonstrate a sharp divergence from the Protestant churches. The individual Catholic also communicates directly with God; the priest does not ultimately forgive sins, but registers the fact of contrition. The main difference is the essential sacramental character of confession.[69] This issue was raised by republicans in their conflict with the hierarchy. Here it should be noted that loyalists, believing the confessional unscriptural, have always insisted that Catholic members of the IRA be excommunicated, in other words compelling confessors to exclude physical-force republicans from the Catholic sacraments, of which many loyalists disapprove.[70]

Similar considerations apply to the home, the book, and the ballot-box. The Catholic hierarchy wishes the law in the Irish Republic to maintain Catholic moral teaching on divorce, abortion and contraception; Dr Paisley's Free Presbyterians want the law in Ulster to prohibit homosexual practices between consenting adults. They are equally hostile to abortion. The Irish Republic has banned Steinbeck;[71] Paisley's supporters work for the exclusion of Steinbeck from Northern Irish schools. In the Irish Republic Catholic clerics pressure government ministers on Catholic moral teaching; in Northern Ireland Protestant clerics lead political parties, stand for, and sit in parliament as well as pressuring government ministers on their churches' moral teaching. These incongruities have long been pointed out. the 'blackmouth' Presbyterian, the Rev. J. B. Armour, celebrated in both Provisional and UVF literature, demonstrated during the first Irish revolution that Ulster Protestants were addicted to authority, not private judgement.[72] Dr Paisley's loyalist critics portray him as a rival pope, or even a rival God. The UDA's *Ulster* depicted a cynical pope in dialogue with an equally cynical Paisley who declared: 'For goodness sake can you not see/That God is Ian Pais-el-ey'. According to McKeague's journal, Ian Paisley 'calls for unity within the Protestants ranks, but forgets to tell the people on my terms only'.[73] In personal style Dr Paisley is nothing if not authoritarian. There is, however,

[69] See Fr Art O'Neill, RN, 6.4.74. and the Liberal Presbyterian Professor J.M. Barkley, *The Roman Church: A handbook for Parents and Teachers*, (Presbyterian Church in Ireland), nd, pp. 7–8. Barkley argues that Protestants do not object to voluntary confession.

[70] PT, 12.5.73., criticised the Church of Ireland for almost accepting the 'Real Presence' in the sacraments like the Catholics.

[71] See Michael Adams, *Censorship: the Irish Experience*, Alabama, 1968, p. 250 for banning of Steinbeck. PT 12.8.78. claimed that Steinbeck's *Mice and Men* had blasphemous sentences.

[72] C, 12.4.74. and RN, 24.11.73. Davis, 'Ulster Protestants'.

[73] U, 2.80.; LN, 9.1.71.

a more important issue, less frequently emphasised. Paisley's claim that he stands unequivocally for the separation of church must be taken alongside his insistence that, unlike modern trendy Presbyterians, he unequivocally adheres to the *Westminster Confession of Faith*, 1646.[74] These are incompatible as the *Westminster Confession* enjoins the civil magistrate to 'maintain piety', suppress 'heresies and blasphemies', and even 'call synods'. The campaign of Paisley's friend, Dr Bob Jones, and others to ensure, contrary to decisions by the United States Supreme Court, that a non-ecumenical translation of the Bible he read in public schools,[75] must be seen in this connection.

Thus the chief aspects of a consensus Protestantism as portrayed in the *Protestant Telegraph* are neither particularly good indicators of the divide between Northern Irish Protestants and Catholics, nor particularly suitable for asserting the leadership of Free Presbyterianism. In another article,[76] P. E. Donovan came closer to the religious reality by declaring the essence of Protestantism to lie in the supremacy of the Bible, private judgement and salvation by faith alone. But here again there were difficulties. On the Bible, ecumenists like Bishop Hanson insisted not only that it was indissolubly linked with church tradition but that old translations were faulty and divisive. The production of new translations acceptable to Roman Catholics and many other churches was clearly an important breakthrough. Free Presbyterians who insisted on the Authorised Version of 1612, rejecting the more modern translations as Bibles of Antichrist,[77] were surely removing themselves even further from leadership of an increasingly hypothetical 'Protestant consensus'. The same may be said for their understanding of 'private judgement'. The *Protestant Telegraph* definition was hardly that of most Protestant churchmen, though certainly rooted in the early Reformation. According to Donovan, it was not private opinion. The individual must accept Christ's teaching from the 'Book'. But what 'Book'? Was the Authorised Version 'indefensibly bad'[78] and incapable of expounding itself? The argument was circular. Republicans and loyalists were equally hostile to the respective scholars undermining their traditions.

The reformation: Freedom of conscience or muscular Christianity?

On Donovan's third point, the issue reverts to Luther and the early

74 See for example Paisley's Stormont speech, PT, 1.8.70. and the Free Presbyterian edition of the WCF.
75 PT, 4.2.67.
76 Rev. P.E. Donovan, 'Why I am, a Protestant', PT, 23.8.75.
77 PT, 17.2.73.
78 Bishop Hanson quoted by PT, 13.3.71.

Reformation. Justification by faith alone appears in popular theology as a radical departure from the Roman Catholic system. Luther had apparently broken with the pope on this issue, refusing to accept any intermediary between his view of the Bible and God. *The Bible* said 'the just shall live by faith' (*Romans* 1, 17),[79] without any mention of works or Masses. Thus the essential revolution was accomplished. But the theological issues are less simple than people in the pews of churches deriving from Luther are encouraged to imagine. It is not necessary to give a detailed examination of how much Luther owed to the medieval church, or the efforts of the Council of Trent to reach a compromise on the various knotty theological issues raised by the Reformers. Suffice it to say that a number of authorities who are not themselves Roman Catholics believe that the doctrinal decisions of the Council of Trent were a victory for common sense.[80] This is not to deny the bitter hatreds aroused by 16th century wars of religion which led to scurrilous language and atrocities like the Massacre of St Bartholomew in France. Dr Paisley compared the latter to the Irish 1641 Rising.[81] If the 16th century has a particular message for Northern Ireland it is surely the discrepancy between the passionate intensity of the physical force struggle and the fine philosophical distinctions ostensibly at issue. Community identity, sociologists tell us, is achieved by submission to a leader, not to theoretical principles.

Leaving aside theological minutiae, did Luther really represent a movement towards greater freedom on which a consensus Protestant position could be based? The radical priest, Fr Desmond Wilson, suggested in 1982 that neither Luther nor Calvin could be regarded as agents of liberty. As for the *Protestant Telegraph*, it demonstrated that Luther freed men from the pope but subjected them to God and the *Bible*. Was he a liberator of human mind and conscience? 'Yes, he was – but only over against the 'other masters'.'[82] The Orange Grand Master, Martin Smyth, agreed that private judgement does not allow any man either to believe or do what he wants irrespective of all other considerations.[83] This was hardly what the average Protestant means by freedom. But Martin Luther, like the two other great Reformers, John Calvin and Huldrych Zwingli, 'developed forms of organisation which closely

79 See I.R.K. Paisley, *Three Great Reformers*, Belfast (Puritan), nd, p. 2.

80 Norman Sykes, *The Crisis of the Reformation*, London (Geoffrey Bles), 1959 p. 103. 'A sounder theological definition than that of the German and Swiss Reformers'. Most Protestant scholars admit 'the service rendered to truth and common sense by the Council of Trent when it repudiated the more emphatic expressions of that quasi-Pauline determinism to which the great Reformers were addicted'.

81 Ian Paisley, *United Ireland: Never!*, Belfast (Puritan), (1972) p. (9) for 1641. John Mckeague's LN, 17.10.70. – 5.12.70., published a series of articles on that massacre.

82 PT, 25.10.69.

83 OS, Belfast, 2.75

identified church and state and shut the door to religious and social dissidence'.[84] Though some of the relatively minor figures of the Reformation, like Sebastian Castellio, advocated a more modern type of tolerance, it can hardly be claimed that freedom of worship or speech derived from the early Protestants, named after the protest at the German Diet of Spires in 1529. The princely protesters involved certainly declared passionately for the individual's direct responsibility to God. But their main objective was to allow prince-bishops, converted to Lutheranism, hereditary rights over their ecclesiastical principalities. The morality of such acquisitions was doubtful. They rejected, moreover, any toleration of Anabaptists or Zwinglian Reformers. In the *Orange Standard* its editor, Church of Ireland Canon S. E. Long, admitted the compulsory worship of the Reformation period but still insisted on a tradition of human equality, citing Thomas Jefferson, a child of the 18th century rationalist Enlightenment rather than the Reformation. To Long, like Smyth, liberty means doing what one *ought*, not what one *wants*.[85]

In asserting the principle of Protestant consensus liberty, some of the Ulster loyalist heroes are revealing. The *Protestant Telegraph* was particularly impressed by the passionate, dynamic, red-haired William Farel, a whirlwind of anti-popery, who travelled from village to village in Switzerland. His tactics were to interrupt the Mass, take over the pulpit, thunder out a sermon, and quickly convert the area to the Reformed faith.[86] This was not simply the power of the Word for, as Kamen points out, 'the ruthless methods of the Protestant soldiery' had a part to play.[87] A mixture of verbal and physical force also characterised the advance of Lutheranism. As a precedent for Ulster in the 1960s and 1970s it was not reassuring; it evoked the tactics adopted by loyalists against NICRA and PD marches in 1968–9, not to mention the British Army in Catholic ghettoes.

Calvinism and politics: An ambivalent legacy

Farel eventually called his more scholarly French compatriot, John Calvin, into Geneva to consolidate his gains. Calvin was another hero of Ulster loyalists in the 1970s. Even the UVF *Combat*, which did not always agree with Paisley, had for a time a columnist, 'Calvin', who preached the predestination of the original, emphasising the total depravity of mankind. Inevitably, the *Westminster Confession* was recommended as the pure expression of this

84 H. Kamen, *The Rise of Toleration*, London (Weidenfeld & Nicholson), 1967, p. 56.
85 OS, 10.73.
86 PT, 13.3.71.
87 Kamen, *The Rise of Toleration*, p. 47.

doctrine. The writer opposed 'authentic Protestants' to Arminians who believed that Christ's sacrifice was intended to make salvation available to all. 'Calvin' inadvertently exposed the weakness of Paisley's consensus advocacy of secular government by insisting that there was no need for the absolute separation of church and state.[88] More surprising was a piece of unconscious ecumenism by 'Calvin' who stated very succinctly an educational philosophy identical to that of the Roman Catholic church. The impossibility of state school neutrality, the priority of parental rights, and the necessity for moulding character were all raised.[89] In the same journal, Hugh Smyth insisted that the Ulster-Scot tradition was basically Protestant and Calvinist.[90]

Such identifications, important when the Church of Ireland is classified as Calvinist,[91] can be double-edged. James Connolly made shrewd nationalist propaganda when he quoted the Irish rationalist and unionist historian, W. E. H. Lecky against the invariable despotism of Anglicanism and the Scottish Presbyterian tyranny buttressed by 'inexorable barbarity' and 'religious terrorism'.[92] F. S. L. Lyons, however, has called attention to that 'kindliness' and 'liberality' in the private lives of North-East Ulster Calvinists which was offset by a history of frontier insecurity.[93]

The other great Calvinist reformer was John Knox, according to Lecky 'this great apostle of murder'.[94] Knox, who broke with his master on non-resistance to ruling powers, was probably more popular with Ulster loyalists who sometimes depicted him on Orange banners. The UDA *Ulster Loyalist* demonstrated that Knox, unlike other Reformers of his time, did not merely criticise Romanist errors, but struck at the very base of the system by declaring the pope Antichrist. Paisley, a master of such rhetoric, was nevertheless criticised for presiding over a congregation that had never manned a road block nor guarded life and property at night.[95] Practice notwithstanding, Paisley included an article on Knox in one of the first issues of the *Protestant Telegraph*.[96] He later compared modern ecumenists unfavourably to Knox. Paisley believed, for example, that the publication of the Presbyterian 'blackmouth' Professor John Barkley by the United States John Knox Press was 'the last straw'.[97] Of greater significance was the

88 C, (1:12, 23–4, 31) 74.
89 C, (1:11, 17–19) 74.
90 C, 6.75.
91 J.T. MacNeill, *The History and Character of Calvinism*, New York (OUP). 1962, pp. 321–2.
92 James Connolly, *Labour in Ireland*, Dublin nd, pp. 156–8.
93 *The Burden of our History*, p. 19.
94 Quoted Kamen, *The Rise of Toleration*, p. 54., from W.E. Lecky, *History of the Rise and Influence of Rationalism in Europe*, London (Longman), 1910., Vol. 2, p. 44.
95 UL, 6.4.75.
96 PT, 6.75.
97 PT, 6.67.

Protestant Telegraph's inclusion of an article discussing the famous confrontation, given in dialogue by Knox's autobiography, between the Reformer and Mary Queen of Scots. Knox, despite Calvin's strictures, promised resistance by 'power' if his sovereign refused to maintain the true kirk.[98] Such was the conditional nature of the Free Presbyterian loyalty; Paisley said much the same to the descendant of Mary Queen of Scots, Queen Elizabeth II, especially when the latter engaged in unacceptable papal visits. Indeed, the *Protestant Telegraph* more than hinted at resistance when commenting in a later article that 'the Stuarts were abominable kings. The virus of that temptress and adultress Mary, Queen of Scots, coursed through their veins'.[99] The article, however, omitted to mention that both William III and Elizabeth II sat on the throne by virtue of 'the virus of that temptress'. This was only a minor problem. The whole issue of resistance to government teems with confusion in Calvinist and Paisleyite thinking. The *Westminster Confession of Faith*, even in the form printed for distribution by Free Presbyterians, shows clearly that the Presbyterian members of the Long Parliament, after Charles I's defeat in the English Civil War, were determined to maintain a strong state which could not be undermined by factious clerics. Hence the stipulation that 'infedility, or indifference to religion, doth not make void the magistrate's just and legal authority'.[100] Nevertheless, Paisley's hero Cromwell had no hesitation in turning out the Presbyterian majority whose Erastianism in the *Westminster Confession* made little appeal to the sectaries of the New Model Army. Paisley, using Carlyle to justify Cromwell's sack of Drogheda,[101] an event celebrated on the banner of at least one Orange Lodge, neglected the tension between Cromwell and the WCF. Cromwell, recognised as 'a man of God', met the requirements for salvation as demanded by the Free Presbyterians.[102]

The 17th century plantations: Towards Derry and the Boyne

This is to move too quickly ahead of chronology. The transference of the Reformation to Ireland aroused relatively little interest amongst the loyalists. The Ulster Plantations of the early 17th century were the essence of the

98 Article by Thomas McGie, PT, 6.1.73.

99 PT, 7.78. and Paisley, *Three Great Reformers*, p. 46, which compares Rome's tactics in the days of Knox to modern attempts at 'papalising our Royal House of Windsor'.

100 *Westminster Confession of Faith*, Glasgow (Free Presbyterian Publications), 1978, p. 19 (XXIII, IV).

101 PT, 17.9.77. For republican use of the Sack of Drogheda as anti-British propaganda see AN, 14.12.74.

102 PT, 17.4.76.

controversy. Here was the key to the 'two nations' question.[103] On the republican side it was generally maintained that an alien element had entered the country at that time, and, as history progressed, these aliens had the choice of identifying with the majority or departing when the majority ultimately came into its own as an independent nation. In mid-19th century, Thomas Davis took up the ideas of Wolfe Tone for a union of peoples of different origins into a new and enriched Irish nation,

As filled by many a rivulet
The stately Shannon flows.

Arthur Griffith later wrote that the declaration in favour of Irish unity by the mainly Protestant Irish Volunteers in 1782 annihilated earlier differences and created one nation. Amalgamation was still the official policy of the republican movement during the first Irish revolution. As already indicated, it was often associated with the concept of the basically good and nationalistic Orangeman. Nevertheless, there were occasional suggestions that the Calvinists of the north-east had as little place in the Irish nation as the English sahebs in India, and would ultimately have to leave.[104] During the Ulster troubles this attitude appears to linger on behind the bland assumption of some republicans that there will be no problem in Northern Ireland after the British departure. 'Freeman' (identified as the southern Irish author, Desmond Fennell) in *An Phoblacht* hinted at two cultural nations, giving allegiance to Ireland and Ulster, might remain for some time before merging in a new Irish nation. This was dangerous ground. On the other side, Michael Dolley, a Queen's University, Belfast, historian sympathetic to the Provisionals, was accused of telling the planters to conform or get out.[105]

The loyalist argument agreed entirely with that of republicans or

[103] Some historians, such as A.T.Q. Stewart in *The Narrow Ground: Aspects of Ulster, 1609–1969*, London (Faber) 1977, p. 41 ('There never was any true confrontation of archetypal Planter and Gael), do not accept the absolute division of this time. See also R.H. Buchanan, 'The Planter and the Gael: cultural dimensions of the Northern Ireland Problem', in F.W. Boal and J.N.H. Douglas, *Integration and Division: Geographical Perspectives on the Northern Ireland Problem*, London (Academic Press), 1982. pp. 67 and 69.

[104] Richard Davis, *Arthur Griffith and Non-Violent Sinn Fein*, Dublin (Anvil), 1974, p. 56, and 'India in Irish Revolutionary Propaganda, 1905–22', *Journal of the Asiatic Society of Bangladesh*, Vol. 22, No. 1, April 1977, pp. 66–89.

[105] AP, 8.72. claims that the republican movement has always accepted the Orangemen as Irish not British. 'Freeman' insisted (AP, 11.7.75) that there were not two nations in Ireland, but two allegiances: The British allegiance did not make a nation but part of a foreign community lodged in Ireland. He later (AP, 5.9.75) qualified this by saying that Provisionals did not offer abandonment of British nationality or departure, foreseeing that two nations would combine with a common Ulster and Irish citizenship, eventually being part of a *new* Irish nation. RN, 4, 5, 6.9.71, compared the pro-British Ulstermen with Algerian colons who must decide between England and Ireland. The historian Michael Dolley was reported by PT, 18.11.72, as saying that planters could take it or leave it.

nationalists, except for the final outcomes. Yes, said the loyalists, we were invaders and intend to remain apart. As the *Protestant Telegraph* put it, if Ulster loyalists were driven out after so long an occupation, then the United States, colonised at about the same time, would have to be given back to the North American Indians. This attitude was to make many loyalists extremely sympathetic towards colonial and settler regimes such as those of South Africa and Rhodesia (Zimbabwe). Dolley was answered by the insistence that the 17th century planters were returning to the home of their ancestors. As for the 'Freeman' position, unionists, originally sure of their British identity, had given a resounding 'no' when asked to become a rivulet feeding the greater Irish Shannon. However, by 1974 when many loyalists, especially in the paramilitaries, felt that they had been sold out by the British espousal of power-sharing, they began to see merits in Davis's racial merger. The contrast with Paisley's *Protestant Telegraph*, which continued to interpret post-plantation 17th century events in terms of total racial-religious polarisation, is sometimes marked.

In the loyalist historical tradition the long contested alleged 1641 massacre of Protestant platners by the native Irish and subsequent rebellion is followed by the Protestant Cromwellian repression and final epiphanies in the Protestant defence of (London)derry against Catholic James II and the latter's ultimate defeat by William III at the Boyne ofn 1 (subsequently 12) July 1690. Against these, nationalists have set the heroism of the Jacobite commander, Patrick Sarsfield, the siege of Limerick, and the broken treaty of that city, which was followed by the anti-Catholic penal laws of the late 17th and early 18th centuries. These nationalist symbols have never become the focus of a cult quite as extensive as that of their loyalist counterparts, but the banners displayed by modern demonstrations of the Ancient Order of Hibernians balance the 17th century history of their Orange counterparts. The Young Irelanders, John Mitchel, considered the period particularly important: the Irish parliament of 1692 ensured that 'the division into two nations became definite' by excluding Catholics form membership.[106] Here the 'two nations' are perceived as political, not racial or cultural.

Propagandist history often lingers without visible means of support. Scientific historians and nationalists since the 1840s may demonstrate that the papist atrocities of 1641 were deliberately exaggerated to justify the seizure of Irish land by the English Long Parliament, but this will scarcely affect the loyalist rabblerouser's anticipation of forthcoming massacres. Ironically, the *Loyalist News* of the post-1974 McKeague was the most balanced: 'Faults on

[106] J. Mitchel, *Ireland from the Siege of Limerick*, London (Washbourne), nd, p. 18.

[107] LN, 29.8.75. adn Davis, *Griffith*, p. 109. S. Nelson, *Ulster's Uncertain Defenders*, p. 33 on the 1641 myth.

both sides swayed back and forth, Protestant Ireland or Roman Catholic Ireland. The native Irish find it hard to forget Cromwell and the Plantation. Ulstermen find it hard to forget 1641 and 1798'. When discussing the siege of Londonderry, Paisley's paper made considerable use of the description from T. B. Macaulay's *History of England*, which John Mitchel had formerly denounced as a bitter attack on the Celtic people.[107] Paisley could revel in the contrast between the 'aboriginal peasantry' harangued by their priests, and the upstanding Protestant settler defenders of the city.[108] As has already been shown, Paisley projected this racial-religious cleavage into the controversies of the 1970s and 1980s.

Protestants and the Gaelic tradition

In 1974 the UVF *Combat* published an appreciative article based on a pamphlet, *The Hidden Ulster*, by Padriag O Snodaigh, with a forword by a retired Church of Ireland cleric, the Rev. Cosslet Quinn.[109] Here it was shown that the cultural gap between the 17th century planter and the native Irish was much less than had been supposed, linguistic and cultural affinities easily bridging the narrow seas between Scotland and Ulster. As for the siege of Derry-Londonderry, analysis if the famous song Lillibulero, which is reputed to have whistled James II out of three kingdoms, demonstrates the title to be, not meaningless gibberish, but perfectly good Irish: 'An Lile ba Leir Dho, Ba Linn an La'. ('The Lily was triumphant, it won the day'.) The celebrated Apprentice Boys who closed Derry against James II, and whose commemoration in 1969 helped to spark off the Ulster Troubles, may have been Irish-speaking. O Snodaigh demonstrated that early 19th century Catholic clerics were more dubious about Gaelic than their Presbyterian counterparts. The Orange leader, R. R. Kane, signed his lodge minutes in Irish.

Cosslet Quinn, a Protestant traitor according to Paisley's paper,[110] showed, moreover, that there was a common Irish-Scottish Gaelic culture shared by Catholic and other churches. The Church of Ireland had produced the first Gaelic *Bible*, while the Scottish Presbyterians had translated major works by Calvin and Knox into Gaelic. Of course, these translations were to facilitate conversion not to perpetuate the cultures themselves. Indeed, the failure of the Reformation in Ireland was partly due to the inability of English churchmen to provide immediately a Gaelic translation of their new prayer

[108] PT, 3.9.77.
[109] C, 25.4.74.
[110] PT, 3.2.73.

book. *Combat*, quoted with interest by the Provisionals,[111] argued that the identification of Gaelic culture with Roman Catholicism should be abandoned, and that loyalists, who could remain unionists like the Scots, should regain their heritage 'in folklore, in music, in literature, in song and in the Gaelic language'. It was not so much that papists had stolen Protestant culture, but that Protestants had foolishly given it away to Roman Catholics. The unionist British and Irish Communist Organisation, which endeavoured to influence Protestant paramilitaries, published a pamphlet in reply to O Snodaigh.[112] But the eminent historian, Professor Oliver MacDonagh, accepted that 'the quest for Gaelic culture was largely Protestant in origin'.

Even the Battle of the Boyne, the most holy of all loyalist commemorations, now came under review. Republicans and nationalists repudiated James II and sometimes argued that celebration was misplaced as William III was leader of a European coalition against Louis XIV the patron of James II. The coalition contained a number of Catholic powers including the pope who was said to have marked his ally's victory with a Te Deum in Rome. Loyalists usually ignored such talk. In 1974, for example, the UDA *Ulster Loyalist* published an article on the battle which adopted the usual depiction of William III as an enemy of Rome. The following year, however, the same journal changed tack. Tongue in cheek, it suggested that the 12th July was not sectarian as 'William of Orange's victory was particularly welcome to the Pope, among other Europeans. Its traditional commemoration nowadays had rather the character of an Independence Day celebration'. The unionist historian, Dr Hugh Shearman, agreed.[113] Paisley, again quoting Macaulay, showed that the pope in question, Alexander VII, was closer to Louis XIV than his predecessor, Innocent XI.[114] A Te Deum was certainly sung in Catholic Vienna, but probably not Rome.

The UDA and Ulster separatism: Adamson's Cruthin

As for other post-1974 loyalists, the UDA through its New Ulster Political Research Group (NUPRG) aimed at the establishment of an independent Ulster. This, it hoped, would reconcile both Protestants and Catholics to a common Ulster identity, opposed both to British and Irish cultural

[111] AP, 5.5.74, talked of important bridges. RN, 25.5.74, quoted the article in full.
[112] See BICO's *'Hidden Ulster' Explored; A Reply to P. O'Snodaigh* (1974). Oliver MacDonagh, *States of Mind: A Study of Anglo-Irish Conflict 1780–1980*, London (Allen and Unwin), 1983, p. 105.
[113] UL, 21.11.74 and 2.3.75. See also Hugh Shearman, *27 Myths about Ulster*, Belfast (Ulster Unionist pamphlet), 1972, p. 5.
[114] PT, 3.4.76.

imperialism. The philosopher of this group was a medical doctor and prolific publicist, Ian Adamson, who appears to have sold his ideas to the UDA commander, Andy Tyrie, and some other leaders. Adamson epitomised his message in a 1982 volume, *The Identity of Ulster*, after previous publications such as *The Cruthin*, 1974, *Bangor, Light of the World*, 1979, and a number of articles in the UDA's Ulster, sometimes under the pseudonym, Sam Sloan. Adamson developed the idea of 17th century Ulster planters as a returning, rather than an alien force. Even Paisley seems to have accepted this. But Adamson went a step further, arguing that the Ulster Protestant community was represented by the pre-Milesian Cruthin, or Picts, who as the original inhabitants were driven to Scotland or absorbed into the invading Gaelic culture which accepted many Cruthnic forms. The Cruthin, unlike the Gaels, were not Indo-European,[115] but contributed to the cultural mix, making Irish an exceptional language. The Cruthnic apogee was reached, according to Adamson, in the foundation of the Bangor monastery in north Down in 555. This produced in Columbanus the Pict the greatest of all Irish missionaries. In 637 the Picts were finally reduced to vassalage by the Gaelic O'Neills. In the 17th century many of the settlers from Scotland had Pictish ancestry; therefore it could be said that they were coming home. what did all this mean politically?

In the 'Sam Sloan' articles in the UDA's Ulster, Adamson is a great deal more explicit than in *The Identity of Ulster*. His message was clear: 'We affirm that Ulster is a Pictish not a Gaelic nation'. Even Cuchulain, the inspiration of Pearse, is annexed as a Pict who defended Ulster against the invading Gaels. Adamson was preceded by the first issues of the *UDA News* in 1971 which used Cuchulain and his famous hound as its emblem: Cuchulain 'particularly symbolises Ulster today ... He was Ulster's one and only hero and he defended Ulster against the rest of the provinces of Ireland. They killed him in the end but only by treachery, deceit and subversion'. This was not the first time that Cuchulain had been put to loyalist use.[116]

Adamson developed the argument by claiming that the six counties of Ulster were not an unnatural unit seized in 1920 by opportunist unionists working through a complaisant British government but a reasonable compromise between the varying frontiers of Chruthnic or Pictish power.[117] The ultimate call was emotional: 'you are the children of the Cruthin, the sons and daughers of the Picts. This is OUR land, YOUR culture, YOUR heritage – You are indeed the people. You are older than the Gaels, older than the Welsh, older even than the English. You have a (right) to belong here, no less than the trees. You have a right to be HEARD here. You have a right to be

115 Cruthin, p. 115.
116 Sam Sloan in U, 8 and 9 78.
117 UDAN, 19.10.71 and Hugh Shearman, *Not An Inch*, London (Faber), 1942, p. 5.

FREE!'[118] Unlike Paisley, Adamson accepted the United Irishmen, including the 'noble' Henry Joy McCracken, as Cruthin.[119]

Winning general support for such an idea was difficult. The Catholic community was totally unwilling to become Ulster Picts with the UDA and preferred to see themselves as Gaels in a united Ireland. Moreover, as Bishop Hanson pointed out in a new study, St Patrick hated the Picts. Once the amalgation of cultures wsa admitted in Ulster, why not accept Irish identity? Some southern Provisional allies seem privately to have been interested.[120] The unionists themselves were not very impressed. Those working for greater integration with Britain rejected the suggestion without consideration, and even on the devolutionist wing Paisley was hostile. When the bicycling traveller, Devla Murphy, published the best-selling *A Place Apart*, accepting the relevance to Ulster of the NUPRG ideas, the book was acclaimed by the UDA (121) but denounced by the *Protestant Telegraph*, not only for misrepresenting Dr Paisley, but for attributing papistical superstition to Protestant working-class ghettoes. An independent Ulster, 'Protestant Sinn Fein', was rejected on the intransigent ground that 'while popery exists in Ireland, there will continue to be trouble'.[122] So much for the NUPGR's 'Beyond the Religious Divide'. Paisley's DUP, however, commanded votes in the loyalist community, but the UDA has always been singularly unsuccessful at the ballot box, probably because of what the *Irish Press* called its 'blood stained history'.[123] John McMichael, one of the progenitors of the New Ulster idea, has proved no vote spinner; like Tyrie, he was arrested, but not convicted, for alleged associations with violence.

19th century Protestant clericalism: Paisley versus UDA and UVF

The discussion of the 17th century plantations has thus ranged far beyond that period and carried the reader rapidly from pre-history to the present day. Such is the diffuse nature of the historical argumentation in unionist and republican self-justification. The 19th century, which saw the development of the Orange Order and the tradition of riot-provoking sermons in Belfast by

[118] U, 10.78.

[119] *Cruthin*, pp. 86–7. For St Patrick and the Picts, R.P.C. Hanson, *The Life and Writings of St Patrick*, New York (Seabury Press), 1983, p. 55.

[120] According to J. Holland, *Too Long a Sacrifice: Life and Death in Northern Ireland since 1969*, New York (Dodd, Mead), 1981, p. 118, PIRA rejected NUPGR but 'privately they played with the idea of Ulster independence'.

[121] U, Christmas '79, published Dervla Murphy's 'A return' praising the UDA's *Beyond the Religious Divide* (29.3.79.).

[122] PT, 29.4.78.

[123] U, 3.79.

preachers like 'Roaring' Hugh Hanna, provided numerous incidents for local folklore. Paisley identified chiefly with churchmen like Hanna[124] and the conservative Presbyterian Henry Cooke[125] who did much to unite Presbyterians and Anglicans against Roman Catholicism. All loyalists were inspired by the resistance to Home Rule in the late 19th and early 20th centuries. Paisley, temporarily dropping the Cooke image, went on 'the Carson trail'. On another occasion he assisted in bringing the *Clyde Valley*, the original UVF gun-running ship, back to Ulster. According to McKeague, Paisley failed to account for the money raised after the project had been literally scrapped.[126]

The 'Protestant heritage' thus confronts the theoretically secular republican ideal. But Paisley's attempt at a Protestant consensus was challenged in the 1970s by a more secular ideal of a cultural Ulster identity. Sometimes there was convergence, though the paramilitary journals increasingly distanced themselves from clerical tutelage. The surprising result was that, though an anachronism in its continued emphasis on racial and cultural divergence in an increasingly cosmopolitan world, the New Ulster idea was a refreshing break with Paisley's naked anti-popery. UVF men who learned Gaelic in gaol and sported the Irish speaker's *fainne* badge lamented that earlier in life they had been cut off from their rightful heritage of Irish history and culture. John McKeague, a peddler of extreme anti-popery, seems to have gone through a type of conversion to a broader view of Ulster identity before being laid low by an assassin's bullet. Tara and the Orange Lodge 1303, which emblazoned Irish mottos on its banners and looked for a Protestant to teach its members Irish, were, however, ludicrously illiberal and anti-ecumenical in their aim of destroying Catholicism throughout Ireland.[127] To adapt Dr Johnson's comment on the woman preacher, the surprise was not the loyalist numbers involved, but that any should participate in Irish culture at such a period. Whatever the precise motives or nature of participators, an alternative to the 'Protestant heritage' was developing.

Prot-stats and Prot-ecums

Analysis of the 'Protestant heritage' as it ransacks history demonstrated many discrepancies. Only verbal sleight of hand could enable Free Presbyterians to pose as defenders of a Protestant consensus. The 'popery barefaced' which consisted of seeking salvation 'by doing no harm, paying every man his own,

124 PT, 15.5.71. on Hanna's great rally in 1862.
125 PT, 8.10.66. Paisley on 'that Great Irish Presbyterian leader'.
126 PT, 28.12.68. Paisley welcomes the return.
127 OS, 7.75. and 4.82. The republican AN, 3.1.73. commended the development.

saying your prayers and going to church and sacrament' probably epitomised the religion of most Protestants.[128] Furthermore, the history of the Reformation is too complex to admit of an easy identification with principles like 'private judgement' and 'the separation of church and state'. The aim of removing popery from Ireland is irreconcilable with peaceful religious coexistence. Indeed, the Paisleyite view of history leads to an exceptionally muscular Christianity. Clarity of thought might be increased by dropping the use of the word 'Protestant' in this connection and using a neologism such as 'Pro-statist' or 'Prot-stat', implying a vigorous political anti-Catholicism. Ecumenical churches, prepared to live and let live, could then be described by their individual names or generally as 'Prot-ecums'. A Methodist, for example, only becomes a 'Prot-stat' when he or she holds strong views on the need to resist the encroachments of Catholicism by political or forceful means. The 'Protestant consensus' view, easily manipulated by Free Presbyterians for their own specific ends, could be quietly phased from popular thought, an operation easier to conceive than translate into reality.

Prot-stats and mirrored republicans

Generally, the still dominant religious 'Prot-statism' mirrors secular republicanism. Both viewpoints are blurred in the details of their rationalisations, and extremely vulnerable to the erosion of revisionists. Their dependence on historicism increases this vulnerability. Antagonistic history results from abandoning the democratic, problem solving, social engineering attitude in favour of absolutist solutions. Force lies at the heart of each credo. Thus we revert again to the old symbiosis. Religion, however, operated differently, or appeared to do so, on the opposing viewpoints. The republican assault on the anti-national traditions of the Catholic hierarchy was at first more forceful than the relatively mild loyalist criticism of Protestant clergy. The UDA, however, excluded clergy from its counsels and the New Ulster proposals were a step towards Protestant secularism. Such differences were less visible in the three-cornered debate on terrorism, involving not only loyalists and republicans but also British Army spokesmen.

[128] PT, 12.7.74.

KITSON VERSUS MARIGHELA: THE DEBATE OVER NORTHERN IRELAND TERRORISM

RICHARD DAVIS

Republicans, loyalists and the British Army

Much has already been written on terrorist violence and the religious strife between Protestants and Catholics in Northern Ireland. Most illuminating, however, is the propaganda war waged between the Provisionals and the British Army, with the loyalist paramilitaries clumsily attempting to establish themselves as an argumentative third force. Liz Curtis, in *Ireland: the Propaganda War*, has described the rival propagandist machines of the British government and the Provisional IRA; her focus, however, is the manipulation of the British media, rather than the intrinsic debate. The semantics of violence have a pathology of their own, sometimes divorced from supportive actions in the real world. The Provisionals were probably more effective with the pen than the bomb.

The Irish revolution of 1919–21 gives perspective. The most eminent Irish propagandist, Arthur Griffith, publisher of several newspapers as well as general overseer of the influential *Irish Bulletin*, had misgivings about Irish violence. He minimised republican force, counter-attacking where possible with stories of English atrocities. The advent of the Black and Tans and Auxiliaries in mid-1920 eased Griffith's task considerably. During the conflict his papers implied that a totally non-violent Irish movement was continually beset by homicidal maniacs in British uniforms. Griffith was adept at revealing British *agents provocateur*. Ruthless actions by the Irish appeared either British lies or deliberate 'felon setting' by the alien government. Only reluctantly did Griffith even admit that the Irish retaliated against outrageous provocation by the Black and Tans.

Footnote abbreviations

Protestant-Loyalist (Prot-Stat)

C	= *Combat* (UVF)
LAW	= *Loyalist Association of Workers*
LN	= *Loyalist News* (variable loyalist)
PT	= *Protestant Telegraph* (Paisley)
UDAN	= *UDA News*
OUDAN	= *Official UDA News*

Catholic-Republican

RN	= *Republican News* (PIRA)
AP	= *An Phoblacht* (PIRA)
UI	= *United Irishman* (OIRA)
SP	= *Starry Plough* (IRSP)
SDLPN	= *SDLP News*

Other

CG	= *Constabulary Gazette* (RUC)
ST	= *Sunday Times*

Justification for such defensive arguments required a conspiratorial theory of some plausibility. Events in India proved invaluable. The Amritsar Massacre of March 1919 was ideal for Irish purposes. Though General R.E. Dyer received something of a hero's welcome from admirers in England, his shooting dead of nearly 400 unarmed Indian demonstrators appeared excessive punishment to all whose patriotic sympathies were not unconditionally engaged on the British side. Griffith denounced mini-Amritsars in Ireland. The incantation of names like Dyer and Amritsar was superb propaganda. Griffith's critics accused him of persistently retailing half-truths or downright lies even when the facts had been clearly established. Some of his tactics appeared dubious: on 'Bloody Sunday' 21 November 1920, a Griffith paper denounced the shooting of twelve members of a football crowd by British troops, but said nothing of the assassination of fourteen intelligence officers by the IRA earlier in the day, despite the editor's personal repugnance for the Irish action.[1] Griffith undoubtedly realised that skilful propaganda was not simply an aid to physical-force rebellion, but rather the essence of revolution. Modern commentators argue that 'the guerilla fighter is primarily a propagandist, an agitator, a disseminator of the revolutionary idea, who uses the struggle itself – the actual physical conflict – as an instrument of agitation'.[2] Griffith scarcely endorsed 'propaganda by deed', previously adopted in 19th century Russia, but was well in advance of colleagues who still hoped that the IRA might eventually triumph over Britain in a set-piece battle, possible armed with the traditional pike.[3]

By the 1970s there was more revolutionary theory to play with, some derived secondhand from Ireland itself. Although Griffith was repudiated by both branches of the post-1969 IRA, Provisional Sinn Fein asserted its continuity with the movement he founded in 1905 and its 1918 objectives.[4] Griffith's tactics as a propagandist were tacitly followed. The emphasis on defence appeared at the start of the Provisional campaign; the Protestant incursions into Catholic areas after 1968 made it entirely plausible. Similarly actions of the British Army after the Falls search in July 1970 enabled the Provisionals to assert their position as guardians of their community. Their

[1] Richard Davis, *Arthur Griffith* (Dublin Historical Association), 1976, pp. 30–33, and Davis, 'India in Irish Revolutionary Propaganda, 1905–22', *Journal of the Asiatic Society of Bangladesh*, 22, 1, April 1977, pp. 66–89.

[2] R. Taber, *The War of the Flea: Guerrilla Warfare – Theory and Practice*, London (Paladin), 1972, p. 23. E. Hyams, *Terrorists and Terrorism*, London (Dent), 1975, p. 165 and H. Lasswell, *Politics: Who gets what, when, how*. Cleveland (Meridian), 1963, p. 55.

[3] G.A. Hayes-McCoy, quoted in Richard Davis, *Arthur Griffith and Non-Violent Sinn Fein*, Dublin (Anvil), 1974, p. 167. 4. RN, 30.4.72. 'The Modern Sinn Fein of 1972 is the same organisation as was founded in 1905 and has the same objectives as it set itself in 1918'.

opponents maintained, on the contrary, that PIRA, far from helping the Catholic community, was deliberately provoking the British violence it claimed to oppose. The papers of the security forces, the *Constabulary Gazette* and *Visor*, played a minor role in the debate. The latter, whose semi-nude pinups upset the Equal Opportunities Commission, sometimes ridiculed 'Seamus the Smear', PIRA's propaganda officer, and the contention that the Provisionals protected the lives of the general population.[5] PIRA and the security forces in effect re-established the pattern of 1919–21 when Arthur Griffith denounced Britain for goading the British into rebellion, and Lloyd George repudiated a tiny murder gang deplored by the Irish people.

The issue is epitomised in the propagandist confrontation between Provisional spokesmen, such Ruairi O Bradaigh, David O'Connell, and Sean MacStiofain, chief of staff before his arrest in 1972, on one side, and General Richard Clutterbuck on the other. In books like *Protest and the Urban Guerilla* and *Living with Terrorism*, Clutterbuck, eventually metamorphosed into an academic, gives a coherent case for the British Army. He is backed by other writers such as Paul Wilkinson and Edgar O'Ballance. The rival interpreters, as will be shown later, endeavoured to associate their opponents, like Griffith's evocation of General Dyer, with a frigthening bogey. To the Provisionals the bogey was Clutterbuck's former student at the British Army staff college, Frank Kitson, by 1982 commander of British land forces.

The Contest of stereotypes: Kitson v. Marighela

Kitson at forty-four the youngest British brigadier, commanded the 39th Brigade in Belfast from September 1970 to April 1972. In 1971 he published a controversial book on counter-insurgency, *Low Intensity Operations*. Copies were soon bought up by Irish republicans and the CIA.[6] Especially in the years 1974–7, Kitson was continually attacked by republicans and others as the mastermind of internment, torture, brutal interrogation, subtle brainwashing, media control, black propaganda, incitement to sectarian murder, SAS assassination, and stealing felt from Thiepval barracks.[7] He became a propaganda byword for all the most hated aspects of the British Army's service in Ulster. On the loyalist side Kiston was sometimes praised – Professor Kennedy Lindsay told a Vanguard meeting that Northern Ireland

5 *Protest and the Urban Guerrilla*, London (Cassell), 1973; *Living with Terrorism*, London (Faber) 1975.

6 *Low Intensity Operations: Subversion, Insurgency, Peace-keeping*, London (Faber), (1971), 1975.

7 UI, 2.76.

needed more Dyers and Kitsons[8] – and sometimes reviled, as indeed by Kennedy Lindsay himself some years later.[9] General Clutterbuck, however, did not mention his former student in the footnotes to his *Protest and the Urban Guerrilla*, which dealt with the early years of the second Irish revolution. He had more to say about the ideas of the Brazilian revolutionary, Carlos Marighela. Marighela's *Minimanual of the Urban Guerrilla* and *For the Liberation of Brazil*[10] were cited to demonstrate how urban guerrillas deliberately provoked government reprisals on their own communities to goad them into support of the revolution. Thus the Provisionals portrayed a war in which Machiavellian fiends like Kitson brutally ill-treated the Catholic community to compel it to desert its natural leaders and defenders; the British Army, on the other hand, saw terrorists, steeped in Marighela, subjecting their own communities to bloodshed and brutality in the interests of a remote and extreme cause. The former PIRA chief of staff, Sean MacStiofain, in his *Memoirs of a Revolutionary*, has thus nothing to say about Marighela, only occasionally mentioned in republican literature, but a great deal on Kitson, 'our deadliest enemy in the north'.[11] These attitudes clearly mirror each other.

Marighela, however, had no direct connection with Ireland, while Kitson was a commander during the exceptionally important early years of the Ulster troubles. Is it possible, in the midst of such a welter of propaganda, to establish the basic facts about his Ulster mission? Very little official documentation is available on Kitson's precise work and influence in Northern Ireland, though paddy Devlin, a member of the power-sharing executive, claims that 'it is clear from public records that his troops were instructed to put the boot into the Catholic section of the community'.[12] Brian Faulkner does not mention Kitson in his memoirs; most accounts of the Kitson period in Ulster give him little attention. Kitson himself does not include a description of his work in Northern Ireland in *Bunch of Five*, an autobiographical account, published in 1977, which indirectly answers some of his Irish critics. Clutterbuck ignores Kitson in his lengthy description of the build-up of terrorism from 1970 to 1972. The only significant hint of the Kitson influence from a semi-official source comes from Roy Bradford, a minister under Faulkner in both the old Stormont regime and the later power-sharing executive. The fictional hero of Badford's novel, *The Last Ditch*, is greatly impressed by Kitson's efforts to modernise the British Army against conservative opposition.[13]

8 Law (2, 39 73).

9 K. Lindsay, *The British Intelligence Services in Action*, Dundalk (Dundrod Press), 1980, p. 84.

10 *For the Liberation of Brazil*, London (Penguin), 1971.

11 S. MacStiofain, *Memoirs of a Revolutionary*, Great Britain (Gordon Cremonesi), p. 72.

12 P. Devlin, *The Fall of the N.I. Executive*, Belfast (P. Devlin), 1975, p. 121.

13 Roy Bradford, *The Last Ditch*, Belfast (Blackstaff), 1981, p. 29.

Generally, however, Kitson appears to have remained in the back ground till the publication of his *Low Intensity Operations* in the months following internment in August 1971. There then appeared a direct connection between theory and practice. But this was not Kitson's first book. As early as 1960 he had published *Gangs and Counter-Gangs* describing his experiences as an intelligence officer in the Mau Mau emergency.[14] His method had been to recruit loyal Kikuyu and Mau Mau prisoners, form them into pseudo-gangs with face-blackened British officers (sometimes himself), and send them into the forest to gather information or eliminate real Mau Mau formations. Though this book was to form the focus of an intense Irish debate, it became generally known only after the publication of *Low Intensity Operations*. The new work was researched at University College, Oxford, 1969–70, under a defence fellowship. From academic cloisters Kitson was sent to apply his research in Northern Ireland. His second book developed his earlier experiences in Kenya, Malaya, Cyprus and Oman into a general theory. It suggested that the British Army, no longer able to rely on force of numbers, needed greater facility for psychological operations, irregular warfare, and co-operation with police at earlier stages in subversion.[15] Clearly the authorities were aware of these conclusions before sending him to Northern Ireland.

Kitson arrived in Belfast at a crucial period of the Troubles. The Conservatives replaced Labour in June 1970, and ended their so-called 'softly, softly' policy. The 'tea for soldiers' period concluded with the Falls arms search in July, after the first main Provisional action in the Short Strand. Even Clutterbuck considered the arms search 'ill-judged'.[16] It was, in fact, close to the force of numbers approach which Kitson criticised in his *Low Intensity Operations*. His appointment to Northern Ireland appears an attempt to introduce greater subtlety. Kitson had the advantage of a lull before the Provisional urban guerrilla campaign began in earnest in February 1971. In the months before February, there were, according to Clutterbuck, discreet meetings between officers and republican leaders.[17] Here Kitson's tactics should have worked most effectively. General Freeland had already established various community projects and clubs, ostensibly to enable the mixing of the different traditions. To Kitson such projects were extremely valuable as sources of information by the Army.[18] Total polarisation and no-

14 *Gangs and Counter-Gangs*, London (Barry S. Rocliffe), 1960.
15 *Low Intensity Operations*, pp. 2, 68, etc.
16 Clutterbuck, *Protest and the Urban Guerrilla*, p. 137.
17 Clutterbuck, *Protest*, p. 71.
18 *Low Intensity*, p. 92.

go areas, on the other hand, made the type of intelligence hunting envisaged in *Gangs and Counter-Gangs* very difficult.

Kitson, however, did not succeed in checking the development of the Provisionals. In early 1971, General Harry Tuzo was appointed the new British Army commander in Northern Ireland. According to MacStiofain, there was tension between Tuzo, a conservative who favoured the establishment of a ring of steel round nationalist areas to provoke all-out confrontation with PIRA, an Kitson who sought fluidity enabling plain clothes officers to infiltrate republican areas and emulate the counter-gangs in the Kenyan forest. Roy Bradford also suggested military opposition to Kitson who 'singlehanded, was attempting to drag the army through a revolution as great as Cardwell's'.[19]

Kitson and internment

By summer 1971 the Faulkner government decided on internment. Was Kitson, as subsequently alleged, the mastermind behind this strategy? Faulkner's memoirs mention Roy Bradford as a hardliner on internment;[20] Bradford approved of Kitson, so the latter may have been one of the military men in favour, especially if opposed to his sceptical superior Tuzo. Kitson's books hint approval of such tactics. In *Bunch of Five* he praises the massive use of internment in Kenya for saving many lives.[21] Republican critics quote Kitson's later comments in *Low Intensity Operations* that an amount of low grade evidence was more useful for subsequent development than a little high grade information.[22] They also noted Kitson's approval of the pro-internment Robert Trinquier, a French general who fought against the Algerian Revolt.[23] Internment was an obvious means for obtaining low grade information when informal contacts between soldiers and nationalist civilians were almost impossible. It therefore seems a fair deduction that Kitson did advocate internment more strongly than Tuzo. MacStiofain suggests an enormous 'shopping list' of information sought at this time.[24] If correct, it indicates just how little was known about the IRA.

The actual implementation of internment in Belfast was certainly Kitson's responsibility. Yet he was clearly dissatisfied with the overall arrangements

[19] *The Last Ditch*, p. 29.

[20] Brian Faulkner, *Memoirs of a Statesman*, (ed. John Houston), London (Weidenfield and Nicholson) 1978, p. 317, and for Tuzo's reluctance, p. 121.

[21] *Bunch of Five*, London (Faber) 1977, pp. 58–9.

[22] *Low Intensity*, p. 72. RN, 6.8.77., MacStiofain, p. 195.

[23] *Low Intensity*, p. 5 and AP 12.7.74.

[24] MacStiofain, p. 195.

for 'Operation Demetrius'. The journalist Simon Winchester points out that Kitson was on holiday when a dry run practice internment was carried out on 23 July. He was, as a result, 'highly irritated' that surprise had been lost and that dozens of suspects escaped. When the crucial day, August 9, came there was further inefficiency. The RUC handed over the suspect list to Kitson, often with the wrong photographs, and the Army sent out three-man snatch squads.[25] This was clearly opposed to Kitson's view as his books insisted that Army and Special Branch should work together in building up information banks, rather than using soldiers simply as police agents.[26] But, as MacStiofain, PIRA chief of staff at the time, points out, Kitson was 'then little known to the public' and correspondingly less influential with his superiors.[27]

Clutterbuck is ambiguous on internment, admitting that it inevitably polarises opinion, but still claiming that it was the only alternative to the intimidatory tactics of vigilantes determined to create a backlash à la Marighela.[28] Thus the arguments are mirror-images; Provisionals see internment as part of a Kitsonian plot; British officers as an attempt to defeat a Marighela plot. What was the achievement? MacStiofain quotes Kitson's desire for low-grade information, but unlike other republicans who are content to attribute to the then brigadier all subsequent ill-treatment, the PIRA chief of staff considers sensory deprivation, effective in eliciting confession, counter-productive for Kitson. MacStiofain in fact suspects tension between officers wishing to obtian counter-insergency leads and those who wanted experimental guinea-pigs. He points out that if one IRA member's name had been obtained from each of 700 detainees, the Provisionals would have been destroyed immediately. That they were not, indicated either the inaccuracy of initial British information or the incompetence of their intelligence officers.

MacStiofain realised that Kitson's object was tactical information enabling the Army to build low-grade sources into contact leads for definite targets, instead of passively waiting for IRA units to appear in an exposed position.[29] This is a sensible reading of Kitson's work. The latter continually emphasised the need to develop background information into operational data capable of beginning a feedback process and 'chain reaction' which 'snowballs'.[30] The use of the latter word in the *Parker Report* on internment was attributed to

[25] Simon Winchester, *In Holy Terror. Reporting the Ulster Troubles*, London (Faber) 1974, pp. 154–5 and 163. Noticed by RN, 8.3.75.

[26] *Bunch of Five*, p. 53 talks of the futility of the blind 'Dante' round-up in Kenya.

[27] MacStiofain, p. 194.

[28] *Protest*, pp. 94–6.

[29] MacStiofain, pp. 195, 198 and 202–3.

[30] *Low Intensity*, p. 98.

Kitsonian influence.[31] But Kitson also talks of obtaining background information through soldiers and police 'in a friendly and civilised way'.[32] Moreover, he laid great stress on the efficient collating of overt information and even reading revolutionary memoirs in public libraries. A Belfast paper correctly asserted that he made war 'with a filing cabinet', or, more accurately, a computer in the Lisburn headquarters.[33]

Kitson and interrogation

Republicans accused Kitson of organising the beating, electric shock treatment, psychological disorientation, and gross humiliation of internees at the Holywood Police Barracks. The Officials published a photograph of Kitson ('the face of a sadist') on their anti-internment pamphlet, *They came in the morning*.[34] Were they making dishonest propaganda? Certainly, they could not deduce it from Kitson's books; he would hardly admit publicly to rough handling of suspects. There is one admission in *Counter-Gangs* of a night spent working over a prisoner 'as tough as nails and very unco-operative'. As Kitson and his assistants 'were not feeling particularly sympathetic' they succeeded in eliciting some useful information. In *Bunch of Five* Kitson repudiated brutality, distinguishing between formal interrogation for immediate tactical information and long-term, and ultimately more valuable, attempts to win a prisoner's friendship. Draughts, parties, horseplay, and a willingness to live without moralising in close proximity to a prisoner, were emphasised. The certainty of capital punishment for the unco-operative was a powerful incentive. Republican insistence that Kitson practised sleep deprivation might be deduced from his Kenyan habit of keeping initially unco-operative prisoners in chains. But Joram Wamweya, a Kenyan guerrilla, ridiculed the naivety of special branch agents attempting to extract confessions by shackles. In formal interrogation Kitson emphasises confrontation with unexpected facts from background sources to 'break down' the prisoner.[35] As MacStiofain admitted, beating and torture were

31 MacStiofain, p. 177. See *Parker Report* (Cmd. 4901) March 1972, p. 5. On the same page it claimed that the interrogator identified 700 IRA men.

32 *Low Intensity*, pp. 130 and 117.

33 *Gangs and Counter-Gangs*, pp. 126–7, *Low Intensity*, p. 199, *Bunch of Five*, pp. 32 (filing cabinet), 47 (changing prisoners' allegiance by use of stick, carrot and appeal to self-respect).

34 UI, 1.72.

35 *Gangs and Counter-Gangs*, pp. 59 (unco-operative prisoner), 126 (chains), and 132 (horseplay etc.). *Bunch of Five*, p. 290, *Low Intensity*, p. 142 (break down prisoner). See Peter Dowling's article on 'Pseudo Gangs', RN, 5.11.77. J. Wamweya, *Freedom Fighter*, Nairobi (East Africa Publishing House), 1971, pp. 185–6.

more useful in forcing confessions than obtaining information.[36]

Revolutionary propaganda lays considerable stress on torture which Hyams sees as standard practice for all counter-insurgents. Britain's 1978 condemnation by the European Court for inhuman and degrading treatment was a considerable victory for the Provisionals. Though they claimed that Clutterbuck on TV justified sensory deprivation,[37] in *Living with Terrorism*, despite emphasis on Pavlovian disorientation as more common than physical torture, he is at pains to insist that 'there is no real antidote to the loathesome techniques of modern interrogation – and they are equally loathesome which ever side uses them'.[38] Kitson's refusal to moralise in his books enabled republicans to invoke his name as a shorthand stereotype for cynical brutality. He became particularly useful, long after he had left Northern Ireland, in the period of Ulsterisation and prison protest.

The English debate Kitson

The publication of *Low Intensity Operations* in the months after internment began this process. The work caused a stir outside the ranks of Irish republicanism. Right-wing officers, lamenting the breakdown of authority in the permissive society, endorsed its views. It became the subject of correspondence in the London *Times*,[39] and a matter of concern to members of the Labour opposition in Westminster. It was a propagandist's godsend to Irish republicans, equivalent to Amritsar in 1919. But what exactly caused the furore?

From the British viewpoint the significance of *Low Intensity Operations* lay not in its scenarios for developing counter-gangs against colonial insurgents, but its implications for the metropolis itself. Kitson defined 'insurgency' not simply as illegal measures, short of violence, to overthrow those in government, but even 'to force them to do things which they do not want them to do'. This came perilously close to suggesting army intervention in politics. Moreover, Kitson included 'pressure, strikes, protest marches, and propaganda' amongst such subversive activities. He envisaged a situation in which a 'genuine and serious grievance arose, such as might result from a significant drop in the standard of living'. The police failing to keep order,

36 MacStiofain, p. 198.

37 RN. 19.1.74.

38 *Living with Terrorism*, pp. 68–70.

39 See Chris Walker, 'Senior Officers concerned about subversive faces', Times, 23.5.72, and letters (Patrick Wall, MP, and James Lindsay pro Kitson; Denis Christian and Brian Stevens worried 26.5.72. Kitson was also quoted in SP, 31.10.71. See also Bruce page and Lewis Chester, 'The Guns of the New Model Army', ST, 14.5.72. and James Kelly, *Genesis of Revolution*, Dublin, (Kelly Lane), 1976, pp. 26 and 35.

the army might have to restore it rapidly. 'The government should be in a position to keep the country running during a prolonged period of strikes and civil disturbance, and to this end either the police or the army should have men available who are capable of operating essential services such as power stations and sewerage systems with relatively little assistance from civilian experts'. Ironically, the Ulster Workers' Strike of 1974 demonstrated that the British Army did not have this capacity. In 1971 Kitson had warned that the Ulster Troubles proved that law and order could not be taken for granted even in the United Kingdom. 'It may be of interest to recall that when the regular army was first raised in the seventeenth century, 'Suppression of the Irish' was coupled with 'Defence of the Protestant Religion' as one of the two main reasons for its existence'.[40]

Such indiscretions were quickly seized on. In early 1972, when violence peaked in Northern Ireland, several Labour MPs, including Roy Hattersley, who as minister for defence had been involved in sending troops to Northern Ireland in August 1969, tabled parliamentary questions on Kitson's book. Kitson's views became particularly important after April 1972 when he left Ireland to become commandant of the school of infantry at Warminster. Were these views to be taught to young officers? Was *Low Intensity Operations* an official publication endorsed by the ministry of defence? The minister, Lord Balneil tried to defuse the situation by stating that the book contained Kitson's private opinions only. It was, however, admitted that he had been given permission to publish. Kitson was now 'a figure of cult hatred on the further left'. In 1974 Colonel George Wigg, another Labour MP, opposed Kitson's view, operational in Northern Ireland, that soldiers should do police work. Roy Hattersley totally disagreed with some of Kitson's conclusions. No Labour man could, in fact, do less. Hattersley insisted that political disputes must be decided by the elected government, not by soldiers.[41] Kitson touched on this issue in his 1971 analysis. He accepted that subversion in a good cause might sometimes be right; the soldier in a democratic country was dependent on electors whose representatives 'will only make war when it is right to do so'.[42] However, the thrust of Kitson's suggestion seemed most appropriate to a Conservative or right-wing government. Indeed, by admitting that the government cause might sometimes be wrong, he nearly insinuated that the soldiers should then take over.

Though Kitson's views were relevant in Britain where the Heath government soon fell after failing to resolve its dispute with the miners, they were even more applicable to Northern Ireland. The revealing reference to

40 *Low Intensity*, pp. 3, 25, 83. 24.
41 See *Times*, 10, 13, 23.6.72. and 8.7.72, and AP, 5.6.74. (Wigg).
42 *Low Intensity*, pp. 8–9.

Cromwell's New Model Army and the suppression of Irish Catholicism, as a prelude to establishing the only military dictatorship in English history, was not allowed to pass unchallenged.[43] It was superb propaganda for both the Provisionals and the Officials, not to mention other groups. Authorities as eminent as Edmund Burke, Karl Marx and Friedrich Engels had warned that England's destruction of liberty overseas would undermine her own freedom. The Officials' *United Irishman* was one of the first to emphasise the idea of Northern Ireland as a laboratory for 'the spillover of repression' into England. Kitson, it claimed, intended to deal with English strikes by rubber bullets and CS gas. As a result, he was the darling of the middle classes.[44] The Provisionals also raised this issue, warning of a 'national plan' for drawing the fangs of the British working class.[45] The socialist, Bob Purdie, writing for *Republican News*, declared Kitson 'the submerged iceberg of British politics'. Purdie attributed to Kitson not only the use of the army in place of police as a forthcoming threat to the British workers (thus agreeing with Wigg) but also an array of psychological and scientific techniques.[46] The message of warning to the British working classes was repeated in subsequent years; incidents such as police repression in Notting Hill (1976) and Lewisham (1977)[47] were cited as examples. The use of troops at London airport was also traced to the use of Northern Ireland for the people to accept army urban activity. The demand for the solidarity of the British working classes was well taken. Marx and Engels in the 19th century had continually emphasised the need for Irish self-government as a means to British emancipation. Marx's letter to Kugelmann, 29 November 1869, for example, not only insisted that the British workers take the initiative in dissolving the Union, but also warned that 'the English republic under Cromwell met shipwreck in – Ireland. Non bis in idem! (Not twice for the same thing!)'.[48] When Kitson was sent to command a BAOR division in Germany, a Provisional paper claimed that his system was being exported to EEC countries.[49] As if in reply, the *Constabulary Gazette: the Ulster Police Magazine* published an article in the *Daily Express* claiming that Northern Ireland was a world Marxist syndicate's 'laboratory for revolution'.[50]

43 Peter Dowling in RN, 20.12.75.
44 UI, 6.72., 5.73.
45 RN, 25.1.75.
46 RN, 20.9.75.
47 RN, 4.9.76. and AP, 24.8.77.
48 K. Marx and F. Engels, *Ireland and the Irish Question*, London (Lawrence & Wishart), 1978, pp. 394–5.
49 RN, 23.4.77.
50 CG, 5.72.

Kitson and Loyalism

Kitson's *Low Intensity Operations* infuriated republicans, but Paisley's *Protestant Telegraph* took a different line, complaining that officers like Kitson who had supported loyalist interests were soon recalled.[51] It thus agrees with opponents who argued that Kitson was in fact sacked when Whitelaw took over after the suspension of Stormont in March 1972.[52] The Kitson reference to the 17th century British Army and its initial task of suppressing Irish Catholicism was more than relevant in this connection. Christopher Hill emphasises the significance of 17th century Ireland in the Puritan hysteria against Antichrist.[53] Kitson was aware that 'certain sections of the Unionist majority are trying to prevent their own government from giving concessions to the Nationalist minority'.[54] However, his success in Kenya and other places was based to a large extent on liaison with the local settlers or loyalist population; the *Protestant Telegraph* was probably correct in asserting Kitson's loyalist sympathies. Republicans later argued that loyalist gangs in Northern Ireland had been sent by Kitson's agents. Whitelaw may well have felt that Kitson's continued presence after the publication of Low Intensity Operations would have been counter-productive, especially when he hoped to conciliate Catholics.

Sean MacStiofain claimed that Kitson's counter-insurgency techniques were actually stepped up after his departure.[55] The Kitson references in republican papers increased sharply between 1974 and 1977. The political situation required such propaganda. Sectarian assassination of Catholics and the use of undercover British agents were increasing but the threat to the Provisionals from a power-sharing SDLP and the emergence of the Peace People were potentially more threatening. The 'Kitson' issues can thus be grouped under the headings of British Army counter-insurgency, loyalist paramilitaries, SDLP on the power-sharing executive, Peace People, government control of the media, and the adoption of Kitson's method in the Irish Republic.

Kitson's theory – (1) Law as a weapon

A backdrop for all 'Kitsonism', and especially for the counter-insurgent British Army, was the treatment of law in *Low Intensity Operations.*

[51] PT, 21.6.75.

[52] J. McGuffin, *Internment*, Tralee (Anvil), 1973, p. 183, ft. 7 and P. Devlin, *The Fall of the N.I. Executive*, p. 119.

[53] C. Hill, *Antichrist in Seventeenth-Century England*, Cambridge UP, 1971 pp. 174 and 177.

[54] *Low Intensity*, p. 88.

[55] MacStiofain, p. 257.

According to Kitson, there were two alternative attitudes to law when dealing with subversion. First, it could be

> just another weapon in the government's arsenal, and in this case it becomes little more than a propaganda cover for the disposal of unwanted members of the public. For this to happen efficiently, the activities of the legal services have to be tied in with the war effort in as direct a way as possible which, in effect, means that the member of the government responsible for law either sits on the supreme council or takes orders from the head of the administration.

Second, law could remain impartial while the government introduced tough legislation, and the legal officers maintained the distinction between the government, the enemy, and the uncommitted. Kitson accepted the second alternative was morally right and expedient for retaining the allegiance of the population, but speed or obstacles to strong legislation might require option number one.[56]

Such a vague and ambiguous passage was manna from heaven to the republicans. As his other books show, Kitson criticised the delays of the Nairobi supreme court during the Mau Mau emergency, which sometimes released, on what seemed frivolous pretexts, guerrillas he had captured. Moreover, the Mau Mau committee members, who seem to have corresponded to overt Sinn Fein leaders, rarely did anything illegal.[57] The short, sharp proceedings of martial law were clearly more to his taste. Republicans, however, who stretch the meaning of admittedly chilling phrases like 'the disposal of unwanted members of the public' to cover wholesale assassination of opponents by plain clothes squads and torture of suspects, clearly exaggerate. Dillon and Lehane, in their *Political Murder in Northern Ireland* (1975) suggested that Kitson's book 'would seem to countenance under certain circumstances a campaign of assassination by the British Army undertaken by plain-clothes troops', but believe he would always insist on sanction at government level. To the fury of the Provisionals, they acquitted Kitson of demanding a wholesale campaign against the Catholic community and believed undercover assassination of Catholics by British Army units, as opposed to loyalist paramilitaries, infrequent. The issue re-emerged after 1982 with the controversial 'shoot to kill' policy. 'Supergrasses' were similarly linked with Kitson's alleged use of law as a weapon.[58]

[56] *Low Intensity*, p. 69.

[57] *Bunch of Five*, pp. 30–31; *Gangs and Counter-Gangs*, 44–5.

[58] M. Dillon and D. Lehane, *Political Murder in Northern Ireland*, Harmondsworth (Penguin), 1973, p. 314 and 318. AP, 15.2.74, regarded Dillon and Lehane as British propagandists, but RN, 24.11.73, and 2.11.74, found them useful, despite their criticism of PIRA, in demonstrating the extent of loyalist assassination. Michael Farrell, *Northern Ireland: the Orange State*, London (Pluto) 1980, p. 390, however, believes them 'sympathetic to loyalists'. Supergrasses, AP, 15.9.83.

(2) Pseudo-gangs in Ulster

Despite the undoubted exaggeration of propagandists, 'Operation Motorman', which ended the no-go areas in July 1972, did make it easier to operate the type of undercover squads which were the Northern Ireland equivalent of the pseudo-gangs simulating the Mau Mau. Mac Stiofain claims, however, that they were badly organised and that Kitson's weakness lay in defence. What if the guerrillas eliminated the special forces sent to eliminate them? MacStiofain ridicules the three-man Military Reconnaisance (or Reaction) Force Squads (MRF), who followed hit lists of Provisionals, posing with old Thompson guns as IRA, or, transparently, as hitch-hikers. Certainly, the Provisionals were able to claim propagandist successes, equivalent to those of Arthur Griffith in the Irish revolution 1919–21. The Four Square laundry service at Twinbrook, designed to obtain forensic evidence of gunshot stains on customers' clothes, and the Gemini Health Studio massage parlour on the Antrim Road were in 1972 put out of business by the Provisionals.[59] The latter were also delighted in 1977 when they caught and eliminated Captain Robert Nairac, an SAS officer posing as a republican sympathiser, complete with assumed Portadown accent, who had assassinated a leading Provisional in the Irish Republic.[60] The destruction of a helicopter by M-60 fire in 1978 allowed *An Phoblacht* to boast of the removal of another Kitson trained intelligence officer.[61] It was not so much the precise score of MRF and SAS success measured against that of the Provisionals, as the fact that the latter could exploit their efforts more effectively in propaganda. Another development, also attributed to Kitson, was the stakeout, resembling the Anglo-Indian tiger shoots under the Raj, when an SAS squad would lie in wait after locating an arms dump or other guerrilla resort. This rough and ready means of dealing with their opponents inevitably led to some mistakes, as in the case of the innocent John Boyle, killed by soldiers who were subsequently found not guilty of murder by Chief Justice Lord Lowry. The verdict, declared an *An Phoblacht* writer, was judicial endorsement of stakeouts which broke every rule of the 'yellow card' supposed to determine the behaviour of the army.[62] SAS assassination policy, it was declared on another occasion, came straight from Kitson's textbook.[63] On the other hand, when

59 MacStiofain, pp. 320, 317, 319–320. See also P. Dowling's article on Kitson. ''Special Operations' from Kiambu to Twinbrook', RN, 29.10.77. MacStiofain, believes the incident a demonstration of Kitson's weakness in defence.

60 RN, 21.5.77, AP, 18.5.77, and 29.6.77. (Little to fear from such a vain and arrogant agent). For Nairac's assassination of John Green, see Duncan Campbell, 'Victims of the 'dirty war'', *New Statesman*, 4.5.84.

61 AP, 8.2.78.

62 AP, 7 and 14.7.79.

63 AP. 17.6.78.

the Provisionals wanted to justify their own assassination of Judge Rory Conaghan and Magistrate Martin McBurney in 1974 they cited Kitson's perversion of law as a weapon in the struggle.[64] An attempt to assassinate Lowry himself failed in 1982.[65]

The Provisionals were not only concerned to expose the security forces. They had also to find an explanation for loyalist assassination of Catholics, especially after Motorman. Given the Provisional philosophy of British troops out before community reconciliation it was essential that they play down the possibility of a Protestant 'backlash' and a civil war after withdrawal. Usually a backlash was simply rejected as government propaganda; it was asserted that the Prot-stats had never previously fought except under British auspices, that the paramilitaries engaged only in assassination, without emulating the IRA in facing the British Army, and that Prot-stats had no stomach for any physical force. Sometimes, however, it was admitted that there might have to be some fighting after British withdrawal. Again, the helpful Kitson showed a way out of any apparent inconsistency. Developing his counter-gang theory, it was argued that the loyalist assassination squads were actually organised or inspired by the British Army. Thus the withdrawal of the latter would automatically end sectarian killing.[66] The mysterious UFF (Ulster Freedom Fighters) almost certainly a cover for the UDA, reluctant to admit illegality, might even mask British counter-insurgency.[67] Peter Dowling, the Kitson expert, writing in *Republican News*, classified the pseudo-gangs into three categories.[68] First, there were British units like the SAS which used various disguises but remained sections of the British Army. Second, came loyalist organisations such as the UVF, RHC, and Tara. These were generally independent, but their actions sometimes backfired on the British. Dowling referred to Kitson's book on Kenya, *Gangs and Counter-Gangs*, now much published, for authority. The independence of groups like the UDA, UVF, and RHC (Red Hand Commandos) was denied. Deliberate British strategy used them to terrorise the nationalist population into deserting the IRA, to divert IRA attention from British forces, to encourage the bloodbath theory, and to drive Catholics into larger and more easily controlled ghettoes.[69]

How much of this can be legitimately deduced from Kitson's *Gangs and*

64 RN, 21.9.74.

65 AP, 4.3.82.

66 See Gerry Adams interview with *Sunday World*, quoted by AP. 10.2.79. He admitted the backlash a real possibility but the superior thought and action of the Provos would deter loyalists experienced only in assassination. See also comments on failure of Paisley's 1977 strike. AP, 18.5.77. SP, 12.76: loyalist bluff never called.

67 AP, 15.2.74. RN, 18.6.77.

68 RN, 7.5.77.

69 RN, 3.4.77.

Counter-Gangs, on which Peter Dowling wrote a lengthy and relatively accurate article for *Republican News* in 1977?[70] On the general intimadation of the Catholic population, a remark attributed to Kitson in 1971 was quoted *ad nauseam*, 'I would squeeze the Catholic population until they vomit the gunmen out of their system'.[71] In *Low Intensity Operations* Kitson says more discreetly that 'conditions can be made reasonably uncomfortable for the population as a whole, in order to provide an incentive for a return to normal life and to act as a deterrent towards a resumption of the campaign'. Commenting on Mao's guerrilla fish swimming in the water of public support, Kitson ominously suggested that something might have to be done to the water.[72] Does this indeed imply that under a façade of minimum force, innocent Catholics would be gunned down by sectarian gangs? In *Gangs and Countergangs* there is nothing quite so sinister, basically because Kitson is dealing with Mau Mau groups in the forest, not urban guerrillas. The counter-gangs, which mixed loyal Kikuyu, Mau Mau turncoats, local white settlers, and expatriate British officers, when they contacted real gangs for information or destruction, do provide some justification for the apparently far-fetched propaganda of the Provisionals. The single man missions, which sometimes ended in the painful death of Kitson's accomplices, were more appropriate in Northern Ireland conditions. Nevertheless, the Provisional argument that loyalist violence was not *sui generis* had some plausibility, though difficult to attribute to Kitson.

(3) Exploiting moderates: SDLP and Peace People

In 1974 and 1977 the Provisionals faced constitutional threats from power-sharing and the Peace People. Kitson again provided a perfect propagandist answer to these advocates of constitutional reform and non-violence. *Low Intensity Operations*, in another well-quoted passage, outlined a strategy for exploiting the non-violent phase of subversion which precedes the outbreak of terrorism. Kitson believed that the movement was then at its most vulnerable. The simplest suppression was by 'naked force', but this was difficult for a British government. Instead, 'the judicious promise of concessions', while 'imposing a period of calm' and promising implementation of reform when normality was achieved, could separate leadership from rank and file. At such a time squeezing the potentially rebellious population becomes possible. The breathing space gained must be used to do

70 RN, 5.11.77.

71 RN, 12.7.75., 10.12.77.; AP, 25.1.77., 7.9.77., 2.11.77.

72 *Low Intensity*, pp. 87 and 49 (Mao's water), commented on by RN, 9.4.77.

> three further things quickly. The first is to implement the promised concessions so as to avoid allegations of bad faith which may enable the subversive leadership to regain control over certain sections of the people. The second is to discover and neutralise the genuine subversive element. The third is to associate as many prominent members of the populaton, especially those who have been engaged in non-violent action, with the government. This last technique is known in America as co-optation ... and is described by Messrs Hoch and Schoenback as drowning the revolution in baby's milk.[73]

Though not used against the SDLP till after the power-sharing attempt had broken down, it was easy to portray that party, via the Kitson quote, as a British stooge dishonestly accepting co-optation from the Westminster government. This must have been particularly galling for the SDLP as it attacked Kitson as vigorously as others for provoking sectarian violence and putting the boot into the Catholic population. Ironically, Paddy Devlin, then a SDLP leader, accused Kitson of being the IRA's 'most powerful recruiting agent'.[74] Similarly, the Peace People, almost immediately after their emergence in 1976, were portrayed as Kitson's stooges. Cartoons reinforced the verbal message.[75] As all nationalists abhorred Kitson, reply was difficult.

(4) Black propaganda

Another major propagandist use of Kitson covered the whole range of media control and 'black propaganda'. This was the most vital area of the war itself which the Provisionals had to win to stay in business. As usual there were quotes allegedly from *Low Intensity Operations*: the government 'must also promote its own cause and undermine that of the enemy by disseminating its view of the situation ... The countering of the enemy's propaganda and putting across of the government's point of view, can be achieved by direct action, as for example the provision of leaflets, or the setting up of an official wireless or television network, or by trying to inform and influence the existing news media ... The real difficulty lies in the political price a democratic country pays in order to influence the ways in which its people think'. Kitson did indeed recommend the training of officers in psychological operations and media persuasion, but republicans elaborated on the implicit threat to free speech. There were a number of complaints about slanted pro-government reporting in the English press and revealing films like 'A Sense of Loss' banned from television. Kitson's accomodating book helped to

73 *Low Intensity*, p. 87. Attacked RN, 28.9.74, 15.2.75, 20.9.75, 21.8.76

74 SDLPN, 5.10.73, and P. Devlin, *The Fall of the N.I. Executive*, pp. 121 and 123.

75 RN, 21.8.76. and 11.12.76.

provide a suitably conspirational perspective.[76]

There was, however, the more positive side of Kitson's influence. 'Black propaganda' was depicted as the attempt to destroy the republican credibility in its own community and abroad through the Thiepval Barracks 'lie machine',[77] and even concocting outrages to attribute to PIRA. How far was it actually used in the second Irish revolution? Full details will not be available for many years, if ever. Liz Curtis, however, provides a number of instances. A precedent from the 1919–21 period was the capture by the British of the *Irish Bulletin* and the dissemination of a false issue. It had been extremely effective for Griffith to attribute to 'black propaganda' some counter-productive Irish action, and this is an inevitable aspect of any war, formal or informal. In 1973 the *Andersonstown News* complained that the Sinn Fein fortnightly *Nation* had also been forged. *An Phoblacht* denounced Kitsonian influence when the UFF detonated a car bomb at Coalisland, apparently with the initial intention of blackening the reputation of the local Provisionals.[78] Kitson was also accused of originating his techniques of black propaganda in Kenya where he endeavoured to denigrate the African insurgents by mutilating beasts and like activities.[79] Needless to say, Kitson admits nothing so specific, yet there are interesting hints in *Gangs and Counter-Gangs*. The Mau Mau emergency certainly saw the extreme vilification of the Kikuyu, but Kitson's work is notable for its lack of emotion in this respect. He laughs at the obscene oaths that were imposed on new members of the 'Mau Mau', itself a term of contempt coined by its enemies. Nor does Kitson show any revulsion from leaders of the revolutionary movement. He had not compunction about using a witch doctor to discover, by some uncanny means, where a suspect had hidden money. 'The whole business was absolutely genuine'. On the other hand he considered that the Christian missionaries were 'discrediting the old without gaining acceptance for the new'. Most important of all, when participating in pseudo-gangs himself, Kitson admits to taking part in the administration of Mau Mau oaths and collecting money, ostensibly on their behalf.[80]

This admission is sufficient to give the Provisionals almost indefinite cover for black propagandist claims. When it is remembered how public revulsion

[76] *Low Intensity*, pp. 71 and 77, 'quoted' by RN, 19.3.77. and Peter Taylor, 'Reporting Northern Ireland', *The British Media and Ireland*, London (The Campaign for Free Speech in Ireland), [1979], p. 22. See also p. 18. There is a considerable discrepancy in the different versions. Liz Curtis, *Ireland: the Propaganda War*, London (Pluto), pp. 229–237, is useful on British policies.

[77] RN, 21.5.77.

[78] AP, 14.12.73. AN, 7.12.73.

[79] RN, 24.11.73.

[80] *Gangs and Counter-Gangs*, pp. 166–9, 14 and 150. *Bunch of Five*, pp. 42–3. Kitson kept guard while his African agents administered the oath.

for the primordial savagery of the Mau Mau oathing was disseminated to the world media during the Kenyan emergency, and that at least 222 Kikuyu were executed for administering illegal oaths, it is difficult to accept Kitson's off-hand announcement that 'sometimes our gang would have to administer the odd oath, or collect some money. Not to have done so would have seemed strange at the time'.[81] Irish republicans have always maintained, and Karl Marx fully agreed,[82] that the 1798 rising was deliberately provoked by the British government to justify the Union. The Presbyterian, William Orr, was not only hanged for administering the United Irish oath in 1797, but convicted on the unsupported word of an informer. 'The odd oath' in his case had grave consequences. Modern republicans, with their long tradition of denouncing 'perfidious Albion',[83] insisted that Kitson-inspired intelligence officers were guilty of every kind of misinformation and villainy. *Gangs and Counter-Gangs*, according to *An Phoblacht*, might provide the answer to the spate of inter-group killings, 'the result of diabolically clever action by enemy '*agents provocateurs*' on Kitson's pattern.[84] Certainly, much 'Kitson' propaganda was made by Provisionals, led by Sinn Fein president, Ruairi O Bradaigh, out of the 1975 splits between the Officials and the IRSP (Irish Republican Socialist Party) on one side, and the UDA and UVF on the other.[85] The Officials were also happy to attribute the IRSP to a Kitson plot.[86] The influence of this evil genius appeared so enormous that even great English universities, like Oxford, which gave him a defence fellowship, could be portrayed as the servants of counter-insurgency.[87] Though fully sustainable only by quotes out of context,[88] Kitson's malign potency in republican eyes mirrored those of the pope in Prot-stat demonology.[89]

The Irish Republic and Kitson

Not only did Kitson's influence extend to EEC countries but it incorporated the collaborationist government of the twenty-six counties. There army officers, said *An Phoblacht*, were trained according to a Kitson-style manual

[81] *Gangs and Counter-Gangs*, p. 118. For executions see Anthony Clayton, *Counter-Insurgence in Kenya, 1952–60*, Nairobi, (Transafrica Publishers), 1976, pp. 15 and 54.

[82] *Ireland and the Irish Question, p. 214.*

[83] See C(4, 4) 77; UDAN, 11.71; OUDAN (1, 12), 72; RN, 5.12.71, and 19.10.74.; PT, 12.6.71., LN, 2.8.75., etc.

[84] AP, 9.5.75.

[85] AP, 11.4.75, 2.5.75.

[86] UI, 5.75.

[87] RN, 17.5.75, 22.1.77.

[88] ST, 14.5.72. Bruce Page and Lewis Chester refer to Kitson's image as 'a systematic and callous anti-democrat'.

[89] PT, 27.5.67 on the pope's visitation of famine on India.

which taught anti-strike action. Justice Minister patrick Cooney was accused of using Kitson's 'law weapon' argument to justify the atrocious treatment of political prisoners in Port Laoghise gaol. When several escaped in 1976, it was revealed that they had been stripped, handcuffed over chairs, and had cigarettes stubbed on their skin. This was regarded as vintage Kitson. Kitson's influence over the Irish government was still claimed in 1984.[90] There appeared to be no object of Provisional invective unlinked with the bloodthirsty brigadier.

Clutterbuck and Marighela – Do guerrillas provoke reprisal?

The use of Kitson by the Provisionals was mildly paralleled by Dr (General) Richard Clutterbuck's use of the Brazilian urban guerrilla theorist, Carlos Marighela. The terrorist profile presented by Clutterbuck, and Kitson himself in parts of his books less emphasised by opponents, is clearly drawn. Though they pay lip-service to the possibility that subversives may sometimes be acting in a good cause, most government spokesmen are reluctant to accept this. They declare alleged grievances are either imaginary or easily reformed by constitutional means. Thus Kitson places much stress on the views of the American J. J. McCuen, who like the brigadier's foreword writer, General Robert Thompson, assumed that revolution starts from nothing.[91] Kitson discusses the 'foco' theory of Castro, Che Guevara and Debray which enables a revolution to begin without the preliminary organisation of the people considered necessary by authorities like Mao.[92] Marighela, killed in late 1969, after a brief career as a Brazilian guerrilla which began only in the previous year, became known in Britain in 1971 when his *Minimanual of an Urban Guerrilla* and *For the Liberation of Brazil* were translated. His significance lies in his transfer of small revolutionary 'focos', gathering support in the country, to the cities, and to the popularisation of the term 'urban guerrilla'. Most established Provisional IRA members have infinitely more practical experience than had Marighela. So far, only MacStiofain, in his underrated 1975 *Memoirs of a Revolutionary*, has produced (1975) a full-scale work of Provisional theory. As indicated earlier, he has much to say about Kitson, but nothing on Marighela; Clutterbuck reversed this emphasis. Both sides were avoiding awkward subjects.

[90] AP, 1.3.74., 12.1.84, RN, 27.3.76., 5.6.76.

[91] J. Kelly, *The Genesis of Revolution*, Dublin (Kelly Lane), 1976, pp. 112–114.

[92] *Low Intensity*, p. 33. For Provisional discussion of focos see RN, 4.9.77, (Debray's *Critique of Arms*) and AP 23.2.80. in 'O'Dowd, 'Cuba –'Tear away the mask'', which refers to Marighela.

Clutterbuck's account of Northern Irish insurgency before 1975, notwithstanding his post at Exeter University, is clearly a defence of the British army. He accepts that the 'Bloody Sunday' shootings of January 1972 were instigated by an IRA determined, despite the restraints of British soldiers, to keep tension high.[93] This contention is of course denied by MacStiofain who insists on the contrary that the Provisionals were ordered to stay away lest the British provoke them into a set battle where they would be destroyed.[94] These accounts are mirror-images in their patterned opposition. Clutterbuck's other arguments are in like vein. He laments Provisional dirty tricks, such as anonymous phone accusations to instigate rough handling of sick, disabled or bereaved innocents, and attacks behind protective walls of children. Nevertheless, he insists that PIRA members are basically stupid, just as MacStiofain ridicules the inefficiency of the British. Clutterbuck, moreover, shows some bias in playing down the loyalists while admitting the UDA as a 'mirror-image' of the IRA. Loyalist Tartan gangs are described with some sympathy, but their Catholic equivalents are 'hooligans'.[95]

The thrust of Clutterbuck's argument thus lies also in provocation. Bloody Sunday[96] is an excellent example. Here Marighela appears useful. According to Clutterbuck the basic terrorist strategy is openly admitted in his works. These are alleged to argue that the best way to ensure the people's support is to force the government to intensify repression: 'The police networks, house searches, arrests of innocent people and of suspects, closing off of streets, make life in the city unbearable. The military dictatorship embarks on massive political persecution. Political assassinations and police terror become routine'.[97] The middle class constitutionalists clamour for free elections, but the masses will see that these are useless and join the revolution.[98]

Clutterbuck considers Marighela, whose comments certainly read like a preview of many aspects of the Ulster conflict, quite specific: 'As soon as a reasonable section of the population begins to take seriously the action of the urban guerrilla his success is guaranteed'. In a more revealing passge, also underlined by Clutterbuck, Marighela states: 'The basic principle of revolutionary strategy in a context of permanent political crisis is to unleash,

93 *Protest*, p. 117.

94 MacStiofain, p. 226.

95 *Protest*, p. 98 (phone calls), 105 (stupidity), 127 (tartans).

96 For criticism of Clutterbuck on Bloody Sunday see AP 6.4.73. quoting G. Glennon in *Irish Press*, 6.3.73.

97 Quoted by *Protest*, p. 248.

98 For Marighela, *Minimanual of the Urban Guerrilla*, np, (Gramvats Publications), nd, p. (39). In a more revealing passage (p. 27) he explains how guerrillas can attack from a mass demonstration. Terrorism he regards (p. 33) as 'armed propaganda'. For *Minimanual* passage see also *Community Forum*, 2.73., p. 6, which quotes it in full. A similar argument appears in 'Handbook for the Urban Guerrilla', quoted in C. Marighela, *For the Liberation of Brazil*, pp. 94–5.

in urban and rural areas, a volume of revolutionary activity which will oblige the enemy to transform the country's political situation into a military one. Then discontent will spread to all social groups and the military will be held exclusively responsible for failures'.[99] Clutterbuck associates these tactics with the efforts of Grivas in Cyprus, in Robert Taber's phrase, 'to create 'the climate of collapse'.'[100] Thus Provisional bombing and other activities can all be seen as efforts to make life unbearable for the ordinary people, either directly or through anti-subversive repression. The ordinary people then vent their rage, not on the terrorists responsible. but on the established authorities.

This theory has often been applied by opponents of terrorism. Student rebels in the late 1960s were adept at provoking authorities into over-reaction and thus ensuring radical leadership of a formerly apathetic mass. It is a theory mirroring that of Provisional propagandists against Kitson.

Clutterbuck argues against allowing insurgency to spread from Northern Ireland, just as his opponents developed a fear of counter-insurgency being used against British workers. Both are zero-sum conspiratorial theories; both believe in attack as the best means of defence; both maintain that ordinary people are being terrorised by unscrupulous opponents; both insist that they themselves work for the good of the masses, not their exploitation for ulterior ends. Can we dissipate this fog of rationalisation, and penetrate the real moral issues dividing the two sides? The last section of this chapter examines republican and loyalist attitudes to their 'give-away' sources and then finally compares the resultant ethical arguments.

Marighela out of context?

In analysing Kitson, it was found that, though some of his arguments and revelations gave reasonable cover to the Provisional propagandists, they grossly exaggerated both his powers and his malignancy. Was this equally true of Clutterbuck's treatment of Marighela, Grivas and others? Marighela in context certainly argued very strongly against the interpretation that he wished to revolutionise the masses by deliberately making their lives unbearable. He repeatedly insisted that 'revolutionary terrorist acts and sabotage are not designed to kill members of the common people, or upset or intimidate them in any way'. Even the passage cited by Clutterbuck on the guerrilla's need to be taken seriously by the masses, was prefaced by declaring that guerrillas must win public support by identifying with popular causes. In a parallel passage, he says 'the stress the guerrilla lays on acting to help

99 Marighela, *For The Liberation*, p. 46. Clutterbuck, *Protest*, p. 219.
100 *The War of the Flea*, p. 31.

ordinary people is the best way of obtaining their support'.[101] This was very similar to the Provisional insistence that they always endeavoured to keep civilian casualties to a minimum by giving adequate warnings when bombs were detonated. What other guerrilla organisation in the world, they asked rhetorically, does that?[102] When eliminating the agents of the repressive government, and in Marighela's case, American imperialism, there was little difference in the ruthlessness prescribed. As for economic warfare, Provisionals would have agreed heartily, that 'the urban guerrilla is not afraid of dismantling and destroying the present economic, political and social system'. Marighela, moreover, had, like the Provisionals, broken with a Marxist non-violent party. He would also have appreciated the Provisional use of Kitson's remarks on making the legal system subservient to repression; that is precisely what he attributed to the repressive government in Brazil. His insistence on small urban 'focos', rather than regular formations with a clumsy chain of command is, probably coincidentally, close to the Provisional reorganisation of the late 1970s. Like Kitson and MacStiofain, Marighela emphasised the importance of good information sources, suggesting that insurgents, despite the need to retain everything in the head, would have an advantage here over government forces. MacStiofain and Marighela both underlined the importance of open media information,[103] which even Kitson did not disdain.

None of this constitutes an admission that the respective revolutionaries deliberately provoked reprisals against the civilian population. This complaint was insinuated by some clerical opponents of the Provisionals and the IRA of 1919–21. In Provisional literature Marighela was mentioned vaguely as a martyr without much attempt to analyse his ideas, but his *Minimanual* seems to have circulated in Northern Ireland.[104] The UDA's *Ulster Loyalist*, on the other hand, was delighted to adopt Clutterbuck's interpretation and to claim that the Provisionals were studying Marighela and Grivas. A higher civilian death rate, it argued, was part of Provisional strategy. Violence would create a clamour for repression which would bear most heavily on the Catholic ghettoes. There PIRA's intimidation would be forgotten when it gave protection against soldiers and police.[105] This exposition invited a reply from the Provisionals, especially as Marighela might have been quoted against loyalist assassination. PIRA preferred to distract by emphasising Kitson.

101 *For the Liberation*, pp. 112 and 94 and *Minimanual, Community Forum.*

102 RN, 9.6.73.

103 *For the Liberation*, pp 63 (economic warfare), 127 (break with Marxists), 105–6 (legal system), 77–8 and 115 (good information). MacStiofain, pp. 101–3.

104 AP, 2 and 23.2.80. Two Marighela passages are quoted in Provisional Sinn Fein's *Notes For Revolutionaries*, Dublin, 1982, pp. 24–5 and 35. These assert the priority of revolutionary action and the duty of revolutionaries to the revolution itself.

105 UL, 14.11.74.

Clutterbuck was certainly attacked in republican journals, but usually alongside Kitson.

Grivas and the IRA

Grivas, however, could be disposed of less easily. In 1974 there was speculation in Dublin's *This Week*, quoted by the *Protestant Telegraph*, that Grivas's EOKA was one of the chief sources of Provisional strategy. Contact between IRA and EOKA in the 1950s at Wakefield prison was emphasised. MacStiofain confirmed this in *An Phoblacht* and in his memoirs. He admitted discussing common ideas but did not develop the Grivas strategy.[106] *An Phoblacht* published an article which showed that EOKA was prepared to kill British civilians, bomb, and execute collaborators and informers. Its stablemate, *Republican News*, commenting on the Grivas *Memoirs*, declared that 'Grivas himself happens to be a rather unpleasant and arrogant old Fascist, however, it is instructive that the Brits have learned nothing'.[107] The Provisionals moreover reversed their opponents' argument by claiming that British squads had assassinated Turks and Cypriots to stir up inter-racial strife.[108] The Officials' *United Irishman* drew the anti-PIRA conclusion that in Cyprus as in Northern Ireland a 'kind of schizophrenia' operated; with both EOKA and the Provisionals, 'people knew that their policy was insane, but national hysteria made them tolerate it'. Ironically, Kitson himself would probably have disagreed with this verdict. He admired Grivas's courage and determination and was happy to salute him in Cyprus when the brigadier, then 'peace keeping', saw Grivas deliberately provoking the Turkish population.[109] Kitson and the Provisionals probably appreciated each other's strategy, but neither could afford to admit it. Sean Cronin, a former IRA chief of staff, is positive that Grivas's 'primitive warfare', also practised by Michael Collins, 1919–21, was the model for the early Provisionals.[110]

PIRA's debt to Taber

Provisionals were less reticent on Taber. The defector, Maria Maguire, claims that, not only were Cyprus and Aden direct models for the Provisionals but that Taber's *War of the Flea* (1969) was studied so closely that Ruairi O

106 PT, 24.8.74., 10.8.74.; UL, 22.3.75., MacStiofain, pp. 77–79. See also AP, 11.71.
107 AP, 12.4.74.; RN, 2.6.73.
108 AP, 9.72.
109 UI, 8.74. *Bunch of Five*, p. 263.
110 Cronin, *Irish Nationalism*, p. 208.

Bradaigh bought copies for the seven members of the PIRA army council.[111] In 1982 it was still on sale in republican shops. The book is particularly appropriate in that it not only analyses Grivas's ruthlessness but relates modern guerrilla techniques to the Irish revolution, which sought 'to create an intolerable situation for the occupying power or its government'. Taber does not quite state the political victory through reactive violence them with the candour of Marighela's two passages, but he describes very clearly how even militarily ineffectual actions by the IRA had powerful psychological results: 'Newspaper ink flowed more freely than blood'. The arrival of the Black and Tans was 'a godsend to the IRA'. Irish propagandists magnified each incident, the *Irish Bulletin* providing reports of ruthlessness with 'sufficient truth ... to make it credible'. This, applied equally to PIRA's use of Kitson and Arthur Griffith's use of Amritsar. Taber is similarly perceptive in his analysis of Grivas's *Memoirs*; in Cyprus the British were goaded into one counterproductive action after another. He does not play down the more controversial aspects of Grivas's ruthlessness, such as the use of school-children as young as ten, for which the Provisionals have also been attacked. But Taber is sympathetic to revolution and insists that it can never be defeated while grievances and guerrillas remain. Grivas didn't simply blackmail the British out. As in Ireland, 'EOKA was an expression of the popoular will, and, this being so, the British could have remained only by making war on the entire population'.[112]

This represents the real difference between Taber and writers like Clutterbuck. They may agree that revolutionaries use ruthless means to win the support of their communities and destroy the morale of the occupying power but they part company on whether grievances are real or artificially created. Hence the Provisionals openly praised Taber's *War of the Flea* as an 'excellent' work and related it to their guerrilla war. They fully endorsed his opinion that extermination was the only answer to insurgents who refused to surrender. Taber helped to educate at least one hunger-striker of 1981. Ironically, Taber was also praised by the *Protestant Telegraph* which used his classification of revolution to summarise Northern Irish events since 1969, but regarded him as a weapon to castigate the weakness of the british government, apparently retreating from terrorism without a fight.[113] At any rate at all – Kitson, Marighela, Clutterbuck, Paisley, O Bradaigh, and MacStiofain – could agree with Taber that guerrilla or revolutionary war 'is the extension of politics by means of armed conflict'.[114]

[111] M. McGuire, *To Take Arms: A Year in the Provisionals*, London (Macmillan), 1973, p. 74. For PIRA papers on Taber see *Tatler*, 4 1971, *Volunteer*, 50 and 59 1972.

[112] Taber, p. 91. (intolerable situation), 95(newspaper ink), 96 (Black and Tans), 107 (Grivas and children), 151 (war on whole population).

[113] Thomas Nelis, RN, 13.7.74., 8.1.77., AP, 19.9.81., PT, 7.2.76.

[114] Taber, p. 26.

Loyalists and the propaganda of violence

So far this chapter has focused mainly on the mutually antagonistic attempts at self-justification by the Provisionals and the British Army. The loyalist paramilitaries were delighted to adopt British Army arguments against the Provisionals, while the latter endeavoured to make loyalist violence appear the result of Kitsonian provocation. But how did the loyalists justify their own actions? There was the usual inconsistency and division. Paisley, for example, approved of Kitson and regarded SAS stakeout killings as 'summary execution'. The assassination of the Provisional Sinn Fein president, Maire Drumm, was 'extermination', according to a letter published in the *Protestant Telegraph*. An article in the paper accused the dead woman of never risking her neck but stirring up trouble with fiery speeches.[115] Similar criticism was applied to Paisley himself. Despite extremely divisive rhetoric, which hinted at ruthless measures against the Catholic population in association with the Third Force and the earlier UPV (Ulster Protestant Volunteers), and contacts with paramilitary leaders, nothing specifically illegal could be proved against him. On the contrary, it was insisted in the *Protestant Telegraph* that 'it is not part of the Protestant ethic or resistance mentality to engage in a murder campaign'.[116] Though Roman Catholics were likely to commit genocide, Dr Paisley declared, 'Let Protestants not imitate Rome'. Killing Roman Catholics and burning their churches 'reduces Protestantism to the level of the Roman Church which the Bible states is drunk with the martyr's blood'.[117] Such a passage, ostensibly deprecating violence while simultaneously encouraging hatred, is typical of Paisley's rhetorical strategy. He could protect himself by claiming that it was their duty to evangelise not terrorise 'our Roman Catholic fellow countrymen'. Even John Knox himself had found it difficult to rein misguided Protestants of the 'rascal multitude'. In practice, however, the genocidal propensities of Roman Catholics impressed Prot-stats more than their convertability to Free Presbyterianism. By maintaining his balancing act between verbal violence and incitement to action, Paisley evaded responsibility for the physical force which he always disavowed. His threats of independent action were designed to goad the security forces into more aggressive action rather than to take it himself. This was a variant of provocation akin to that attributed to his opponents. Yet Paisley's endorsement of the most ruthless action by the security forces was conditional. When counter-subversion was exercised on loyalists, Paisley reacted as vigorously as any Provisional.

115 PT, 11.3.78., 13.11.76.
116 PT, 6.1.73.
117 PT, 15.9.73.

Prot-stats' indiscretions

The Protestant paramilitaries grew dissatisfied with Paisley. Unlike him, they needed to justify their undoubted violence. Like the republicans, they argued that it was minimal and defensive. The UDA may have used the UFF as a cover to evade the issue: its paper published a letter from a Long Kesh prisoner insisting that the UFF was a Provisional organisation.[118] This was scarcely convincing propaganda. The UDA and UVF followed the Provisionals and emphatically denied making war on civilians. They rejected, however, each other's human claims. Similarly, the Officials insisted that Provisionals attacked Protestant workers, not military targets. The UVF denounced 'the 'romper room' where men, women and innocent teenagers have been brutalised and murdred in filthy secret UDA courts'. The UDA dismissed the UVF as delinquents who 'spent all night long polishing their leather jackets, and robbing milkmen, old-aged pensioners and kiddies' piggy-banks',[119] often in aliance with the Official IRA. Neither Prot-stat paramilitary was as sophisticated in its defence of violence as the Provisionals. Presenting a petition against the power-sharing executive, the *Ulster Loyalist* roared; 'WHY THE HELL SHOULD WE WORRY WHETHER WE ARE ACCUSED OF INTIMIDATION OR NOT'.[120] In May 1974 when the UVF blew thirty Dubliners into eternity, Sammy Smyth, the UDA spokesman, gloated on television that he was 'very happy about the bombings in Dublin'. Two years later he gave the most ferocious interview of the period to *Gown*. Legitimate targets, he said, were 'people who act against the state or give passive or active support to those who do'. As for innocent Catholics, 'war exists in Northern Ireland and in a war situation there are no innocent people'. No prisoners would be taken in the almost inevitable civil war. 'There will be no room for R.C.s in a new state'.[121] Paisley agreed that no neutrality was possible.[122] As late as 1981, the UDA Commander, Andy Tyrie, admitted that his organisation had originally killed Roman Catholics indiscriminately, believing them all to be Provisionals.[123] As for the UVF, 'We are not particularly concerned whether world opinion is on our side or not. We are not particularly concerned about the effects of the war effort on the economy – we would rather be paupers and free than rich men in chains'.[124] There was

118 UL, 21.3.74.
119 UDAN (1, 29) 72., C, 6.75., UI, 10.71., UL, 22.3.75.
120 UL, 31.1.74. For loyalist paramilitary rivalries, see S. Nelson, *Ulster's Uncertain Defenders*, Belfast (Appletree), 1984, p. 190, etc.
121 R. Fisk, p. 233. SP, 4/76. For *Gown* see RN, 14.2.76.
122 PT, 18.9.76.
123 AP, 6.6.81. quotes *Washington Star* interview with Mary McGory.
124 C, 10.75.

no need to seek indirect revelations from Brazil to demonstrate how loyalist paramilitaries treated the community.

The UVF, to a greater extent than the initially more reticent UDA, did sometimes try to justify itself. It presented at times an image of regular warfare, reminiscent of Pearse and the insurgents of 1916 on the republican side. Car bombs, booby traps and executions were out. UVF rifle platoons would decide the day. *Combat* was scandalised at the idea of killing teenage girls. 'No Protestant worthy of his high calling as a Soldier of the Faith would justify the slaughtering of an innocent girl and no Papist worthy of his Faith could justify a similar act of treason against God'. This was considerably more ecumenical than Paisley. *Combat*, however, agreed with the latter that the tactics of the enemy were not to be copied and that Protestant tradition from Calvin to William of Orange required ruthlessness against the enemy, but 'the greatest charity and compassion' towards non-combatants. Resistance was legitimate, retaliation (as the pope had said at Drogheda in 1977) unacceptable. But what were legitimate targets? Killing a young Queen's University student, Michael Adamson, for IRSP membership, was justified by the ICA's excecution of Che Guevara, a hero to Provisionals and some loyalists. Besides, Adamson was an atheist, so the assassination was clearly non-sectarian. Nor was there anything wrong in bombing pubs frequented by the IRA. Innocent people should stay away. Furthermore, civilians inevitably suffered from aerial bombardment in war.[125] This argument, popular with Provisionals, was extended shortly afterwards when the UVF had to justify killing members of the Miami Showband, claiming at least two as Provisionals. The thrust of the previous argument on the humane Protestant tradition of warfare was blunted by the unconscious quotation from James Connolly that 'there is no such thing as humane or civilised war ... Now I ask you, what is the difference between the UVF volunteer's bullet and the British soldier's bullet, what is the difference between a UVF man shooting a traitor or gunman and the executioner at Crumlin Road Goal hanging his victim by the neck until dead?' More generally, 'what, may I ask, is the difference between the bombing of a public house in Belfast and the blockbusting pattern-bombing of German and British cities during the last war?'[126]

Kitson's cynicism

Some loyalists had thus arrived at the same position as the British Army and the Provisionals. Was there any means of distinguishing between the moral

[125] C, (1,33) 74 and 7,75.
[126] C, 9.75.

arguments? Kitson is illuminating here. In the introduction to *Gangs and Counter-Gangs*, Kitson's commander in Kenya, General George Erskine, explicitly denied that rules were suspended to accomodate the special operations described. Only in the forest could the security fores 'act in unrestricted manner'. This proviso, instead of closing, opens up the whole debate. Are there in fact areas where normal laws and morality do not apply? Do the Ten Commandments lose validity in forests south of Suez and building sites west of the Lagan? In the book itself, Kitson admits that some people (he does not mention himself) took the law into their own hands. His comment could hardly be more ambiguous. 'Looking back, I am sure that this was wrong. Certainly this sort of conduct saved countless loyalist lives and shortened the Emergency'. Nevertheless, such conduct was frowned upon and rare. Britain's good name was lost for 'a few thousand Africans and a few million pounds of taxpayers' money'. Kitson's attitude mirrored that of his Mau Mau opponents. Moreover, his identification with opponents emerges in the comment on Mau Mau who 'thought it would be fun to be a gangster and carry a pistol and kill their acquaintances. Their outlook was not far from many young men of spirit anywhere else in the world'. Opponents, perhaps sharing the same 'spirit', have not quoted this give-away passage. Kitson admitted disappointment when his most resourceful enemies were killed. He conceded himself beaten in argument by a young guerrila, *en route* for the gallows. Accused of murdering white boys, the Mau Mau retorted that the youth of armed Kikuyu would not have secured mercy from the British Army. According to Kiston, 'I had already decided in my own mind that it was rebellion which was wrong. It is no use trying to be critical of the individual incidents which civil war brings in its wake. What is murder from one point of view may be unavoidable unpleasantness from another and even a triumph from a third'. This is the crux. In his subsequent *Bunch of Five* Kitson himself adopts the classic justification of the Provisionals, the UVF, and many other revolutionary organisations. From his Cyprus experience he admits that guerrillas must use any means available, even assassination. This, the future commander of British land forces declares, is more selective than the saturation and nuclear bombing of World War II; the assassin moreover runs more risk.[127]

[127] *Gangs and Counter-Gangs*, pp. 46 (law in own hands), 179 (thinking like Mau Mau), 126 (fun to be gangster), 287 and 72 (disappointment), 174 (worsted in argument); Bunch of Five, p. 236. RN, 25.1.75. quoted Frederic Raphael, reviewing E. Hyams' *Terrorists and Terrorism*, London (Dent) 1975, in the *Observer* (19.1.75.) that terrorists are feared because of their courage.

Republican moralism

The surprising conclusion that the Provisionals' worst enemy provided a final accolade for their actions is unavoidable. Kitson punctured the Marighela bogey raised by Clutterbuck. Why did the Provisionals fail to quote this passage with glee? Because, unlike Kitson, they could not afford to regard their operations as a 'game', though Dervla Murphy has emphasised their popular song by Dominic Behan, 'The Patriot Game'.[128] They had to appeal always to the highest standards of morality. The contention that 'terrorists, like great powers, fight dirty' was inadmissible. Provisionals needed to use Kitson against the Catholic church, and indeed asked the bishops why they did not condemn his views instead of Provisional actions.[129] Kitson had to be totally blackened to provide suitable propaganda. He assisted by asserting that the decline in official religion had disintegrated moral standards. The individual soldier could therefore be guided only by legality or expediency.[130] When Kitson conceded that insurgency may sometimes be justifiable, the moral problem dissolved into a matter of individual conscience, in which revolutionary and government agent start at par. Who then has the right to cast the first moral stone?

Here Marighela suggests that the urban guerrilla has 'one enormous advantage' over conventional soldiers and police. 'He is defending a just cause, the cause of the people – whereas they are on the side of an enemy the people hate'.[131] This is to turn Clutterbuck's argument on his head. Northern Ireland differs in many ways from South American dictatorships like Brazil. Nevertheless, there is a common factor, fully recognised by Marighela – nationalism. Provisionals possessed separate schools, logically opposed by Clutterbuck,[132] to instill the nationalist tradition into the Catholic community. They were not left stranded in the wilderness of Columbia, like the left-wing 'focos' of their inspiration, Che Guevara, a hero even to some UDA men.[133] The notion that the Provisionals are simply a small 'murder gang' provoking an otherwise contented population in West Belfast, the Derry Bogside and the rural areas west of the Bann collapses on analysis. The people there are not, like Kitson, playing a 'game'. He has nothing in fact to offer

[128] *Low Intensity*, p. 131. D. Murphy, *A Place Apart*, Harmondsworth (Penguin), 1980, p. 190. RN, 4.6.77. quotes 'game'. Rona Fields, *Society under Siege: A Psychology of Northern Ireland*, Philadelphia (Temple), 1977, p. 27, argues that Dominic Behan's poem is lived, not sung, by the children of Belfast and Derry.

[129] AP, 12.4.77 and RN, 2.11.74.

[130] *Bunch of Five*, p. 302.

[131] Marighela, *For the Liberation*, p. 64.

[132] *Protest*, p. 50.

[133] RN, 24.8.75. (UDA man with Che on cage locker), 6.3.74. (linked with Pearse, etc.), 8.10.77. (Juan Sosa's article uses him to justify violence), 15.10.77.; UI 9.71.; AP, 5.7.74.

them, having himself rejected both moral and religious principles. Kitson appears to be a victim of what Taber has called the 'methods fallacy' of the American Army: 'the old-fashioned notion that guerrilla warfare is largely a matter of tactics and techniques, to be adopted by almost anyone who may have need of them, in almost any irregular warfare situation.[134]

To sum up, we have seen how the British Army and the Provisionals did indeed confront each other with mirror-image attitudes. Both were less than candid in their propaganda but agreed to a surprising extent. Both glossed over the delicate question of their own provocation and in their polemic tried to concentrate all attention on the foe's misdeeds, seen in both cases as a conspiracy likely to spread from Northern Ireland to England. The indiscretions of General Kitson's works gave the Provisionals a distinct advantage in the propagandist war, an advantage which could hardly be neutralised by raising the distant and less convincing spectre of the late Carlos Marighela. The latter was cited as late as 1984 by Sir John Biggs Davidson, Conservative spokesman on Northern Ireland, to justify an RUC rubber bullet killing.[135] Kitson's phrases were similarly twisted out of context, but he contributed sufficient revealing give-away passages to render even far-fetched assertions credible. The loyalists were no help to the British in view of their confusion over counter-insurgency, welcomed against the Provisionals but totally repudiated when 'Perfidious Albion' turned it on them. Other loyalist arguments tended to be clumsy versions of Provisional propaganda with too many 'give-away' lapses. In the morality debate, Provisional propagandists have, surprisingly, more than held their own, mainly because of the weakness and errors of the opposition. The Provisionals are a goal ahead in the great 'game' of psychological warfare.

[134] Taber, p. 20.

[135] For John Biggs Davidson, see interview with Janet Cohen on BBC Radio 4 World Tonight, 13 August 1984.

MILITARISING A SOCIETY: THE ULSTER VOLUNTEER FORCE, 1913–1914

JOSEPHINE HOWIE

This essay is partly based on a paper given to Brian Bond's Military history seminar at the Institute of Historical Research, London University.

The research carried out in Belfast, Dublin, Oxford, Edinburgh and London was financed by the Central Research Fund, University of London, to whom grateful acknowledgement is made.

Political Background

The second General Election of 1970 returned a minority Liberal government to office, dependant on support in Parliament from the Irish Nationalist Party under the leadership of John Redmons; in the following year the Parliament Act limited the powers of delay of the House of Lords, thus removing the last constitution/al barrier to the government's declared policy of Home Rule for Ireland. Faced with this situation the northern province of Ulster embarked upon a policy of resistance. This paper will attempt to trace the stages by which this resistance, originally political, developed a military wing, the Ulster Volunteer Force: how it was financed, armed and organised; and how its policies and strategic plans ensured that, from 24 July 1914, the Nine Counties could consider themselves reasonably safe from rule by Dublin.

On 9 April 1912 a huge demonstration was held in the Balmoral district of Belfast in protest against Home Rule, the 3rd Bill being introduced in the House of Commons two days later. A Liberal Amendment to exclude the four almost wholly Protestant Ulster counties (Antrim, Down, Londonderry and Armagh) was defeated on 18 June. On 28 September (later to be known as 'Ulster Day') a Solemn Leage and Covenant to defend ' ... our cherished position of equal citizenship in the United Kingdom ... using all means which may be found necessary to defeat the present conspiracy to set up a Home Rule Parliament in Ireland ... ' was signed in Ulster by several thousand people. On 1 January 1913 Sir Edward Carson's Amendment to exclude Ulster was defeated. On 16 january the Bill passed in the Commons but was defeated (predictably) by the Conservative-Unionist majority in the Lords on 30 January. The Ulster Volunteer Force was formally established the following day. The Bill again passed the Commons on 7 July, to be defeated again in the Lords on 15 July. Plans for a Provisional government for Ulster were made public on 23 September. During October, November and December talks which attempted some compromise took place between members of the government, the Conservative opposition and Irish Nationalist leaders and members of the Ulster unionist Parliamentary Party. In the course of these Carson, the latter's leader, privately let it be known that the might consider the exclusion of only 6 of the 9 counties; which meant that Cavan, Monaghan and Tyrone would have to be abandoned to Home Rule as the price of agreement. A British Covenant was launched on 4 March 1914. Asquith, the Prime Minister, made what he regarded as his government's final offer on 9 March: exclusion on a temporary basis. This was rejected by Carson. The 3rd reading of the Bill passed the Commons on 25 May, followed by a Lords Amendment to exclude the whole of Ulster permanently, which was passed on 8 July. The Buckingham Palace all-party Conference, the King's last-minute initiative to achieve a political settlement and avoid what seemed to be the certainty of civil war, took place from 21 to 24 July. It proved abortive.

Origins and Organisation of the U.V.F.

A contingent of men from Co.Tyrone stood out for their smartness and military bearing from among the thousands of Ulstermen who paraded in Captain James Craig's grounds in September 1911; they had, on their own initiative, been drilling. Soon afterwards most of the Lodges of the Orange Order began to follow their example and on 5 January 1912 Colonel R. Wallace, who had previously commanded the 5th Royal Rifles in the South African war, and who was then Secretary of the Grand Orange Lodge of Ulster, enabled legal drilling to be organised by fulfilling the requirement of obtaining the permission of two magistrates for the area under their jurisdiction; other Lodges rapidly following this example. [1] In December 1912 the Ulster Unionist Standing Committee decided to combine these units into a single body to be known as the Ulster Volunteer Force which would be organised and administered by individual Unionist County Committees. Antrim, Armagh, Cavan, Down, Tyrone, Monaghan and Fermanagh supplied their lists of County and Divisional representatives, together with Secretaries, during that month, such speed suggesting organisations which had been formed a good deal earlier. North Derry supplied its list on 24 April 1913, followed by Belfast North in May and South Belfast in June. The lists of occupations and adresses suggest largely upper and middle class membership: in Antrim, for example, the list included 5 'Gentlemen', 3

[1] A.T.Q. Stewart: *The Ulster Crisis*, page 71

'Managing Directors', 4 'merchants', 2 'landagents', a 'landowner', a 'manufacturer', a doctor, a Justice of the Peace and a retired General.[2] This decision to form the U.V.F. was publicly announced at the annual U.U.C. meeting in January 1913 when it was also stated that recruitment would be limited to those men who had signed the Covenant (approximately 100,000) and were aged between 17 and 65. According to Captain Wilfred Spender, who had retired from an army Staff appointment to serve as A.Q.M.G. with the U.V.F., Carson realised that unorganised resistance would not only be ineffective, but would almost certainly lead to riots and disturbances which might cause grave loss of life and indiscriminate massacres. [33] Craig seems to have agreed, and in March he and his wife had a meeting with Field-Marshal the Earl Roberts of Kandahar who had already given his advice on how best to turn a locally-based protest movement into a trained and disciplined army under centralised control.[4] On 4 June Roberts wrote to Colonel T.E. Hickman, M.P. for South Wolverhampton and a member of the Executive of Lord Willoughby de Broke's British League for the Support of Ulster, that he had obtained the services of Lieutenant Sir George Richardson, K.C.B., to command the U.V.F.,[5] the appointment being announced on 18 September. Colonel Hackett-Pain was at the same time appointed Chief of Staff.[6]

The U.U.C. held a meeting on 24 September at the Old Town Hall, Belfast (the U.V.F. Headquarters) for the purpose of setting up a Provisional government for Ulster in the event of 'Home Rule' becoming law. The Council delegated its powers to the Provisional government of 77 members, with Carson as Chairman. In addition a number of committees were established, their titles and functions suggesting that Ulster had now been put on a war footing, most of the Province's activities being subordinated to military objectives. The chief of these, the Military Council, consisting of Carson, Richardson and Hackett-Pain, was to determine military policy. The Ulster Volunteer Committee with 39 members including Carson as Chairman, Craig and 16 other M.P.'s, the Mayor of Belfast R.McMordie J.P., M.P.; and the U.V.F.'s senior officers – Richardson (G.O.C.) and Spender – were to execute the Military Council's policies. For this purpose it was sub-divided into the following Boards:

a. The Volunteer Advisory Board, to deal with such questions as might be referred to it by the Military Council concerning the U.V.F. Its members included Carson, Craig, Hackett-Pain, Richardson, Captain Frank Hall

2 1327/4/18
3 Sir Wilfred Spender: *Unionist*
4 D1415/B/38 (Lady Craigavon's Diary)
5 Roberts 7101/23
6 D1415/B/38

(Military Secretary), Lieutenant-Colonel T.V.P. McCammon (i/c Administration), Colonel Wallace, Colonel Sharman Crawford and officers currently commanding U.V.F. divisions and regiments.
b. The Personnel Board, responsible for keeping in contact with those in Ireland and elsewhere who were sympathetic to Ulster's military preparations; and for investigating anyone whose qualifications might be useful to the U.V.F.
c. The Finance Board, to produce estimates of military expenditure, supervise monies allocated for military purposes and audit U.V.F. accounts and contracts.
d. The Railway Board, to make recommendations to H.Q. regarding railway policy.
e. The Transport Board, with the responsibility of registering all steam, horse and motor transport, and all horses suitable for military purposes.
f. The Supply Board, which was to collect information regarding supplies of food, forage, implements and accessories, and to advise on supplies for military uses.
g. The Medical Board, to obtain information on existing medical resources, and to advise on military medical questions.

In addition to these, an Intelligence Board was arranged, but no information on it appears in the minutes of this meeting. Five other Committees were set up: Finance and Business; Legal; Education, Publications and Literary; and Customs, Excise and Post Office. The purpose of these was to organise civilian passive resistance, such as the witholding of taxes, and to produce alternatives to the British government's functions in these areas. Carson's name headed the lists of all Boards and Committees, but ill-health and heavy Parliamentary duties meant that his control in many instances was only nominal.[7]

One of Richardson's first actions was to replace the county organisation of 'sub-divisions' and 'districts'[8] with a more complex structure Regimental and Battalion Commanders were to be responsible for discipline, efficiency, the engagement of paid instructors, the awarding of proficiency certificates in musketry and drill, and the canvas Battalion Armlet (an important status symbol) which they were empowered to withold at their discretion. Battalion Commanders also had the responsibility of appointing their own officers, or of confirming in their rank those who were chosen by election. The order of seniority of officers was decided either by agreement or by ballot. Their names had to be submitted via Regimental Commanders to H.Q. for approval before inclusion in the Volunteer Army List. Military intelligence was to be obtained

7 D1327/3/21
8 CAB/37/116 October 1913

from each Regiment's locality, and Battalions had to organise their own corps of signallers and bicycle and horse riders for local communications. Those functions more suited to civilians were to be carried out by members of the County Committees. Co.Down's Regimental files give detailed information as to how Richardson's reorganisation was applied in that area. On 10 November 1913 the Down County Committee consisted of five Representatives, sixteen 'other members', and five battalion Commanders co-opted as ex-officio members. At the same time the military units were composed of the North Down Regiment of two battalions, the South Down Regiment of four battalions, the East Down with three battalions and the West Down with two battalions.[9] By March 1914 Down was recruited some 10,330 men. (10) The Down battalions were divided into companies, each having a commander and two sub-commanders as officers, four N.C.O.'s as section leaders and approximately 100 men including squad leaders. It was considered to be of great importance that the organisation should be as localised as possible so that the men would not have to travel long distances for training; moreover a territorial base helped cohesion.

The County Committees had to deal with finance, documentation and the distribution of the canvas arm band. Where there was not already an organised Battalion they had power to withold its issue. Divisional, regimental and battalion commanders were nominated by them but had to be approved by the G.O.C. so as to ensure centralised control. The County Committees appointed and paid their own Secretaries and instructors. The organisation of transport and the requisition of food and other essential supplies was to be carried out on a county basis if mobilisation was ordered, the Committee being responsible for arranging payment.

In collaboration with the military wing an intelligence appraisal had to be made of the strength of the Nationalist inhabitants, the amount of force required to meet 'a possible eruption' in the border areas, and an estimate of the amount of outside help which might be required. In addition, mounted sections were to be organised, together with a Cadet Bicycle Corps (for boys under seventeen) and local Transport and Supply Corps.[11]

There were variations in this basic scheme in accordance with local conditions. In County Antrim, for example, General Sir William Adair, the Officer Commanding, sent an order dated 21 October that each C.O. must endeavour to make his own district financially self-supporting (Antrim's Regimental files suggest it was chronically short of funds); as to intelligence, a survey was to be undertaken of the coast and Coastguard Stations, and information was to be undertaken of the coast and Coastguard Stations, and

9 D1327/4/15
10 CAB/37/119 March 1913
11 D1238/120/124

information was to be sought as to those places where it would be possible to land troops and police.[12]

In Belfast there were four regiments divided into twenty battalions of unequal size, totalling about 25,000 men. In january 1914 it was decided to raise from these a 'Special Service Force' of about 3,000 men, each Battalion supplying about 150 Volunteers, of whom the largest proportion were to be ex-Regulars, Special reservists or Militia. This 'spearhead' force was designed to be mobile at all times, so that it could go rapidly to the assistance of any County area in peril without having to deplete the scattered/local country forces. The members of this Force were required to serve anywhere and under any officers appointed by H.Q. They were to be well armed and equipped and, when called out, were to be paid £I.00 per week (equal to about £11.00 today) in addition to their 'rations'; they were expected, however, to supply their own clothing and boots.[13]

By 2 january 1914 a Despatch Service had been organised by H.Q. to cover almost the whole of Ulster, with a network of post-houses, usually run by women who received, decoded, encoded and arranged for messages to be sent. The Playfair code was used and the keywords were frequently changed. This system was arranged because of the intention in the event of war to immobilise official communications, and also because the government postal, telephone and telegraph services employed a large proportion of Roman catholics (reflecting the government policy of non-discrimination in employment) and so were not considered secure. At that time it was widely believed in Ulster that mail was opened and telephones 'tapped', so it was common practice to send even overseas mail by hand.[14]

The U.V.F. Motor Corps was described in an intelligence report from the Irish Command sent to General Sir Neville Macready at the War Office on 21 January 1914 as well-organised. Cars were provided voluntarily by U.V.F. members and their supporters. It now had twenty Companies, each consisting of twenty four four-seater cars for transporting other ranks; four two-seater cars for officers; and six motor cycles. The Companies were divided into three sections of eight cars so that each one could carry four officers and 100 men. However, the U.V.F. had only a small number of cavalry: County Derry a Troop, and Fermanagh a force of two hundred of whom all but six men belonged to the North Irish Horse.[15]

On 16 May 1914 an order was sent to Regiments from H.Q. requiring where possible the organisation of local formations of cyclists, so that ' ... in the event of military operations being undertaken a body of cyclists would be

12 D1238/121
13 D1327/3/21
14 D1238/27
15 Mottistone 22/176

invaluable, pushed ahead of marching columns they would free a large number of mounted men, they could be moved quickly forward to hold selected points, keep up road communications as orderlies, and be used in many useful ways ... ' Volunteers were to provide their own machines.[16]

By March 1914 the Province's medical arrangements were near completion. A first aid and ambulance service was organised throughout Ulster, with field and base hospitals. Most of the large country houses participated, providing a specified number of beds per house. Large supplies of medical materials were stockpiled.[17]

Towards the end of June 1914 the threat presented by growing numbers joining the Irish Volunteers – the rival paramilitary force formed to support Home Rule – was being taken very seriously, and special plans were formulated. It was proposed to begin recruiting again in order to form 'battalions de marche' for service outside their own areas, wherever the opposing force was estimated to be superior. Local commanders were asked for their opinions of the proposal, and the reply of Captain the Honourable arthur O'Neill M.P., who commanded the North Antrim Regiment, illustrates some of the problems which faced this unofficial army. He claimed that it was impossible to supply the 1,100 men which H.Q. had asked for to serve outside their own locality because, he wrote, ' ... The Regimental District is situated at a very much greater distance from Belfast (the probable centre of any operations) than either of the other Regiments. There are more Nationalists – and proportionately less Unionists and Ulster Volunteers – than in any other part of the Country. The Regimental area is about twice as large as either the Central or South, and contains only two Battalions as against three in each of the others ... I informed the Commander, 2nd Battalion that he should endeavour to furnish 100 men, but he is evidently not of this opinion ...'[18]

Finance.

Initially, however, the worst problem facing the U.V.F. was finance. For a succesful resistance campaign large sums of money were required, far beyond the Province's own resources, for propaganda, payment of personnel, arms and ammunition, stores of food, fuel, medical and other essential supplies (a blockade was anticipated), indemnity for the families of men killed or injured, and the proposed evacuation of non-combatants.

Between 29 November 1910 and 18 February 1913 £1,761.7.6 had been raised privately in Ulster and used towards the purchase of 2,000 rifles and

16 D1238/149
17 D1633 (Lady Spender's Diary)
18 D1238/121

50,000 rounds of ammunition for training purposes.[19] In January 1912 a central fund – the Sir Edward Carson Unionist Defence Fund – was established, management being undertaken by the Belfast Banking Company.[20] It was said to have spent £50,000 by 23 March 1913 on propaganda, chiefly in England.[21] In the following month house-to-house collections began, and subscribers were invited to earmark their donations for 'Home Defence' or 'Work in Great Britain'. Most subscribers seem to have followed Craig's advice, given in a public speech, and chose the former. According to police reports 'The working classes are contributing more zealously than any other, and are making great sacrifices to help the movement ... '[22]

The U.U.C. meeting on 24 September, as well as making arrangements for a Provisional Government, decided to set up an Indemnity Fund with a target of £I,000,000. Two days later it was announced that half this sum had been guaranteed.[23] By 2 October the Fund had reached £400,000 which had been contributed almost entirely by members of the Council. As yet no appeal had been made to the public, and members of the Unionist Clubs and Orange Lodges had not been approached for guarantees.[24] However, on 17 october a secret letter from U.V.F. H.Q. notified the Regimental Commanders of Counties Antrim, Donegal, cavan and Tyrone that Craig had undertaken to contribute £I.00 towards the cost of each rifle they purchased out of their own resources, provided it took .303 ammunition.[25]

Meanwhile, financial and other support was forthcoming from England. On 21 July 1913 Roberts wrote to Lord Milner suggesting that the time had come for him to end his isolation and take part once more in politics. Milner's public support of Ulster proceeded to take the form of pressure group organisation, the most spectacular part of which was his launching on 4 March 1914 a British Covenant. However, his covert financial activity would seem to have been at least as important. Towards the end of 1913 Walter Long, a Unionist M.P. and one of Milner's principal aides, supplied a list of contributors to the Ulster cause. In included Lords Rotschild and Iveagh: £10,000 each; Lord Astor: £25,000; the Duke of Bedford: £10,000; three contributions of £5,000 and 'many ... of £1,000 ... '[26]

Economy had still, however, to be practised. Volunteers were expected to

[19] D1327/4/21. According to information supplied by Lloyds Bank Ltd, £I,00 in 1913 is worth approximately £II.00 today (October 1977).

[20] P. Buckland: *Irish Unionism 1885–1923. A Documentary History*. page 208.

[21] CAB/37/115 April 1913

[22] CAB/37/115 17 April 1913

[23] Breandan Mac Giolla Choille (ed.): *Intelligence Notes* page 30.

[24] CAB/37/116, October 1913

[25] D1327/4/8

[26] Milner 16/204 and PRB/987

provide their own '... boots, socks, underclothing ... blankets and pocket-knife ...' Battalions would purchase haversacks, mess-tins, possibly greatcoats and water bottles ' ... but it is a mistake to spend money on Caps and uniform of this nature ... until the more important articles such as Haversacks have been aquired ... '[27] Much of the secret fund was being earmarked for guns and ammunition. On 28 February 1914 Carson told Craig that he had given major Frederick Crawford, the U.V.F's Director of Ordnance, £55,000 for their purchase.[28] Other U.V.F expenses included instructor' pay, the Signals Corps, County Secretaries and Headquarters staff. For the financial year beginning 1 August 1913 this totalled £3,607. [29] A further expence of £20,000 was incurred at the beginning of March 1914 with the formation of the Special Service Force [30] but by then the Indemnity Fund had exceeded its £I,000,000 target [31] and Carson suggested to Milner that the British Covenanters might consider organising a similar fund.[32] By 24 March the amount aquired or promised from this source was £144,000 which included £45,000 from Australian sympathisers.[33]

There is evidence which suggests that from about this time financial constraints upon the U.V.F. were becoming less severe. On 10 March 1914 regimental commanders were notified that they could claim a refund on all .303 rifles purchased by them since 1 April 1913, but not for rifles of other bores, and ammunition was not to be purchased with the idea of getting a refunds without specific permission from Divisional Commanders. However, arms and ammunition still took priority in the allocation of funds. The North Antrim Regiment, for instance, was being told at the same time that it would have to make do with 1/-per day for all its men succesfully completing their course at the regimental camp, amounting to £35.00 per 100 men per week. County Tyrone had to manage with the pro rata sum of £25.00. Even this was only a subsidy as the Antrim men had to make a contribution of 7/- for three days themselves.[34] Moreover, the Carson Fund was now beginning to suffer as money raised in the Counties was going towards arming and equipping their own local forces.[35] These contribitions were relatively large. In Armagh, for instance, with its large proportion of Nationalist sympathisers, one

27 D1238/9/5
28 D1415/B7/43
29 D1327/4/23
30 D1415/B/38
31 CAB/37/119 5 March 1914 and Milner 41/55
32 Milner 41/55
33 Milner 41/70
34 D1238/49
35 D1238/143, memorandum dated 15 May 1914.

meeting of local people raised some £700.00 to equip the Portadown Battalion.[36]

But money continued to pour into the secret fund in England. On 10 May 1914 Walter Long stated that he now had £170,000 in sums ranging from £30,000 to £100. His target was £250 – 300,000. Lord Northcliffe was mentioned as being among the contributors.[37] According to Captain George Berkeley, then commanding the Irish Volunteers' Belfast Brigade, he had contributed £250,000 by July 1914.[38]

Arms and Ammunition

For the U.V.F. to be an effective fighting force and thus able to achieve its prime objective of defending Ulster, it was essential that it should be adequately armed. The enthusiasm which had led to large numbers of recruits was in danger of evaporating unless guns could be provided for all those trained to use them. Given the part-time characteristics of most of the Force, the personal inconvenience of drilling after work (men often had to walk several miles to the drill centre), and the doubtful legality of the enterprise, it was essential for morale as well as self-defence that the Volunteers were able to convince themselves as well as the world in general, that they were a fighting army to be taken with the utmost seriousness.

At first only small quantities of arms were brought into Ulster, mainly on the initiative of individuals acting unilaterally. For example, a police report of 26 September 1913 stated that twenty rifles from Hamburg of an out-of date pattern had been imported by Hunter and Sons of Belfast.[39] By 31 December the police believed that the Unionists had a total of 17,051 rifles of which only 4,000 were up-to-date; but since the police estimates for recruits totalled 76,757 by the end of November 1913, it may be seen that there were not nearly enough rifles to go round.[40] nevertheless, enthusiasm was still apparent: 20,000 of these recruits had joined since the end of September. Making a virtue out of necessity, strict rationing of rifles was carried out by regimental officers. Arms were only issued to men who had attended drills regularly and could handle and take care of weapons – thus the status of being allowed a gun acted as an incentive to continue with military training. The Bangor and Holywood Battalions were allowed the exceptional privelege of keeping their arms at home. The reasons for this were first, they had a full

36 CAB/37/119, March 5 1914
37 Gwynne
38 Berkeley 10923
39 CAB/37/116, October 1913
40 Choille, page 33

complement of arms: at least I,000 rifles, bayonets and ample ammmunition had been smuggled in by one of their officers in his motoryacht the *Doreen*; second, there were fears that police might sieze the arms if they were left in store; and third, the men were 'steady and respectable ... with few if any of the rowdy element, and they can be trusted with arms ...'[41] Other Volunteers were not so fortunate. On 6 January 1914 General Adair, his three Regimental Commanders and the County Committee of Antrim expressed 'very great dissatisfaction' at the 'indequate supply of arms – even for instructional purposes ...' Only a hundred .303 rifles and carabines and fifty Vitterlis had been issued for their force of I0,700, and to make matters worse there was no ammunition suitable for the Vitterlis. Battalion commanders reported their men as 'manifesting considerable disappointment ... and are tiring of elementary dril ...' Moreover, Antrim's problems were exacerbated by four of their senior officers being M.P.'s; the ex-officers they had expected to be forthcoming from England to deputies for them had not so far materialised. At a meeting with Carson and Craif on 20 January 1914 they protested that other counties had received a larger share of the available arms and demanded an explanation, pointing out that they, unlike some others, had given donations to the Carson Fund instead of buying arms for themselves. They now required a grant to make up their deficiencies.[42]

Meanwhile, the government issued on 5 December 1913 a Proclamation banning the importation of arms into Ireland and their traffic coastwise. Confronted with this action the political leaders of the U.V.F. decided during January 1914 to request Crawford to organise a massive gun-running operation. This was succesfully completed at Larne during the night of 24 April under cover of a practice mobilisation. Some 35,000 rifles and 5,000,000 rounds of ammunition were now in the U.V.F's possession.[43] In addition, individual smuggling had brought the supply of rifles to approximately 24,900 by 31 March.[44] But even with the post-Larne total which approached 60,0000 weapons, 84,540 men had enrolled by this date, so the arms shortage was still acute.[45]

The arms stores now contained Lee-Enfield, Martini-Enfield and other miscellaneous modern makes, and a small quantity of older models of Italian manufacture. In addition, Crawford had obtained 20,000 Mausers costing £63,000. The total expenditure in the Larne operation was £102,000.

The Royal Navy was now ordered to patrol the Irish coasts to prevent further smuggling, but their operations do not seem to have been completely

41 CAB/37/117, November 1913
42 D1238/108. Also cited in Buckland, pages 243–258
43 This account is based on Stewart, chapter 14–16 and Buckland, pages 243–258
44 Choille, page 34.
45 Choille, page 37.

succesful. One such evasion seems to have taken place on 20 May 1914 when Frank Hall and Spender led a convoy of six five-ton lorries to Fermanagh, each with a full load of rifles and ammunition, and escorted by sixteen cars with armed men riding on their roofs.[46]

In addition to rifles, Tyrone and Down had each one Maxim gun.[47] During June and July 1914 the police reported that they had information concerning an unspecified number of machine-guns (most of these were believed to be in Belfast) and there were unconfirmed reports of light artillery and aircraft.[48]

By the end of May 1914 there were enough rifles to enable the up-to-date types to be distributed to the now highly-trained mobile forces and specialist sections such as the Ballymena Horse, the older makes being allocated to those Volunteers (usually the less able man) whose duties were guarding and protection. As the prospect of civil war loomed menacingly towards the end of July 1914, H.Q. ordered on 16 July that not more than five per cent of service ammunition was to be used for target practice, and when recruiting was thrown open, from I August, to men who had not signed the Covenant, they were to be warned that it might not be possible to arm them all. The numbers anticipated were large – Antrim, for example, expected some 13,000 additional men.[49]

Military Policies and Plans

On 26 july 1913 Craig wrote a secret memorandum, probably intended for the U.V.F.'s chief political leaders, setting out his view of the situation facing Ulster and the military moves which would have to be undertaken to ensure that the government's Home Rule policy could be defied:

> You say that you intend to sit tight until the Bill becomes law, and then to act if it is enforced. If the government dares not face real fighting of course this will do all right, but they would be forever discredited and ridiculous, and fear of ridicule is the thing that drives men to fight. If they fight at all, they will surely fight to win, and to get it over as soon as possible. The British Army will hate it, but as a whole I believe they will fight against you. Anyhow, is it not safer to assume that they will fight? The Government will probably wait as long as they dare in the hope of things quieting down, and at last suddenly move 20,000 to 30,000 men into Ulster, secure railways, bridges etc. and reinforce weak police posts ... (with the help of the Navy they could certainly do it in two days) ... I do not see how you can hope to get your men out, and concentrate them in suitable positions. Must you give up the enormous advantage of the first move? I assume that you have say 30,000 ... rifles and enough ammunition for a big fight (say 21/2 million rounds). To impress the English and get real support from them, you must not only put up a fight,

46 D1633/2/19
47 D1327/4/21 Also quoted in Buckland, page 246
48 CAB/117
49 D1238/148 and D1238/198

you must put up a good fight, and I cannot see how you can put up a good fight unless you sieze the first move. Your speeches say you will wait etc. ... all so much to the good, the Art of War, including Civil War is to deceive your enemy and try to hit him hard before he is ready ... you and your men are suited to a stubborn stand up fight. Neither this country or your men are suited to 'Guerilla warfare', 'Boer tactics' and so on. If you stake all on a big fight, there will be no doubts or hesitations. Subordinate leaders can be told something of where to go and what to do, and will be spared the heavy responsibility they will have to bear if you fight all over the place. If you make it one big fight you may well get beaten but you will make a great name for the men who fight under you and, beaten or not, you will probably attain your great object. I don't advocate moving in a hurry – I advocate moving before the Government move. They have very able ambitious men on the Army Council – and if they move at all, they'll pounce ... [50]

This appraisal, together with subsequent secret plans, suggests that at least until May 1914 the British Army was the U.V.F.'s contemplated enemy. The Nationalist threat at this stage was seen in terms of civil disorder which could be contained by police-type measures.

The U.V.F. was, however, anxious to project an image of respectability so as to make a favourable impression on British opinion, and to this end Craig announced in a public speech on 13 November 1913 that the U.V.F. would be willing to make up the deficiency of 35,000 men in the British Territorial Force and, in public, an impression was forward by the Ulster leadership which was somewhat at variance with its secret war plans. General Sir Arthur Paget, C.-in-C. of the Irish Command appears to have been aware of the real nature of the Force and as early as 19 October 1913 he was considering recommending partial mobilisation to the Government.[51]

From about this time the U.V.F. began to be given advice by sympathisers within the British Army. On 15 November Lieutenant-General Henry Wilson warned Edward Sclater (one of the 'inner ring' who had formulated the constitution of the Provisional Government, the others being Carson, Craig, Wallace, Sharman Crawford and Thomas Sinclair) of '... such pitfalls as siezing depots where there are arms, and any action hostile to the Army which was most sympathetic to the Ulster movement ...' [52] Spender was given similar advice at a staff College dinner the following February. It thus became a fundamental policy to maintain tight discipline in order to avoid any action which could be construed as civil disorder, in which troops could legitiamtely be ordered to intervene. Nevertheless, undercover planning went ahead which envisaged the use of the British Army in a coervice role. The U.V.F. had its 'hawks' and one of these, probably Spender, put forward a plan entitled 'The Coup' in December 1913. This recommended that '... a sudden, complete, and paralyzing blow should be struck at the right moment, i.e. simultaneously ...' Bridges and railway lines, it continued, by which forces of police or

50 D 1633/2/19

51 Mottistone 22

52 Wilson Diaries, 15 November 1913

soldiers could be sent into Ulster should be destroyed by members of H.Q. Special Force Intelligence 'scouts' who were conversant with explosives; likewhise telephone, telegraph and cable lines would be cut. Depots of arms, ammunition and military equipment would be captured. All roads which could be used by troops for entering Ulster should be closed by 'isolated detachments of men occupying defensive positions commanding these roads ...' Field artillery should be captured by direct attack, or by 'previous arrangement with the gunners concerned ... Where possible, secret negotiations should be made with troops guarding depots for these to be handed over without fighting – but if this occurs, the force for attack should be overwhelmingly superior to the defending force ...' Railways were to be immobilised with minimum damage; for instance the bridge at the rail junction town of Drogheda was planned for destruction instead of the four bridges on the lines out of Drogheda.[53] (It was later agreed with the three railway companies that engine drivers would be issued with bars of soap to put in their boilers, so that bubbles would be produced instead of steam.) Communications wires would be cut at night if they had been repaired after the initial destruction, so that the men could carry on with their usual jobs by day, thus avoiding suspicion.[56]

Normally, there were only about 9,000 troops stationed in Ulster, and they evidently included U.V.F. sympathisers. The rest of the 5th Division at the Curragh and the 6th Division at Cork totalled 14,000 soldiers including cavalry and artillery.[57] The U.V.F. therefore by March 1914 were numerically. The U.V.F. had another function: internal security. It was anticipated that the Irish Nationalists in Ulster might create trouble if a Provisional government was declared. Therefore part of the Special Service Force was to stay in Belfast for '... police work, and the safety of the Town against any Rioting or destruct or incendiarism from the Nationalist inhabitants, or from irresponsible youths and unenlisted men of the Orange side ...' Entrance into and egress from the city must be denied '... to the enemy ... every man will know which stone, ditch, wall or building he has got to be behind and fire from ...'[58] In a police report dated 8 January 1914 it was stated that plans existed for the R.I.C. to be disarmed without bloodshed,

[53] Sir Wilfred Spender: *Unionist, April 1949*. (The PRONI believes that all copies of this publication were recently destroyed in a fire at the Unionist Party's H.Q. in Belfast. Dr. A.T.Q.Stewart kindly allowed me to see the extract he had made from the paper. It is not in the British Library's collection at Colindale, nor in the N.L.I.) Spender
D1295/14B/I

[54] Sir James Ferguson: *The Curragh Incident*, pages 19–23

[55] D1327/4/21

[56] CAB/37/119 5 March 1914

[57] D1327/4/21

[58] CAB/37/119

military barracks in Ulster were to be seized, and wax impressions of their store room keys were believed to be in the U.V.F.'s possession. Loughs Swilly, Carlingford and Belfast were believed to have been mined. Finally the report stated that if attempts were made by the police to sieze the Volunteers arms, then armed resistance would be offered.[59]

On 7 February 1914 plans for partial and full mobilisation were sent out by H.Q. to each regiment. The orders were to be sent by despatch riders or the Motor Corps, and then locally by horse, motorbike or on foot. Assembly was to take place at each man's nearest drill centre, and everyone had to bring with him two days' supply of food, and his arms and ammunition. Entrenching tools would be issued from the centre's supply.[60] Practise mobilisations were frequent as, for example, the one which covered the Larne gun-running.[61]

The British Adjudant-General, Sir Spencer Ewart noted in his diary on 15 February 1914: 'Gleichen (the Brigade Commander in Belfast) ... is quite sure the Ulster loyalists will fight. They will be quite unlike their Presbyterian ancestors if they don't ...'[62] But the policy of discipline and restraint was carried out at all times and in consequence there were no disorders or riots provoked by Ulster Unionists. On 16 May 1914 orders were given to the U.V.F. to cope with the anticipated demonstrations from Nationalists celebrating the third reading of the Home Rull Bill, due on 25 May, which might be provocative. Battalion commanders were to consult with their local R.I.C. Inspector and offer their Battalion's services to assist in preserving the peace, ' ... prior to calling out troops for that purpose ...' Commanders were to use their own discretion concerning full or partial mobilisation, but arms were not to be carried initially, and ' ... no violence used except in self-defence; also that any demonstrations of force of numbers which you may make is to be made in such a way as not to provoke the offensive on the part of the Nationalists. Should troops be called upon by Magistrates or others to assist in the preservation of the peace, the U.V.F. will take no part in the proceedings unless called upon by the officer in command of the Troops to assist in their capacity as citizens; otherwise they are to be dismissed from duty but kept collected so that they may not interfere individually ...'[63] In Co.Antrim the Ballymena Horse were to be put under the Command of one of the Battalions so that they could be used quickly to quell a riot. (This area contained a relatively high proportion of Nationalists).[64]

Careful precautions were taken to hide arms and ammunition. Caches were small, and known to very few people; orders were that the arms were to be

59 Lwart, Diaries, 126
60 D1238/141
61 D1238/142
62 D1327/4/8
63 Choille, pages 71–79
64 D1238/160

protected with minimal violence; the aim was to try to overawe the police by weight of numbers. Only if this was not effective was violence to be used, and then only of the same kind as had to be met. Volunteers were forbidden to fire on the police unless the latter had first fired on them. The same tactics were to be used if attempts were made to arrest civilian leaders or officers. If, however, communication with H.Q. broke down during an emergency, local commanders could use their own discretion as to the action taken.[65] It is noticeable from May 1914 onwards that the emphasis shifted from dealing with troops, to police and Nationalists. This may have been a consequence of the Curragh 'incident' and the subsequent changes in the Army Council which now had in Sir Charles Douglas (the C.I.G.S.) and Sir Henry Sclater (Adjutant-General) two officers who were, to say at least, doubtful about coercive military intervention in Ulster.[66] The U.V.F.'s war plans from about this time suggest that the Nationalists were now the contemplated enemy; their own paramilitary force, the Irish Volunteers, was becoming formidable in the South, although in the North the military balance overwhelmingly favoured the U.V.F. On 17 July Colonel Maurice Moore, Inspector-General of the I.V., advised against giving any of their limited supplies of arms to the northern brigades: '... We are not and will not be in a position to resist an attack in the North and it will just be handing the arms over to the Ulstermen. If the Carsonites do nothing the arms are no use; if they do they will simply surround any force we have and take away the arms ...'[67]

Nonetheless the Nationalist threat, perhaps overestimated, was regarded with increasing seriousness. On 11 June County Secretaries were notified that they should now plan to set up stores of coal, flour and animal fodder, each county to be responsible for its own supplies. Interference with rail communications from the south was anticipated, so canals were recommended as more secure supply routes.[68] By 13 June arrangements were completed for anyone who wanted evacuate his family to England, where a network of houses by then existed ready to receive them.[69] On 27 June battalion commanders were given permission by H.Q., with Carson's concurrence, to carry arms openly and an assurance was given them that the '... Leaders are prepared to take full responsibility for any collision with the Authorities that the carrying of arms may entail ...'[70] Instructions were given

65 D1238/161
66 D1327/4/10
67 Moore 10545
68 D1238/174
69 D1415/B/34
70 Berkeley, Diary 73

for dealing with Nationalist raids on arms depots which were anticipated for 12 July.[71]

By the beginning of July Crawford, Richardson and the businessmen members of the Council decided to break into the Customs and Inland Revenue offices and steal their documents, [72] the 'passive resistance' part of the Ulster Campaign. Active measures against the Nationalists were also contemplated. Captain Berkeley, in command of the Belfast Brigade of the I.V. discovered a plan to take over the Catholic quarter of Belfast by cutting off the water supply, thus forcing the I.V. to surrender. In such an event Berkeley felt that the only course of action open to him would be retreat down to the south leaving the women and children in the care of the authorities (whoever they then might be), for they would be gravely endangered in close quarter fighting in the city.[73] This problem faced by the I.V. illustrates the farsightedness of the U.V.F.'s evacuation plans which, on 10 July 1914, were extended to 'prority categories': those living in isolated places and the families of the 'Fighting Force' whose soldiers would be operating away from their own areas. It was envisaged that this evacuation should take place before hostilites began.[74]

On 21 July the Buckingham Palace Conference began, called on the King's initiative as a last resort to prevent civil war. Carson's terms were the exclusion of all Ulster. He demanded '... a clean cut, or come and fight us ...' Predictably the Conference broke down, on 24 July, but the object of the U.V.F.'s formation seemed to have been fulfilled: there was now no question of forcing Ulster to accept the rule of a Dublin Parliament, until the outbreak of the Great War transformed the Irish situation along with so much else.

CONCLUSION

Northern Ireland today is not a militarised society. Great efforts are made by many of the inhabitants to live as normal a life as possible in the face of continuing terrorism.

There are several groups who are extreme, and have carried out a number of outrages. These compromise the Provisional IRA and the Irish National Liberation Army, both of whom attempt to achieve union with Eire by violent means. They are probably small in number. It has been estimated that active

[71] D1238/176

[72] Robert Fisk, *The Strike that Broke the British in Ulster* gives an account of these events.

[73] The survey was conducted among a quota sample of 1,983 respondents in 150 contituencies in Britain between 25 April and 5 May 1984. It is quoted in *The Economist*, June 1984.

[74] Claire Sterling, *The Terror Network*, Weidenfeld and Nicholson, 1981, chapter 9.

IRA membership is probably no more than some three hundred, although many of their weapons which have been found show a high degree of sophistication.

The known terrorist groups which support the Union are the 'new' UVF, the Ulster Freedom Fighters and the Red Hand Commando, all of which are illegal. Other extreme supporters of the Union include the Ulster Defence Association, the Orange Volunteers and the Reverend Ian Paisley's 'Third Force', set up in 1981. It may be suggested that some or all of these groups possess weapons, but very little is known about them, except perhaps to army intelligence, and is probably classified.

There is no equivalent today to the 'old' UVF. Several reasons for this may be suggested.

First, there is no threat at present to the Unionist majority of integration with Eire. Successive British governments have reiterated their policy of keeping the six counties within the United Kingdom for as long as this remains the wish of a majority of the inhabitants. However, it must be said that attempts by Westminister even to talk to the government of Eire have been greeted with deep suspicion by Unionist supporters.

The most important example of this opposition was shown by the general strike organised by the Ulster Workers' Council in 1974, which paralised public utilities and effectively undermined the power sharing Northern Ireland Executive.[72]

Secondly, support for the Unionist cause from mainland UK does not appear to be as strong as that enjoyed by the 'old' UVF. In a recent opinion poll conducted by *The Economist*/MORI, less than one third of the respondents felt that Northern Ireland should remain part of the UK; union with Eire was supported by 21% and an independent state was supported by 31%. These figures suggest that financial and moral support might not be forthcoming for a paramilitary force dedicated to keep the six counties in the UK as it was from 1913 to 1914. It is difficult to see, therefore, that funds could be raised to arm and train an 'army' comparable in size and strength. In any case it is probable that no necessity for such a force is envisaged in Northern Ireland given Westminister's contuing policy of respect for the wishes of the Northern Irish majority.[73]

It has been suggested that Colonel Qaddafi of Libya invited the UDA to Libya in 1973 with the possible intention of offering arms and other support, but nothing appears to have come of this. There is evidence, however, that Nationalist terrorists have obtained assistance from other countries.[74]

At present the armed personnel in Northern Ireland are (apart from the terrorist groups already mentioned) members of the security forces, having therefore legal and constitutional status.

These consist of three parts. First, there is the British Army, numbering some 7,060 on two years tours of duty, and about 2,070 on four month tours. In addition to this force there is the Ulster Defence Regiment, consisting of fulltime and part-members. It is an integral part of the British army, except that it has no overseas role. It numbers about 7,000.

Most police in Northern Ireland carry arms for self defence. The Royal Ulster Constabulary has some 8,000 men and women members, with a part-time reserve of 4,500. It carries out normal police duties, similarly to its counterparts on the mainland, assisted by the army in its role of aiding the civil power. (The Territorial army is part of the UK armed forces, and Territorials only serve overseas, for example in support of NATO forces in West Germany).

Simon Jenkins quotes a membership figure for the UDA of 40,000,[75] but it probably stands much lower, at about 5,000.[76] Thus, it is outnumbered by the security forces. It is probable that any attempt to build up a paramilitary army along the lines of the 'old' UVF would be immediately prevented. In any case, Westminister's commitment to the present constitutional position of Northern Ireland, guaranteed by the security forces, is probably perceived as being of sufficient protection by most of the Unionist majority. No one can predict the outcome, however, were this guarantee to be withdrawn.

THE ULSTER VOLUNTEER FORCE

ABBREVIATIONS

Roberts. The papers of Field-Marshal Lord Roberts of Kandahar, in the National Army Museum, London.

CAB. Cabinet papers, in the Public Record Office, London.

Mottistone. The papers of Lord Mottistone, in Nuffield College, Oxford.

Milner. The papers of Lord Milner, belonging to New College, Oxford. Deposited in the Bodleian Library.

Gwynne. The papers of H.A. Gwynne in the Bodleian Library, Oxford.

Berkeley. The papers of Captain George Berkeley, in the National Library of Ireland, Dublin.

75 Ulster Survey, *The Economist*, June 1984

76 The lower figure was supplied by the Northern Ireland Office in London.

Wilson. The papers and diaries of Field-Marshal Sir Henry Wilson, in the Imperial War Museum, London.

Ewart. The papers and diaries of Sir Spencer Ewart, in the Scottisch Records Office, Edinburgh.

D 1327, D1415, D1238, D1633 are deposited in the Public Record Office of Northern Ireland, Belfast.
Moore. The papers of Colonel Maurice Moore, in the National Library of Ireland.

BRITISH GOVERNMENTS AND THE 'PROTESTANT BACKLASH' 1969–74

HENRY PATTERSON

Towards Direct Rule

A few months after the Ulster Workers' Council strike which destroyed the British Government's attempt to establish a new 'power-sharing' regime in Northern Ireland, the *Ulster Loyalist*, a newspaper representing the viewpoint of the Ulster Defence Association (UDA) the major Protestant paramilitary grouping, commented on the decision of the Official Unionist Party to adopt Enoch Powell as one of its parliamentary candidates:

> ... The spokeman they have chosen is just the man most guaranteed to convince British trade unionists that the Ulster worker is a right wing fanatic. It is a sad state of affairs and until we can procedure our own politicians there is nothing that we, the working people of Ulster, can do about it.[1]

This response indicates the heterogeneity of what commentators, politicians and civil servants had been referring to as the 'Protestent backlash'. It will be the argument here that one important index of the inadequacies of British government's policies since the increase in involvement in the late sixties has been the failure to adequately perceive the nature of popular Protestant politics. This lacuna has been reproduced in most left wing and radical nationalist critiques of government policy and analyses of the situation. Thus in an influential, if slight, work, Geoff Bell argues 'the determining factor throughout Northern Ireland's latest political crisis has been the way the ordinary Protestant has thought and reacted'.[2] According to Bell the Protestant working class has a reactionary political consciousness which has expressed itself in a virulent, even pathologically violent, opposition to the main political changes which British governments and Unionist reformers have attempted to introduce. Bell's thesis is established by a rather selective use of quotations from loyalist papers which focuses only on the secretarian and reactionary themes whilst ignoring those like the one quoted above. It would be simply reproducing this incorrect approach if we concentrated instead on the progressive themes. What needs to be analysed is the unstable combination of progressive and reactionary elements and their political conditions of existence.

1 *Ulster Loyalist* 5 September 1974.
2 Geoff Bell *The Protestants of Ulster* (London, 1976) p121.

These political conditions were crucially influenced by British government policy towards the unfolding crisis of the Unionist regime. A central characteristic of Labour and Conservative governments' policies from the onset of the 'Troubles' was the attempt to minimise involvement. The Stormont-Westminister relation in the 1921–69 period has been based on a mutually reinforcing desire to maintain the insulation of Northern Ireland and its peculiarities from the political system in the rest of the UK. The response of the first Wilson government, despite a certain anti-partitionist rhetoric on his own part, was to maintain this insulation as far as possible. A prerequisite for this was the maintenance in power of a Unionist regime of a reformed sort. Thus, although at various times after 1966 Unionist prime ministers were threatened with radical changes in the relationship with London if reforms were not implemented, there was a consistent tendency for the British government to recoil from action of this sort. The effect of leaving the Unionist regime in power was effectively to discredit those reforms that were introduced in catholic eyes whilst at the same time allowing the intra-governmental and party divisions within Unionism over the questions of reform and security to reach crisis proportions. The clear British desire to keep the problems of the province at arms length gave Brian Faulkner, the last Unionist prime minister, considerable leverage with the Heath government which he used to persuade them of the necessity of the internment operation in August 1971.

A significant and influential analysis of the effects of internment on the political viability of the reform programme was put forward by Wilson in the Commons debate on the aftermath of internment. The reform programme inaugurated with the Downing Street Declaration in 1969 was now clearly inadequate: 'Many of the reforms have been implemented or are in the process of implementation, but they are as dust in the wind in terms of adequacy for a political solution.' The inadequacy was defined solely in terms of a changed perception of the situation by the Catholic community,

> ... following internment nothing can ever be quite the same again ... It is a basic elemental question of lack of confidence created by an ever-increasing sense of fear, which no word, no speech, no different delineation of reforms ... almost no action can change ... I believe that the situation has now gone so far that it is impossible to conceive of an effective long term solution which is not in some way directed to finding a means of achieving the aspiration towards a United Ireland.[3]

What must be noticed here is how Wilson transforms a structural problem – the bipartisan disinclination to get more directly involved which predated the Conservative's coming to power, into a narrowly partisan and self-serving

[3] House of Commons *Debate* vol.826, 25 November 1971, col.1580.

critique of the obviously disastrous internment decision. (It should be noted that Wilson did not demand the ending of internment). It was precisely the disinclination of Labour as well as Tory governments to get more involved that had done much to undermine any positive effects the reforms may have had. More importantly the question of whether the reforms were themselves adequate to deal with the substantive grievances raised by the Civil Rights movement is avoided completely. Wilson effectively conceded the ground of argument to those who were already claiming that it was impossible to reform the Northern state and that therefore the 'national question' should become the central issue for Catholics. By identifying the question of the possibility of reforming and democratising the Northern state with that of the clearly piecemeal and minimalist reforms that were introduced after August 1969, Wilson ensured that what was an essentially nationalist definition of the problem increasingly set the tone of debate at Westminster. Heath's government, profoundly disillusioned with Faulkner as the violence intensified after internment, was clearly deeply divided over the question of to what extent a change of course was necessary.[4] The very lack of a coherent Tory position meant that the terms of the public debate were increasingly set by the Labour party and Wilson in particular.

Internment had propelled Wilson into a much more thorough reaffirmation of his traditional anti-partitionist rhetoric. In an adjournment debate in November when after a whirlwind visit to both Irish states, he put forward his 'Fifteen Point Plan' for a final solution to the Irish question, he was predictably hailed by Roy Hattersley as changing 'permanently and fundamentally the whole character and nature of the Irish debate.'[5] When by the time of the Bloody Sunday Killings at the end of January the government had still not gone beyond Maudling's invitation to the main constitutional Catholic party the SDLP to get involved in talks – an invitation which the party had repeatedly made clear it was not going to accept, the desire of government and opposition to maintain some sort of bipartisanship on Ulster was clearly in danger of disintegrating. In March the labour Party had divided the House on a motion criticising the government for its failure to announce a political initiative. Wilson urged an initiative,

> ... capable of firing the imagination of those who have been increasingly driven, wrongly but remorselessly, to the point where they believe that their grievances cannot be assuaged, that their aspirations can be made a possibility only by the invocation of violence.[6]

[4] see for example Keith Kyle, 'How Direct Rule came to Ulster' in *The Listener*, 30 March 1972.

[5] House of Commons *Debates* vol.827, 29 November 1971, col.68.

[6] *Ibid* vol.833, 20 March 1972, col.1079.

This speech was made shortly after he had a meeting in Dublin with three leaders of Provisional Sinn Fein where he had made clear to them his belief that any solution must involve an Irish dimension. Later in the debate on the implementation of direct rule he reiterated this position,

> This is now the occasion for a conference and all-party talks ... with the fullest programme of consultation with all the Irish parties in the Dail.[7]

The development of Wilson's proposals after internment was favourably received far outside the Labour Party. The *Financial Times*, in a leader on his Fifteen Point Plan referred to it as ' ... by far the most constructive contribution he has made since he left office.' It considered it a suitable basis for discussion and added, 'The great thing about the Wilson plan is that for the first time it mentions the unmentionable.' (Irish unity as a policy objective.)[8]

If Heath had none of Wilson's traditional identification with Irish nationalist aims, his own profound distaste for what he saw as a messy a new chronism could result in a willingness to consider radical measures which could at least hold out the possibility of eventually extricating Britain from the whole Irish quagmire. Increasingly there was a tendency for ministers to air privately their distaste for the idea of prolongation of the Union for more than was absolutely necessary. In January 1972 the *Economist* could report,

> ... ministers have made little secret of their belief that the most satisfactory solution in the end would be if a political solution were created over the years in which the Protestant majority in the north could come to recognise a future for itself in a united Ireland.[9]

Although the announcement of the suspension of Stormont was coupled with the promise of ten yearly prebiscites on the border issue, the wider conjuncture in which these announcements took place did little to stem a growing Protestant feeling that bipartisanship had been restored at Westminster on Harold Wilson's terms. As the *Newsletter* put it on the day after the imposition of direct rule,

> The plot was laid behind the backs of the Ulster government and it was hatched within days of Mr Wilson making a secretive assignment with Republicans in Dublin.[10]

The Protestant Response

The first significant manifestations of what began to be referred to as the

[7] *Ibid*. vol.833, 24 March 1972, col.1865.
[8] *Financial Times* 27 November 1971.
[9] *The Economist* 12 January 1972.
[10] *Belfast Newsletter* 25 March 1972.

'Protestant backlash' came in the emergence of local defence groups in areas like north and west Belfast where, since August 1969, there had been frequent violent confrontations between Protestants and Catholics. The UDA would eventually emerge through a fusion of these groups. Whilst having a primarily paramilitary role they related to the intensifying crisis of the state in terms of an ideology which blamed the Unionist leadership groups for a policy of 'appeasement'. An early example of this first attempts in this period to mobilise Protestants at their places of work. It called on all 'loyalists' to write to their MP s demanding the 'full restoration of law and order' or their resignations and continued,

Appeasement is cowardice and on looking back over the past few months we ask 'what about the republican mobs from the Bogside' and compare this treatment to the use of CS gas by the army in Belfast on loyalists ...[11]

The Provisionals' adoption of an intense campaign of bombings in the spring of 1971 stimulated ideologies of embattlement and the main Unionist daily speculated that such a threat would reproduce the classical Unionist pan-class unity of the Home Rule period and the IRA's 1918–21 offensive:

They (Provos) have brought together with one mind and one purpose all sections of pro-government opinion, from the humble labourer to the clergyman in his pulpit, from shipyard technician to surgeon in a hospital.[12]

Such attempts to conjure up the unities of the past fundamentally misconceived the nature of the current unfolding crisis. The one lesson which the British government and opposition were clearly learning was the impossibility of even managing the situation if any attempt was made to go back on the reforms of the state apparatuses initiated in 1969. Unionist unity was a chimera given the realisation of at least some sections of the leadership of the Unionist party that 'reform' was irrevocable.

Nevertheless the intensification of the Provisional campaign and the concomitant strengthening of the reactionary element in Unionist politics at all levels, did enable Brian Faulkner to persuade Heath's government that a radical anti-Provo measure was necessary if 'moderate' Unionism was to be preserved at all. By failing miserably in dealing with the Provos, internment also sealed the fate of Protestant 'moderation' and its last attempt to preserve the Stormont regime.

The months after internment saw intra-Protestant divisions over how to react to the Provos capacity to fight on, reach a critical level. In September and October William Craig the dominant Unionist 'antiappeaser' was only the

11 Leaflet produced by *Ulster's Committee for the Defence of the Constitution* (1970).
12 *Belfast Newsletter* 2 September 1971.

most prominent of a group of Protestant politicians who addressed a series of large rallies (often composed of workers on their luch hours) the main theme of which was to demand the creation of a 'third force'. This in effect meant that the British government sanction a recreation of the Protestant militia – the B Specials. Craig was the most hysterical, claiming in one mass rally near the shipyards and aircraft factory that there were '1,500 armed terrorists backed by 3,000 auxilliaries in the Falls Road alone.[13] John Taylor, a junior minister of Home Affairs, publicly supported these demands.[14] Craig took these demands to the annual conference of the Unionist party in October. He opposed any further reforms, demanded full Stormont control over security, and proposed a resolution that was strongly critical of government security policies. This was defeated after a significant speech from Faulkner who set out clearly the limits that the need to maintain British government support placed on them,

> Let us face realities. Legislative arguments about Northern Ireland's constitutional responsibility for law and order is truly beside the point. Either we follow common security policies or we go it alone... our aim is not just to defeat the IRA. This is the first necessity but beyond it we must look to an Ulster united on a basis of common purpose rather than existing in a state of armed truce.[15]

But as the year drew to its close it became clearer that not only was Faulkner correct in pointing to Westminster's inevitable refusal to contemplate Craig's demands, but also that his own aim of being able to maintain a Unionist regime in power was unlikely to be realised. Already in November he was forced to react to speculation about a new and radical initiative.[16] As the year ended the press began to carry stories on how the Army was at last beginning to deal with the Provos. But this was of little comfort to Faulkner as it was also reported that the army was one of the main forces pressing the government for a political initiative to complement what the Bloody Sunday killings were to show had been the illusory nature of all talk of military progress.[17]

Once direct rule became a clear possibility the lack of unity amongst Protestant politicians on the question of what their response should be became obvious. Paisley, who had participated in rallies demanding a 'third force', at once differentiated his position from the rest by arguing for full integration in the event of the abolition of Stormont. Craig's Vanguard movement articulated an Ulster nationalist response treating direct rule as one

13 *Ibid* 7 September 1971.
14 *Ibid* 14 September 1971.
15 *Ibid* 14 October 1971.
16 *Ibid* 6 November 1971.
17 See article by Peter Jenkins, *Guardian* 17 January 1972.

symptom of the degeneration of Britain's traditional ruling class. In a pamphlet produced soon after direct rule the *Economist* article referred to above, which claimed that most government ministers favoured a united Ireland as the ultimate solution, was quoted as one indication of the rot which had set in,

> The leftward shift in Westminister politics has produced a Conservative party tired, even bored with Irish politics from which they wish to extricate themselves.[18]

But although Vanguard had a significant amount of support from Protestant paramilitary groups this was more a reflection of their affinity with Craig's intransigent record as an opponent of republicanism and security hardliner, than with identification with the specific policy of breaking the link with Britain in order to preserve some vague notion of Ulster 'nationhood'. Vanguard's talk of 'betrayal' had a clear resonance amongst the masses – to quote one early UDA paper,

> You, the Loyalist population have been sold to the terrorist. We were once a proud and happy nation, who sacrificed many of our best on far-away battlefields. They died in defence of a country that has now betrayed us. Ulster, another Palestine, another Suez, another Cyprus, another Aden. Our friends let us down, they broke under pressure.[19]

However in practise there was no natural tendency for such feelings of betrayal to develop into demands for UDI. The UDA was still very much a set of local organisations which lacked any clear strategy. It was symptomatic that after direct rule their primary concern was to put pressure on the new administration to act against the 'No Go' areas – the areas like the Bogside and Creggan in Derry and parts of West Belfast which were effectively out of bounds for the police and army. Such demands whilst embarrassing the first secretary of state for Northern Ireland, William Whitelaw, demonstrated that the paramilitaries still defined their function as putting pressure on the administration to act in particular ways rather than attempting to radically resist the new constitutional framework.[20]

It had been the clear evidence of divisions amongst Protestant political organisations and the localistic and politically primitive nature of Protestant paramilitarism which had persuaded the Heath administration that any

18 *Ulster a Nation* (April 1972).

19 *The Attack* (Bulletin No.2) March 1972.

20 The Englishman who played a leading role in the UDA in this period and later sold his story to the *Sunday Times* gives a graphic description of the political primitiveness of the organisation. Thus of an early meeting between the UDA's Army Council and Whitelaw: 'There we were with the top man and everyone started contradicting each other. They talked about their individual areas rather than general issues. Very naive. It probably helped Whitelaw.' 'Big Dave lifts the Mask' *Sunday Times* 28 January 1973.

Protestant reaction to direct rule would be relatively easily containable.[21] These divisions and the incoherence of the Protestant working class response allowed the Whitelaw regime to under-estimate the problems they were facing, and to treat the question of Catholic disaffection as the primary consideration. It also appears to have encouraged a tendency amongst the SDLP and southern politicians to urge the Heath administration to press on with even more radical constitutional initiatives, irrespective of Protestant opposition.

The reaction of the main southern parties and the SDLP to the development of British policy from the time of Wilson's plan was dangerously optimistic. The plan was viewed as a major Irish diplomatic coup.

The partition question has now been made respectable in British politics.[22]

The SDLP's refusal to meet Maudling to discuss interparty talks was based on belief that this would force a radical reopening of the 'Irish question'. When a leading member told a Civil Rights Association meeting in January 1972 that 'within the next six months Brian Faulkner and his rotten Unionist system will have been smashed'[23], he was reflecting a mood of semi-millenarianism that reunification would soon be on the agenda. The leader columns of the main Catholic daily made it clear throughout the winter of 71–72 that reform of the state was no longer the issue – 'Direct Rule would be a legitimate step to reunification which must come.'[24] It saw divisions within Unionism as simply an indication of its weakness and hence of its inability to effectively resist.

Such views were not new. They reflected a very traditional Irish nationalist perspective: that partition was not based on substantial and real divisions in Ireland but rather on elite manipulation of popular Protestant prejudices. The implication was clear – if the Protestant political elite was deprived of its control of the local state its capacity to mobilise the masses would be severely damaged and movement towards reunification would be relatively smooth. From the constitutional nationalists of the SDLP to the Provisionals there was a consistent tendency to ignore the possibility of a substantial, and relatively autonomous, Protestant working class reaction to anything savouring of moves towards reunification. This view interacted in what was to prove an explosive manner with a serious misapprehension about the dynamics of Unionism on the British side.

21 *Observer* 26 March 1972.
22 *Financial Times* 8 December 1971.
23 *Irish News* 3 January 1972.
24 *Ibid* 2 February 1972.

The central problem here was a constricted set of assumptions about the nature of the political crisis which treated it as capable of resolution through a series of concessions and compromises organised by the direct rule team between the Catholic and Protestant communities. Though it was recognised that the initial package would necessarily be seen as a victory for the Catholics, it was thought that the Protestants could be pacified by the reaffirmation of the guarantee in the 1949 Ireland Act, plus a system of regular plebiscites on the border – the idea of taking the constitutional issue out of politics.[25] Any residual Protestant resentment would be confronted with the facts of the extent of Britain's financial commitment to the province. Thus, in a debate just after the Vanguard strike against direct rule Whitelaw, whilst expressing a degree of sympathy for the feeling of Protestants outraged by the effects of IRA violence and the shock of losing their parliament, immediately followed this with a clear reminder of their material dependence on Britain:

> It is important when considering these facts to remember what this country, ... has provided, not only in terms of our troops, but in many other ways, for the Northern Ireland economy. Since 1970 we have given extra financial support which overall represents an additional £100 per head of population ... [26]

This type of political calculation was more appropriate to the bargaining relationship between government, employers' organisations and unions which had done so much to colour modern British politics. But this way of dealing with social forces in the rest of Britain was based on the development of corporatist structures which served to articulate existing forms of organisation of capital and labour to the state. In Northern Ireland the crucial effect of direct rule was precisely to disorganise the dominant existing form of organisation of Protestants – the Unionist party. This meant that the chances of ministerial appeals to 'all reasonable people' in the Protestant population being heeded were much slimmer than they realised. For all succesful processes of bargaining and compromise entail the prerequisite of an institutional means by which consent can be organised and mobilised. They also require an over-arching framework of consensus between the parties to the bargaining process. This was non-existent in Northern Ireland. British policy was retrospectively described by one of Whitelaw's ministers, David Howell, as aimed 'to build up, by every means available, a band of moderate opinion drawn from both sides'.[27] The appeal was a negative, not to say

25 House of Commons, *Debates* vol.837, 24 March 1972, col. 1861.
26 *Ibid* vol.837, 24 March 1977, col.241.
27 *The Times* 19 February 1975.

Hobbesian, one. Protestants should support the initiative, for although it meant sacrifices on their part, it would have the eventual effect of turning the Catholic masses away from support for the IRA and bind them to the new state structure in the north. They would realise 'that a united Ireland could not be achieved by violence and certainly not in the foreseeable future by any means.'

That this appeal was to find so little response was not due to any incorrigibly reactionary tendencies amongst the Protestant masses, but to the dissociation between the proclaimed ends of British policy and the means by which Northern Ireland was governed for six to seven months after direct rule. Unionist political domination in the period of Stormont had been centrally related, as far as the Protestant working class was concerned, to a particular form of organisation and ideological representation of the security apparatuses. Unionist hegemony had as one of its most enduring ideological effects the identification of stability and security with a particular type of Protestant political control of repression. At the centre of the problems created by direct rule, as it was developed by the Whitelaw team, was the need to reconstruct the ideological relationship of the Protestants to the key questions of security and stability. The Union which had for fifty years been indissociably linked with a real material reality – the form of organisation of the Unionist state apparatuses – was now to be guaranteed by the much less substantial reality of bargaining and compromise. More critically it was soon clear that in order to get the Catholic masses interested in the process, Whitelaw would have to make concessions and negotiate in just those areas that an important ideological tradition amongst the Protestant masses defined as crucial to the maintenance of the Union. It was because of this that despite the repeated assertions of commitment to respect the will of the majority, the sincerity of which can not seriously be doubted, the Whitelaw administration was continuously accused of plotting the destruction of Northern Ireland.

Soon after direct rule the *Economic* speculated 'it is entirely probable that neither Mr. Heath nor Mr. Whitelaw knows yet what their policy is really aiming at'.[29] This is true in the sense that it was clearly difficult to calculate just how many concessions it would take to win the 'hearts and minds' of the Catholics. At this time the main constitutional voice of Catholics, the SDLP, was refusing to talk with Whitelaw because internment was still in existence. Its leadership was also clearly euphoric about the possibilities that direct rule held for its long term aims. Thus in an RTE interview John Hume claimed 'the possibility of an unreconstructed North is as impractical as was Stormont itself.'[30]

[28] *Ibid.*
[29] *The Economist* 25 April 1972.
[30] *Ibid* 20 May 1972.

Although it was subsequently claimed by David Howell that the process of negotiating with the Provisionals was designed to demonstrate their incorrigible incapacity for compromise to the Catholic masses, this appears doubtful. There is first of all the evidence that there were some at least of the Provisional leaders, with whom serious negotiation was believed possible. A *Times* leader was symptomatic,

The Provisionals, who are now under able political leadership are bent upon having a say in any Northern Ireland settlement proportionate to their power. And that power has not been extinguished ... The concessions that Mr. Whitelaw is making to the IRA in particular and the Catholic community in general are not yet complete.[31]

The problem for British policy was clearly revealed when it added, 'it also becomes necessary for Mr Whitelaw to mend his fences with the Protestant community'.

The idea that Whitelaw could 'mend his fences' by making some concessions to the Protestants whilst continuing to pursue a policy of negotiations with the Provisionals, demonstrates the inability of informed opinion in Britain to grasp the true significance of the security issue for popular Protestant ideology. That this incapacity was shared by Whitelaw was made revealingly clear in a meeting he had with the UDA after the Provisional ceasefire had come into operation and they had treatened to barricade loyalist areas. During the meeting he had offered to set up an employment exchange on the Shankill Road and take more drastic action against those on rent and rates struke.[32] The offer was treated contemptuously by those it was designed to placate and early July was to see a serious outbreak of sectarian murders and a major confrontation between the Army and the UDA in west Belfast.[33]

The degree to which Whitelaw was prepared to consider dealing with the Provisionals only became clear when they leaked to the press details of a secret meeting he had had with six of their leaders in London in early July. As David Wood, the *Times* political correspondent described it,

... it was intended to be a coup at the level where politics overlaps with diplomacy. He had reason to calculate that the meeting might procedure gains and could not produce losses ... He needed to know through the test of political negotiations whether the most militant leaders could be moved towards traditional political methods ... [34]

Despite the failure of the talks and the ending of the Provisional ceasefire, it appears that the idea that the Provos would still have to be involved in any political settlement was not dead. According to the FT's Lobby

31 *The Times* 28 June 1972.
32 *Ibid* 29 June 1972.
33 *Ibid* 3 and 4 July 1972.
34 *Ibid* 17 July 1972.

correspondent, 'some ministers were not too depressed by the attitude displayed by the team's leader, Mr. David O'Connell. They also seen Rory O'Bradaigh and even Joe Cahill, as possible 'men of reason'.'[35] This optimism was in rather stark contrast to the situation in Northern Ireland where the paper's reporter claimed 'not since the troubles of 1920 has there been a more dangerous situation ... the mood of the people is uglier than at any time within memory.' He was referring to the intensification of sectarian murders and the paramilitary organisation of Protestants which 'has made enormous progress in the past two weeks.'[36]

In the middle of July Whitelaw sanctioned the adoption of a harder military line which was to culminate in Operation Motorman against the 'No Go' areas at the end of the month. In part, this was a response to Provisional intransigence but it also was clearly an attempt to respond to increasingly vocal criticism of his policies within the Conservative party. However, this did not lead to any basic reassessment of the overall aims of policy. According to Wood, Whitelaw still believed that he could sell his policies for a political solution in Northern Ireland to some of the Provisional leaders as a step towards their ultimate objective.[37] Now that the most tangible sign of Catholic militancy – the 'No Go' areas – was removed, it was thought that the business of organising a political settlement could begin. However, the effect of the previous concentration on the 'hearts and minds' of the Catholic population had been to greatly strengthen the elements of popular Protestant resistance to any process of accomodation. By September the UDA was involved in violent conflict with the army involving the deaths of two Protestants.[38] By October violent conflict between the army and Protestants had become almost endemic in parts of east and north Belfast. It was at this time that the UDA issued a statement, 'To hell with the British Army. To hell with Whitelaw. The British army and the British government are now our enemies.'[39] The response of the government was a series of hints that British patience was not inexhaustible and in the words of a clearly inspired lack, 'the price of non-cooperation will be withdrawal of the Army and subsidies'.[40] Rather than relate Protestant violence to the kind of policies adopted since March, there was a tendency to blame the government for not being hard enough with them.[41] However, the problem with this sort of approach was

35 *Financial Times* 15 July 1972. Tory perceptions of O'Connell's 'statemanship' May have been influenced by Harold Wilson who had met him earlier that year Joe Haines *The Politics of Power* (London 1977) p.126.
36 *Financial Times* 11 July 1972.
37 *The Times* 15 July 1972.
38 *Ibid* 8 September 1972.
39 *Ibid* 18 October 1972.
40 *Financial Times* 25 October 1972.
41 *Ibid* 'Putting the Question to the Protestants' 3 November 1972.

made clear in a *Times* leader which tried to construct a balance sheet on seven months of direct rule. It concluded, 'despair and bewilderment are now more prevalent than they were before'. It bleakly commented that there were few indications that better conditions had been created for political reconstruction. But crucially it gave a clear diagnosis of the major threat to progress,

Those who now govern Northern Ireland are losing control of the crucial section of the Protestant community without having gained control of the Catholic community. The possibility must now be reckoned with that the political and military authority in the province may find themselves lacking friends sufficient to enable them to succeed in their task.[42]

The Sunningdale Strategy and the Irish Dimension

In his analysis of British policy in this period Michael Farrell describes Sunningdale as ' ... the high point of British strategy in Ireland. It was a masterpiece of balance and ambiguity.' It foundered on the determination of the Loyalists 'to restore Orange supremacy at all costs'.[43] What this analysis ignores is the degree to which the Protestants mobilisation against the power-sharing Executive focussed much more on the plans to set up a Council of Ireland which would have included representatives from the Executive and the government of the Republic than on power-sharing. It was the Council of Ireland, and the related questions of its executive functions and role in policing, which had been at the centre of negotiations between Whitelaw and the SDLP since the Assembly elections in the summer of 1973. It was these issues which were at the heart of the inter-party negotiations which began in October 1973 and culminated in the Sunningdale Conference between the British and Irish governments and the power-sharing parties in December 1973.

Seen from this viewpoint it is clear that Farell *exaggerates* the degree of strategic thinking behind all these developments. Serious strategic thinking would have considered the implication of the Council of Ireland proposals for *all* the political forces involved. There is little evidence of this in relationship to either of the main blocs but this is especially the case with the Protestants.

The 'Irish Dimension', like the decision to implement direct rule were geared above all to getting the SDLP directly involved in negotiations. The SDLP had refused to attend the Darlington Conference in September 1972 primarily because of the government's failure to end internment and take action against the UDA. Robert Fisk clearly summed up Whitelaw's problem.

42 *The Times* 14 October 1972.
43 *Northern Ireland The Orange State* (London, 1976), p311 and 331.

Since direct rule, he argued, Whitelaw had attempted the pacification of both blocs by the distribution of 'political gifts' – direct rule for the Catholics; plebiscites on the border for Protestants. He was, however, now in a situation where 'to satisfy one group of extremists the Army are expected to break up the other groups'.

He then quoted a member of the SDLP who said there could be no political progress until Whitelaw 'took on' the UDA. [44] Given the violence of the feelings of large sections of the Protestant population to Whitelaw's security policies, it was impossible to give the SDLP what they wanted on internment or the UDA. The 'Irish Dimension' was, therefore, the only area in which apparently substantial concessions to the SDLP could be made.

A broad spectrum of political opinion from Brian Faulkner to Michael Farell would agree that these concessions were little more than window-dressing, that, as Faulkner was to say of the Sunningdale proposals on the Council of Ireland, 'if this nonsense was necessary to bring their supporters along I did not see why we should be difficult.'[45] It is highly likely that this is how British policymakers saw this issue – as concessions to nationalist sentiment which would help to ensure Catholic support for the Executive and Southern government support for more effective all-Ireland action against the IRA.

What Farell ignores, largely because of his reductionist treatment of the SDLP as the party of the Catholic middle class interested only 'a share in power patronage', was the real commitment of the SDLP to an all-Ireland solution as the only viable one. A reading of the minutes of the meetings of nineteen SDLP Assembly members from July to October 1973 makes it clear that they attached central importance to three issues – internment, the restructuring of the police force and the Council of Ireland seen as the central transitional stage to a united Ireland. In their negotiations with Whitelaw's civil servants it was these issues, particularly the Council of Ireland, that dominated discussions.

The SDLP's expectations of a radical solution were high. This is evident in everything discussed, from the early symbolic demand that the Assembly should meet at Armagh instead of Stormont, to the disquiet expressed with the speech, by Liam Cosgrave the leader of the new Coalition government in the Republic, which appeared to accept that reunification was not on – at least in the medium term: 'Equivocation similar to that emanating from Coalition government spokesmen could be demaging to us at a time when we appear to be on the verge of a breakthrough'.[46]

[44] *The Times* 21 August 1972.

[45] Brian Faulkner *Memories of a Statesman* (London, 1978) p229.

[46] *Minutes* of the first meeting of the SDLP Assembly party held at Dungannon on 6 July 1973.

After a delegation to see Cosgrave and a joint seminar on their respective views on the Council of Ireland question in September, the SDLP appear to have convinced the Cosgrave government of the need for *simultaneous* advance on both the power-sharing and Council of Ireland fronts. It is clear that this was not envisaged by the British who wanted an Executive set up first.

However, the realisation that the more the Council of Ireland proposals figured in any settlement, the less likely it was to find Protestant acceptance was subordinated to the desire to get some from of agreement acceptable to the SDLP. The British government continued to behave as if it would be possible to progress by relying on the one hand on the experiences of office to moderate the more unrealistic ambitions of the SDLP whilst on the other continuing to hope that intra-Protestant divisions and an unwillingness to confront the 'sovereign' Parliament would ensure their compliance. The result was the Sunningdale agreement which clearly undermined the support base of that section of the Unionist party led by Faulkner which was willing to share office with the SDLP. The insistence of leading members of the SDLP after Sunningdale that the Council of Ireland was a stage on the road to a united Ireland simply confirmed popular Protestant perceptions that the whole post-direct rule strategy was aimed at extricating the British state from a burdensome responsibility.[47]

Conclusion

The 'Protestant backlash' which destroyed the power-sharing executive was clearly an enigmatic phenomenon for many commentators. Neal Ascherson who had been in Belfast during the UWC strike was one of many who were surprised by the radicalism of the ideas being expressed by some prominent paramilitary leaders: 'The UDA is only one of the sources of a fountain of radical ideas which clearly terrify the more traditionally-minded bodies dedicated to maintaining Protestant supremacy'. He was obviously so entranced that he informed his readers that its leader, Andy Tyrie, 'has a suprising resemblance to the novelist Gunter Grass'.[48]

Merlyn Rees, the labour Secretary of State, who had refused to meet the UWC leadership during the strike was subsequently to see in it the rise of 'Ulster Nationalism' as a political force. The paramilitary discussion of

[47] Paddy Duffy, the party's treasurer told a meeting in Co Tyrone that the party was committed to getting Britain out of Northern Ireland on a 'satisfactory financial basis'. *Belfast Newsletter* 1 February 1974.

[48] Neal Ascherson 'The Republic of Hawthorden Road' *The Observer* 2 June 1974.

solutions may have exhibited naïveté – as Ascherson pointed out the supporters of independence 'are inventing a Catholic population eager to abandon republicanism and the Irish Dimension for the sake of a reborn Ulster'.[49] But what was significant about Protestant paramilitarism was not the undoubted support for some form of 'independent Ulster' solution but rather the very fact of serious political discussion taking place, discussion which took it as its point of departure that no return to pre 69 conditions was possible. The UDA's paper had informed its readership before the strike that opposition to the Executive did not mean that powersharing was to be ruled out in all circumstances:

> The present arrangement in the Northern Ireland Assembly is not power-sharing. It is government by appointment ... Power-sharing is anathema to some of our people but unless you go for a Protestant Ulster for a Protestant people – that is you exclude the Roman Catholics, if they are not willing to go then they will have to be pushed out, it is difficult to see how you can get around the issue.[50]

The same paper would argue after the strike that the fragmentation of the Protestant politics into seven parties was a progressive development.[51] This was just another indication of how a significant current of popular Protestantism did not hanker after the 'good old days' of monolithic Unionism.

The crisis and distintegration of the Unionist state inevitably set free many reactionary and sectarian elements. What is significant is that these were far from dominant in the discourse of popular Protestantism. Direct Rule by breaking the link between the Unionist Party and the central state apparatuses guaranteed that the intra-Unionist divisions manifest since the mid-60s would become institutionalised – the hegemonic Unionist Party was finished. At the same time there was increasing evidence of independent politics amongst the Protestant working class. Although this popular Protestantism was a contradictory mixture of reactionary and progressive elements it did have a potential for positive development. British government policy did little to help that potential to develop.

The bipartisan consensus on Northern Ireland frayed by internment and 'Bloody Sunday' was restored with direct rule but on the basis of the questionable assumption that reform of the situation had been tried and found inadequate and that now the nationalist aspirations of Catholics must be satisfied to some degree. A more appropriate response would have seriously questioned the adequacy of the reform programme for dealing with the structural inequality that did much to fuel Catholic disaffection. But the

49 *Ibid.*
50 *Ulster Loyalist* 14 March 1974.
51 *Ibid* 4 July 1974.

option of a more thoroughgoing reform programme came up against the deeply ingrained bipartisan disinclination to do anything more than manage the situation.

Direct rule, by destroying the substance of the Unionist state, was a radical measure. There is little evidence that British policy-makers were prepared to accept all of its implications. In particular, it was inevitable that it was interpreted by Nationalist and Unionist ideologies as re-opening the constitutional question. Instead of making it clear that what was at stake was a process of reconstitution of the Northern Ireland state along more democratic and equitable lines, the desire to return as quickly as possible to a situation where British involvement was minimised, led to an attempt to create a nonsectarian coalition. This meant, at the very least, appearing to take nationalist aspirations seriously. The result was predictably disastrous. For while it might have been possible to at least secure Protestant acquiescence to a more substantial programmes of *internal* reform, reforms, which appeared to be linked to a process of gradual British disengagement were quite a different matter.

THE EXPERIENCE OF THE BRITISH ARMY IN NORTHERN IRELAND

BRIAN HOLDEN REID

The deployment of the British Army in Northern Ireland as an aid to the civil power in August 1969 raised a number of difficult problems. Although the British Army had gained considerable experience in counter-insurgency since 1945, this had been acquired in former colonial territories. Also, long before in 1918–21 it had engaged in a guerrilla war in Ireland and against the same enemy – the IRA. Though this conflict had left no lasting impact on the Army, it had left a potent republican mythology which would eventually rebound on the Army, despite the pleasing impressson the initial deployment of troops had made on the Catholic community. Consequently, the doctrine and experience that the Army had built up under extremely difficult circumstances in other parts of the world was of little use in Northern Ireland, an integral (though hardly normal) part of the United Kingdom. Nevertheless it had to cope with a Republican political and social heritage that refused to accept that unity and viewed the British Army as an occupying force. This essay seeks to explore the way the Army coped with the political tensions arising from the 'troubles' in Northern Ireland and assess the degree of adaptability it has shown in coming to terms with its complex task of countering terrorism in the province. It will also suggest that the mounting of a counter-subversion campaign with the expectation of totally defeating the terrorists in military terms within the context of Northern Ireland politics was not possible. In retrospect it is clear that the task of the Army has been an unenviable one and the manner in which its operations have constantly been readjusted has tested its professionalism.

The essential aim of a counter-subversion campaign is simple: counter-insurgency seeks to reduce and eventually destroy the subversive influence of a terrorist group – in this case the IRA (but also later the Irish National Liberation Army) – which has worked to increase its influence over the population either formally or informally and undermine the fabric of the existing social and political order in the province. The way in which intelligence is collated has a direct bearing on these operations, as it is supremely important in identifying and eliminating members of a clandestine military organization, and the success terrorists enjoy in extending their control over the populace will determine the flow of information. As General Sir Frank Kitson observes in his influential book *Low Intensity Operations*, 'the problem of defeating the enemy consists very largely of finding him, [and] it is easy to recognise the paramount importance of good information'.

Such a simple formulation obscures the complexity of realising the end. The fact that Northern Ireland is a part of the United Kingdom is not the least of the problems facing planners of any such campaign. The Army has to destroy any measure of influence that the IRA had acquired over the civil population, simultaneously increase its flow of information and either eliminate or render the IRA ineffective by capturing its arms, explosives, places of refuge and drying up its source of recruits and intelligence. This required the Army to wage a psychological war on its own territory, for which it was initially quite unprepared, and its success could not be measured merely in military terms. Its operations had to be conducted with due regard to the requirements of the mass media, a vociferous concern for civil liberties of British citizens, and the state of international opinion, especially in the Irish Republic and the United States.[1]

One area in which the Army did not reveal any great adaptability was in handling the media. In the early days in Northern Ireland, the Army naïvely assumed that the truth will 'always out'. Before 1970 handling reporters had not received a very high priority in the training manuals of the British Army. As one recent critic has observed, 'an Army officer selected for a PR appointment is more likely to receive commisserations rather than congratulations from his colleagues'.[2] The Army overlooked that it is the *first* reports of any given incident that make a real impact and no number of retractions or amendments can compensate for the initial effect of an event or presentation of that event by a skilful propagandist. A thorough investigation of an incident takes time (which is of the essence in Fleet Street or on television) and the effect of the most fair minded inquiry, taking into account all the relevant factors, is muted by comparison with the dramatic *political* reactions which accrue from an originally garbled (and frequently distorted, or sometimes inaccurate) news story. Newspaper reports and television coverage of 'Bloody Sunday' especially was used to discredit the Army. Only in 1977 did it develop an information policy that emphasised its own version of events in a more positive manner, only commenting on specific incidents when directly questioned about them. The training and resources of the Army were quite inadequate to cope with the pressures of news reporting. In 1970 it only had 30 trained for 'psychological' warfare, and half of these were posted overseas. One intelligence officer was reported to say that after the events of 1970, 'It would take an advertising agency of genius to sell the British Army in the Catholic ghettoes', and after the first honeymoon with the Catholics was over, it was clear that the British Army would have to rethink

[1] See David Charters, 'Intelligence and Psychological Warfare Operations in Northern Ireland', *RUSI Journal*, 122 (1977), 23–24.

[2] Alan Hooper, *The Military and the Media* (London 1982), 214.

its public relations. But by the time this was completed, the pressure of events had set these efforts at nought.

Although the Army moved slowly on the public relations front, its adaptability in responding to operational needs was much more impressive. In 1972 the *Sunday Times* 'Insight' team published a book arguing that the commitment of the Army was a major blunder because its training and outlook did not in any way equip it for a counter-subversion campaign. Certainly in 1969 the Army was not trained for use on a large scale within the United Kingdom. Even though the IRA had conducted a sporadic campaign of bombing in 1968, Northern Ireland was considered a 'cushy' number by most soldiers. The garrison numbered only 2,168 men. By 1971 numbers had increased to 21,300 and a year later they rose to 22,000. In Malaya the Army had successfully developed a counter-subversion strategy in the jungles of Malaya, an area of the world where the attentions of the media were far less insistent than in Northern Ireland. As well as politicians at Westminster, the views of Ulster politicians had also to be taken into account. Pleas for the maintenance of civil liberties could not be ignored, and no serious attempt was made to control the movements of the population. Attempts at controlling the border were less rigorous than many Unionist politicians would have liked because the Army realized that local residents would be put to a great deal of inconvenience. In the long run such efforts would have been counter-productive. Likewise, as the level of street violence rose so did calls for a general curfew. Some local curfews were introduced. But to be really effective a general curfew required a large number of troops on the ground and moreover, these would present clear targets for terrorist snipers. Troops would have to be empowered to shoot curfew breakers – a move that the Army calculated would heighten tensions and prove unacceptable to public opinion.

When compared with the Army of 1919–21, the contemporary British Army is shown in a favourable light. It is much better trained and equipped for its task and has shown greater ability to adapt. The points forcefully argued by the 'Insight' team underline that Britain is virtually alone in the Western world in lacking a paramilitary third force equipped and trained for riot control. There is no force to compare with the French CRS, the Dutch Marechaussee or the American National Guard. The arguments for raising such a force are persuasive. The police would be relieved of tedious duties, and as riot police could be concentrated against rioters quickly, they could handle riots more effectively and economically. The immediacy of a third force would relieve the Army of the necessity to support the civil power. The problem with such a view is that it goes against the grain of British policing, which has ostensibly eschewed the organization of a national police force, and has always been hostile to paramilitary organizations, as witness the widespread hostility to a step in that direction – the Special Patrol Group. At any rate, reliance on the Army involved immediately the resuscitation of historic anti-British feeling that could be focused on the Army. Perhaps the introduction of a third force would only have deflected such criticism on to itself, but it would have had a less potent appeal and phrases such as 'Bloody Sunday' would have had a reduced emotional effect.[3]

For good or ill British Governments have relied on the direct intervention of the Army in the event of a break down in law and order. this has been a costly burden for the Army to bear in Northern Ireland. Many of the troops have been drawn from the British Army of the Rhine (BAOR). They are either sent to the province on 18 month garrison tours with their wives and families or on four month emergency or roulement tours without their families. The troops on four month tours are stationed in the most troublesome areas. These have averaged up to 92–100 hours of patrolling per week. In the period 1 January 1974–30 June 1976 up to 50 units and 80,000 men were in the province at some time; 2nd Light Infantry having served on seven separate occasions. Although rapid tours have a drawback in that they prevent troops from becoming thoroughly familiar with their duties, the psychological and physical strain of more extended tours might prove too much for officers and men. In any case, by the summer of 1978 the garrison tours had been extended to 14 months for units based in Britain and 22 months for those from BAOR. The only alternative was to increase the emergency roulement tours from four to six months which was rejected on the grounds that it was likely to erode morale. On this kind of duty men simply patrol, eat, sleep and watch television. Such tedium could not be accepted for long periods.

The training of British soldiers, especially those from BAOR, is totally different from that required by the special conditions of Northern Ireland. Consequently, the drain on the Army's reserves has been considerable because it is frequently forgotten that their absence from Germany consumes much more time than the four months they are stationed in Northern Ireland. One month is assigned for the unit to prepare itself for special assignments, followed by another month so that troops can become accustomed to their 'normal' duties, followed by another month's leave – a fortnight before leaving for Ulster and another fortnight after they have returned. These preparations were very important to the men of the Royal Armoured Corps and the Royal Artillery who leave behind their tanks, self-propelled guns and artillery to support the infantry, and as many as seven units of these troops have been borrowed simultaneously from BAOR. The Army's manpower reserves have been so stretched that occasionally even members of the R.A.F. Regiment and the Royal Marines have been sent to the province. Such a

[3] Richard Clutterbuck, *Protest and the Urban Guerrilla* (London 1973), 33–34.

deployment on a large and improvised scale, the hurried manner in which training schemes have changed, displays a skill in coping with the unexpected that was not allowed for in the early, rather hasty, criticisms of the British Army's ability to cope with an urban guerrilla war in Northern Ireland. It is proof of professionalism in the widest sense and has reaffirmed that the morale of the Army is high. As John Baynes has written, 'The frustrating and difficult task of preserving law and order in Ulster may have given little pleasure to those carrying it out, but it has reassured them [the soldiers], and others, of the essential requirement for their particular skills.[4]

The Army has also shown impressive abilities of improvisation and adaptability in improving old or developing new equipment for urban guerrilla warfare. For instance, the one ton armoured personnel carrier, the 'pig' has had its armour thickened to offer protection against high velocity American and East European rifles which have now superceded Thompson machine guns as the basic terrorist weapon. A new version of the Saracen armoured care has been introduced which can fire without opening a hatch – a change that was introduced in time for Operation 'Motorman'. Other more advanced technological developments include the use of image and seismic surveillance equipment to find and listen to terrorists at night, and 'sniffers' to trace explosives in suspects; 'nitesun' is an 800 candlepower searchlight which can light up the ground at night from helicopters. But highly refined military technology cannot be produced like rabbits from a hat; the development time for special weapons is so long that it is rarely possible to order particular weapons for use in special operations. The tag 'Operational Emergency' will confer on an item a measure of high priority but this is no guarantee of any precise solution being found to an operational problem, as the difficulties surrounding the faltering advances in developing suitable body armour for the infantry shows, which at the time of writing is far from proving reliable.[5]

What of the task that the Army was set? It has coped well with the institutional strains that have been imposed upon it. But has it developed a coherent anti-terrorist strategy given the political constraints which have hedged it in at every turn? It is well known that the Bogside Riots of August 1969 led to the deployment of the Army in Northern Ireland. It is of no small symbolic significance that in this very same area over two years later, street confrontations led to 'Bloody Sunday'. This transformation of Catholic opinion from regarding the troops as their protectors to execrating them as oppressors resembling their forebears of 1919–21 illustrates the general

4 J.C.M. Baynes, *The Soldier in Modern Society* (London 1972), 70, 92, 99.

5 Henry Brandon, *The Soldiers* (London 1979), 137–39; also see Norman L. Dodd, 'The Corporal's War: internal security operations in Northern Ireland', *Military Review*, 56 (July 1976), 59–68.

intractability of the Army's dilemma. The initial 'honeymoon' was to last from the adoption of the Hunt Report, which advocated disarming the RUC and the disbandment of the 'B' Specials, in an attempt to create a truly bisectarian police force and 'territorial' force in the Ulster Defence Regiment, until April 1970 when it ended abruptly after 400 Catholic youths attacked the Royal Scots injuring 25 men. During this period the Army was anxious to show that it dealt with crime and violence in an 'even handed' way. The attitude of the IRA was more complex. They probably hoped that the Army would act in such a way that any major military intervention would eventually stimulate widespread hatred. The new GOC, Northern Ireland General Sir Ian Freeland predicted that the 'honeymoon' would end once an act of violence provoked really firm action.

During this lull the Army developed a whole series of community projects: the Magnet Club in Mulhouse Street and the paradise Club in Coates Street were both very successful in attracting large numbers of youths on a bisectarian basis. organizing discoes, sporting events and the like. The laudable aim of bringing together young people of both denominations initially succeeded because neither political grouping interfered. Once violence began – one club was blown up in Londonderry in 1971 – these well intentioned efforts at influencing the 'hearts and minds' of the younger generation crumbled as a 'laager mentality' largely reasserted itself. Such efforts would only have had a faint hope of success over the long term if the surrounding political culture had developed in such a way as to sustain them; it did not, and they were doomed to failure.

By the summer of 1970 friction between the Army and the Catholic community was increasing. Throughout the period of the 'honeymoon', and indeed after, a measure of cooperation with the Army had been sought by the IRA. Both sides seem to have thought that they could gain intelligence from such contacts. It ended temporarily in February 1971 with the launching of the IRA's urban guerrilla campaign. Countering this immediately highlighted the kinds of problems that the Army faced while operating in a part of the British Isles. A curfew introduced into the Falls Road certainly confirmed the view that curfews antagonise those they are in part designed to protect. All efforts to send 'meals on wheels' to elderly Catholics and generate good will dissolved in face of hard political realities. As the Catholic community had decided that the IRA was its most reliable form of protection against the Protestants and that the Army had not done enough to protect them, the Army faced formidable problems in increasing its quality and quantity of intelligence in the Catholic areas. Army intelligence corps personnel were seconded to the RUC; local censuses were undertaken to complete a street by street register of the population, and card indexes were built up so that fairly complete dossiers on suspected terrorists were put together, including relevant cross references to their family and friends. Initially frequent mobile foot patrols were encouraged so that the troops could familiarize themselves with their areas and gain background knowledge and contacts. After the imposition of Direct Rule in May 1972 these were discouraged and a 'low profile' patrolling policy was introduced, largely at the request of the Northern Ireland office.

Outbreaks of violence in January 1971 were precipitated by street attacks on Army dance halls. On 14 January 700 troops were launched into a detailed house-to-house search of Catholic areas and were met by 42 petrol bombs and three bottles of sulphuric acid; fresh rioting ensued. The experience of the Brixton riots of 1982 has confirmed that the technique of 'swamping' an area with forces only hardens existing antagonisms and provokes renewed violence. The 'innocent' citizen looks askance when his every move is monitored and he is more likely than formerly to sympathise with those who violently oppose such activity. On 6 February the first British soldier was shot dead and seven were wounded in two gun battles. The attempt to reduce the level of violence by a combination of a 'hearts and minds' attempt to win over the Catholic community, and the restrained use of force had clearly failed against those who were determined to use violence for political ends. In retrospect hopes placed in the community schemes were hopelessly exaggerated and were symptomatic of a fundamental ignorance of conditions prevailing in Northern Ireland. *Military* success against terrorists could have been possible if armed force had been deployed against the terrorist organizations while they were still weak. In 1969–71 this option was not acceptable to the British Government and not consistent with its well intentioned efforts to bring 'peace' to Northern Ireland. Judged by the veracity of its motives the policy of the British Government evokes admiration; but the half measures that were deployed to support it only resulted in an increase in that very violence that had sought to check.[6]

At this stage the most vexed problem facing the Army was crowd control. In an attempt to control crowd violence the RUC had suffered 368 casualties before 1971. Between 1970–1975 almost one quarter of its entire strength was killed or injured at some time in civil strife. Until the middle of 1970 the Army tended to meet trouble from crowds head on. The IRA could easily produce a crowd at short notice which could be used to intimidate or even overwhelm a small patrol. Sniper fire was immediately returned and crowds were confronted as they gathered. After the first appearance of gunmen in 1970 the IRA manipulated crowds so as to cover them. While rioters pelted the troops with stones, petrol or nail bombs, snipers hid behind them and took 'pot

[6] Frank Wright, 'The Ulster Spectrum', David Carlton and Carlo Schaerf (eds), *Contemporary Terror* (London 1981), 195; J. Brian Garrett, 'Ten Years of British Troops in Northern Ireland, *International Security*, 4 (1979–80), 80–104.

shots'. Often soldiers preferred the 'fire right' to crowd control, and care had to be taken so that their enthusiasm did not carry them into ambushes. One sniper managed to kill five soldiers from the Green Howards in the Ardoyne area later in 1971. The usual ploy was to create a disturbance, after which a British patrol would arrive; once they emerged from behind cover, the gunman would fire a couple of shots and scurry away into the urban jungle behind him. Another variant of the ambush technique was to dig a Claymore mine into the side of the hedge or culvert and detonate it as a patrol passed. Thus by the winter of 1971–72 the Army had to match a four fold threat: the hit and run sniper; bombs in public places; concealed mines; and the murder of off-duty soldiers.

The escalation of these forms of terrorist violence increased the pressure to suspend habeas corpus and introduce internment without trial. This policy illustrates the dangers of introducing a punitive form of policy in a democracy. In purely military terms internment was a striking success. The RUC Special Branch listed those they wanted arrested or wanted for questioning and the Army interned them. 342 people were arrested immediately and the total eventually rose to over 700. Twelve of these were subject to what was officially described as 'interrogation in depth'. This was perhaps the most controversial aspect of the whole policy. The British Army had developed a form of intense interrogation in Cyprus and Aden (based on that used by the Communist Chinese), which attempted to manipulate the victim's sense of isolation and vulnerability and push him into responding to stress and ostracism. Those interrogated in depth offered information on 700 members of the IRA and identified those involved in 85 unsolved incidents. Discoveries of considerable stores of arms and explosives were made – more than any previously located. This information was extremely vulnerable, and furthermore, the fuss caused among members of the IRA that 'torture' was being used, frightened those undergoing interrogation to offer information in an attempt to escape torture – at least for a time.

But success in counter-insurgency cannot be judged simply by reference to a military balance sheet. The overall effect of internment was a propaganda success for the IRA. Internment runs counter to the second of Sir Robert Thompson's principles of waging a successful counter-insurgency campaign, namely the '*The government must function in accordance with law*'.[7] Although internment achieved considerable disruption of the IRA's leadership, it proved a major embarrassment for the British Government. To be really effective, internment should have been applied ruthlessly. It was actually applied half heartedly, and it is difficult to see how the Army could have acted otherwise. In a well publicized stunt, Joe Cahill, chief of staff of

7 Robert Thompson, *Defeating Communist Insurgency* (London 1966), 52 (my italics).

the Provisional IRA, held a press conference which simultaneously ridiculed the efficiency of internment as a coercive measure and allowed him to attack 'torture' and other draconian measures. Reports of ill treatment of detainees filtered through from the Irish press and were given wide coverage in the *Sunday Times*. Even though British public opinion seemed to rally in support of the Army's position, the British Government found the matter embarrassing and set up the Compton inquiry. The majority report concluded that under the conditions of an urban guerrilla war 'the techniques used were necessary and should be permitted provided that they were used only when it was essential to obtain information quickly'. But the report only underlined the problem facing the Army, namely that half measures only stimulated violence without eradicating it. If an escalation of violence was risked while the IRA leadership was bruised but still intact, then a momentum would be injected into the urban guerrilla war, and this could hardly compensate, over the long term, for the embarrassment caused the Government.

The new Secretary of State for Northern Ireland, William Whitelaw, appointed after the imposition of Direct Rule in May 1972 decided that the Army would have to adopt much less provocative tactics. Though internment was not overturned, the number of patrols in the Catholic areas of Belfast were reduced and patrolling was often allowed only at night. The 'hot pursuit' of terrorists was discouraged and strict limits were placed on the number of random searches and arrests made. This constituted in many soldiers' view a classic example of the dangers of 'political' interference in operations. It was nevertheless inevitable once the decisive step had been taken of introducing internment without trial within one part of the United Kingdom and Westminster took upon itself the burden of governing the province. Militarily, the Army's sources of intelligence were endangered, as contacts were isolated and prevented from offering information. Fewer patrols led to the creation of so-called 'no go' areas. Indeed many of the gains of the previous two years were in danger of being lost. The discrediting of internment required the development of more subtle methods of counter-subversion. There was an increase in positive policing. Although the IRA had lost many of its most able leaders, the initiative in the urban guerrilla war, which had been promised by the introduction of internment, was lost. After the imposition of Direct Rule the Prime Minister, Edward Heath, promised to phase out internment. Thus a paradox developed. As the price of internment proved too high, the Heath Government back tracked and urged a more conciliatory policy on the Army. The IRA was thus given an opportunity to set up areas which excluded the security forces and where the writ of the British Government did not run. Consequently, a build-up of forces was required – some 22,000 men – for the mounting of Operation 'Motorman' and the dismantling of these areas. The employment of military force was conducted with a haphazard inconsistency.

But again, the opportunity which was presented by this concentration of military force in the Catholic areas to destroy the IRA militarily was lost, if the option was ever available. The British Government had undertaken a political initiative which resulted in the Sunningdale agreement. This, in brief, attempted to bring together the 'moderate' political parties and hammer out an agreement for peace which was virtually imposed from Westminster. It assumed that the determination to restore devolved, constitutional government was as strong in Ulster as it was in Westminster. But certain political elements were not included under the general rubric 'moderate' and the Sunningdale agreement did not reflect political reality in Ulster. At any rate, its formulation had an important effect on the 'campaign' against terrorism in that it became much less ambitious in character. If the Sunningdale agreement was successful, the political 'atmosphere' of Ulster would be greatly improved, the Dublin Government could be persuased to join in the attempt to contain IRA terrorism, and SDLP could be reconciled to a restrained and judicious use of emergency powers until the security problem could be resolved.

But it is clear that the security problem was to be improved largely by *political* means; the Army would be an auxiliary to this and it would be used to *contain* terrorist violence. These ambitious political proposals were torpedoed by the Loyalist General Strike of May 1974 which followed in the wake of the fall of the Heath Government. The succeeding Labour Government realized that the attempt to develop and impose a solution from Westminster had failed and that the political problem would have to be solved by Ulster politicians themselves. The new Secretary of State for Northern Ireland, Merlyn Rees, set up a constitutional Convention; direct rule would continue and so would the campaign against terrorist violence. This policy was sound so long as it was based on a correct estimate of the political spectrum in Ulster; if this was unsound however it ran the risk of promoting political conditions that would render the Army's task more difficult and therefore, over the long term, render the political task more intractable. Rees wanted the Army to hold the line against terrorism, maintain order in a restrained manner and thus pave the way for some form of political settlement. Consequently, the general guide line was laid down that the level of intensity of the security campaign against the IRA *would be regulated by the level of intensity of terrorist offensive operations*. If the IRA refrained from violence, then the Army would refrain from responding and a 'low profile' could be maintained. Such a policy, of course, left the initiative in the hands of the terrorists. The Army responded by pointing out that there would be no prospect of troops being confined to their barracks and terrorist crimes would continue to be prosecuted mercilessly. Nevertheless some subtle changes were introduced. Rees suspended the practice of issuing interim custody orders, and well known IRA leaders were allowed to walk the streets of Belfast unmolested. Given its task in maintaining public order, the Army's room for manoeuvre against terrorism was strictly limited.

The ceasefire with the IRA, evidence of a distinct improvement in 'atmosphere', reduced this room for manoeuvre further. Rees believed that if detention was phased out it would excite the enthusiasm of Catholics and reduce the general level of violence. All remaining detainees were released by December 1975, though this was accompanied by an increase of violence by December of the following year. There appeared to be little substance in the 'carrot and stick' theory. The ceasefire itself only returned the Army to the position that it had enjoyed before 1970 of co-operating with the IRA in an attempt to keep the fiction that the ceasefire was a unilateral act of the IRA. The various 'incident centres' set up and manned by members of Provisional Sinn Fein, in which incidents of alleged 'harrassment' by the security forces were reported, opened the Government to the charge that it was recognizing that the IRA had legitimate authority over its members, whatever it might say officially. At any event it seemed an odd way to carry out a counter-subversion campaign against an organization that the British Government continued to deny had any legitimacy. It still searched for a political solution that this policy of co-operating with the IRA made more difficult to attain, as the influence of the IRA was strengthened.

At the same time efforts were made to reduce the degree of Army participation in the law enforcement process and increase the role of the R.U.C. The Army had been introduced as an aid to the civil power when those forces had become overstretched; it was never meant to suborn or replace that power. The yellow card carried by every British soldier, which provided guidelines explaining under what conditions troops could open fire, does not exempt British soldiers from the law, even though the Special Powers Act does confer some concessions in extenuating circumstances. Building up the strength of the police was difficult because of its small size. For instance, in Malaya the Army deployed 40,000 troops and were assisted by 66,000 police. In Northern Ireland the average number of troops before 1978 were 12–14,000, but these were assisted by only 6,000 police and 2,000 reserves, plus the Ulster Defence Regiment, a body that by 1981 had formed the R.U.C.'s first reserve if military help was required. It has also been complicated by the growth of Protestant paramilitary organizations as a response to the IRA. In October 1975 the Ulster Volunteer Force was implicated in several sectarian murders and was proscribed. The somewhat more orderly Ulster Defence Association and the Ulster Service Corps (largely composed of members of the disbanded 'B' Specials) were left alone as they claimed to be purely defensive. But this excuse omits one important factor, namely, that however defensive these organizations might be, a clash between them and the IRA might lead to an outbreak of inter-communal violence which has markedly declined since the mid-1970s. It is also true that the presence of the R.U.C. is still resented in Catholic areas where the IRA is strong. Nevertheless it is hoped to reduce the strength of the Army in Northern Ireland by the mid-1980s to 7,000 men.[8]

The overall thrust of these policies was to introduce an element of stalemate in the urban guerrilla war in Northern Ireland. The police took over many of the tasks of the army, though not without some quarrelling between the two branches of the security forces. 'Police primacy' resulted in some successes with the 'supergrass' prosecutions. As this occurred the struggle took on a more overt political form. The political wing of the IRA has become increasingly adept at gaining political advantage from the stalemate, especially during the Maze hunger strikes. The military campaign has moved away from the urban areas to the border rural areas, where the Army must guard against sporadic bombings. Movement by road is dangerous, and patrols are usually transported by helicopter. The IRA has become adapt at placing 1000 pound bombs under roadside culverts, and detonating them by radio control once vehicles pass by. Even the thick armour of the Saracen armoured car cannot withstand such enormous explosions. The Army has had to come to terms with the hard fact that no matter how hard it tries, it cannot eliminate the possibility that a radio controlled bomb has been placed under a culvert. Research into a radio jamming device has not proved very successful. If they operate at night there is little prospect of capturing terrorists moving about in sparsely populated rural areas.

Any effort which seeks to find a political solution to the Northern Ireland problem which ignores the political power of the IRA, no matter what position is adopted by the Protestants, will fail; and conversely, military efforts which try to hold the line, or improve the 'atmosphere' of the province are liable to foster the political influence of the IRA at the ballot box. The immense complications of this political equation are belied by the simplistic political solutions which the British Government has attempted to impose. Under these circumstances the failure of the British Government to follow a consistent policy of counter subversion has greatly hamstrung the efforts of the Army, and has resulted in an oscillating and opportunistic character of the campaign against terrorism in Ulster. This has only contributed to the growth of the political influence of the IRA, while only reducing the security problems to manageable proportions without solving it. The only uncertainty in the confusion and contradictions of Ulster politics is that terrorism will continue.

[8] For an excellent discussion of the most recent developments, see Josephine Howie, 'Britain's Irish Problem', *RUSI & Brassey's Defence Yearbook 1984* (London 1984), especially 75–76.

SELECTED BIBLIOGRAPHY

Adelson, Alan. *SDS: Profile*. New York: Charles Scribner's Sons, 1972.
Aizcorbe, Roberto. Argentina *The Peronist Myth*. Hicksville, New York: Exposition Press, 1975.
Alexander, Robert J. *The Bolivian National Revolution*. New Brunswick, New Jersey: Rutgers University Press, 1958.
Alexander, Yonah. *The Role of Communications in the Middle East Conflict: Ideological and Religious Aspects*. New York: Praeger Publishers, 1973.
-, ed. *International Terrorism: National, Regional and Global Perspectives*. New York: Praefer Publishers, 1976.
-, Browne, Narforie Ann and Names, Allan S., eds. *Control of Terrorism*. New York: Crane, Russak & Company, 1979.
-, Carlton, David and Wilkinson, Paul, eds. *Terrorism: Theory and Practice*. Boulder: Westview Press, 1979.
-, and Friedlander, Robert A., eds. *Self-Determination: National, Regional and Global Perspectives*. Boulder: Westview Press, 1979.
-, and Kilmarx, Robert A., eds. *Political Terrorism and Business: The Threat and Response*. New York: Praeger Publishers, 1979.
-, and Kittrie, Nicholas, eds. *Crescent and Star: Arab-Israeli Perspectives on the Middle East Conflict*. New York: AMS Press, 1972.
-, and Nannes, Allan, eds., *The United States and Iran: A Documentary History*. Frederick, Maryland: University Publications of America, 1980.
-, and Seymour, M. Finger, eds. *Terrorism: Interdisciplinary Perspectives*. New York: John Jay Press, 1977 and Maidenhead: McGraw Hill Book Co., 1978.
Ali, Tariq, ed. *The New Revolutionaries: A Handbook of the International Radical Left*. New York: William Morrow and Co., 1969.
Alves, Marcio Moreira. *A Grain of Mustard Seed*. Garden City, New York: Doubleday Anchor Press, 1973.
American University, Washington, D.C. Special Operations Research Office. *Human Factors Considerations of Undergrounds in Insurgencies*. Washington, 1966.
Andreski, Stanislav. *Parasitism and Subversion: The Case of Latin America*. New York: Pantheon, 1967.
Annual of Power and Conflict 1979–80. London: Institute for the Study of Conflict, 1980.
Arey, James A. *The Sky Pirates*. New York: Charles Scribner's Sons, 1972.
Ariel, Dan. *Explosion!* Tel Aviv: Olive Books, 1972.
Avineri, Shlomo, ed. *Israel and the Palestinians: Reflections on the Clash of the Two National Movements*. New York: St. Martin's Press, 1971.
Avner (Pseudo.) *Memoirs of an Assassin*. New York:Yoseloff, 1959.

Avrich, Paul. *The Russian Anarchists*. Princeton: University Press, 1967.
Bassiouni, M. Cherif, ed. *International Terrorism and Political Crimes*. Springfield, Illinois: Thomas, 1975.
Baudovin, Jean. *Terrorisme et Justice*. Montreal: Editions du Jour, 1970.
Baumann, Bommi. *Terror or Love? Bommi Baumann's Own Story of His Life as a West German Urban Guerrilla*. New York: Grove Press, 1979.
Baumann, Carol Edler. *The Diplomatic Kidnappings: A Revolutionary Tactic of Urban Terrorism*. The Hague: Martinus Nijhoff, 1973.
Bayo, Alberto. Translated by R. I. Madigan and Angel de Lumus Medina. *150 Questions to a Guerrilla*. Montgomery: Air University, n.d.
Becker, Jillian. *Hitler's Children: The Story of the Baader-Meinhof Terrorist Gang*. Philadelphia: Lippincott, 1977.
Bell, J. Bowyer. *A Time of Terror: How Democratic Societies Respond to Revolutionary Violence*. New York: Basic Books, 1978.
-. *The Myth of the Guerrilla: Revolutionary Theory and Malpractice*. New York: Knopf, 1971.
-. *On Revolt*. Cambridge: Harvard University Press, 1976.
-. *The Secret Army: The IRA 1916–1974*. Cambridge: MIT Press, 1974.
-. *Terror out of Zion: The Irgun, Lehi, Stern & the Palestine Underground, 1929–1949*. New York: St. Martin's Press, 1977.
-. *Transnational Terror*. Washington, D.C.: American Enterprise Omstotire. 1975.
Beres, Louis Rene. *Terrorism and Global Security: The Nuclear Threat*. Boulder, Colo.: Westview Press, 1979.
Berkman, Alexander. *Now and After: The ABC of Communist Anarchism*. New York: Vanguard Press, 1929.
-. *Prison Memoirs of an Anarchist*. New York: Schocken Books, 1970.
Berry, Steve. *The Prevention of Terrorism Act: Legalized Terror*. London: Socialist Work Printers and Publishers, 1977.
Bewaffneter Kampf in Iran. Isari Komitte, 1975.
Black, Cyril E. and Thornton, Thomas P. *Communism and Revolution*. Princeton: University Press, 1964.
Blackstone Associates. *Risk Assessment for Italy*. Washington: Blackstone Associates, 1978.
Bloomfield, Louis M. and Fitzgerald, Gerald F. *Crimes Against Internationally Protected Persons: Prevention and Punishment: An Analysis of the U.N. Convention*. New York: Praeger Publishers, 1975.
Bocca, Geoffrey. *The Secret Army*. Englewood Cliffs: Prentice-Hall, 1968.
Bodelsen, Anders. Translated by Joan Tate. *Operation Cobra*. New York: Elsevier Nelson books, 1979.
Borisov, J. *Palestine Underground: The Story of Jewish Resistance*. New York: Judea Publishing Co., 1947.

Boston, Guy D., Marcus, Marvin and Wheaton, Robert J. *Terrorism: A Selected Bibliography*. Washington, D.C.: National Criminal Justice Reference Service, March, 1976.
Botha, Andries Jakob. *SWAPO*. Sandton, South Africa: Southern Africa Freedom Foundation, 1977.
Bowden, Tom. *The Breakdown of Public Security*. London, Beverly Hills: Sage, 1977.
Brigham, Daniel T. *Blueprint for Conflict*. New York: American-African Affairs Association, 1969.
Brinton, Crane. *The Anatomy of a Revolution*. Englewood Cliffs: Prentice-Hall, 1965.
Broehl, Wayne G. *The Molly Maguires*. Cambridge: Harvard University Press, 1964.
Brown, Richard M. *Strain of Violence: Historical Studies of American Violence and Vigilantism*. London: Oxford University Press, 1975.
Burton, Anthony M. *Revolutionary Violence: The Theories*. New York: Crane, Russack & Co., 1978.
-. *Urban Terrorism: Theory, Practice and Response*. New York: Free Press, 1975.
Button, James W. *Black Violence: Political Impact of the 1960's Riots*. Princeton, New Jersey: Princeton University Press, 1978.
Canadian Council on International Law. *International Terrorism*: Proceedings of the Third Annual Conference held at the University of Ottawa, Ottawa, Canada, October 18–19, 1974. Ottawa: Faculté de droit de l'Université d'Ottawa, 1974.
Carlton, David and Schaerf, Carlo, eds. *International Terrorism and World Security*. London: Croom Helm, 1975.
Carmichael, Joel. *Stalin's Masterpiece*. New York: St. Martin's Press, 1976.
Carr, E.H. *Studies in Revolution*. New York: Grosset and Dunlap, 1964.
Catholic Commission for Justice and Peace in Rhodesia. *Civil War in Rhodesia: Abduction, Torture, and Death in the Counter-insurgency Campaign*. Salisbury: The Commission, 1976.
Chailand, Gerald. *The Palestinian Resistance*. Baltimore: Penguin, 1972.
Chase, L.J., ed. *Bomb Threats, Bombings and Civil Disturbances: A Guide for Facility Protection*. Corvallis, ORE: Continuing Education Publications, 1971.
Clark, Michael K. *Algeria in Turmoil*. New York: Praeger Publishers, 1959.
Clark, Richard C. *Technological Terrorism*. New York: Devin-Adair Co., 1978.
Clark, Robert P. *The Basques: The Franco Years*. Reno, Nevada: University of Nevada Press, 1980.
Clutterbuck, Richard L. *Guerrillas and Terrorists*. London: Faber and Faber, 1978.

-. *Kidnap and Ranson: The Response*. London and boston: Faber and Faber, 1978.
-. *Living with Terrorism*. London: Faber and Faber, 1975.
Clyne, P. *Anatomy of Skyjacking*. London: Abelard-Shumann, 1973.
Cole, Richard B. *Executive Security*. New York: John Wiley & Sons, Inc., 1980.
Conquest, Robert. *The Great Terror*. New York: MacMillan, 1968.
-. *The Human Cost of Soviet Communism*. Washington: U.S. Government Printing Office, 1970.
Contemporary Terrorism. Gaithersburg, Maryland: Bureau of operations and Research. International Association of Chiefs of Police, 1978.
'Convention to Prevent and Punish the Acts of Terrorism taking the Form of Crimes Against Persons and Related Extortion that are of International Significance'. U.S. Government Printing Office, 1971.
Coogan, Tim Patrick. *The IRA*. New York: Praeger Publishers, 1970.
Council of Europe. *Explanatory Report on the European Convention on the Suppression of Terrorism*. Strasbourg: Council of Europe, 1977.
Crelinsten, Ronald S., Laberge-Altmeja, Danielle, and Szabo, Denis, eds. *Terrorism and Criminal Justice*. Lexington: Lexington Books, 1978.
Cormier, Robert. *After the First Death*. New York: Pantheon Books, 1979.
Crooty, William J. *Assassination and the Political Order*. New York: Harper and Row, 1971.
Crozier, Brian, ed. *Annual of Power and Conflict, 1973–1974: A Survey of Political Violence and International Influence*. London: Institute for the Study of Conflict, 1975.
-. *Annual of Power and Conflict, 1974–1975: A Survey of Political Violence and International Influence*. London: Institute for the Study of Conflict, 1975.
-. *Annual of Power and Conflict, 1975–1976: A Survey of Political Violence and International Influence*. London: Institute for the Study of Conflict, 1976.
-. *Annual of Power and Conflict, 1976–1977: A Survey of Political Violence and International Influence*. London: Institute for the Study of Conflict, 1977.
-. *South-East Asia in Turmoil*. Baltimore, Penguin Books, 1965.
-. *The Study of Conflict*. London: Institute for the Study of Conflict, 1976.
-. *Ulster: Politics and Terrorism*. London: Institute for the Study of Conflict, 1973.
Cunningham, William C. *Prevention of Terrorism*. McLean, Virginia: Hallcrest Press, 1978.
Curtis, Michael. et al., eds. *The Palestinians: People, History, Politics*. Edison, New Jersey: Transaction books, 1975.

Dallin, Alexander and Breslauer, George W. *Political Terror in Communist Systems*. Stanford: University Press, 1970.
Davies, Dave. *The Ustasha in Australia*. Sydney: Communist Paryt of Autralia, 1972.
Davies, Jack. *Political Violence in Latin America*. London: International Institute for Strategic Studies, 1972.
Davies, James C., ed. *When Men Revolt and Why*. New York: Free Press, 1971.
Davis, James R. *The Terrorists*, San Diego, California: Grossmont Press, 1978.
Debray, R. *Revolution on the Revolution*. New York: Monthly Review Press, 1967.
DeGrazia, Sebastian and Stecchini, Livio C. *The Coup d'Etat: Past Significance and Modern Technique*. China Lake: U.S. Ordinance Test Station, 1965.
Demaris, Ovid. *Brothers in Blood: The International Network*. New York: Scribner, 1977.
Dillon, Martin and LeHane, Denis. *Political Murder in Norhtern Ireland*. Baltimore: Penguin Books, 1974.
Dobson, Christopher. *Black September: Its Short, Violent History*. New York: MacMillan, 1974.
-. *The Terrorists*. New York: Facts on File Publications, 1979. -, and Payne, Ronald. *The Carlos Complex: A Study in Terror*. New York: Putnam, 1977.
Dortzbach, Karl and Debbie. *Kidnapped*. New York: Harper and Row, 1975.
Draper, Theodore. *Castro's Revolution: Myths and Realities*. New York: Praeger, 1962.
Duncan, Patrick.*South Africa's Rule of Violence*. London: Methuen, 1964.
DuPlessis, Jan A. *South Africa*. Pretoria: Foreign Affairs Association, 1977.
Eckstein, Harry, ed. *Internal War*. New York: Free Press, 1964.
Elliot, John D. and Gibson, Leslie K., eds. *Contemporary Terrorism: Selected Readings*. Gaithersburg: International Association of Chiefs of Police, 1978.
Ellis, Albert and Gullo, John. *Murder and Assassination*. New York: Stuart Lyle, 1971.
European Convention on the Suppression of Terrorism. Strassbourg: Council of Europe, 1977.
Evans, Alona E. and Murphy, John F., eds. *Legal Aspects of International Terrorism*. Lexington: Lexington Books, 1978.
Evans, Ernst. *Calling a Truce to Terror: The American Response to International Terrorism*. Westport, Conn.: Greenwood Press, 1979.
Evans, Robert D. *Brazil, The Road Back from Terrorism*. London: Institute for the Study of Conflict, 1974.

Fairbairn, G. *Revolutionary Guerrilla Warfare: The Countryside Version.* Middlesex, England: Penguin Books, 1974.
Fanon, Franz. *Toward the African Revolution: Political Essays.* Translated by Haadon Chevalier. New York: Grove Press, 1967.
-. *The Wretched of the Harth.* New York: Grove Press, 1968.
Farhi, David. *The Limits to Dissent.* Palo Alto, California: Aspen Institute for Humanistic Studies, 1978.
Faul, Denis. *SAS Terrorism.* Dungannon, The Authors, 1976.
Ferguson, J. Halcro. *The Revolution of Latin America.* London: Thames and Hydson, 1963.
Fitzgerald, Charles P. *Revolution in China.* New York: Praeger, 1952.
Fleming, Marie. *The Anarchist Way to Socialism.* Totowa, New Jersey: Rowman and Littlefield, 1979.
Footman, David. *Red Prelude.* Westport, Conn.: Hyperion Press, 1979.
Frank, Gerold. *The Deed.* New York: Simon and Schuster, 1963.
Freed, Donald and Landis, Fred. *Death in Washington: The Murder of Orlando Letelier.* London: U.S. Distributors for Zed Press, 1980.
Friedlander, Robert A. *Terrorism: Documents of International and Local Control.* Dobbs Ferry, New York: Oceana Publications, 1979, 2 vols.
Fromm, Erich. *The Anatomy of Human Destructiveness.* new York: Rinehart and Winston, 1973.
Fuqua, Paul Q. and Wilson, Jerry. *Terrorism – The Executives Guide to Survival.* Houston: Gulf Publishing Company Book Division, 1978.
Gablonski, Edward. *Terror from the Sky: Airwar.* Garden city, New York: Doubleday, 1971.
Gale, William. *The Compound.* New York: Rawson Associates Publishers, 1977.
Galula, Davis. *Counterinsurgency Warfare: Theory and Practice.* New York: Praeger, 1964.
Gaucher, Roland. *The Terrorists: From Tzarist Russia to the O.A.S.* Translated by P. Spurlin. London: Secker and Warburg, 1968.
Gellner, J. *Bayonets in the Streets: Urban Guerrilla at Home and Abroad.* Ontario: Collier-MacMillan Canada, Ltd., 1974.
Giap, Vo-nguyen. *People's War, People's Army: The Viet Cong Insurreciton Manual for Underdeveloped Countries.* New York: Praeger, 1962.
Gibson, Brian. *The Birmingham Bombs.* Chichester: Rose, 1976.
Gillo, M.E. *The Tupamaro Guerrillas.* New York: Ballantine, 1970.
-. *The Tupamaro Guerrillas.* Translated by Anna Edmondston. Introduction by Robert Alexander. New York: Saturday Review Press, 1972.
Goode, Stephen.*Guerrilla Warfare and Terrorism.* New York: F. Watts, 1977.
Goodhart, Philip. *The Climate of Collapse.* Richmond: Foreign Affairs

Publishing Co., 1975.
Gott, Richard. *Guerrilla Movements in Latin America*. London: Thomas Nelson and Sons, 1970.
Graham, Hugh D. and Gurr, Ted R., eds. *Violence in America: Historical and Comparative Perspectives*. Washington, D.C.: National Commission of the Causes and Prevention of Violence, 1969.
Great Britain. Committee of Privy. Counsellors Appointed to Consider Authorized Procedures for the Interrogation of Persons Suspected of Terrorism. Report. London: H. M. Stationary Off., 1972.
Great Britain. Foreign Office. *Report by Mr. Roderic Bowen, Q. C., on Procedures for the Arrest, Interrogation and Detention of Suspected Terrorists in Aden*. London: H.M.S.O., 1966.
Greene, T.N., ed. *The Guerrilla: And How to Fight Him*. New York: Praeger Publishers, 1962.
Grimshaw, Allen. *Racial Violence in the United States*. Chicago: Aldine, 1970.
Gross, Feliks. *Violence in Politics: Terror and Political Assassination in Eastern Europe and Russia*. The Hague: Mouton, 1972.
Grundy, Kenneth W. *Guerrilla Struggle in Africa: An Analysis and Preview*. New York: Grossman, 1971.
Guevara, Che. *Reminiscences of the Cuban Revolutionary War*. Translated by V. Ortiz. New York: Monthly Review Press, 1968.
Guevara, Ernesto. *Che Guevara on Guerrilla Warfare*. Translated by Harries-Clichy Peterson. New York: Praeger, 1961.
-. *Obra Revolucionaria*. 4th ed. Mexico: Ediciones Era, 1971.
Guillaume, Gilbert and Lerasseur, Georges. *Terrorisme International*. Paris: A Pedone, 1977.
Guillen, Abraham. *Philosophy of the Urban Guerrilla*. Translated by D.C. Hodge. New York: Morrow, 1973.
Gurr, Ted Robert. *Why Men Rebel*. Princeton: University Press, 1970.
Gusman, Campos, et al. *La Violencia en Columbia*. Bogota: Ediciones Tercer Mundo, 1963.
Gwyn, David. *Idi Amin: Death-Light of Africa*. Boston: Little, Brown, 1977.
Hacker, Frederick F. *Crusaders, Criminals, Crazies: Terror and Terrorism in Our Time*. New York: Norton, 1976.
Hackey, Thomas, ed. *The Problem of Partition: Peril to World Peace*. New York: Rand McNally, 1972.
-. *Voices of Revolution: Rebels and Rhetoric*. Dryden Press, 1973.
Hale, H.W. *Political Trouble in India, 1917–1937*. Allahabad: Chush Publications, 1974.
Halperin, Ernst. *Terrorism in Latin America*. Beverly Hills: Sage Publications, 1975.

Harkabi, Y. *The Arab's Position in Their Conflict with Israel.* Jerusalem: Israeli Universities Press.
Havens, Murray Clark. *Assassination and Terrorism*. Manchaca, Texas: S. Swift Publishing Col, 1975.
Heilbrunn, Otto. *Partisan Warfare.* New York: Praeger Publishers, 1962.
Hills, Denis Cecil. *Rebel People.* New York: Africana Publishing Co., 1978.
Hodges, Donald Clark. *National Liberation Fronts: 1960–1970.* New York: Morrow, 1972.
-. *Philosophy of the Urban Guerrilla.* New York: Morrow, 1973.
The Human Cost of Communism in Vietnam. Washington: U.S. Government Printing Office, 1970.
Hofstadter, Richard and Wallace, Michael, eds. *American Violence: A Documentary History.* New York: Knopf, 1970.
Horn, Stanley. *Invisible Empire: The Story of the Ku Klux Klan, 1866–1871.* Boston: Houghton Mifflin Co., 1939.
Horrell, Muriel, *Terrorism in South Africa.* Johannesburg: South African Institute of Race Relations, 1968.
Horowitz, Irving Louis, ed. *The Anarchists.* New York: Dell Publishers, 1964.
-. *The Struggle is the Message: The Organization and Ideology of the Anti-War Movement.* Berkeley: Glendessary Press, 1970.
Hosmer, Stephen T. *Viet Cong Repression and Its Implications for the Future.* Lexington: Heath Lexington Books, 1970.
The Human Cost of Communism in Vietnam: A Compendium. Washington: U.S. Government Printing Office, 1972.
Humberman, Leo and Sweezy, Paul M. *Cuba: Anatomy of a Revolution.* 2nd ed. New York: Montly Review Press, 1960.
Hutchinson, Martha Crenshaw. *Revolutionary Terrorism: The FLN in Algeria, 1954–1962.* Stanford, California: Hoover Institution Press, Stanford University, 1978.
Hyams, Edward. *Terrorist and Terrorism.* New York: St. Martin's Press, 1974.
Hyde, Douglas Arnold. *The Roots of Guerrilla Warfare.* Chester Springs, PA: Dufour Editions, 1968.
The Impact of Terrorism and Skyjacking on the Operations of the Criminal Justice System. Montreal: International Centre for Comparative Criminology. Université de Montreal, 1976.
Indira Devi, M.G. *Terrorist Movement in South India.* Trivandrum: Kercila Historical Society, 1977.
Institute for the Study of Conflict. *Ulster, Politics and Terrorism.* London: Institute for the Study of Conflict, 1974.
International Defence Aid Fund. *Terror in Tete.* London: International Defence Aid Fund, 1973.

International Terrorism. Milwaukee: Institute of World Affairs, University of Wisconsin-Milwaukee, 1974.
Israel. Misrael ha-huts. ha-Lish kah le-hasbarah Jerusalem: Israel Ministry for Foreign Affairs, Information Division, 1972.
Irish Republican Army. Provisional IRA. *Freedom Struggle*. London: Red Books, 1973.
Jackson, Sir Geoffrey. *Surviving the Long Nights: An Autobiographical Account of a Political Kidnapping*. New York: Vanguard, 1974.
Jacobs, Walter Darnell. *Terrorism in Southern Africa: Portents and Prospects*. New York: American African Affairs Association, 1973.
Jenkins, Brian, M. *The Five Stages of Urban Guerrilla Warfare*. Santa Monica: Rand, 1974.
-.*International Terrorism: A New Kind of Warfare*. Santa Monica: Rand Corp., 1974.
-. *International Terrorism*. Los Angeles, California: Crescent Publications, 1975.
-. *Numbered Lives*. Santa Monica, Cal.: Rand Corp., 1977.
-. *Terrorism and Kidnapping*. Santa Monica, Cal.: Rand Corp., 1974.
-. *Soldiers versus Gunmen: The Challenge of Urban Guerrilla Warfare*. Santa Monica: Rand Corp., 1974.
-. *Terrorism Works – Sometimes*. Santa Monica: Rand Corp., 1974.
-, and Johnson, Janera. *International Terrorism: A Chronolgoy, 1968–1974*. A Report prepared for the Department of State and Defense Advanced Research Projects Agency. Santa Monica, Cal.: Rand Corp., 1975.
Johnson, Chalmers A. *Revolutionary Change*. Boston: Little, Brown, and Co., 1966.
Johnson, John H. *The Military and Society in Latin America*. Stanford: University Press, 1964.
Joll, James. *The Anarchists*. New York: Grossett and Dynlop, 1964.
Joyner, Nancy D. *Aerial Hijacking as an International Crime*. Dobbs Ferry. New York: Oceana, 1974.
Jurjevie, Marjan. *Ustasha Under the Southern Cross*. Melbourne: M. Jurjevie, 1973.
Kaplan, Morton A., ed. *The Revolution in World Politics*. New York: Wiley, 1962.
Karagueuzian, Dikran. *Blow It Up!* Gambit: Boston Press, 1971.
Katz, Robert. *Days of Wrath: The Ordeal of Aldo Moro, the Kidnapping, the Execution, the Aftermath*. Garden City, New York: Doubleday, 1980.
Kautsky, Karl. *Terrorism and Communism: A Contribution to the Natural History of Revolution*. Translated by W.H. Kerridge. London: George Allen and Unsin, 1920.
Kirkham, J.F. and Levy, S. *Assassination and Political Violence*. National

Commission on the Causes and Prevention of Violence. Washington, D.C.: GPO, 1969.
Kitson, Frank. *Low Intensity Operations: Subversion, Insurgency, Peace-Keeping*. London: Faber Publishers, 1972.
Kobeertz, Richard W. *Target Terrorism*. Gaithersbuty, Maryland: Bureau of Operations and Research: International Association of Chiefs of Police, 1978.
Kohl, J. and Litt, J. *Urban Guerrilla Warfare in Latin America*. Cambridge: MIT Press, 1974.
Kuper, Leo. *The Pity of It All: Polarisation of Racial and Ethnic Relations*. Minneapolis: University of Minnesota Press, 1977.
Kupperman, Robert H. *Facing Tomorrow's Terrorist Incident Today*. Washington, D.C.: Law Enforcement Assistance Administration, Office of Operations Support, 1977.
-, and Trent, D. *Terrorism: Threat, Reality, Response*. Stanford, Cal.: Hoover Institution Press, 1979.
Laffin, John. *Fedayeen*. New York: MacMillan, 1973.
Lambrick, H.T. *The Terrorist*. London: Rowman, 1972.
Laqueur, Walter. *Guerrilla: A Historical and Critical Study*. Boston: Little, Brown and Co., 1976.
-. *Terrorism*. Boston: Little, Brown and Co., 1977.
-. *The Terrorism Reader: A Historical Anthology*. Philadelphia: Temple University, 1978.
Lasswell, Harold, and Lerner, Daniel, eds. *World Revolutionary Elites: Studies in Coercive Ideological Movements*. Cambridge: MIT Press, 1965.
Laushey, David M. *Bengal Terrorism & the Marxist Left*. Calcutta: Firma K.L. Mukhopadhyay, 1975.
Leach, Edmund Ronald. *Custom, Law and Terrorist Voilence*. Edinburgh, University Press, 1977.
Legal and Other Aspects of Terrorism. New York: Practicing Law Institute, 1979.
Leiden, Carl and Schmitt, Karl M., eds. *The Politics of Violence*. Englewood Cliffs: Prentice Hall, 1968.,
Leites, Nathan and Wolf, Charles, Fr. *Rebellion and Authority: An Analytical Essay on Insurgent Conflicts*. Chicago: Markham, Lieuwen, Edwin Publishing Co., 1970.
Lens, Sidney. *Radicalism in America*. New York: Thomas Y. Cromwell Co., 1966.
Lesch, Moseley. *The Politics of Palestinian Nationalism*. Los Angeles: University of California Press, 1973.
Lewytzkyj, Borys, comp. *The Stalinist Terror in the Thirties: Documentation from the Soviet Press*. Stanford, Cal.: Hoover Institution Press, 1974.
LiBonachea, Ramon. *The Cuban Insurrection*. Brunswick, New Jersey:

Marta San Martin, 1964.
Lineberry, William P., ed. *The Struggle Against Terrorism*. New York: H.W. Wilson, 1977.
Liston, Robert A. *Terrorism*. Nashville: Nelson, 1977.
Livingston, Maurius, ed. *International Terrorism in the Contemporary World*. Westport, Conn.: Greenwood Press, 1978.
Lorch, Netanel. *The Edge of the Sword: Israel's War of Independence, 1947–1949*. New York: Putman, 1961.
Lun, Dyer. *A Concise History of the Great Trial of the Chicago Anarchists*. Chicago: Socialistic Publishing Co., 1887.
MacDonald, Peter G. *Stopping the Clock*. London: Hale, 1977.
MacStiofain, Seam. *Revolutionary in Ireland*. London: G. Cremonesi, 1975.
Maksimov, Grigorii Petrovich. *The Guillotine at Work*. Brooklyn, New York: Revisionist Press, 1975.
Mallin, Jay, ed. *Terror and Urban Guerrillas: A Study of the Tactics and Documents*. Coral Gables, Florida: University of Miami Press, 1971.
-. *Terror in Vietnam*. Princeton, New Jersey: D. Van Nostrand Co., 1966.
Malloy, James M. *Bolivia: The Uncompleted Revolution*. Pittsburg: University Press, 1970.
Mao Tse-Tung. *Basic Tactics*. New York: Praeger Publishers, 1966.
-. *On Guerrilla Warfare*. New York: Praeger Publishers, 1961.
Mardor, Munya. *Haganah*. New York: New American Library, 1966.
-. *Strictly Illegal*. London: Robert Hale, 1964.
Marighella, Carlos. *For the Liberation of Brazil*. Harmondsworth: Penguin, 1972.
-. *Minimanual of the Urban Guerrilla*. Havana: Tricontinental, n.d.
Masotti, Louis H. and Bowen, Don R., eds. *Riots and Rebellion: Civil Violence in the Urban Community*. Beverly Hills: Sage Publications, 1968.
Matekalo, Ivan. *Les Dessous du Terrorisme International*. Paris: Jilliard, 1973.
Mathur, L.P. *Indian Revolutionary Movement in the United States of America*. Delhi: S. Chand, 1970.
Max Alphonse. *Guerrillas in Latin America*. The Hague: International Documents and Information Center, 1971.
-. *Tupamaros – A Pattern for Urban Guerrilla Warfare in Latin America*. The Hague: International Documentation and Information Center, 1970.
McDonald, Lawrence Patton. *Trotskyism and Terror: The Strategy of Revolution*. Washington, D.C.: ACU Education and Research Institute, 1977.
McKnight, B. *Mind of the Terrorist*. London: Michael Joseph, Ltd., 1974.
McWhinney, E.W., ed. *Aerial Piracy and International Law*. Eiden: A.W. Sijthoff, 1971.

The Media and Terrorism. Chicago: Field Enterprises, 1977.

Mercader, A. and de Vera, J. *Tupamaros: Estratagia y Accion*. Montevideo: Editorial Alfa, 1969.

Merleau-Ponty, Maurice. *Humanism and Terror: An Essay on the Communist Problem*. Boston: Beacon Press, 1969.

Metrowich, F.R. *Terrorism in Southern Africa*. Pretoria: Africa Institute of South Africa, 1973.

Mickolus, Edward F. *The Literature of Terrorism: A Selectively Annotated Bibliography*. Westport, Conn.: Greenwood Press, 1980.

-. *Transnational Terrorist: A Chronology of Events, 1968–1979*. Westport, Conn.: Greenwood Press, 1980.

Milbank, David L. *International and Transnational Terrorism*. Washington, D.C.: Central Intelligence Agency, 1976.

Miller, Abraham H. *Terrorism and Hostage Negotiations*. Boulder, Colo.: Westview Press, 1980.

Miller, Michael J. and Gilmore, Susan. *Revolution at Berkley*. New York: The Dial Press, 1965.

Momboisse, R.M. *Blueprint of Evolution: The Rebel, The Party, The Techniques of Revolt*. Springfield, Ill.: Charles C. Thomas, 1970.

Morf, Gustave. *Terror in Quebec*. Toronto: Clarke, Irwin, 1970.

Morris, Michael. *Armed Conflict in Southern Africa*. Cape Town: Jeremy Spence, 1974.

-. *Terrorism*. Cape Town: Howard Timmins, 1971.

Morton, Marian J. *Terrors of Ideological Politics*. Cleveland: Case Western Reserve, 1972.

Mosbey, John C. *The Prison-Terrorist Link*. Bessemer, Ala.: Cerberus, 1977.

Moss, Robert. *Urban Guerrillas*. London: Temple Smith, 1972.

-. *The War for the Cities*. New York: Coward, 1972.

Naipaul, V.S. *Guerrillas*. New York: Alfred A. Knopf, 1975.

Nasution, Abdul Haris. *Fundamentals of Guerrilla Warfare*. New York: Praeger Publishers, 1965.

National Advisory Committee on Criminal Justice Standards and Goals. Task Force on Disorders and Terrorism. *Disorders and Terrorism*. Washington, D.C.: National Advisory Committee on Criminal Justice Standards & Goals, 1976.

National Council for Civil Liberties. *Prevention of Terrorism (Temporary Provisions) Act, 1974*. London: National Council for Civil Liberties, 1975.

Nieburg, H.L. *Political Violence: The Behavorial Process*. New York: St. Martin's Press, 1969.

Nkrumah, Kwame. *Handbook of Revolutionary Warfare*. New York: International Publishers, 1972.

Nolin, Thierry. *La Haganah: L'Armée Secrète d'Israel*. Paris: Ballard, 1971.

Nomad, Max. *Aspects of Revolt: A Study in Revolutionary Theories and Techniques*. New York: Noonday Press, 1959.
Norton, Augustus R. and Greenberg, Martin H. *International Terrorism: An Annotated Bibliography and Research Guide*. Boulder, Colo.: Westview Press, 1980.
O'Ballance, Edgar. *Language of Violence: The Blood Politics of Terrorism*. San Rafael, Dal.: Presidio Press, 1979.
O'Farrell, Patrick. *Ireland's English Question*. London: Batsford, 1971.
O'Flaherty, Liam. *The Terrorist*. London: E. Archer, 1926.
O'Neill, Bard E., Heaton, William R., and Alberts, Donald J., eds. *Insurgency in the Modern World*. Boulder, Colo.: Westview Press, 1980.
Oppenheimer, Martin. *The Urban Guerrilla*. Chicago: Quadrangle Books, 1969.
Oruka, H. Odera. *Punishment and Terrorism in Africa*. Kampala: East African Literature Bureau, 1976.
Osanka, Franklin Mark. *Modern Guerrilla Warfare: Fighting Communist Guerrilla Movements 1941–1961*. New York: Free Press, 1962.
Paine, Lauran. *The Terrorists*. London: Hale, 1975.
Paret, Peter and Shy, John W. *Guerrillas in the 1960's*. rev. ed. New York: Praeger Publishers, 1962.
Parry, Albert. *Terrorism: From Robespierre to Arafat*. New York: Vanguard Press, 1976.
Payne, Pierre Stephen Robert. *The Terrorists: The Story of the Forerunners of Stalin*. New York: Funk and Wagnals, 1967.
-. *Zero, The Story of Terrorism*. New York: Day, 1950.
Peres, Shimon, *David's Sling*. New York: Random House, 1970.
Piasetzki, J. Peter. *Urban Guerrilla Warfare and Terrorism*. Monticello, Ill.: Council of Planning Librarians, 1976.
Pike, Douglas Eugene. *Hanoi's Strategy of Terror*. Bangkok, Thailand: South-East Asia Treaty Organization, 1970.
Pisano, Vittorfranco S. *Contemporary Italian Terrorism*. Washington, D.C.: Library of Congress, Law Library, 1979.
The Politics of Terrorism. New York: M. Dekker, 1979.
Pomeroy, William J. *Guerrilla Warfare and Marxism*. New York: International Publishers, 1968.
Porzicanski, A.C. *Uruguay's Tupamaros: The Urban Guerrilla*. New York: Praeger, 1973.
Pasadas, J. *Terrorism and the Struggle for Democratic Rights and Socialism in Germany*. London: Fourth International Publications, 1978.
Possony, Stefan T. and Bouchey, L. Francis. *International Terorrism – The Communist Connection*. Washington, D.C.: American Council for Freedom, 1978.

Pryce-Jones, David. *The Face of Defeat: Palestinian Refugees and Guerrillas*. London: Weiderfeld and Nicholson, 1972.
Pustay, John S. *Counterinsurgency Warfare*. New York: The Free Press, n.d.
Pye, Lucian. *Guerrilla Communism in Malaya: Its Social and Political Meaning*. Princeton: University Press, 1956.
Radvanyi, Miklos K. *Anti-Terrorist Legislation in the Federal Congress Republic of Germany*. Washington, D.C.: Library of Congress, Law Library, 1979.
Radwanski, George. *No Mandate But Terror*. Richmond, Ont.: Simon and Schuster of Canada, 1971.
Rapoport, David C. *Assassination and Terrorism*. Toronto: Canadian Broadcasting System, 1971.
The Red Brigades. New York: Manor Books Inc., 1978.
Reed, David. *111 Days in Stanleyville*. New York: Harper and Row, 1965.
Regush, Nicholas M. *Pierre Vallieres: The Revolutionary Process in Quebec*. New York: Dial, 1973.
Rotberg, R.J. and Mazrui, Ali, eds. *Protest and Power in Black Africa*. New York: Oxford University Press, 1970.
Russell, D.E.H. *Rebellion, Revolution and Armed Force*. New York: Harcourt, Brace Jovanovich Publishers, 1974.
Sale, Kirkpatrick. *SDS*. New York: Random House, 1973.
Schiff, Zeev and Rothstein, Raphael. *Fedayeen: Guerrillas Against Israel*. New York: David McKay, 1972.
Schreiber, Jan Edward. *The Ultimate Weapon: Terrorists and World Order*. New York: Morrow, 1978.
Scorer, Catherine. *The Prevention of Terrorism Acts, 1974 and 1976*. London: The Council, 1976.
Selzer, Michael. *Terrorist Chic*. New York: Hawthorn Books, Inc., 1979.
Shay, Res. *The Silent War*. Salisbuty, Rhodesia: Galaxie Press, 1971.
Shultz and Sloan, eds. *Responding to the Terrorist Threat*. Elmsford, New York: Pergamon Press, Inc., 1981.
Silvert, Kalman H. *Reaction and Revolution in Latin America*. New Orleans: Hauser Press, 1961.
Sinclair, Andrew. *Guevara*. London: William Collins and Sons, 1970.
Skobnick, Jeromw, ed. *The Politics of Protest*. New York: Ballantine Books, 1969.
Sobel, Lester A., ed. *Palestinian Impasse: Arab Guerrillas and International Terror*. New York: Facts on File, 1977.
-. *Political Terrorism*. New York: Facts on File, 1975.
-. *Political Terrorism, 1974–1978 vol. 2*. New York: Facts on File, 1975.
Sorel, George. *Reflections on Violence*. New York: Collier Books, 1961.
South Africa Department of Foreign Affairs. *South West Africa: Measures*

Taken to Combat Terrorism. Cape Town, 1968.
Stewart, Anthony Terence Quincey. *The Ulster Crisis*. London: Faber and Faber, 1967.
Studies in Nuclear Terrorism. eds., Norton and Greenberg. Boston: G.K. Hall, 1979.
Styles, George. *Bombs Have No Pity*. London: Luscombe, 1975.
Suchlicki, Jaime. *University Students and Revolution in Cuba, 1920–1968*. Coral Gables: University of Miami Press, 1969.
Taber, Robert. *The War of the Flea*. New York: Lyle Stuart, 1965.
Tanham, George Kilpatrick. *Communist Revolutionary Warfare*. New York: Praeger Publishers, 1961.
Ten Years of Terrorism: Collected Views. ed., Jennifer Shaw. London: Royal United Services Institute for Defense Studies, New York: Crane, Russak, 1979.
Teixeira, Bernardo. *The Fabric of Terror: Three Days in Angola*. New York: Devin-Adair, 1965.
Terror in East Pakistan. Karachi: Pakestan Publications, 1971.
The Terrorism Reader. New York: New American Library, 1978.
Trautman, Frederic. *The Voice of Terrorism: A Biography of Johann Most*. Westport, Conn.: Greenwood Press, 1980.
Trelease, Allen W. *White Terror: The Ku Klux Klan Conspiracy and Southern Reconstruction*. New York: Harper and Row, 1971.
Trotsky, Leon. *Against Individual Terrorism*. New York: Pathfinder Press of New York, 1974.
Truby, J. David. *How Terrorists Kill: The Complete Terrorist Arsenal*. New York: Paladin Press, 1978.
Turi, Robert T., et al. *Descriptive Study of Aircraft Hijacking*. Huntsville, Texas: Institute of Contemporary Corrections and the Behavioral Sciences, 1972.
United Nations. General Assembly. Ad Hoc Committee on International Terrorism. Report. New York: United Nations, 1973.
United States Central Intelligence Agency. *Annotated Bibliography on Transnational and International Terrorism*. (Prepared by Edward F. Mickolus) Washington, D.C.: CIA, 1976.
United States Central Intelligence Agency. Directorate of Intelligence. *International Terrorism in 1976*. Washington, D.C.: CIA, 1977, 1978.
United States Congress. House. Committee on Foreign Affairs, Subcommittee on the Near East and South East Asia. *International Terrorism*. Ninety-third Congress, second session. Washington, D.C.: U.S. Government Printing Office.
United States Congress. House. Committee on International Security. *The Symbionese Liberation Army: A Study*. Ninety-third Congress, second

session. Washington, D.C.: U.S. Government Printing Office, 1974.

United States Congress. House. Committee on Public Works and Transportaion, Subcommittee on Aviation. *International Terrorism*. Ninety-fifth Congress, second session on H.R. 13261. Washington, D.C.: U.S. Government Printing Office, 1978.

United States Congress. Senate. Committee on Foreign Relations. *Combatting International and Domestic Terrorism*, Ninetyfifth Congress, second session on S. 2236, June 8, 1978. Washington, D.C.: U.S. Government Printing Office, 1978.

United States Congress. House-Committee on Internal Security. Terrorism: Hearings before the Committee on Internal Security, House of Representatives. Ninety-third Congress, second session. Washington, D.C.: U.S. Government Printing Office, 1974.

United States Congress. Senate. Committee on Foreign Relatins, Subcommittee on Foreign Assistance. *International Terrorism*. Ninety-fifth Congress, first session. Sept. 14, 1977. Washington, D.C.: U.S. Government Printing Office, 1977.

United States Congress. House. Committee on Internal Security. *Terrorism: A Staff Study*. Ninety-third Congress, second session. Washington, D.C.: U.S. Government Printing Office, 1974.

United States Congress. Senate. Committee on Governmental Affairs. *An Act to Combat International Terrorism*. Ninety-fifth Congress, second session, on S. 2236. Washington, D.C.: U.S. Government Printing Office, 1978.

United States Congress. Senate. Committee on the Judiciary, Subcommittee to Investigate the Administration of the Internal Security Act and other Internal Security Laws. Ninety-third (Ninety-fourth, second session) Congress. Washington, D.C.: U.S. Government Printing Office, 1974.

United States Congress. Senate. Committee on the Judiciary, Subcommittee on Criminal Laws and Procedures. *The Terrorist and his Victim*. Ninety-fifth Congress, first session. July 21, 1977. Washington, D.C.: U.S. Government Printing Office, 1977.

United States Congress. Senate. Committee on the Judiciary, Subcommittee on Criminal Laws and Procedures. *West Germany's Political Response to Terrorism*. Ninety-fifth Congress, second session. April 26, 1978. Washington, D.C.: U.S. Government Printing Office, 1978.

United States Congress. Senate. Committee on the Judiciary, Subcommittee to Investigate the Administration of the Internal Security Act and Other Internal Security Laws. *Trotskyite Terrorist International*. Ninety-fourth Congress, first session. July 24, 1975. Washington, D.C.: U.S. Government Printing Office, 1975.

United States Congress. Senate. Committee on the Judiciary. Washington, D.C.: U.S. Government Printing Office, 1973.

United States Embassy (Vietnam) *Viet Cong Use of Terror*. Saigon, 1967.
United States. Private Security Advisory Council. *Prevention of Terroristic Crimes*. Washington, D.C.: The Administration, 1976.
Vajpeyi, J.N. *The Extremist Movement in India*. Allahabad: Chush Publications, 1974.
Values in Conflict: Blacks and the American Ambivilance Towards Violence. ed., Frye, Charles A. Washington, D.C.: University Press of America, 1980.
Van den Haag, Ernest. *Political Violence and Civil Disobediance*. New York: Harper and Row, 1972.
Waddis, Jack. *New Theories of Revolution*. New York: International Publishers, 1972.
Walker, Walter. *The Bear and the Back Door*. Richmond, Surrey: Foreign Affairs Publishing Co., 1978.
Wallace, Michael, ed. *Terrorism*. New York: Arno Press, 1979.
Walter, Eugene Victor. *Terror and Resistance: A Study of Political Violence*. New York: Oxford University Press, 1969.
Walzer, Michael. *The Revolution of the Saints: A Study in the Origins of Radical Politics*. Cambridge: Harvard University Press, 1965.
Watson, Francis M. *Political Terrorism: The Threat and the Response*. Washington, D.C.: R.B. Luce Co., 1976.
Weigert, Gideon. *Who So Killeth a Believer*. Jerusalem: Israel Communications, 1971.
Whelton, Charles. *Skyjack!* New York: Tower Publications, 1970.
Wilkinson, Paul. *Political Terrorism*. London: MacMillan Press, 1974.
-. *Political Terrorism and the Liberal State*. New York: John Wiley and Sons, 1977.
Woodstock, George. *Anarchism*. New York: World Publishing Co., 1971.
Wright, C.D. *Terrorism: Poems*. Fayetteville, Ark.: Lost Roads Publishing Co., 1979.
Yaari, Ehud. *Strike Terror*. New York: Sabra Books, 1970.
Zwiebach, Burton. *Civility and Disobediance*. New York: Cambridge University Press, 1975.

NOTES ON CONTRIBUTORS

Yonah Alexander (co-editor) is Professor of International Studies and Director of the Institute for Studies in International Terrorism at the State University of New York at Oneonta, New York, and a Senior Research Member at the Center for Strategic and International Studies at Georgetown University.

D.G. Boyce is Reader and Acting Head of the Department of Political Science and Government at University College Swansea, in the University of Wales.

Patrick Buckland is Reader in the Department of Modern History at the University of Liverpool.

Richard Davis is Reader in the Department of History at the University of Tasmania in Australia.

Sheridan Gilley is Senior Lecturer in the Faculty of Theology at the University of Durham.

Maureen Hartigan is Executive Secretary of the Brent Irish Cultural Centre in London.

Ken Heskin is Senior Lecturer in the Department of Psychology at Trinity College Dublin.

John Hill is Lecturer in Communication Studies at the University of Ulster.

Josephine Howie is a former graduate student at the London School of Economics and Political Science and is now a private writer living in Cyprus.

Jonathan Kelley is in the Institute of Advanced Studies at The Australian National University.

John Kirkaldy is Tutor-Counsellor for The Open University, South West Region, and Lecturer in Teacher Training, Salisbury College of Technology.

Ian McAllister is in the Institute of Advanced Studies at The Australian National University.

Alan O'Day (co-editor) is Senior Lecturer in the Department of History, Philosophy & European Studies at the Polytechnic of North London.

Henry Patterson is Senior Lecturer in the Department of Politics and Philosophy at the University of Ulster.

Roland Quinault is Senior Lecturer in the Department of History, Philosophy & European Studies at The Polytechnic of North London.

Brian Holden Reid is Editor of the Royal United Services Insitute *Journal*. He also lectures in the Department of War Studies at King's College, University of London.